T0391863

Light is Sown

OXFORD STUDIES IN WESTERN ESOTERICISM

Series Editor
Henrik Bogdan, University of Gothenburg

Editorial Board
Jean-Pierre Brach, École Pratique des Hautes Études
Carole Cusack, University of Sydney
Christine Ferguson, University of Stirling
Olav Hammer, University of Southern Denmark
Wouter Hanegraaff, University of Amsterdam
Ronald Hutton, University of Bristol
Orion Klautau, Tohoku University
Jeffrey J. Kripal, Rice University
Michael Stausberg, University of Bergen
Egil Asprem, Stockholm University
Gordan Djurdjevic, Independent scholar
Peter Forshaw, University of Amsterdam
Jesper Aa. Petersen, Norwegian University of Science and Technology
Manon Hedenborg White, Malmö University

CHILDREN OF LUCIFER
The Origins of Modern Religious Satanism
Ruben van Luijk

SATANIC FEMINISM
Lucifer as the Liberator of Woman in Nineteenth-Century Culture
Per Faxneld

THE SIBYLS OF LONDON
A Family on the Esoteric Fringes of Georgian England
Susan Sommers

WHAT IS IT LIKE TO BE DEAD?
Near-Death Experiences, Christianity, and the Occult
Jens Schlieter

AMONG THE SCIENTOLOGISTS
History, Theology, and Praxis
Donald A. Westbrook

RECYCLED LIVES
A History of Reincarnation in Blavatsky's Theosophy
Julie Chajes

THE ELOQUENT BLOOD
The Goddess Babalon and the Construction of Femininities in Western Esotericism
Manon Hedenborg White

GURDJIEFF
Mysticism, Contemplation, and Exercises
Joseph Azize

INITIATING THE MILLENNIUM
The Avignon Society and Illuminism in Europe
Robert Collis and Natalie Bayer

IMAGINING THE EAST
The Early Theosophical Society
Tim Rudbog and Erik Sand

MYSTIFYING KABBALAH
Academic Scholarship, National Theology, and New Age
Boaz Huss

SPIRITUAL ALCHEMY
From Jacob Boehme to Mary Anne Atwood
Mike A. Zuber

THE SUBTLE BODY
A Genealogy
Simon Cox

OCCULT IMPERIUM
Arturo Reghini, Roman Traditionalism, and the Anti-Modern Reaction in Fascist Italy
Christian Giudice

VESTIGES OF A PHILOSOPHY
Matter, the Meta-Spiritual, and the Forgotten Bergson
John Ó Maoilearca

PROPHECY, MADNESS, AND HOLY WAR IN EARLY MODERN EUROPE
A Life of Ludwig Friedrich Gifftheil
Leigh T.I. Penman

HÉLÈNE SMITH
Occultism and the Discovery of the Unconscious
Claudie Massicotte

LIKE A TREE UNIVERSALLY SPREAD
Sri Sabhapati Swami and Śivarājayoga
Keith Edward Cantú

FRIENDSHIP IN DOUBT
Aleister Crowley, J. F. C. Fuler, Victoria B. Neuburg, and British Agnosticism
Richard Kaczynski

THE UNKNOWN GOD
W. T. Smith and the Thelemites
Martin P. Starr

AMERICAN AURORA
Environment and Apocalypse in the Life of Johannes Kelpius
Timothy Grieve-Carlson

THE LADY AND THE BEAST
The Extraordinary Partnership between Frieda Harris and Aleister Crowley
Deja Whitehouse

THE MAGICAL DIARIES OF LEAH HIRSIG 1923–1925
Aleister Crowley, Magick, and the New Occult Woman
Manon Hedenborg White and Henrik Bogdan

LIGHT IS SOWN
The Cultivation of Kabbalah in Medieval Castile
Avishai Bar-Asher and Jeremy Phillip Brown

Light is Sown

The Cultivation of Kabbalah in Medieval Castile

AVISHAI BAR-ASHER

AND

JEREMY PHILLIP BROWN

OXFORD
UNIVERSITY PRESS

OXFORD
UNIVERSITY PRESS

Oxford University Press is a department of the University of Oxford.
It furthers the University's objective of excellence in research, scholarship,
and education by publishing worldwide. Oxford is a registered trade mark of
Oxford University Press in the UK and certain other countries.

Published in the United States of America by Oxford University Press
198 Madison Avenue, New York, NY 10016, United States of America.

© Oxford University Press 2025

All rights reserved. No part of this publication may be reproduced, stored in a retrieval system, transmitted, used for text and data mining, or used for training artificial intelligence, in any form or by any means, without the prior permission in writing of Oxford University Press, or as expressly permitted by law, by license or under terms agreed with the appropriate reprographics rights organization. Inquiries concerning reproduction outside the scope of the above should be sent to the Rights Department, Oxford University Press, at the address above.

You must not circulate this work in any other form
and you must impose this same condition on any acquirer.

Library of Congress Cataloging-in-Publication Data
Names: Bar-Asher, Avishai, 1980– author. |
Brown, Jeremy P. (Jeremy Phillip) author.
Title: Light is sown : the cultivation of Kabbalah in medieval Castile /
Avishai Bar-Asher & Jeremy Phillip Brown.
Description: New York, NY : Oxford University Press, [2025] |
Series: Oxford studies in Western esotericism |
Includes bibliographical references and index. |
Identifiers: LCCN 2025412023 (print) | LCCN 2025002291 (ebook) |
ISBN 9780197744819 (hardback) | ISBN 9780197744826 (epub) | ISBN 9780197744840
Subjects: LCSH: Zohar. | Moses ben Shem Tov, de Leon, 1250–1305. |
Cabala—Spain—Castile—History—To 1500. |
Judaism—Spain—Castile—History—To 1500.
Classification: LCC BM525.A59 B36 2025 (print) | LCC BM525.A59 (ebook) |
DDC 296.1/62—dc23/eng/20250402
LC record available at https://lccn.loc.gov/2025412023
LC ebook record available at https://lccn.loc.gov/2025002291

DOI: 10.1093/oso/9780197744819.001.0001

Printed by Marquis Book Printing, Canada

The manufacturer's authorized representative in the EU for product safety is
Oxford University Press España S.A., Parque Empresarial San Fernando de Henares,
Avenida de Castilla, 2 – 28830 Madrid (www.oup.es/en).

MIX
Paper | Supporting responsible forestry
FSC® C103567

Contents

List of Figures ix
Acknowledgments xi
Note on Translations xiii

1. Sowing the Zohar 1
 1.1 Introduction 1
 1.2 Who Was Moses de León? 9
 1.3 Structure 18
 1.4 Sources 20
 1.5 The Zohar 22
 1.6 Itineraries 29

2. An Order of Penitents 33
 2.1 Rabbinic Pietism in Medieval Castile 33
 2.2 Moses de León's Penitential Writings 34
 2.3 Kabbalah as a Penitential Movement Within Judaism 43
 2.4 Homeward Birds: Penitents on the Thirteenfold Path 56
 2.5 Inducement from the Mendicants 63
 2.6 A Social Vision for Kabbalah 67

3. Secrets of the Hebrew Language 73
 3.1 From Catalonia to Castile 73
 3.2 The *Sefer ha-Ne'lam* Corpus 78
 3.3 *Alef*: One, Two, Three, and Four 83
 3.4 The Four Israelite Banners 85
 3.5 *Alef*: Three Worlds 89
 3.6 *Ḥokhmah*: Nine and Ten 95
 3.7 *Yod*: The Noetic Point 99
 3.8 The Andalusi Legacy of Arabic Lettrism 106
 3.9 An Early Dispute with Joseph Gikatilla 110
 3.10 A Generative Reconciliation of Paradigms 114

4. The Rose of Testimony 116
 4.1 The Transition to Gender in Castilian Kabbalah 116
 4.2 *Alef*: Three Worlds (Again) 121
 4.3 Female Shall Compass Male: *Binah* as the Mother of a Son 127
 4.4 Solomon's Sea: Standing in Eternal Femininity 132
 4.5 Male Between Two Females, Female Between Two Males 137

4.6 Solomon's Sea (Again): The Pattern of Female Superordination 139
4.7 *Dalet/Heh*: Shifting Index of the Female 142
4.8 *Sub Rosa*: Migrations of de León's Earliest Speculation on Gender 150

5. Light of the West: Moses de León of Guadalajara 161
5.1 The Thirteenfold Pattern 162
5.2 *Sabios Antiguos*: Wisdom and Its Contexts 171
5.3 Wisdom of the Zohar from Rav Hamnuna Saba 184

Bibliography 199
Hebrew Bible Index 219
Index 221

Figures

1.1 Incipit of the longest fragment from de León's earliest theosophical composition, the "Nameless Composition," attributed here to "Rabbenu Moshe"—not de León, but Naḥmanides; MS Munich, Bayerische Staatsbibliothek, Cod. hebr. 47, fol. 335b, copied in 1551 by Meir ben Isaac ha-Levi of Prague in Venice. 5

1.2 Moroccan witness to "Nameless Composition," copied seventeenth century (commentary on divine names); MS New York, Jewish Theological Seminary of America, 1777, fol. 26a. 6

1.3 Moses de León's "Nameless Composition" (commentary on Rabbi Ishmael's thirteen hermeneutical principles); MS New York, Jewish Theological Seminary of America, 1609, fol. 131a. 7

1.4 First known attestation of the romanized term "cabala" referring to Jewish esotericism; from the prologue to Juan Manuel's early fourteenth-century *Libro de la caza*; MS Madrid, Biblioteca Nacional de España, S. 34, fol. 201a. 17

2.1 Moses de León's "Order of Penitents" (*Siddur ba'ale teshuvah*), kabbalah's earliest regimen vitae; MS Munich, Bayerische Staatsbibliothek, Cod. hebr. 47, fol. 349a. 37

3.1 Secret of the *alef*, comprising three worlds: *yod*, *vav*, and *dalet*; MS Munich, Bayerische Staatsbibliothek, Cod. hebr. 47, fol. 361b. 91

4.1 "Secret of the female world" (*sod 'olam ha-neqevah*); MS Munich, Bayerische Staatsbibliothek, Cod. hebr. 47, fol. 373b. 131

4.2 Early eighteenth-century rendering of Solomon's Sea resting upon twelve oxen; Conrad Mel, הים מוצק, *dissertatio theologico-philologica, de Mari Aeneo, seu labro magno templi Salomonis, 1 Reg. VII. & II. Chron. IV.* (Regiomontum [=Königsberg]: Reusnerus, 1702), 2–3 (interleaf). 133

5.1 Patio de los Leones, Alhambra Palace, Granada, Spain; lithograph by Francisco Javier Parcerisa Boada; Francisco Pi y Margall, *Recuerdos y bellezas de España: Reino de Granada* (Madrid: Jose Repullés, 1850), 384–385 (interleaf). 175

5.2 "And it is already stated in the Book of Rav Hamnuna Saba," presumably referring to the "Nameless Composition"; from the final part of Moses de León's 1292 *Sheqel ha-qodesh*; MS Jerusalem, National Library of Israel, Heb. 8°2066, fols. 100b–101a. 187

Acknowledgments

The partnership that gave rise to this book began when we first met in 2013. At that time, we each learned that the other was engaged in doctoral research dealing in part with Moses de León's "Nameless Composition" and agreed the text would reward collaborative study. Through the course of our work together, the world kept turning. Children born. Vaccines distributed. Wars begun. Amid the changes, the joy of intellectual fellowship has been a constant. How fortunate we have been to learn from each other, and from the Castilian Jew who has so vigorously seized our attention from beyond the grave.

We express our gratitude to Henrik Bogdan for featuring *Light Is Sown* in Oxford Studies in Western Esotericism, to the Oxford editorial team for shepherding the book through production, and to Ginny Faber and Maud Kozodoy for their expert help in preparing the manuscript.

This book has received support from the Memorial Foundation for Jewish Culture, the Estate of Simon and Ethel Flegg (McGill University), the Israel Science Foundation, the Institute for Research in the Humanities (University of Madison–Wisconsin), and the Mandel Institute for Jewish Studies (Hebrew University). We acknowledge several collections for granting us the permission to feature several images in the book. Figures 1.1, 2.1, 3.1, 4.1, and 4.2 appear courtesy of Bayerische Staatsbibliothek, Munich; figures 1.2 and 1.3 appear courtesy of the Jewish Theological Seminary of America, New York; figure 1.4 appears courtesy of Biblioteca Nacional de España, Madrid; figure 5.1 appears courtesy of Boston Public Library; and figure 5.2 appears courtesy of National Library of Israel, Jerusalem.

We acknowledge the support of our colleagues at the Hebrew University of Jerusalem and at the University of Notre Dame, especially Khaled Anatolios, Gary Anderson, Ann Astell, Thomas Burman, John Cavadini, Jonathan Garb, Moshe Idel, Reimund Leicht, Daniel Machiela, Avigail Manekin-Bamberger, Timothy Matovina, Maren Niehoff, Tzvi Novick, Benjamin Pollock, Caterina Rigo, Gabriel Said Reynolds, Mun'im Sirry, Alexis Torrance, Joseph Warykow, and Abraham Winitzer.

We are grateful for the encouragement of numerous additional scholars. We acknowledge especially Emma Abate, Adam Afterman, Mohamad Ballan, Na'ama Ben-Shachar, Jonatan Benarroch, Yoram Biton, Travis Bruce, Dylan Burns, Eric Caplan, Yossi Chajes, Jonathan Dauber, Ofer Dynes, Samuel Fleischacker, Esther Frank, Carlos Frankel, Pinchas Giller, Guadalupe González Diéguez, Arthur Green, Joel Hecker, Marc Herman, Susannah Heschel, Gershon Hundert (of blessed memory), Boaz Huss, Lawrence Kaplan, Patrick Koch, Daniel Matt, Ariel Mayse, Ronit Meroz, Yehudah Liebes, Elke Morlok, Steven Nadler, Biti Roi, Naomi Seidman, Omri Shasha, Assaf Tamari, Tanja Werthmann, and Oded Yisraeli.

Lastly, it is thanks to the love of our families that we find the strength and clarity to stay the course of our studies.

A. B.: With love and gratitude for my dear Miki, Nehora, Ayala, and Naomi.

J. B.: For my beloved Valeria, Rafael Emilio, and Amalia Hanna, with gratitude and admiration.

Note on Translations

Light Is Sown features quotations from English translations of zoharic texts produced by Daniel C. Matt, Joel Hecker, and Nathan Wolski (*The Zohar: Pritzker Edition*, 12 vols. [Stanford, CA: Stanford University Press, 2004–2017]). Unless otherwise indicated, these typically appear for the texts covered by the Pritzker project, albeit with modifications based on contextual emphases, interpretive priorities, and alternate readings of the Hebrew and Aramaic sources.

1
Sowing the Zohar

1.1 Introduction

> I kept my silence, placing hand to mouth until . . . I saw that the days of my life were setting before me, that old age was rapidly approaching. Therefore, I pressed forward to disseminate . . . mysteries and secrets whose memory was lost to scripture's interpreters, neglecting its perdurance and splendor.[1]

With these dramatic remarks, Ezra ben Solomon of Girona announced the dawn of a written discourse. Near the turn of the sixth millennium (ca. 5000 AM / 1240 CE), the author expressed his determination to avert the loss of a religious-intellectual heritage. His words preface one of the first known works of the kabbalah, an oral domain of Torah wisdom that Ezra saw as threatened by the vicissitudes of memory. In committing this wisdom to writing, the author saw himself engaged in a delicate operation of rescuing ancient secrets from oblivion.

Efforts to breathe new life into endangered knowledge are not just the stuff of a medieval mentality clinging—whether faithfully, creatively, or opportunistically—to the epistemic authority of the ancients. Modern scholarship has its own stories about the improbable salvage of uniquely instructive documents all but destined to evade the historical record. This book, too, tells the story of a loss averted—that of knowledge concerning a pivotal moment in the development of kabbalah. Indeed, a series of factors conspired against any awareness of the exceptional document to which we dedicate this book.[2] It comes to light only by the grace of a string of accidents and scholarly interventions.

[1] Translation adapted from Ezra ben Solomon of Gerona, *Commentary on the Song of Songs and Other Kabbalistic Commentaries*, trans. Seth Brody (Kalamazoo, MI: Medieval Institute Publications, 1999), 24; on the basis of Ezra ben Solomon of Girona, "Perush Shir ha-Shirim," in *Kitve Ramban*, ed. Charles B. Chavel (Jerusalem: Mossad ha-Rav Kook, 1964), 2:479–480. See the discussion in Jonathan Dauber, *Knowledge of God and the Development of Early Kabbalah* (Leiden: Brill, 2012), 38–39.

[2] MS Munich, Bayerische Staatsbibliothek, Cod. hebr. 47, fols. 335b–386b.

Light is Sown. Avishai Bar-Asher and Jeremy Phillip Brown, Oxford University Press.
© Oxford University Press 2025. DOI: 10.1093/oso/9780197744819.003.0001

Gershom Scholem (Berlin, 1897–Jerusalem, 1982) was the first modern scholar to note the significance of the document that is at the heart of this book. As a young student in Munich during the early 1920s, Scholem labored to master the sizable inventory of Hebrew codices held by the Bavarian State Library. It was through a painstaking process of working through this collection that the scholar first honed his skill at Hebrew manuscript research.[3] One of the codices found in the kabbalah-rich collection contained the single known witness to our text, about which Scholem would publish a pioneering German-language article in 1927, four years after migrating to British Mandatory Palestine.[4] The article showed that this large fragment, bearing no extant title, had been composed by the prolific Castilian writer Moses ben Shem Ṭov de León of Guadalajara (fl. ca. 1280–1293). More than a decade after the publication of this 1927 article, Scholem would ascribe to the same Moses de León the authorship of the voluminous *Sefer ha-Zohar*—the vast repository of esoteric and pietistic exegesis that, since the late thirteenth century, has served as the authorized corpus of kabbalah.[5] Thanks to a telltale clue from the great bibliographer Moritz Steinschneider (1816–1907),[6] Scholem was able to cite substantial evidence for de León's authorship of the Munich fragment, based on the appearance of the author's signature

[3] The initial bibliographic yield of his work on the Munich catalog is documented in Gershom Scholem, "He'arot ve-tiqqunim li-reshimat kitve ha-yad she-be-Minkhen," *Kiryat Sefer* 1 (1925): 284–293.

[4] Gerhard [Gershom] Scholem, "Eine unbekannte mystische Schrift des Mose de Leon," *Monatsschrift für Geschichte und Wissenschaft des Judentums* 71, nos. 3–4 (1927): 109–123, esp. 123. It is clear that Scholem had reached the conclusion endorsed in this article at least as early as 1925 (at which time, it appears, the article had already been completed); in the entry on MS Munich, Bayerische Staatsbibliothek, Cod. hebr. 47 in his corrigendum to Moritz Steinschneider's catalog of the Munich collection, he affirmed that the fragment comprised "part, approximately half, of an unknown book by R. Moses de León, and it appears to be from *Sefer Shushan ha-'edut*—his first fruits," and he noted, "On this important manuscript I have prepared a special article, as was needed, and there you will find all of the details" (Scholem, "He'arot ve-tiqqunim," 287).

[5] Gershom Scholem, *Major Trends in Jewish Mysticism* (New York: Schocken Books, 1995), 156–204. For a detailed account of the long fermentation of this ascription, see Daniel Abrams, "Gershom Scholem's Methodologies of Research on the Zohar," in *Scholar and Kabbalist: The Life and Work of Gershom Scholem*, ed. Mirjam Zadoff and Noam Zadoff (Leiden: Brill, 2018), 3–16. For a recent assessment of de León's relationship to the Zohar, see Avishai Bar-Asher, "Kabbalah and Minhag: Geonic Responsa and the Kabbalist Polemic on Minhagim in the Zohar and Related Texts" [in Hebrew], *Tarbiz* 84, no. 1 (2016): 195–263.

[6] When Steinschneider assessed the material, he observed that the text's chapter headings followed a convention familiar to him from de León's 1293 *Mishkan ha-'edut*. The fact that the composition used the idiosyncratic chapter title *sha'ar ha-ḥeleq* known elsewhere from the writings of de León was another factor that caught Steinschneider's eye: Moritz Steinschneider, "Die sonderbare Benennung שער חלק (der Kapitel) stammt wahrscheinlich aus Mose de Leons משכן העדות, welches 13 מדות der Büßenden behandelt, während hier 13 סדרים aufgezählt werden," *Hebräische Bibliographie* 9, no. 49 (1869): 28–29, cited in Scholem, "Eine unbekannte mystische Schrift," 110. Compare the 1869 description of the codex's contents, published in *Hebräische Bibliographie*, with a later one, which makes no mention of de León. Steinschneider, *Die hebräischen Handschriften der K. Hof- und*

style and terminology, and on further connections with his other Hebrew works.[7] Though he correctly identified the Munich fragment's author, the young scholar misjudged its place within de León's corpus. This book shall demonstrate that the document first analyzed by Scholem preserves the earliest traceable evidence of de León's immersion in the zoharic project. The large Munich fragment is a unique witness to the lion's share of a work that Scholem called the "Nameless Composition" (*ḥibbur le-lo shem*), a designation we retain.[8] Our single witness to the largest portion of this composition owes its unlikely survival to the handiwork of a Venetian scribe (see Figure 1.1). This scribe was commissioned, through the mediation of an enterprising Jew, by a wealthy Christian [!] book collector who eventually sold his extensive collection to Albrecht V, Duke of Bavaria (1528–1579). Had Scholem labored at another library, the work might have languished in obscurity. These contingencies are rendered even more tenuous by the fact that de León himself contributed to the obscurity of this text. Though the author's later works are full of expressly intertextual references to his other titled and signed compositions, we find no overt mention of this early theosophical composition in the large portion of de León's Hebrew corpus that we possess. However, we will hold the critical question of covert references to the work in reserve until our conclusion. It will prove fruitful for pinpointing the text's precise relationship to the Zohar.[9]

Staatsbibliothek in München (Munich: Commission der Palm'schen Hofbuchhandlung, 1895), 31–32. See also Aliza Cohen-Mushlin, *Selected Hebrew Manuscripts from the Bavarian State Library* (Wiesbaden: Harrassowitz, 2020), 203–208 ("Cod. hebr. 47: Biblical and Kabbalistic commentaries, Venice, c.1552"; the attribution [there, 203] to de León of a short commentary on the prayer "Barukh she-amar" ["8. Treatise on Kabbalah"], fols. 228a and 228b, is mistaken. The text is a fragment from Isaac [ben] Todros's Maḥzor commentary [MS Paris, Bibliothèque nationale de France, héb. 839, fols. 191b–192b]. Other errata include the text cataloged as "7. Commentary on *Sefer Yezirah*," 326b–327b, which corresponds in fact to material from the Fifth Gate of Joseph Gikatilla's *Sha'are orah*, and the text cataloged as "11. On Metempsychosis," fols. 332b–333a, which belongs to Meir Aldabi's *Shevile emunah*).

[7] Scholem, "Eine unbekannte mystische Schrift," 114–115. Subsequently, Wolfson's edition of de León's *Sefer ha-Rimmon* (Elliot R. Wolfson, ed., *The Book of the Pomegranate: Moses de Leon's* Sefer ha-Rimmon [Atlanta, GA: Scholars Press, 2020] = Moses de León, *Sefer ha-Rimmon*) noted several parallels between that work and the MS Munich, Bayerische Staatsbibliothek, Cod. hebr. 47 fragment. See 8, 28, 56–57, 75, 86, 114, 329. See, too, the parallels noted throughout Charles Mopsik, ed., *R. Moses de León's* Sefer Sheqel ha-Qodesh (Los Angeles: Cherub Press, 1996) = Moses de León, *Sheqel ha-qodesh*.

[8] In this respect, it is like other documents bearing sole witness to individual Hebrew compositions by de León, for example, Jochanan H. A. Wijnhoven, ed., "Sefer Maskiyyot Kesef" (MA diss., Brandeis University, 1961) = Moses de León, *Maskiyyot kesef*.

[9] In terms of authorship, it is possible that de León never signed this composition to begin with, though this cannot be determined without the first half of the work.

Notwithstanding the lack of explicit external references to the composition, we have now identified a second witness to a significant portion of the material preserved in the Munich fragment. This discovery illustrates that the journey of de León's composition from medieval Castile into our hands was not, after all, limited to a single trajectory. The work's transmission may now be characterized as a ramified itinerary, by which information has reached us via multiple channels. Neither Scholem nor the few others who have examined the Munich fragment since were aware that an integral portion of the text had been preserved in a miscellaneous North African codex, copied in seventeenth-century Morocco, containing rare and unique material from medieval Iberia (see Figure 1.2). In fact, the Moroccan manuscript boasts a more reliable witness than the Munich codex, which was copied, as we established, in sixteenth-century Venice (see Figure 1.3).[10] The composition to which these documents attest has an important, if hidden, reception history that is of special significance for demonstrating the deep roots of the Zohar in medieval Castile. Although the attribution of the Zohar to de León dates from the early modern period, no scholar before Scholem had presented the hypothesis with as much documentary rigor. Still, for all his eventual confidence in de León's authorship, Scholem conceded that "the acceptance of this theory [of de León's authorship] still leaves a number of questions unanswered."[11] Indeed, basic questions about de León's intellectual development and its chronology remain unresolved, questions whose investigation could provide firmer traction on the large, stratified, bilingual, and multiauthor repository of works that make up the greater zoharic literature (i.e., the complex of texts composed in the late thirteenth and fourteenth centuries that constitute the anthology printed as *Sefer ha-Zohar* in the sixteenth century). Because no body of work is more constitutional for the kabbalah than the zoharic literature, and no author has been more demonstrably associated with a greater portion of that material than Moses de León,

[10] MS New York, Jewish Theological Seminary of America, 1777 (formerly Enelow 699), fols. 22b–27a. This text bears witness to the portion of the composition preserved in MS Munich, Bayerische Staatsbibliothek, Cod. hebr. 47, fols. 372a–385a, which comprises most of the composition's last (and what we identify as the tenth) chapter (not including the appendices present in the Venice manuscript). With the help of the Moroccan witness (see Figure 1.2), which is based on a more reliable manuscript tradition, it is possible to fill in several lacunae and to correct a host of corruptions preserved in the Venice witness. MS New York 1777 also contains de León's *Sod darkhe ha-otiyyot ve-ha-nequddot*, another early text, to be discussed in Chapter 3.

[11] Scholem, *Major Trends in Jewish Mysticism*, 193.

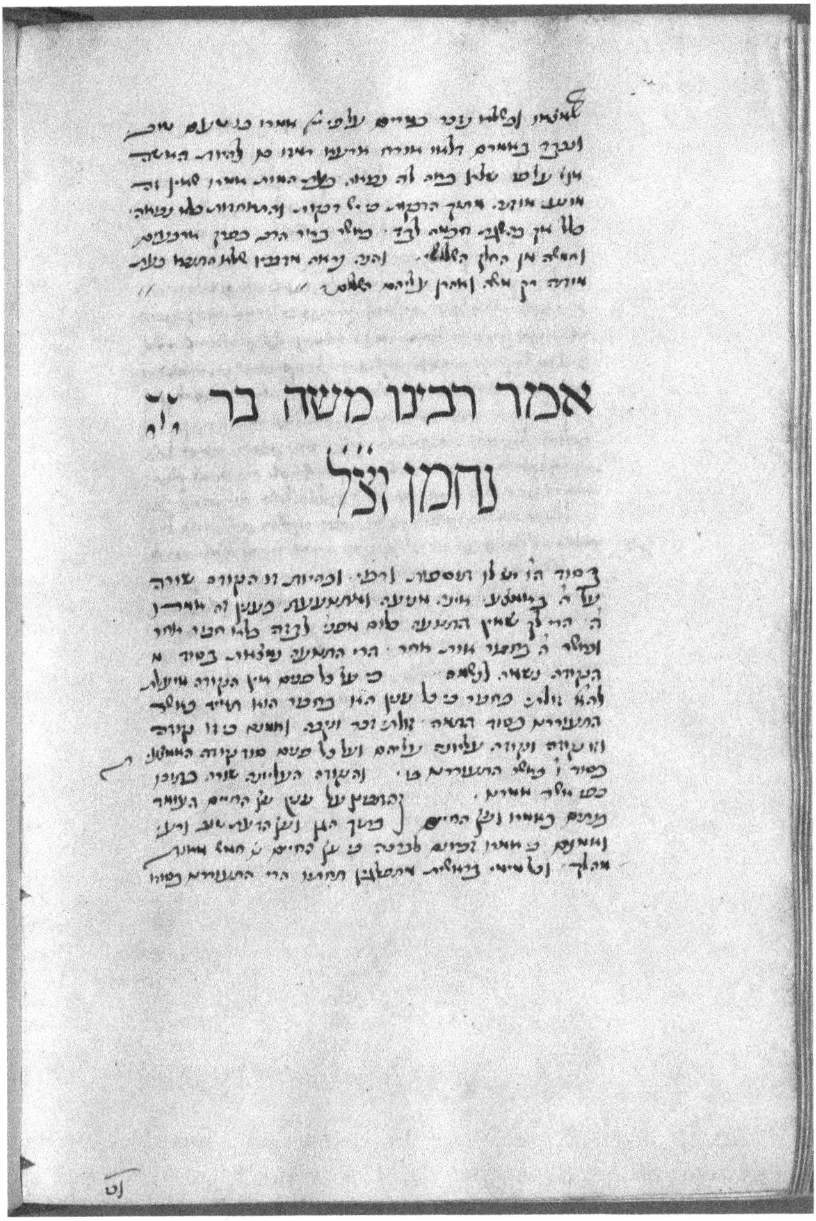

Figure 1.1 Incipit of the longest fragment from de León's earliest theosophical composition, the "Nameless Composition," attributed here to "Rabbenu Moshe"—not de León, but "Naḥmanides"; MS Munich, Bayerische Staatsbibliothek, Cod. hebr. 47, fol. 335b, copied in 1551 by Meir ben Isaac ha-Levi of Prague in Venice.

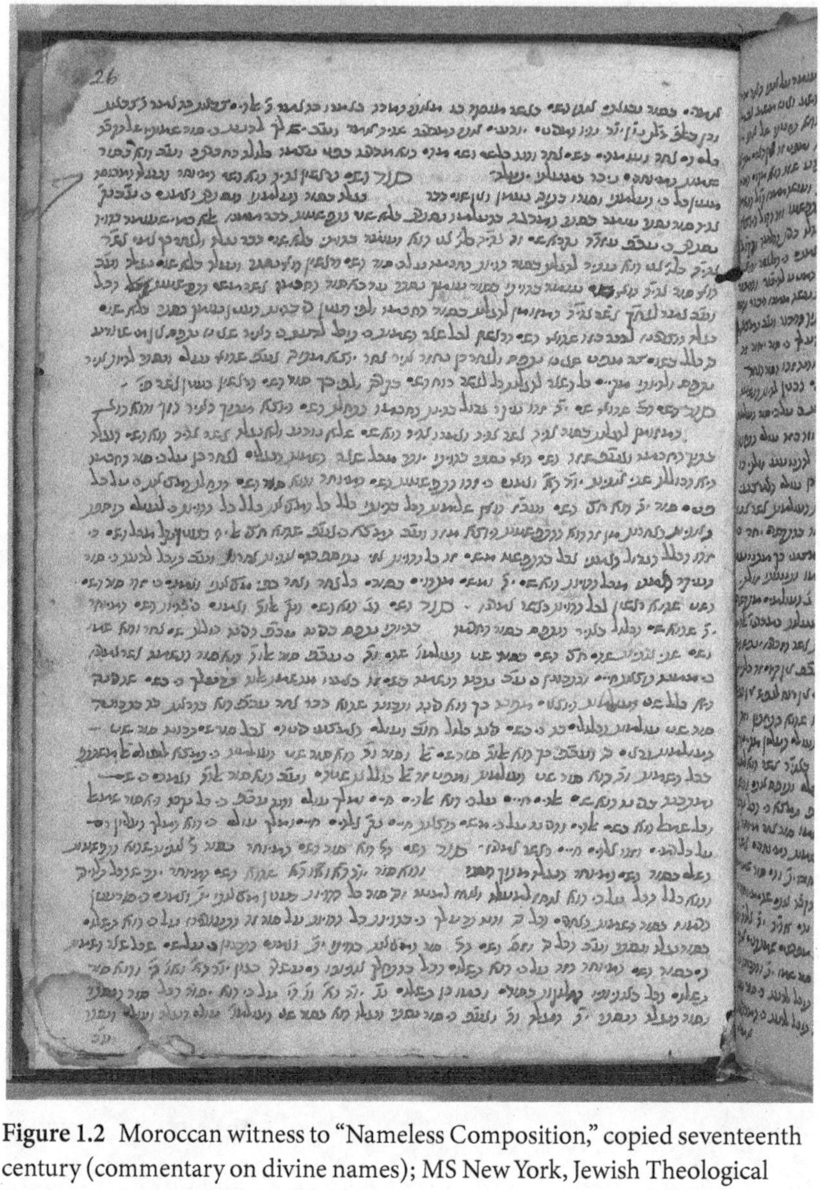

Figure 1.2 Moroccan witness to "Nameless Composition," copied seventeenth century (commentary on divine names); MS New York, Jewish Theological Seminary of America, 1777, fol. 26a.

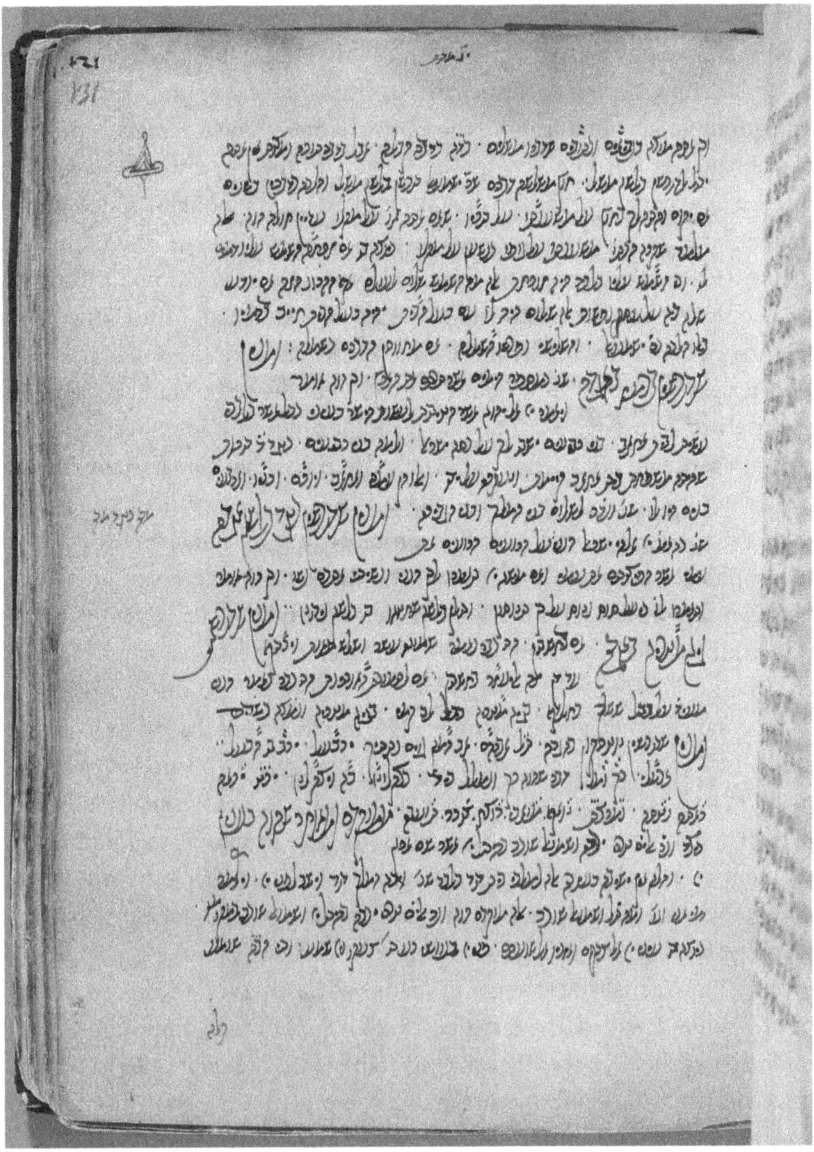

Figure 1.3 Moses de León's "Nameless Composition" (commentary on Rabbi Ishmael's thirteen hermeneutical principles); MS New York, Jewish Theological Seminary of America, 1609, fol. 131a.

scholars are saddled with the bewildering task of conducting their labors of textual archeology with this hopelessly obscure figure in the foreground.

Without presuming to dispel the darkness once and for all, this book inaugurates a new inquiry into the career of one of the foremost exponents of kabbalah in the Middle Ages and, truly, to the present day. Our study offers a new paradigm for the evolution of de León's thought, which hinges on the large, unpublished fragment that seized Scholem's attention back in the 1920s. We distinguish this work, the "Nameless Composition," as de León's first extensive effort to promulgate a kabbalah of the sefirot and the first of his works to corroborate his involvement in the zoharic project. This text, roughly half of which is preserved in the large Munich fragment, is loosely structured as a commentary on the ten sefirot. It is an early exemplar of a genre unique to the kabbalah literature, with which it is nonetheless out of step. Moreover, the composition is one of the first thematic (rather than strictly exegetical) treatises to promote the "new-ancient" wisdom of theosophical speculation.[12] Notwithstanding the many correspondences between this work and other known and authoritative texts, the composition exhibits a host of teachings that are underrepresented or simply lacking elsewhere. These rare and distinctive teachings concern the central topics of repentance, language, and gender. The treatments of these basic topics of kabbalistic speculation comprise most of the surviving portion of our composition and occasion the three thematic explorations we shall undertake here. The explorations afoot will allow readers to glimpse an embryonic moment in the emergence of Castilian kabbalah. It is for these reasons, and others that we will adduce, that our text merits a position of hermeneutical privilege for tracking the peculiar course of de León's thinking, the general evolution of kabbalistic thought in medieval Castile, and the long gestation of the Zohar. Even so, the fact that roughly half of the composition is lost underscores the darkness that shrouds our effort. It is nonetheless possible to reconstruct, however provisionally, some of the material that has not reached our hands from various clues at our fingertips.

[12] Daniel C. Matt, "New-Ancient Words: The Aura of Secrecy in the Zohar" [in Hebrew], in *Gershom Scholem's Major Trends in Jewish Mysticism: 50 Years After*, ed. Peter Schäfer and Joseph Dan (Tübingen: J. C. B. Mohr, 1993), 181–207.

1.2 Who Was Moses de León?

We still know precious little about the life of Moses de León. The dates ventured by Scholem, 1240–1305, are no longer reliable. In truth, we have only the dates de León inscribed in some of his major Hebrew works, a thirdhand anecdote about de León allegedly composed in the early fourteenth century by Isaac ben Samuel of Acre,[13] and what little contextual evidence we can recover about his associates and milieu. For example, his association with the family of the Toledan sage and crown rabbi Ṭodros ben Joseph ha-Levi Abulafia is gleaned from the dedication of de León's works to Ṭodros's son Joseph, and a responsum addressed to the same.[14] Scholars have surmised that Joseph ben Ṭodros, who, like his illustrious father, held a position at the royal court, served as de León's patron. This consideration, to which we will return, is meaningful for positioning de León within a specific Castilian political milieu.

The compositions for which we have explicit dates range from 1286 to 1293, covering less than a single decade. It is known that de León authored unsigned texts that predate 1286, some of which are only now beginning to reach a scholarly audience. These compositions belong to de León's *Sefer ha-Ne'lam* (*The Concealed Book*) corpus, a body of unsigned texts that share a distinctive intellectual orientation. The most familiar work from this corpus is the Genesis commentary called *Or zarua'* (*Light Is Sown*).[15] These pre-1286 compositions treat the Hebrew Bible as the matrix of an elaborate nexus of esoteric correspondences among the celestial spheres, the angelic intellects, and the forms of the Hebrew letters. While these early writings share much in common with de León's mature speculation, they do

[13] Adolf Neubauer printed a transcription of the text from MS Oxford, Bodleian Library, Hunt. 504 (Neubauer 2202) in his "The Bahir and the Zohar," *Jewish Quarterly Review* 4 (1892): 361–363; Abraham Zacuto, *Sefer Yuḥasin*, ed. A. Ḥ. Fraymann (Frankfurt am Main: A. Vohrmann, 1925), 88–89. See Yaacob Dweck, *The Scandal of Kabbalah: Leon Modena, Jewish Mysticism, Early Modern Venice* (Princeton, NJ: Princeton University Press, 2011); and Avishai Bar-Asher, "The Earliest *Sefer ha-Zohar* in Jerusalem: Early Manuscripts of Zoharic Texts and an Unknown Fragment from *Midrash ha-Ne'lam*[?]" [in Hebrew], *Tarbiz* 84, no. 4 (2016): 575–576.

[14] See Avishai Bar-Asher, ed., *R. Moses de León's* Sefer Mishkan ha-'edut [in Hebrew] (Los Angeles, CA: Cherub Press, 2013), 4–8 (editor's introduction). See, too, Yehuda Liebes, "The Date of Rabbi Moshe de Leon's Death" [in Hebrew], in *Meir Benayahu Memorial*, vol. 2: *Studies in Kabbalah, Jewish Thought, Liturgy, Piyut, and Poetry*, ed. Moshe Bar-Asher, Yehuda Liebes, Moshe Assis, and Yosef Kaplan (Jerusalem: Carmel, 2019), 745–750.

[15] Published by Alexander Altmann in his "*Sefer Or Zarua'* by R. Moses de Leon: Introduction, Critical Text, and Notes" [in Hebrew], *Kobez al Yad* 9, no. 19 (1980): 219–293. Subsequent chapters, and Chapter 3 in particular, will address research on this corpus since the pioneering work of Altmann.

not exemplify "kabbalah" in the typical sense; that is, they do not engage in theosophical discourse about the stratified inner dimensions of Israel's divinity (i.e., the sefirot, gradations, worlds, etc.). Based on a statement from *Sheqel ha-qodesh* to which we will return below, Scholem took 1286's *Shushan ha-'edut* (*The Rose of Testimony*)—another partially preserved composition—to be de León's first treatise on the kabbalah of the sefirot. Indeed, this composition already exhibits the same speculative outlook as much of the main homiletical stratum of the Zohar.

To the explicit dates de León provided for his works, which range from 1286 to 1293, we can now add an important coordinate for de León's earliest activity: 3 Tammuz, 5044 AM (June 25, 1284). Such was the date indicated by a Ferrarese scribe when copying a text belonging to de León's unsigned pretheosophical corpus. This date attests to the consumption and reproduction of de León's writings in the Italian peninsula during the author's lifetime. It also indicates that the author's work mediated a transregional network of scribal industry well beyond Castile, already during the earliest known phase of his career.[16] Though the author was evidently active as a writer of pretheosophical speculation prior to this date, we have, at present, no reliable guidelines for precisely how much earlier to establish his activity. Even if one may extend de León's floruit to predate 1284, we are nonetheless confronted by the reality that the total range of our explicit dates for his literary activity covers less than a single decade. The fact, overlooked by previous research, that this period is nearly coterminous with the reign of Sancho IV of Castile ("el Bravo"; r. 1284–1295) demands attention.

Concerning the placement of the "Nameless Composition" within de León's oeuvre, Scholem's 1927 article tendered an argument he would later disavow. He claimed there that the large Munich fragment constituted the missing portion of de León's *Shushan ha-'edut*.[17] But de León, we propose,

[16] Avishai Bar-Asher, "The Punctiform Deity: Theological Debates Among the Masters of Niqqud in the Works of Joseph Gikatilla's 'Disciples'" [in Hebrew], *Kabbalah: Journal for the Study of Jewish Mystical Texts* 53 (2022): 103–236, esp. 112n.32 and 14–15n.39.

[17] Scholem, "Eine unbekannte mystische Schrift," 123 (see already Scholem, "He'arot ve-tiqqunim," 287; and Gershom Scholem, "Ha-im ḥibber R. Moshe de León et Sefer ha-Zohar?" [in Hebrew], *Madda'e ha-Yahadut* 1 (1926): 24. Yet in the annotations to 1941's *Major Trends in Jewish Mysticism* (395n.115), we find this comment: "The lengthy fragment in Ms. Munich 47 which I believed for some time to contain this book [*Shushan ha-'edut*], is certainly from a work of Moses de Leon's but not the שושן עדות"; and in 1976, Scholem corroborated this revised view of the "Nameless Composition" when he finally transcribed a large portion of *Shushan ha-'edut* from a Cambridge manuscript for publication; the published text was evidently incongruent with the extant Munich material, making the provenance of the latter once again an open question. Gershom Scholem, "Shene quntresim shel Rabbi Moshe de Leon," *Kobez Al Yad* 8, no. 18 (1976): 325–384. See, too,

authored the "Nameless Composition" prior to *Shushan ha-ʿedut*. Adopting this key shift in the chronology solidifies our interpretive perspective that the large Munich fragment preserves the author's first work of kabbalah proper (i.e., kabbalah of the sefirot, or "theosophical kabbalah," to adopt a phrase popularized by Scholem). In contrast to subsequent kabbalistic treatises by de León, however, our text is still very much a transitional work. The thinking embodied in this text exhibits a tentative shift away from the cosmological orientation of his early writings and an advance toward the theosophical framework of his mature theology. And yet, among all de León's writings, our text embodies the most thorough synthesis of the early and late paradigms. In the extant portion of this work, we observe de León in the process of amalgamating ideas, testing their coherence with his early speculation, and generally experimenting, without the constraints that a signed corpus can exert upon an author.

In contrast to the scholarly tendency to isolate de León's writings into oppositional categories, such as early versus late, or "kabbalah of divine names" versus "kabbalah of the sefirot,"[18] we propose to assay de León's creativity

Scholem's discussion of our text in his "Farben und ihre Symbolik in der jüdischen Überlieferung," *Eranos Jahrbuch* 41 (1972): 46–47, and there n. 103.

[18] On the emic typological distinctions espoused by de León himself— as well as those made by Jacob ben Sheshet, Abraham Abulafia, Moses of Burgos, and Ṭodros Abulafia, see Wolfson, *Book of the Pomegranate*, 70. In terms of scholarship, Asi Farber-Ginat built upon Alexander Altmann's earlier analysis of a large fragment from *Or zaruaʿ* to organize the kabbalist's career into pretheosophic and posttheosophic periods. She categorized the large Munich fragment as a "theosophic composition" composed on the heels of the early "pretheosophical" works *Or zaruaʿ* and "Sod ha-eṣbaʿot" ("Secret of the Fingers"); Asi Farber-Ginat, "On the Sources of Rabbi Moses de Leon's Early Kabbalistic System" [in Hebrew], *Jerusalem Studies in Jewish Thought* 3, nos. 1–2 (1983–1984): 67–92, here 87–88. She claimed that the text's reference to "custodians of the secret of letters" (*baʿale sod ha-otiyyot*) could refer to "a kabbalist of the kabbalah of letters from the circle within which *Sefer Or zaruaʿ* sprouted." Farber-Ginat, "On the Sources," 79–80n.28. Wolfson divided de León's career into three successive phases: "philosophy, linguistic mysticism, and theosophy" (*Book of the Pomegranate*, 3) but also upheld a twofold periodization (pre-zoharic vs. zoharic periods) and conjectured that de León authored the Munich text once he had already begun composing portions of the Zohar. Elliot R. Wolfson, "Moisés de León y el Zohar," in *Pensamiento y Mística Hispanojudía y Sefardí* (Cuenca: Ediciones de la Universidad de Castilla-La Mancha, 2001), 165–192, esp. 166; Wolfson, *Luminal Darkness: Imaginal Gleanings from Zoharic Literature* (New York: Oxford University Press, 2007), 27n.98; printed initially in Wolfson, "Left Contained in the Right: A Study in Zoharic Hermeneutics," *AJS Review* 11, no. 1 (1986): 27–52, here 49n.98; Wolfson, *Book of the Pomegranate*, 15–16 (English pagination); Wolfson, *Through a Speculum That Shines: Vision and Imagination in Medieval Jewish* Mysticism (Princeton, NJ: Princeton University Press, 1994), 353, 381; Wolfson, "The Image of Jacob Engraved upon the Throne: Further Speculation on the Esoteric Doctrine of the German Pietism" [in Hebrew], in *Massuʾot: Studies in Kabbalistic Literature and Jewish Philosophy in Memory of Prof. Ephraim Gottlieb*, ed. Michal Oron and Amos Goldreich (Jerusalem: Mossad Bialik, 1994), 137n.35; and Wolfson, *Along the Path: Studies in Kabbalistic Myth, Symbolism, and Hermeneutics* (Albany: State University of New York Press, 1995), 119n.55. See, too, Moshe Idel, *Kabbalah: New Perspectives* (New Haven, CT: Yale University Press,

as a graduated continuum.[19] This book adopts a threefold periodization,[20] with the aim of softening past attempts to draw a hard "before and after" fault line bisecting de León's intellectual biography.[21] Our periodization situates the "Nameless Composition" at a transitional middle phase, after the composition of de León's *Sefer ha-Ne'lam* corpus and prior to the composition of *Shushan ha-'edut*.[22] This approach, again, places our text—a work exhibiting the most intensive synthesis of linguistic and theosophical speculation of any work in de León's corpus—in a pivotal position.

The impetus for scholars' initial assumption that *Shushan ha-'edut* was de León's first Hebrew work is this statement from the opening lines of *Sheqel ha-qodesh*, dated to 1292:

> Among the first of the compositions that I fashioned (*bi-teḥillat ha-ḥibburim asher 'asiti*) I composed a book called *Shushan* [*ha-*]*'edut* according to the need of the enlightened person to penetrate further into the correct matter. I was compelled to compose this composition [i.e., *Sheqel ha-qodesh*] for the honor of the great and mighty Prince, the magnificent Rav Joseph ha-Levi, may his splendor be exalted, the glorious son of the great, mighty, and magnificent Rav Ṭodros ha-Levi.

A close examination of this 1292 statement clarifies that its author did not claim *Shushan ha-'edut* (1286) as his first work, but as merely one of his earliest writings. But why name this work, rather than other texts known

1990), 140. A kabbalistic commentary on the thirteen hermeneutical principles of Rabbi Ishmael was published by Ronit Meroz from MS New York Jewish Theological Seminary of America 1609, fols. 129b–131a (see Figure 1.3), a shorter version of which is found at the end of the Munich fragment (MS Munich, Bayerische Staatsbibliothek, Cod. hebr. 47, fols. 385a–386b). Though Meroz weighed both the possibility that this commentary was compositionally integral to the rest of the Munich 47 material and the possibility that it belonged to the lost portion of *Shushan ha-'edut*, she ultimately deemed the commentary an autonomous unit, independent from both our text and *Shushan ha-'edut* (Ronit Meroz, "Kabbalah, Science and Pseudo-Science in Ramdal's Commentary on the Thirteen Attributes," in *And This Is for Yehuda: Studies Presented to Our Friend, Professor Yehuda Liebes, on the Occasion of His Sixty-Fifth Birthday*, ed. Maren R. Niehoff, Ronit Meroz, and Jonathan Garb [Jerusalem: Mossad Bialik, 2012], 123–143, here 125–126; for earlier assertions of the independence of this unit, see Wolfson, "Moisés de León y el Zohar," 166; and Wolfson, *Through a Speculum*, 20).

[19] Avishai Bar-Asher, "*Sefer ha-Ne'lam*, New Parts of *Sefer Or Zarua* and Clarifications Regarding the Early Writings of R. Moses de León: Studies and Critical Editions" [in Hebrew], *Tarbiz* 83, nos. 1–2 (2015): 197–329, esp. 252. For the suggestion that the complex development of de León's corpus may defy scholarly attempts to impose a fixed linear sequence of composition, see Daniel Abrams, "Divine Yearning for Shekhinah— 'The Secret of the Exodus from Egypt: R. Moses de León's *Questions and Answers* from Unpublished Manuscripts and Their Zoharic Parallels,'" *Kabbalah* 32 (2014): 7–34, esp. 18–19.

[20] Avishai Bar-Asher, "The Earliest Citation from *Sefer ha-Zohar* and from Whence the *Book of Zohar* Received Its Name" [in Hebrew], *Kabbalah* 39 (2017): 79–156, here 111–112, also 124.

[21] Bar-Asher, "Earliest Citation," 111–112, 124.

[22] Bar-Asher, "*Sefer ha-Ne'lam*," 57–58.

to precede the 1286 work? Did de León truly wish to sabotage the legacy of his earliest writings? The hypothesis that the author's turn toward theosophy militated against the memory of his earlier works would not explain his failure to mention the early theosophical composition to which we devote our study. The author's singling out of *Shushan ha-'edut* may rather be interpreted as the premise for the statement of dedication. We know that in 1286 de León had dedicated *Shushan ha-'edut* to the same "Prince,"[23] a reference to Joseph's appointment by the court of Sancho IV to succeed his father as crown rabbi over Castilian Jewry.[24] It appears that our author named only *Shushan ha-'edut* among his early works because it was the first he composed under the aegis of Joseph's patronage. He did this, it seems, with the intention of invoking the loyalty of his long-standing benefactor, which began, if our interpretation is correct, in 1286. Although we lack the first half of de León's earliest theosophical work where we might expect to locate the kind of information we find in the prologues to his subsequent books—title, authorship, date, location, dedication[25]—our reading of de León's bibliographic remark suggests that his suppression of earlier titles was a function of the loyalty owed to his benefactor. In fact, the Hebrew works that de León dedicated to his patron are largely interreferential, exhibiting a preference for the direct citation of other titles underwritten by Joseph; this preference is matched by a countertendency to downplay, omit, or misattribute allusions to the writings produced by de León outside the (quasi-)contractual terms of his patronage. These considerations have critical implications for rethinking de León's citation practices generally, and, more specifically, for reassessing the motivations for the author's pseudepigraphic pretenses, and especially his attribution of the zoharic homilies to ancient rabbis of the Galilee. For our present purposes, they help us to account for the baffling disappearance of the "Nameless Composition."[26]

If we thus soften the narrative of de León's sudden and decisive departure from his earliest speculation, do we then propose that the mature author continued to value his pretheosophical worldview? With some qualifications, the answer is yes. Our transitional text provides the clearest illustration of de

[23] Gershom Scholem, "Shene quntresim le-R. Moshe de León," *Kobez al Yad* 8, no. 18 (1976): 325–384, 327, and 332–333 in the text = Moses de León, *Shushan ha-'edut*, 332–333.

[24] On the office of crown rabbi in Castile, see Jonathan Ray, *The Sephardic Frontier: The "Reconquista" and the Jewish Community in Medieval Iberia* (Ithaca, NY: Cornell University Press, 2013), 113–123.

[25] See Michal Oron, ed., *Sha'ar ha-razim le-Rav Ṭodros ben Yosef ha-Levi Abulafia* (Jerusalem: Mossad Bialik, 1989), 35; Bar-Asher, *Mishkan ha-'edut*, v.

[26] It seems that de León's patronage during the reign of Sancho IV accounts more effectively for the author's livelihood than the story found in the letter purportedly authored by Isaac of Acre of de León's selling of quires containing handwritten portions of the Zohar.

León's laborious reworking of elements from his earliest teachings (esoteric teachings related to the basic building blocks of the Hebrew language, the divine names, the causal flow of emanation through the angelic ranks, the celestial spheres, etc.) and the integration of such material into his sustained explorations of the intradivine order. The composition exhibits a complex process of "theosophization," if we may, whenever de León reprised topics treated in his *Sefer ha-Ne'lam* corpus.[27] It becomes clear just how well our text exemplifies this transitional profile when it is studied alongside early compositions belonging to the pretheosophic phase of de León's project.[28] Rather than an erasure of earlier speculation, the "Nameless Composition" embodies a dynamic negotiation between seemingly incompatible worldviews that underlies the text's treatment of basic themes of kabbalistic piety and speculation.

What kind of audience did the author anticipate for this work? As in many of his mature writings, de León expected that his reader would be a *maskil*, a term usually translated as an "enlightened" person. No run-of-the-mill intellectual, the projected reader would be an intrepid wayfarer upon the hidden pathways of wisdom, one who had already attained a high degree of learning and was prepared to expend significant intellectual and spiritual resources in the vigilant pursuit of truth. But what kind of wisdom and truth? Our author expected that his reader would have a general knowledge of, and reverence for, the early curriculum of theosophical speculation produced in Catalonia. This was a sacred body of knowledge likewise enshrined in the writings of Ṭodros ben Joseph ha-Levi Abulafia of Toledo,[29] crown rabbi in the court of Alfonso X (r. 1252–1284) and the father of de León's patron. Like the writings of Ṭodros, our text identifies the wisdom represented by the Catalonian sources as the theological substance of the rabbinic oral tradition ostensibly revealed at Sinai. In other words, it regards what we call "kabbalah" as the core intellectual content disseminated by means of the great *shalshelet ha-qabbalah* (chain of transmission). In Castile, during the 1280s, this was still a relatively novel ideology of Oral Torah, an ideology to which de León first declared his zealous allegiance in our nameless text. Such ideological alignment between the latter text and the works of Ṭodros may have ingratiated de León with the family that would ultimately secure his patronage.

27 See Avishai Bar-Asher, *Journeys of the Soul: Concepts and Imageries of Paradise in Medieval Kabbalah* [in Hebrew] (Jerusalem: Magnes Press, 2019), 198–203, 269–273.

28 See Bar-Asher, "*Sefer ha-Ne'lam*," 8, 17, 18, 32, 35, 41, 52, 55, 57–58. Also, see Bar-Asher, "Earliest Citation," 96, 105, 111.

29 On Ṭodros's sources, see Oron, *Sha'ar ha-razim*, 30–36.

As with the writings of Ṭodros, our text does not instruct its students to bow in obsequious deference to the sages of Catalonia. Just as Ṭodros innovated upon the wisdom from Girona when, for example, carrying forward the tradition of composing commentaries on the talmudic *aggadot*, and therewith guiding "enlightened" readers of such texts down novel highways of knowledge, so too did de León innovate. He aimed, with his first theosophical work, to produce an unprecedented type of pious intellectual. The work's projected reader would possess not only speculative knowledge, but also ritual knowledge of Jewish praxis. In other words, its "enlightened" reader would also be a righteous person. However, the text is not satisfied with its reader's intellectual and religious diligence, which are merely prerequisites. It is, rather, eager to impart a supererogatory, or even angelic, character, aspiring ultimately to the formation of pious penitents (*ba'ale teshuvah*) through the acquisition of godly attributes.

The text frequently engages its reader in a volley of questions and answers (e.g., "If you shall ask ___, you shall know that ___"). While such back-and-forth may be merely rhetorical, it is possible that in some such contexts, de León took the opportunity to respond in writing to the questions of actual students. Another text describes de León holding court with a group of students, fielding their questions, and subsequently responding to them in writing: "The fellows (*he-ḥaverim*) with whom I was present, and whose souls thirsted to enter the orchard of this awesome wisdom, asked me about this, and I recalled what they inquired of me, . . . and I was compelled to write."[30] The statement suggests that its author engaged his students directly, and that unexhausted questions from an oral mode of inquiry spilled over into de León's writings, where he expatiated in greater detail. What we possess of our composition does not name any particular student, but subsequent works name Joseph ben Ṭodros, as we have already mentioned, and one "Jacob," whom our author characterized in 1290 as a paragon of virtue.[31] It is not known if teaching came as an obligation related to de León's patronage or, for that matter, if Joseph was not just a patron but a student as well (as suggested by an extant responsum on the soul addressed by the author to Joseph dating from ca. 1287).

[30] MS Jerusalem, Schocken Institute, 13161, fol. 78a–b.

[31] See Adolph Jellinek, *Moses Ben Schem-Tob de Leon und sein Verhältnis zum Sohar: Eine historisch-kritische Untersuchung über die Entstehung des Sohar* (Leipzig: Heinrich Hunger, 1851), 20; Jochanan H. A. Wijnhoven, ed., "*Sefer ha-Mishkal: Text and Study*" (PhD diss., Brandeis University, 1964), 22, 27–28; Bar-Asher, *Mishkan ha-'edut*, v n. 24.

If de León did instruct Jewish courtiers of Sancho IV, whose reign coordinates almost perfectly with the known dates for our author's activities, it is nearly certain that the rabbinic author from Guadalajara did not initiate Christians, high ranking or otherwise, into the hidden wisdom, or intend his writings for the consumption of Christians, let alone Muslims. He nonetheless assumed his Jewish readers had at least rudimentary knowledge of both Christian and Muslim practices and beliefs.[32] Even though our author was the indirect beneficiary of a Christian king, through the mediation of Joseph ben Ṭodros, his signed compositions grapple polemically with Christianity, and his zoharic writings baldly prohibit disclosing secrets of the Torah to Christians. On these and other grounds, there is adequate reason to doubt the claim that Alfonso X had already gained access to kabbalistic secrets by means of translation. This highly rhetorical assertion was advanced by a renowned literary figure educated in the court of Sancho IV, namely, the latter's cousin Don Juan Manuel, in the context of a hyperbolic encomium to the ostensibly boundless translation project of his learned uncle, King Alfonso X (see Figure 1.4):

> And so much did he [i.e., Alfonso X] desire for those of his kingdoms to be very wise, that he had translated into this Castilian language (*lenguaje de Castiella*) all of the sciences, as well as theology and logic, and all of the seven liberal arts, as well as the craft that is called "mechanics" (*mecanica*). Furthermore, he had translated the entire religion of the Moors (*toda la secta delos moros* [i.e., the Qur'ān]), so that the errors into which their false prophet Muḥammad led them, in which [errors] they remain today, would become apparent. Moreover, he had translated all of the Law of the Jews and even their Talmud and another science that the Jews keep very hidden, which they call "cabala" (*Otrosi fizo trasladar toda ley delos judios e avn el su talmud E otra sçiençia que an los judios muy escondida a que llaman cabala*).[33]

There is clear evidence of Jews facilitating the Alfonsine project of translation, which may have included the rendering of pre-kabbalistic works of Jewish esotericism into the Castilian vernacular.[34] But, even if it were

[32] Such knowledge will be discussed in the course of our study; on Islam in particular, see Ronald C. Kiener, "The Image of Islam in the Zohar," *Jerusalem Studies in Jewish Thought* 8 (1989): 43–65.

[33] MS Madrid, Biblioteca Nacional de España, S. 34, fol. 201a; Juan Manuel, *El libro dela caza*, ed. G. Baist (Halle: Max Niemeyer, 1880), 1; Juan Manuel, *Don Juan Manuel y el* Libro de la caza, ed. José Manuel Fradejas Rueda (Tordesillas: Instituto de Estudios de Iberoamérica y Portugal; Seminario de Filología Medieval, 2001), 129.

[34] See, for example, Alejandro García Avilés, "Alfonso X y el *Liber Razielis*: Imágenes de la magia astral judía en el *scriptorium* alfonsí," *Bulletin of Hispanic Studies* 74, no. 1 (1997): 21–40.

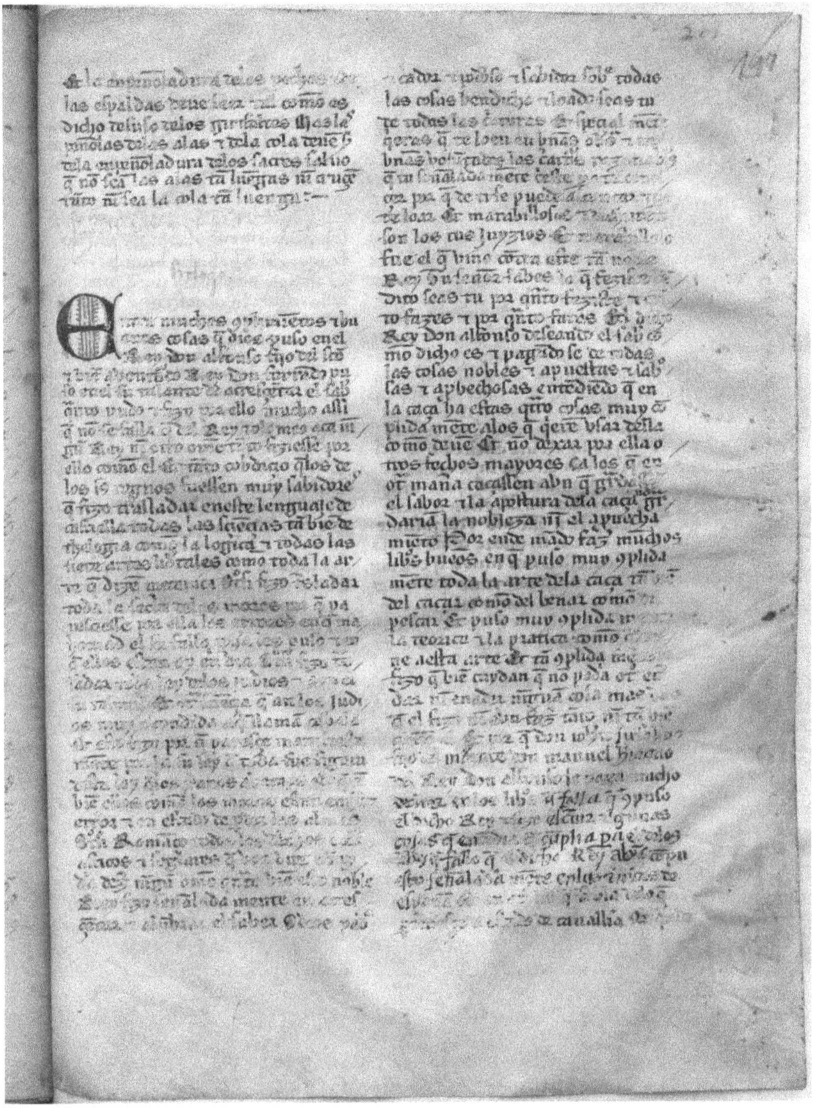

Figure 1.4 First known attestation of the romanized term "cabala" referring to Jewish esotericism; from the prologue to Juan Manuel's early fourteenth-century *Libro de la caza*; MS Madrid, Biblioteca Nacional de España, S. 34, fol. 201a.

trustworthy, Juan Manuel's boast would have nothing to teach us about the vernacular translation of de León's works—which we can scarcely date earlier than Alfonso's death in Seville on April 4, 1284. The text is nonetheless problematic as a testament to Castilian translations of the Qur'ān, the

Talmud, or kabbalistic writings composed prior to de León's time.[35] If this early fourteenth-century text cannot verify the possession by Christians of the Jews' *cabala* (which is certainly among the earliest attestations of this sense of the word outside of Hebrew usage),[36] it nonetheless indicates an uninformed awareness of kabbalah's existence some three decades after de León composed his earliest theosophical text.

1.3 Structure

Above we characterized the "Nameless Composition" as a commentary on the ten sefirot. In this characterization we do not, however, follow Scholem's designation of the composition as a ten-chapter work that exemplifies the conventions of the genre as defined by the encyclopedic organization of *Sha'are orah* (*Gates of Light*) by Joseph ben Abraham Gikatilla of Medinaceli—a contemporary and associate of de León.[37] The work does not use the term "sefirot" often,[38] preferring, as elsewhere in de León's Hebrew corpus, designations like *middot* (attributes, virtues, measures, or qualities), *ma'alot* (gradations, levels, tiers), or *madregot* (rungs, or steps). Though the text seeks to explain the gradations of divinity,[39] its explanations are interspersed with lengthy meditations on various topics of religious knowledge associated with the individual sefirot.[40] Such digressions include an

[35] See, for example, L. P. Harvey, "The Alfonsine School of Translators: Translations from Arabic into Castilian Produced Under the Patronage of Alfonso the Wise of Castile (1221–1252–1284)," *Journal of the Royal Asiatic Society of Great Britain and Ireland* 1 (1977): 109–117; Thomas Burman, *Reading the Qur'ān in Latin Christendom, 1140–1560* (Philadelphia: University of Pennsylvania Press, 2007), s.v. "Qur'ān, Castilian translations of." On the self-authorizing rhetoric of *Libro de la caza*, and the dating of the work, see Germán Orduna, "Los prólogos a la *Crónica abreviada* y al *Libro de la caza*: La tradición alfonsí y la primera época en la obra literaria de don Juan Manuel," *Cuadernos de historia de España* 51–52 (1970): 123–144.

[36] On the near contemporaneous use of the term by Alfonso de Valladolid, see Guadalupe González Diéguez, "Kabbalistic Traditions in the Castilian Vernacular: R. Moshe Arragel's Glosses to the Alba Bible," *eHumanista* 50 (2022): 538–557, esp. 538–540.

[37] For the suggestion that, stylistically, the large fragment resembled the late writings of Gikatilla, see Scholem, "Eine unbekannte mystische Schrift," 144n.2; he made this suggestion because, like Gikatilla's *Sha'are orah*, the fragment expounds the hierarchy of sefirot from below to above, rather than the reverse top-down order attested in de León's mature theosophic writings. Scholars have tended to date *Sha'are orah* to 1293 or prior on the strength of an apparent reference to that work in de León's *Mishkan ha-'edut*; manuscript evidence, however, shows that the supposed reference is a late scribal interpolation and thus unreliable for dating the works of Gikatilla; see Bar-Asher, *Mishkan ha-'edut*, 53n.280.

[38] MS Munich, Bayerische Staatsbibliothek, Cod. hebr. 47, fols. 338b, 339b, 363a–364a.

[39] Asi Farber too referred to the work as such a commentary in her "On the Sources," 87–88; in this, the bibliography of the Pritzker Zohar follows suit.

[40] See Scholem, "Eine unbekannte mystische Schrift," 114.

extensive exhortation to repentance occasioned by the author's theosophical reflections on *binah/teshuvah*, as well as a disquisition on the forms and properties of the Hebrew letters set within the author's account of *ḥokhmah*. In addition to these meditations, we must also account for the text's competing speculative frameworks. As with other kabbalists of his time, de León was not content to limit the theosophical speculation on the divinity to a fixed tenfold formula. He thus infused the text with iterations of a thirteenfold pattern (*dugma*) pervading the divine world, the celestial hierarchies, as well as the cosmos. These teachings about the thirteenfold pattern preserve a theosophical-cosmological tradition in tension with the well-known tenfold discourse of the sefirot.[41]

The extant portion of the composition begins abruptly, in the midst of what appears to be the work's sixth chapter dedicated to *tif'eret* (beauty), *raḥamim* (compassion), and *emet* (truth)—the fifth sefirah, counting from below to above. This is followed by the seventh chapter (*sha'ar ha-ḥeleq*) treating *ḥesed*, the seventh gradation (counting from below), and its relationship to the "left side" of divinity, that is, *paḥad/gevurah*, the sixth sefirah.[42] The next gate, the eighth, discusses the eighth sefirah that is called *binah* (understanding), *'olam ha-ba* (the coming world), but primarily *teshuvah* (repentance). This chapter, as mentioned, provides the theosophical scaffolding of the thirteen-step program for penitents (*Siddur ba'ale teshuvah*). Ascending to the next level of divine wisdom, the reader enters the "gate" of the ninth sefirah, that is, *ḥokhmah*. This ninth chapter deals extensively with letter speculation (for de León, the Hebrew letters are rooted in this aspect of divinity).[43] It also touches on the source of *ḥokhmah* in *keter 'elyon* (supernal crown), or *ayin* (nothing). But in contrast to the view that *keter*

[41] See Jeremy Phillip Brown, *A World of Piety: The Aims of Castilian Kabbalah* (Stanford, CA: Stanford University Press, 2025), esp. chap. 3; Brown, "Distilling Depths from Darkness: Forgiveness and Repentance in Medieval Iberian Jewish Mysticism" (PhD diss., New York University, 2015), 218–221; and Avishai Bar-Asher, "R. Isaac ben Solomon Ibn Sahula's Commentary on Psalms" [in Hebrew], *Kobez al Yad* 26, no. 36 (2018): 39 (ll. 235–241).

[42] Notably, this phase of de León's thought does not deal with the sinister powers of excess judgment erupting from the left side. On the emanation of judgment from the left side, see, for example, MS Munich, Bayerische Staatsbibliothek, Cod. hebr. 47, fols. 341a–342b (concerning the mitigation of harsh judgment by mild judgment, and later joy), fol. 346a–b (on the emanation of judgment and punishment from the attribute of *gevurah* on those who transgress Torah; on the need of balancing left with right), fol. 368a (the emanation of judgment from the left), 383b–384a (linked to the divine name Elohim).

[43] See Elliot R. Wolfson, "Letter Symbolism and Merkavah Imagery in the Zohar," in *Alei Shefer: Studies in the Literature of Jewish Thought Presented to Rabbi Dr. Alexandre Safran*, ed. Moshe Hallamish (Ramat Gan: Bar-Ilan University Press, 1990), 195–236; and Avishai Bar-Asher, "From Alphabetical Mysticism to Theosophical Kabbalah: A Rare Witness to an Intermediate Stage of Moses de León's Thought," *Revue des études juives* 179, nos. 3–4 (2020): 351–384.

is the tenth sefirah, the text argues that this transcendental ground of all things divine and otherwise should not be counted together with the other nine.[44] The text's tenth chapter explores the concatenation of the imperceptible *avir qadmon* (primordial ether) from *keter* traversing the divine world and descending into the realm of creation. Here the composition elaborates on the thirteenfold pattern at length using the central image of Solomon's Sea. To this tenth chapter are appended two further units that are preserved elsewhere, namely, a commentary on the ten divine names whose erasure is prohibited,[45] and a discussion of the thirteen hermeneutical principles of Rabbi Ishmael that breaks off prematurely (see Figure 1.3). We conjecture that the text originally contained an additional final unit, giving the composition, like Solomon's Sea, a thirteenfold structure. This conjecture is further supported by the fact that de León adopted such a structure for organizing 1292's *Sheqel ha-qodesh*.

1.4 Sources

A vigorous confluence of religious, cultural, and intellectual factors infuses the kabbalah of medieval Castile. The placement of the large Munich fragment at the crossroads of de León's Hebrew corpus recommends our text as an unusually illustrative index for this confluence. In addition to its vestiges of the early phase of León's project—itself owing much to Maimonidean cosmology and epistemology,[46] as well as esoteric speculation on the Hebrew letters cultivated in other rabbinic textual communities in the Middle Ages[47]—the text carries forward many other facets of traditional Jewish knowledge. These include, of course, the wisdom of the rabbis to which the text refers on nearly every folio—especially dicta from the Babylonian

[44] MS Munich, Bayerische Staatsbibliothek, Cod. hebr. 47, fol. 378b; compare fol. 362b (in reference to the alef, the monistic source of all and holistic singularity, that is both counted, and not counted). Avishai Bar-Asher, "Decoding the Decalogue: Theosophical Re-engraving of the Ten Commandments in Thirteenth-Century Kabbalah," in *Accounting for the Commandments in Medieval Judaism: Studies in Law, Philosophy, Pietism, and Kabbalah*, ed. Jeremy Phillip Brown and Marc Herman (Leiden: Brill, 2020), 156–174.

[45] Moses de León, *Sheqel ha-qodesh*, 98–102.

[46] On de León and Maimonides, see Wolfson, *Book of the Pomegranate*, 25n.63, 27–34, 36–38 (English pagination); and Wolfson, *A Dream Interpreted Within a Dream: Oneiropoiesis and the Prism of Imagination* (Cambridge, MA: Zone Books, 2011), 256n.161; Jeremy Phillip Brown, "Gazing into Their Hearts: On the Appearance of Kabbalistic Pietism in Thirteenth-Century Castile," *European Journal of Jewish Studies* 14 (2020): 177–214, esp. 198–199; Brown, *World of Piety*, s.v. "Maimonides."

[47] Bar-Asher, "From Alphabetical Mysticism," 352–362.

Talmud and classic midrashic collections.[48] Sometimes, as was de León's practice elsewhere, the text brings medieval teachings known exclusively from the Aramaic Zohar in the name of the ancient sages.[49] The authority of *Sefer Yeṣirah* is likewise well established throughout the text. We will return to the specific motifs and themes from *Sefer Yeṣirah* that feature prominently, such as the language of "sefirot,"[50] "a flame bound to a coal,"[51] the generative character of the Hebrew alphabet, the four elements, and the six extremities (above, below, east, west, north, and south).

Most significant are the kabbalistic traditions incubated by the sages of Girona, though de León does not refer by name to any specific kabbalistic authors of previous generations (nor, for that matter, does he name contemporary kabbalists).[52] The importance of Ezra ben Solomon's writings is evident from phraseology that de León adopts verbatim, as he does elsewhere in later compositions.[53] Moreover, the theosophy and symbolism promoted by de León owe much to the conventions of Ezra's kabbalah. Though our text makes occasional reference to kabbalistic rationales of the commandments (*ṭaʿame ha-miṣvot*) in the style of Ezra, this is not a main preoccupation (in contrast to *Sefer ha-Rimmon* of 1927).[54] The work bears a scribal attribution to Naḥmanides (see Figure 1.1),[55] but the great sage of Catalonia is obviously not its author. Still, de León is much indebted to Naḥmanides's oeuvre, and even deploys the latter's characteristic rhetoric and teachings. One example of this is our author's adoption of the phrase "by the way of truth" (*ʿal derekh ha-emet*), a phrase Naḥmanides used to preface the disclosure of a kabbalistic

[48] Wolfson, *Book of the Pomegranate*, 34–35 (English pagination); Bar-Asher, *Mishkan ha-ʿedut*, 51–52 (introduction).

[49] Wolfson, *Book of the Pomegranate*, 43–55 (English pagination); Bar-Asher, *Mishkan ha-ʿedut*, 28–45 (introduction).

[50] *Sefer Yeṣirah*, 1:2–1:8, 1:14; compare MS Munich, Bayerische Staatsbibliothek, Cod. hebr. 47, fols. 363a–364a.

[51] *Sefer Yeṣirah*, 1:6 (*ke-shalhevet qeshurah le-gaḥelet*); compare MS Munich, Bayerische Staatsbibliothek, Cod. hebr. 47, fol. 375b (*ke-lahav ha-qeshurah le-gaḥelet*).

[52] Though the text refers generically to "custodians" of esoteric wisdom, it does not cite any contemporary authors or titles by name; compare Scholem, "Eine unbekannte mystische Schrift," 116–117.

[53] For example, MS Munich, Bayerische Staatsbibliothek, Cod. hebr. 47, fols. 337b–338a, where de León uses unattributed language taken directly from Ezra's commentary on the talmudic *aggadot*; *Commentarius in Aggadoth auctore R. Azriel Geronensi* [in Hebrew], ed. Isaiah Tishby (Jerusalem: Mekize Nirdamim, 1945), 6, 38–39; Abraham ben Judah Elmalik, *Liqqute shikheḥah u-feʾah* (Ferrara, 1556), 7b. Compare Menaḥem Recanati, *Sefer Ṭaʿame ha-miṣvot ha-shalem*, ed. Simḥah Lieberman (London: Mekhon oṣar ha-ḥokhmah, 1962), 72a (there attributed to "Azriel").

[54] Scholem overstated this point to the erroneous degree of denying that the Munich fragment contains any single "Halachadeutung"; Scholem, "Eine unbekannte mystische Schrift," 121. See, for example, the rationale of the Levitical incense offering, MS Munich, Bayerische Staatsbibliothek, Cod. hebr. 47, fols. 346b–347a.

[55] MS Munich, Bayerische Staatsbibliothek, Cod. hebr. 47, fol. 335b.

tradition.[56] Another is de León's assertion that "all of the Torah in its entirety is the secret of the name of the Blessed Holy One" (*kol ha-torah kullah sod shemo shel ha-qadosh barukh hu*).[57] The author reproduced this axiom almost precisely from the Torah commentary of Naḥmanides: "All of the Torah in its entirety is [composed of] names of the Blessed Holy One" (*kol ha-torah kullah shemotav shel ha-qadosh barukh hu*).[58] Though the kabbalists of Girona studied and cited *Sefer ha-Bahir*, only faint traces of it are attested in the "Nameless Composition,"[59] which, furthermore, attributes no oral traditions to Isaac the Blind. Though, as mentioned, the topic of repentance is a focus of our text, the large portion of the work in our possession does not dwell upon the problem of evil; at least, it does not discourse about the sinister emanations that so preoccupied earlier and contemporary kabbalists active in the territories of Castile.[60] While the text is the first of de León's writings to articulate the goal of harnessing the "left side" of the Godhead to the right, this mandate does not posit a phalanx of impure forces paralleling the stratified realm of divine holiness.[61] Lastly, the text demonstrates subtle engagements with Maimonides and the early, pretheosophical speculation composed by both Joseph Gikatilla and de León himself.

1.5 The Zohar

The relationship of de León's first theosophical work to the Zohar merits special consideration. The copious scholarship on Scholem's evolving views on the Zohar ignores the catalyzing role the Munich fragment played in this

[56] MS Munich, Bayerische Staatsbibliothek, Cod. hebr. 47, fols. 343b, 358b, 376b.

[57] MS Munich, Bayerische Staatsbibliothek, Cod. hebr. 47, fol. 381b.

[58] Naḥmanides, *Commentary on the Torah*, ed. Charles B. Chavel (Jerusalem: Mossad Harav Kook, 1959–1963), 1:6.

[59] Though the text uses a bahiric idiom referring to the "flourishing souls" (*umimenu porḥot ha-neshamot*; MS Munich, Bayerische Staatsbibliothek, Cod. hebr. 47, fol. 338b) from the river going forth from Eden, in the Bahir, the phrase refers instead to the souls flowering from the tree. See Avishai Bar-Asher, "The Bahir as It Once Was: Transmission History as a Tool for Reconstructing and Reassessing the Text, Format, and Ideas of the Original Composition" [in Hebrew], *Tarbiz* 89, no. 1 (2022): 73–225 = *Sefer ha-Bahir*, sections IX 1 (14), pp. 174–175; XVII 7 (39), p. 181; XXVII 3–4 (85), p. 195. It is possible that de León adopted this phrase, which occurs here and there throughout his corpus, from another source, such as Naḥmanides's commentary to Genesis 24:1. On the Bahir in *Sefer ha-Rimmon*, see Wolfson, *Book of the Pomegranate*, 39.

[60] For example, Isaac ha-Kohen, Moses ben Simeon of Burgos, Ṭodros ben Joseph ha-Levi Abulafia, Joseph Gikatilla, and, in other instances, de León himself. See Avishai Bar-Asher, "'Samael and His Female Counterpart': R. Moses de León's Lost Commentary on Ecclesiastes" [in Hebrew], *Tarbiz* 80, no. 4 (2012): 539–566; and Moshe Idel, *Primeval Evil in Kabbalah: Totality, Perfections, Perfectibility* (New York: KTAV Publishing, 2020), 189–236.

[61] Brown, "Gazing into Their Hearts," 22–23.

story. In fact, his examination of our text caused Scholem to revisit the possibility that de León was indeed the author of the Zohar after all, or, at least, its first Hebrew translator.[62] Our Hebrew text contains a host of clear parallels to Aramaic material from the zoharic homilies on the Torah, and these are noteworthy for being the earliest unambiguous parallels to the main homiletical stratum of the Zohar in de León's Hebrew corpus (or anywhere, for that matter). The historiography has lavished much attention on the "quotations" from the Zohar's *Midrash ha-Ne'lam* found in the writings of Isaac Ibn Sahula—*Meshal ha-qadmoni* (*Parable of the Ancient*) and the theosophical commentary on the Song of Songs.[63] Though some follow Scholem in dating *Meshal ha-qadmoni* to 1281,[64] its precise date is unknown. We can only determine that Ibn Sahula completed his collection of moralistic parables at some point after his repentance in 1281 and before composing his kabbalistic commentary on the Song of Songs (ca. 1284).[65] Whatever the precise date, the "quotations" brought by Ibn Sahula only establish parallels to pre-kabbalistic portions of the Zohar. However, if we seek to date the homilies containing the bulk of the Zohar's kabbalistic teachings, we must consider the terminus ante quem we have set for the "Nameless Composition," namely, 1286, as our starting point. This is because the earliest extrinsic evidence for "zoharic kabbalah" that is roughly datable is precisely our text, which, again, de León composed prior to *Shushan ha-'edut*. Coordinating the material in this way is instructive in many respects—not least because it teaches that at least some portion of de León's zoharic activity coincided with the transitional phase of his intellectual journey.

This intermediate material also furnishes our earliest examples of de León's practice of attributing dicta known from the Zohar to the talmudic rabbis. The author persisted in this practice in virtually all his subsequent

62 Scholem, "Eine unbekannte mystische Schrift," 119–120. Noteworthy is the departure from the outlook expressed in Scholem, "Ha-im ḥibber R. Moshe de León et *Sefer ha-Zohar*?"

63 Gershom Scholem, "The First Quotation from the Zohar's *Midrash ha-Ne'lam*" [in Hebrew], *Tarbiz* 3, no. 2 (1931–1932): 181–183; Scholem, "A New Passage from the *Midrash ha-Ne'lam* of the Zohar" [in Hebrew], in *Louis Ginzberg: Jubilee Volume*, ed. Alexander Marx et al. (New York: American Academy for Jewish Research, 1946), 2:425–446; Arthur Green, "R. Isaac ibn Sahola's Commentary on the Song of Songs" [in Hebrew], *Jerusalem Studies in Jewish Thought* 6, nos. 3–4 (1987): 393–491, esp. 400; Nathan Wolski, "Moses de León and *Midrash ha-Ne'elam*: On the Beginnings of the Zohar," *Kabbalah* 34 (2016): 27–116; Bar-Asher, "Earliest Citation," 83–84; Bar-Asher, "R. Isaac ben Solomon ibn Sahula's Commentary on Psalms," 1–45.

64 Scholem, *Major Trends in Jewish Mysticism*, 187–188.

65 Isaac Ibn Sahula, *Meshal Haqadmoni: Fables from the Distant Past*, ed. and trans. Raphael Loewe (Portland, OR: Littman Library of Jewish Civilization, 2004), xv–xvii; Green, "R. Isaac ibn Sahola's Commentary on the Song of Songs"; Bar-Asher, "R. Isaac ben Solomon Ibn Sahula's Commentary on Psalms," 6–10 (for a bibliography, see 6–7n.21).

Hebrew works.[66] To illustrate the point, we will adduce two examples of de León's practice of placing his exegetical innovations on the lips of the ancients, where we have clear parallels from the ostensibly ancient Zohar.[67] The first concerns a correspondence between the social hierarchy of ancient Israel and the tenfold arrangement of the sefirot; the second explains the ritual efficacy of the Levitical incense offering in arousing joy within the divine world.

MS Munich BSB Cod. hebr. 47, 341a	Zohar 2:82a
Our sages of blessed memory suggested [that] ten ascending ranks of Israel stood upon Mt. Sinai, five from the right and five from the left, as it is written: "You stand this day all of you before the Lord your God, your captains of your tribes, your elders, and your officers, with all the men of Israel" (Deuteronomy 29:9); thus here are the five ranks to the right side. And what are the five ranks to the left? It is written: "Your little ones, your wives, and your stranger that is in your camp, from the hewer of your wood to the drawer of your water" (Deuteronomy 29:10); here are the five that are to the left side.	We have learned that they stood [upon Mt. Sinai] in rows and in groups and divisions, and each one saw [the theophany] as befitted him. Rabbi Simeon said that the chiefs of the tribes [stood] by themselves and all the women by themselves. And five ranks [stood] on the right and five ranks on the left, as it is written: "You stand this day all of you before the Lord your God, your captains of your tribes, your elders, and your officers, with all the men of Israel" (Deuteronomy 29:9). These are the five ranks to the right. And what are the five ranks to the left? It is written: "Your little ones, your wives, and your stranger that is in your camp, from the hewer of your wood to the drawer of your water" (Deuteronomy 29:10). These are the five ranks to the left.

[66] One scholar commented that the kabbalist "toyed with his readership" in citing the Zohar in this manner. See Daniel Abrams, "The Only Sefirotic Diagram of the Zohar Manuscript Witnesses and Its Absence in Print," *Daat* 87 (2019): 7. He nonetheless affirmed, on a less cynical note, that de León's persistence in this practice reflected his "total identification with the [ancient] rabbinic milieu," and that the kabbalist's adoption of "its literary norms and mindset was an organic result of such immersion" (8). Whether the reader assumes a suspicious or sympathetic hermeneutical mood, it is critical to survey the earliest evidence for this kind of activity as it emerges from the "Nameless Composition."

[67] Compare also MS Munich, Bayerische Staatsbibliothek, Cod. hebr. 47, fol. 376a with Zohar 1:105b (= Simeon bar Yoḥai [attr.], *Sefer ha-Zohar*, 3 vols., ed. Reuven Margaliyot [Jerusalem: Mossad Harav Kook, 1964]) and there, 3:58b (also with a close parallel in Moses de León, *Sefer ha-Rimmon*, 169); see MS Munich, Bayerische Staatsbibliothek hebr. 47, fol. 338b compared with Zohar 3:39b; de León, *Sefer ha-Rimmon*, 86, where Wolfson identifies a parallel to MS Munich, Bayerische Staatsbibliothek, Cod. hebr. 47, fol. 347a, and cites a tradition also attested in Zohar 1:230a, and 3:11b; and see Wolfson, *Language, Eros, Being*, 451. For a parable on repentance attested in both the Munich fragment (fol. 350a–b) and the *Midrash ha-Ne'lam* stratum of the Zohar, see *Zohar ḥadash* 22b; see Wolski, "Moses de León and *Midrash ha-Ne'elam*," 65–68.

MS Munich BSB Cod. hebr. 47, 346b–347a (compare *Sefer ha-Rimmon*, 86–87)	**Zohar 1:230a** (compare 3:11b)
And thus you can know the secret of the matter of incense found in the hand of the priest according to the matter of joy; as our sages of blessed memory taught, incense comes not but upon joy, as it is written: "Oil and incense gladden the heart" (Proverbs 27:9). And contemplate the verse: "And Moses said to Aaron, Take the fire pan and place upon it fire from the altar. Add incense (and take it quickly to the community and make an expiation for them). For wrath has gone forth from the Lord: the plague has begun" (Numbers 17:11). Because the incense, which is joy, soothes the wrath and the stringency.	It is said, "Let my prayer be set forth before You like incense" (Psalms 141:2), that incense comes not but upon joy, as it is written: "Oil and incense rejoice the heart" (Proverbs 27:9).... Incense is ever a sign of joy. Come and see how incense ties knots. It is attached above and below and removes death, accusations, and anger so they will have no power over the world, as it says: "And Moses said to Aaron, 'Take the fire pan and place upon it fire from the altar. Add incense and take it quickly (to the community and make expiation for them. For wrath has gone forth from the Lord: the plague has begun.' Aaron took it, as Moses had ordered) and ran (to the midst of the congregation, where the plague had begun among the people. He put on the incense) and made expiation for the people"; and it is written: "He stood between the dead and the living until the plague was checked" (Numbers 17:11–13). For no evil aspect or accuser can stand before incense; thus, it is the joy of everything and knot of everything.

Another illustration of this phenomenon is a parable attributed generically to the purveyors of "the midrash," a tradition that is also known from the Zohar. This parable about the ninth name of God is attested in a commentary on the ten divine names whose erasure is forbidden (a commentary appearing again with minor modification as an appendix to the 1292 *Sheqel ha-qodesh*). Both the iterations of this parable about the homecoming of an exiled queen to her king's palace concern the reconciliation of male and female poles of divinity—*tif'eret* and *malkhut*. Accordingly, the reestablishment of the Jerusalem Temple restores the wayward *shekhinah* to her rightful home and to her proper relation within the Godhead.

MS Munich BSB Cod. hebr. 47, 385a (compare *Sheqel ha-qodesh*, 101–102)[68]	**Zohar 3:53b** (compare 3:21b; 2:22b)
And they taught in the midrash a parable about a king who had a lady, but her palace fell down. After some days, an attendant of the lady said to the king, "My lord, rebuild that palace that fell down for the lady so that she will not dwell outside of it, and that she will not be dispersed from her place." And this is: "and cause Your face to shine on Your sanctuary that is desolate, for the sake of Adonai" (Daniel 9:17). And this is, "Then Moses returned to the Lord and said, O Adonai, why did You bring harm upon this people?" (Exodus 5:22). And they [the sages] taught concerning this [in Aramaic], "It is because Moses is the master of the house (*mare de-veta*) that he spoke in these terms, which would have been impossible for another." Thus contemplate how this name [Adonai, i.e., *malkhut*] ascends to the secret of lordship (*adnut*, i.e., conjunction with *tiferet*).	When the Temple stands below, the name [Adonai] stands above. This is like one who says to the king, "Build this house and this temple, so that the queen shall not dwell outside of her palace." Here also, "and cause Your face to shine on Your sanctuary that is desolate, for the sake of Adonai" (Daniel 9:17). Why "for the sake of Adonai"? So that [the name Adonai, i.e., *malkhut*] will not find itself outside of its abode.

Remarkably, de León's Hebrew version of this parable switches into Aramaic to quote the ancient sages, as it were, who describe Moses as the "master of the house" (*mare de-veta*). This epithet identifies Moses with the male sefirah *tiferet*—the proprietor of the divine domain. In this sense, the prophet is vested with special privileges, which others do not possess. More specifically, the prophet's status as "master of the house" means that he is the paterfamilias vis-à-vis *malkhut*, the attribute of sovereignty personified as queen. This distinction founds Moses's prerogative to speak brazenly to her (i.e., to God as *malkhut*), to ask, in reference to Israel, "Why did You bring harm upon this people?" In fact, this characterization of Moses is attested throughout the zoharic homilies on the book of Exodus.[69]

68 Moses de León, *Sheqel ha-qodesh*, 287n.1042.

69 Zohar 2:99b, 235b, 238b, 244b; *Zohar ḥadash*, 20b; see Yehuda Liebes, "Zohar ve-eros," *Alpayim* 9 (1994): 67–119, here 98; Wolfson, *Circle in the Square*, 17. On the figure of Moses in Castilian kabbalah and his identification with *tiferet*, see Wolfson, *Through a Speculum*, 351–354, 378–380, 390–391.

The culminating example of parallelism between our fragment and the Zohar does not typify the practice of ascribing zoharic wisdom to the ancients, but it is outstanding for the extensive degree of its alignment. Like our prior example, this passage describes the conjunction of *tiferet* and *malkhut*. But here, de León imagines their conjunction in terms of the unification of (1) subtle light that is only perceptible by the intellect (intelligible light, i.e., *tiferet*) with (2) a denser gradation of light that the senses may apprehend (sensible light, i.e., *malkhut*). The full spectrum of colors appearing within the flame illustrates this hierarchy of divine attributes, from the white or clear appearance of a flame at its uppermost tip to the indigo appearance at its base (or, more basically, to the black appearance of the coal fueling the flame).[70]

MS Munich BSB Cod. hebr. 47, 375b–376b	**Zohar 1:50b–51a** (compare MS Vatican ebr. 62, folio 9b)
When the flame is attached to its light, they observe [that the] light above does not separate from its bond with the coal, as we mentioned, when the intelligible light is bound with the sensible light.	Come and see. Whosoever wants to learn the wisdom of Holy unification may observe the flame that ascends from a coal or a kindled lamp, because the flame does not rise unless it is united with a coarse thing.
. . . That is the light that you will always find within the flame, which is white and clear above, and the light that is below is a shade of indigo or black, though the colors are one.	Come and see. In the ascending flame, there are two lights. One is a white and radiant light. And one is black or indigo light that unites with the former.
But that light that looks indigo or black is a throne below the white light above, and this is the light of intellect, whose nature is to bind above and below. And if it did not ever have what to attach with below, the white light would not extend and attach itself to [the lower light].	The white radiant light is above and ascends on a straight path. And below, it is the indigo or black light that is a throne for the white one. And that white light extends over it, and they unite one with the other, becoming entirely one.
And so the light that is indigo or black when it is attached with something dense and sensible always extends the light above. . . . For the white light is never consumed.	And that black light or the shade of indigo beneath it is a throne of glory for that white [light]. And so is the secret of the indigo. And this indigo-black throne unites with another thing to cling to that which is below, and that arouses it to unite with the white light.

[70] This is de León's theosophical rendering of the "flame bound to the coal" image from *Sefer Yeṣirah*, 1:6. See Scholem, "Eine unbekannte mystische Schrift," 120; Scholem, "Farben und ihre Symbolik," 46–47 and n. 103; Avishai Bar-Asher, "The Zohar and Its Aramaic: The Dynamic Development of the Aramaic Dialect[s] of the Zoharic Canon," *Leshonenu* 83 (2021): 221–287, esp. 264–270.

MS Munich BSB Cod. hebr. 47, 375b–376b	**Zohar 1:50b–51a** (compare MS Vatican ebr. 62, folio 9b)
But this is the light that is below and is attached to [the white], whose way is always to consume whatsoever arouses it.	. . . Come and see. Even though the path of that indigo-black light annihilates all of what it clings to from below, Israel clings to it from below and endures.
. . . And from this, you will find the secret of the verse, "And you did cling to the Lord your God." When Israel [clings to] the sensible thing. When [Israel] arouses the black light and binds itself to it. And the white light has compassion upon it so that all is one without separation.	And thus it is written: "And you that did cling to the Lord your God," . . . and not "*our* God," [i.e., the verse concerns clinging] to that indigo-black light that consumes and annihilates all which clings to it from below. But you cling to it and endure, as is written [in the continuation of the verse], "all of you are alive today."

Here we have two parallel iterations of a spectral model for envisioning the intradivine conjunction. Both agree on the same polemical point—based on an identical proof-text. The point is that Israel has a unique propensity to thrive while clinging to the very black light that consumes other nations. According to the text, holding fast to this otherwise destructive facet of divinity is an aptitude unique to Israel's religious peoplehood.

These parallels—which communicate the same ideas through a shared exegetical concept—will suffice to show that the Munich fragment moves within the same discursive atmosphere as much of the main homiletical stratum of the Zohar. Stylistic and terminological equivalences likewise abound. Other examples of equivalent terminology include the phrase "secret of faith," referring to a tenet of esoteric doctrine (*sod ha-emunah*;[71] *raza de-mehemanuta*); the phrase "the first supernal pious ones," which may be compared to "ancient pious ones" (*ḥaside ʿelyon ha-rishonim*;[72] *ḥasidai qadmaʾi*);[73] the application of the term "worlds" to refer to tiers of divine, angelic, and mundane being (*ʿolamot*; *ʿalmin*); the specific terms for the three worlds that constitute the Godhead: the phrases "the supernal (or primordial) world that is the hidden one" (*ʿolam ʿelyon she-hu ha-ganuz*;[74] *ʿalma qadmaʾa ha-hu illaʿaʾa temira*),[75] the "middle world" or "second world" (*ʿolam*

[71] MS Munich, Bayerische Staatsbibliothek, Cod. hebr. 47, fol. 344a.
[72] MS Munich, Bayerische Staatsbibliothek, Cod. hebr. 47, fol. 343a; see Scholem, "Eine unbekannte mystische Schrift," 116.
[73] Zohar 1:10b, 94b; 3:98a.
[74] MS Munich, Bayerische Staatsbibliothek, Cod. hebr. 47, fol. 361a.
[75] Zohar 3:159a.

ha-emṣa ʿi;[76] *ʿalma tinyana)*,[77] and the "lower world" (*ʿolam ha-taḥton*;[78] *ʿalma tata*);[79] phrases referring to the attribute of judgment, the phrase "the left side" (*ṣad ha-semol*;[80] *siṭra de-semala*),[81] or, more generally, the related expressions of orientation within the divine world (*ṣedadin*; *siṭrin*), etc.[82]

Beyond these equivalences in terminology, many more of which could be adduced, the theosophical wisdom propounded by our text (as with subsequent Hebrew texts authored by de León) is often identical to that of the Zohar. As scholars have long observed about de León's mature Hebrew corpus, its exegetical sensibilities and symbolic networks of correspondence are shared with those of the Zohar. If this is the case, what is special about the relationship of the Munich fragment to the Zohar? It is not only the earliest work to exemplify robust parallelism to specifically kabbalistic portions of the Zohar, but it is unique, as we have stressed, in terms of the ideation that typifies de León's middle period. This, again, allows us to synchronize the development of the zoharic anthology with the emergence of de León's theosophical speculation, and even to locate instances where our author's transitional ideation features within the authoritative Zohar. The full course of our study will yield even more consequential insights into the Zohar's relation to de León's initial exposition of kabbalah.

1.6 Itineraries

If the "Nameless Composition" is so critical, why did it not play a more conspicuous role in the development of kabbalah? Whatever the explanation, it is possible to reconstruct some of the trajectories of its hidden reception. We can recover at least three such pathways. The first is the text's concealed reception within de León's subsequent Hebrew corpus. Though the author never, so far as we can discern, referred to the text by name, he repurposed many of its teachings in later works—such as *Shushan ha-ʿedut* (1286), *Sefer ha-Rimmon* (1287), *Sheqel ha-qodesh* (1292), and *Mishkan ha-ʿedut* (1293).

76 MS Munich, Bayerische Staatsbibliothek, Cod. hebr. 47, fol. 361a.

77 Zohar 3:159a–b.

78 For but one of many examples, see MS Munich, Bayerische Staatsbibliothek, Cod. hebr. 47, fol. 361a–b.

79 This term is ubiquitous; for example, Zohar 3:37a, 55b, 117a, 159a–b.

80 MS Munich, Bayerische Staatsbibliothek, Cod. hebr. 47, fol. 384a.

81 This term is ubiquitous; for example, Zohar 1:174b, 230b, 2:68b, 98a, 206b, 231b, 252a, 267b.

82 Compare Wolfson, *Book of the Pomegranate*, 47–48.

Although these compositions never achieved a status remotely comparable to the authority assumed by the Zohar, they certainly contributed to the production of the latter and also shaped the development of subsequent kabbalah, eschatology, and so forth.[83] The second pathway may be recovered by examining the zoharic anthology itself as a site of reception. In this case, it will prove rewarding to seek out the veiled presence of our text permeating a major source of Jewish theology, exegesis, wisdom, hagiography, and more—a source deemed canonical by traditional Jews through the ages. In the third case, we can clarify how the composition itself has reached our hands. Here we may speak of pathways in the plural, since not one but two known trajectories exist, which begin with our author in medieval Castile. In one case, the text proceeded from Iberia to northern Italy, where it reached the hands of a sixteenth-century Ashkenazi scribe whom we have identified as Meir ben Isaac ha-Levi. It is this scribe's witness to the text that is singly responsible for the survival of the greater portion of its contents—produced around 1551 during the same decade that the first printings of the Zohar came to light in northern Italy. Meir ben Isaac produced his copy at the workshop of the printer Israel Cornelio Adelkind in Venice, under the auspices of Johann Jakob Fugger of Augsburg (1516–1575).[84] The latter

[83] Much of their impact on subsequent kabbalah comes through the mediation of Meir Ibn Gabbai, who availed himself of teachings from de León's Hebrew corpus without attribution. See, for example, Wolfson, *Book of the Pomegranate*, 57.

[84] Ilona Steimann, "Jewish Scribes and Christian Patrons: The Hebraica Collection of Johann Jakob Fugger," *Renaissance Quarterly* 70 (2017): 1235–1281. Of the Venice workshop in which Meir ben Isaac copied our manuscript, one scholar notes, "This was an industrial enterprise: . . . the scribes who took part in this enterprise were for the most part of Germanic origin [i.e., they employed an Ashkenazic script] and they clearly worked very fast, no doubt because they undertook piecework and were paid by the quire. Accuracy was not part of their job: the texts were not corrected . . . . What is more, the head of the workshop knew that these scientific, philosophical and kabbalistic texts were intended for Christians, who could hardly tell the difference: some texts, surely copied to order, have the title of one work and the text of another." Colette Sirat, *Hebrew Manuscripts of the Middle Ages* (Cambridge, UK: Cambridge University Press, 2002), 211. Our study can corroborate that the work of Meir ben Isaac on our text exhibits precisely the kind of carelessness that would seem to correspond with Sirat's description (on corruptions within the text, see Chapter 4). Of special interest are three early catalogs of Fugger's Hebraica collection; two prepared by Wolfgang Prommer and a nameless Jewish scribe in 1575 or before (but apparently after their acquisition for the Ducal Library of Bavaria in 1571); and one produced ca. 1574 by Paulus Aemilius; all three catalogs feature roughly the same incomplete entries on the codex now shelf-marked as MS Munich, Bayerische Staatsbibliothek, Cod. hebr. 47 (our fragment likely belongs to miscellany indicated in all cases by "devarim aḥerim"); for Prommer's entries, see MS Munich, Bayerische Staatsbibliothek, Cbm Cat. 36, fols. 16b–117a; and MS Munich, Bayerische Staatsbibliothek, Cbm Cat. 37, fol. 44; for Aemilius's catalog, see MS Munich, Bayerische Staatsbibliothek, Cbm Cat. 36 m, fol. 66a. See, too, Otto Hartig, *Die Gründung der Münchener Hofbibliothek durch Albrecht v. und Johann Jakob Fugger* (Munich: Verlag der Königlich Bayerischen Akademie der Wissenschaften, 1917), especially, an undated Prommer-Fugger correspondence, edited on 319–320, containing Prommer's unsympathetic account of an unnamed Jew's hire to help in preparing one of the catalogs.

invested significant funds into the copying of Hebrew manuscripts, as well as Latin and Arabic texts, in his efforts to amass a universal library of the world's wisdom. The second instance is the path of transmission leading from de León, through the hands of the unknown scribe who copied part of the composition in seventeenth-century Morocco. The scribe's handiwork found its way into a collection of codices acquired by the Lithuanian-born North American scholar Hyman Enelow, who, in turn, bequeathed the codex to the Jewish Theological Seminary of America in New York (see Figure 1.2).

In the course of examining the central themes of the "Nameless Composition," we will have ample opportunities to travel these hidden paths of reception. Our second chapter, "An Order of Penitents," argues that de León originally viewed kabbalah as a penitential-pietistic movement within Judaism. It profiles the unique penitential program promoted by the "Nameless Composition," which proves to be the earliest *regimen vitae* in the history of kabbalah—predating the earliest known examples of that discourse by several centuries. The material illustrates de León's expectation that the contemplation of divinity would give rise to a life of piety and his ambitious projection of kabbalistic speculation into the social realm. De León envisioned, not just a path for individuals, but a community organized under his regimen in competition with those of the mendicant orders that were flourishing in Iberia at the time of the text's composition. Our third chapter, "Secrets of the Hebrew Language," analyzes the complex transition from pretheosophical to theosophical speculation in Castilian speculation on the Hebrew language. The rich evidence for this phenomenon from de León's "Nameless Composition" shows that this process involved a delicate and creative negotiation of structurally incommensurable bodies of speculation. The chapter also details de León's doctrine of the *nequddah maḥshavit*, the "noetic point," identified with the sefirah of *ḥokhmah*. According to this doctrine, all letterforms emerge from a primordial grapheme, a single point holding all language, intelligence, and existence in a concentrated state of potential within the divine mind (a precursor to the Lurianic doctrine of *ṣimṣum*, or divine self-contraction). Additionally, the chapter reveals an early debate between Moses de León and Joseph Gikatilla, which attests to the theological stakes involved in their respective approaches to the Tiberian vowel system. It likewise discusses parallels between de León's letter speculation and the Islamic science of lettrism (*'ilm al-ḥurūf*) indicated by the author himself. The fourth chapter, "Rose of Testimony," charts the course of de León's speculation on divine androgyny, distinguishing the earliest phase of his thinking about "male and female" as attributes of the divine world from both earlier and later developments in the kabbalistic discourse on gender. Redressing a glaring omission in the copious scholarship on the construction of "male and female" in Castilian kabbalah, the chapter highlights a double nexus of thirteenfold speculation supporting de León's personification of the upper female sefirah (*binah/teshuvah*) as the maternal source of life as well as the author's doctrine of "eternal femininity" (*neqevut 'olamit*)—the notion that the femininity of the lower female sefirah (*malkhut*) pervades the order of creation eternally. The chapter likewise demonstrates the enduring vestiges of this early speculative paradigm in de León's later writings and the Zohar, focusing on the recurring thirteenfold themes of Solomon's Sea and "the rose of testimony." Our fifth and final chapter, "Light of the West," discusses the theological background of the thirteenfold speculation that structures both the form and content of de León's earliest kabbalah, and the elaboration of related speculation by Joseph Gikatilla. It also surveys several historico-cultural contexts of wisdom for interpreting de León's "Nameless Composition"—including the esoteric wisdom contexts of al-Andalus, Catalonia, and Castile, the Alfonsine wisdom culture of Castile, and the reception of kabbalistic wisdom by Christian Hebraists in Renaissance Italy. The chapter likewise synthesizes arguments concerning the importance of Moses de León's development as an author for grounding a broader historical assessment of the Castilian kabbalah and the Zohar. The book concludes by revealing a concealed mechanism of interreferentiality that links the Zohar to de León's earliest theosophical work.

2

An Order of Penitents

2.1 Rabbinic Pietism in Medieval Castile

Historians have studied the novel forms of rabbinic pietism that developed during the medieval period. From the Judeo-Arabic writings of Baḥya Ibn Paquda (eleventh-century al-Andalus) and Abraham ben Maimonides (thirteenth-century Egypt) to the Hebrew writings of the Ashkenazi pietists (twelfth and thirteenth centuries), multiple corpora have helped scholars to track the emergence of new modes of practical knowledge. How does kabbalah fit into this picture? Till now, scholarship has promoted the consensus that the appearance of kabbalah in thirteenth-century Castile did not give rise to a characteristic pietism of its own—not, at least, until the sixteenth-century kabbalists of Ottoman Safed began to integrate the expiatory techniques of the Ashkenazi pietists as a means of living in accord with theosophical paradigms of purity.[1] Some have argued that the appearance of such practical knowledge in the kabbalistic fraternities of Safed is such a novelty in the history of Judaism that it should be viewed as nothing short of revolutionary, even as a harbinger of "Jewish modernity."[2] Nonetheless, these conclusions perpetuate the assumption that kabbalah, in the first three hundred years of its development, never brought forth its own distinctive program of penitential pietism. In fact, evidence from de León's writings points

[1] Asher Rubin, "The Concept of Repentance among Hasidey Ashkenaz," *Journal of Jewish Studies* 16 (1965): 161–176, here 162, 175; Lawrence Fine, "Purifying the Body in the Name of the Soul: The Problem of the Body in Sixteenth-Century Kabbalah," in *People of the Body: Jews and Judaism from an Embodied Perspective*, ed. Howard Eilberg-Schwartz (Albany: State University of New York Press, 1992), 117–142; Fine, *Physician of the Soul, Healer of the Cosmos: Isaac Luria and His Kabbalistic Fellowship* (Stanford, CA: Stanford University Press, 2003), 167–186; Fine, "Penitential Practices in a Kabbalistic Mode," in *Seeking the Favor of God*, vol. 3: *The Impact of Penitential Prayer beyond Second Temple Judaism*, ed. Mark Boda, Daniel Falk, and Rodney Werline (Atlanta, GA: Society of Biblical Literature, 2008), 127–148.

[2] Roni Weinstein, *Kabbalah and Jewish Modernity* (Portland, OR: Littman Library of Jewish Civilization, 2016); and Jonathan Garb, *Yearnings of the Soul: Psychological Thought in Modern Kabbalah* (Chicago: University of Chicago Press, 2015), 24. For a critical reassessment of the attribution of penitential austerities to the kabbalists of Safed, see Patrick B. Koch, "Of Stinging Nettles and Stones: The Use of Hagiography in Early Modern Kabbalah and Pietism," *Jewish Quarterly Review* 109, no. 4 (2019): 534–566.

Light is Sown. Avishai Bar-Asher and Jeremy Phillip Brown, Oxford University Press.
© Oxford University Press 2025. DOI: 10.1093/oso/9780197744819.003.0002

to the opposite conclusion. Already, in the cradle of thirteenth-century Castile, the author sought to develop a penitential program of supererogatory living as witness to the truth of his theosophical speculation.

We now have the opportunity to account for de León's penitential campaign, a phenomenon that scholarship has sorely overlooked. We will begin by surveying considerable evidence across a range of texts composed by de León. Then we will proceed to a detailed analysis of the "Nameless Composition," which provides the most explicit testimony to the author's construction of kabbalah as a Jewish penitential movement guided by a didactic thirteenfold regimen of repentance. We will examine the parallels between this movement and the contemporaneous mendicant piety, which de León spurred his pious readers to surpass. Lastly, we will consider the importance of this material for assessing our author's communitarian aims.

2.2 Moses de León's Penitential Writings

At least three and possibly four works attributable to de León show that, from the very earliest to the latest datable phases of his literary activity, the author strove to develop a novel program of penitential pietism that he could integrate into his speculative theology. The first piece of evidence is by far the most obscure, dating still from the pretheosophical phase of de León's writing: the eighth chapter of the author's *Or zarua'*. Little survives of this chapter save for the title ("Chapter of the Soul Who Knocks Upon the Doors of Repentance" [*dalte ha-teshuvah*]), a brief description, and a few opening sentences. What scanty text remains suggests that the missing material would have instructed the reader concerning "the soul that seeks the doors of repentance (*teshuvah*), which knocks upon the gates of light and compassion (*raḥamim*), that it may ascend to the level of its desire and aim, to dwell in the tents of the palaces on high."[3] Although this description alone provides us

[3] Avishai Bar-Asher, "*Sefer ha-Ne'lam*, New Parts of *Sefer Or Zarua* and Clarifications regarding the Early Writings of R. Moses de León: Studies and Critical Editions" [in Hebrew], *Tarbiz* 83, nos. 1–2 (2015): 197–329, here 256–318 = Moses de León, *Sefer Or zarua'*, 318. It is noteworthy that the revised version of *Or zarua'*, preserved in the unicum in MS Vatican, Biblioteca Apostolica Vaticana, ebr. 212 (see Bar-Asher, "*Sefer ha-Ne'lam*," 203–207) incorporates an additional discourse on repentance into a commentary on Gen. 3:19 (fols. 193a-203b). Beginning on folio 195b, we find a concise treatise on penitence, exhibiting characteristics of de León's language, instructing the reader in the ways of *teshuvah*, including spiritual circumcision, confession, diet, fasting, dress, and *imitatio Dei*. A Hebrew text presenting close parallels to de León's penitential writings that may also stem ultimately from the same author is the moralistic composition known as *Orḥot ḥayyim*, or alternatively *The Testament of R. Eliezer the Great*, which instructs the reader in a host of practical directives

with only vague information, the opening of the chapter may be helpful for the tentative work of reconstructing what has been lost:

> I have already informed you about the topic of the human body,[4] which is called "the material," and [about] that which is immaterial. For you shall know that there is [a substance] in the human body that is pure and clean, and it is as brilliant as the radiance (*bahir ka-zohar*), and "its appearance is like the appearance of bdellium" (Numbers 11:7). Not because it is beautiful with beauty, nor unsightly with ugliness. But rather [because it is] a pure body without material substance and devoid of perceptible filth. It is that which always conducts itself in the beauty of its deeds (*ve-hu ha-mitnaheg tamid be-yofi ma'asav*) like the glorious and awesome deity that is beautified in its regimens (*ha-meyupeh be-tiqqunav*).[5]

By emulating the rigorous order of God's own actions, one's immaterial body or soul, according to the text, becomes beautiful like God. One may hypothesize that such an account prefaced a penitential regimen that de León had already composed during the pretheosophical period of his activity—one similar in form to the *Siddur ba'ale teshuvah*, or "Order of Penitents," to which we will turn next. These few brief sentences suggest that a pietistic theology of *imitatio Dei*, already articulated in de León's earliest writings, anticipated the author's later exposition of specifically theosophical knowledge concerning repentance. If one supposes that "the soul who knocks upon the doors of repentance" would need to know how to repent, and that such knowledge hinges on discerning God's example, then the exposition of detailed knowledge concerning God's ways and attributes would be a natural development.

The second piece of evidence is extensive and serves as the focus of the chapter. It comes from the "Nameless Composition," which has the historical distinction of being the earliest work of theosophical kabbalah to contain a penitential regimen vitae. The penitential treatise preserved in

using the genre of the ethical will; an edition and translation of the text appears in Israel Abrahams, ed., *Hebrew Ethical Wills* (Philadelphia: Jewish Publication Society of America, 1926), 1:31–50; on the work and its authorship, see Avishai Bar-Asher, *Journeys of the Soul: Concepts and Imageries of Paradise in Medieval Kabbalah* [in Hebrew] (Jerusalem: Magnes Press, 2019), 315–326, 417, 422, 472.

[4] Moses de León, *Sefer Or zarua'*, 295.
[5] Moses de León, *Sefer Or zarua'*, 318.

this composition is titled the "Order of Penitents" (*Siddur ba'ale teshuvah*; see Figure 2.1). In a didactic fashion, the "Order" instructs penitents in conducting their affairs according to thirteen behavioral attributes of repentance, the *middot* of *teshuvah*, which correspond to attributes of divinity. Just as the "Chapter of the Soul Who Knocks Upon the Doors of Repentance" is the eighth chapter of *Or zarua'*, the "Order" is located within the presumed eighth chapter of the "Nameless Composition." Fittingly, the latter eighth chapter, in which the didactic treatise on repentance appears, profiles the eighth sefirah—counting from below to above.[6] This eighth sefirah is the divine gradation known as *binah* (understanding). But the text emphasizes another name for *binah* that is attested as early as the kabbalistic prayer intentions from Provence—namely, *teshuvah* (repentance). Even prior to the eighth chapter, however, the composition contains instructions on how to conduct oneself according to a paradigm of *ḥasidut*—that is, the piety modeled by God's own gracious comportment toward creation (and, especially, toward penitents).[7]

We can observe the shared investment of these texts in the elaboration of penitential wisdom concerning the evil inclination (*yeṣer ha-ra'*). For example, a critical passage from *Or zarua'* equates the predicament of being ruled by the evil inclination with the knowledge of good and evil that humankind acquired through its act of disobedience in the Garden of Eden. This predicament is characterized by an inability to behold the sublime realities and, as a result, an incapacity to repent. In this passage, the text builds tacitly on Maimonides's interpretation of the primordial sin in *Guide of the Perplexed* 1:2, which identifies Adam's punishment as his loss of metaphysical knowledge.[8]

[6] Notwithstanding the correlation that both *Or zarua'* and the "Nameless Composition" dedicate their eighth chapters to *teshuvah*, there is cause for disambiguation. In the case of the later work, the eighth place corresponds to the ordinal placement of *teshuvah/binah* as the eighth gradation, counting from below to above; whereas in *Or zarua'*, in which the eighth chapter is the final chapter, the number of eight bears no correspondence to *binah*. Note, too, that de León distinguished the penitential eighth chapter of *Or zarua'* from the rest of the composition: "[U]ntil now we stood [before] the sown light... but now we must investigate the shoot which the sown seed produces").

[7] MS Munich, Bayerische Staatsbibliothek, Cod. hebr. 47, fol. 346a.

[8] See, for example, Lawrence Berman, "Maimonides on the Fall of Man," *AJS Review* 5 (1980): 1–15; Warren Zev Harvey, "Maimonides on Genesis 3:22" [in Hebrew], *Daat* 12 (1984): 15–21; Sarah Klein-Braslavy, *Maimonides' Interpretation of the Adam Stories in Genesis: A Study in Maimonides' Anthropology* [inHebrew] (Jerusalem: Reuben Mass, 1986); Klein-Braslavy, "On Maimonides' Interpretation of the Story of the Garden of Eden in the *Guide of the Perplexed* I.2," in *Maimonides as Biblical Interpreter* (Boston: Academic Studies Press, 2011), 21–69; Shlomo Pines, "Truth and Falsehood versus Good and Evil," in *Studies in Maimonides*, ed. Isadore Twersky (Cambridge, MA: Harvard University Press, 1990), 95–157.

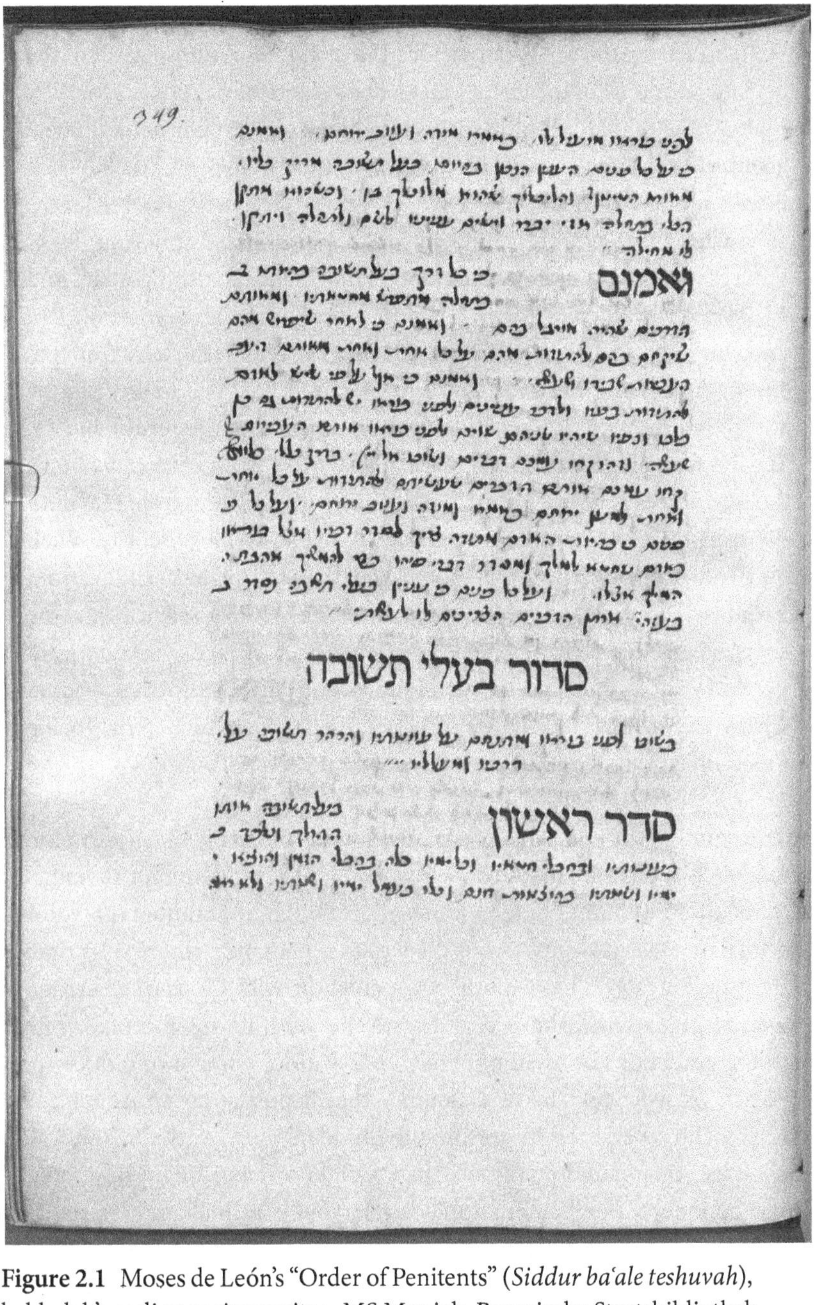
ואמנם
סדור בעלי תשובה
סדר ראשון

Figure 2.1 Moses de León's "Order of Penitents" (*Siddur ba'ale teshuvah*), kabbalah's earliest regimen vitae; MS Munich, Bayerische Staatsbibliothek, Cod. hebr. 47, fol. 349a.

> When Adam sinned, the exalted Creator withheld from him all of the supernal sciences and the true radiance (*ha-zohar ha-amitti*) and all of the gradations and all of the virtues that he had [theretofore] possessed. Why [did God withhold] all of this? So that he [Adam] would not ruminate about wisdom and the secrets of Torah and [thus] do repentance. For such is the way of God, since repentance is withheld from whomsoever [even] ruminates upon such an evil [deed—i.e., the primordial sin]. And this is the secret of the verse [indicating God's rationale for banishing Adam and Eve from the Garden of Eden]: "[Now that the human has become like Us, knowing good and bad], lest he stretch out a hand and take [also from the tree of life and eat and live forever]" (Genesis 3:22). As if to say, "lest he stretch out his hand [to grasp] the way of repentance (*teshuvah*) and eat and live forever." . . . And this is [the explanation of] "lest he stretch out his hand . . . and eat"; He, be He exalted, withheld [repentance] from him until his entire body became obscure and dark as if given over to obscurity. When He [God] had withdrawn from him [Adam] the brilliant light exuding from Eden, and the true radiance (*ha-zohar ha-amitti*), and the sciences, and the supernal gradations, he remained obscured and darkened. . . . And he did not know any hidden and revealed [knowledge] nor any supernal wisdom whatsoever as initially, and [thenceforth Adam] became material, being preoccupied with the concerns of his body.[9]

This account of the consequences of primordial sin, many of whose colorful details exceed our direct concern, is telling in its correlation of repentance with the discernment of hidden knowledge. It takes for granted that knowledge of paradisiacal secrets opens the way to repentance, whereas ignorance thereof militates against a moral reconciliation with God. In referring to "supernal gradations," the text indicates the separate intelligences, rather than the gradations of divinity per se, as a distinct domain of hidden, prelapsarian knowledge. The text assumes that if postlapsarian Adam could have somehow persisted in grasping the hidden wisdom, the metaphysical knowledge squandered by his sin, then such knowledge might have helped him to conquer the evil inclination—to reign in his animalistic materiality—and thus to repent. This assumption—that discerning hidden knowledge engenders repentance—pervades much of de León's oeuvre. It is therefore understandable why the project of elaborating such knowledge—the project

[9] De León, *Sefer Or zarua'*, 298.

that occupied de León from his earliest to his latest writings—would involve inculcating penitential praxes predicated on the control, or even nullification, of bodily impulses.

The third piece of evidence of de León's penitential program is an informative discussion of repentance in *Sefer ha-Rimmon*, a lengthy exposition on the kabbalistic rationales of the commandments composed in 1287. There the author referred his reader to his earlier writings to locate a specific set of protocols (including the subjugation of the evil inclination) that teach how to repent in a way that empowers penitents to fashion their own souls.[10]

> And we already clarified in *Sefer Shushan ha-'edut* instructions concerning the proper [way of] repentance (*ha-teshuvah ha-nekhonah*). And truly, the secret of the matter of repentance is a great thing that concerns when a person acquires a [new] soul from an awesome place by a heavenly secret. You must know that whoever sets out upon the no-good path, power from the left side emanates upon him. And it emanates upon him [from] the attribute by which he conducts himself.[11] But when turning from his sins and subjugating his [evil] inclination, there emanates upon him another supernal power and he obtains another soul.... For verily, the person acquires another spirit by returning to his Creator to make his soul. And since now [while returning to God] he is making his soul, he must subdue the heights of his heart, to turn in complete repentance according to those matters that [constitute] the correct regimen of repentance (*lashuv bi-teshuvah shelemah kefi otam ha-'inyanim asher hem tiqqun ha-teshuvah ha-nekhonah*).[12]

The motif of penitential soul-making recalls the radiant immaterial body that the penitent manifests, according to the account in *Or zarua'*. Nonetheless,

[10] Maimonides's formulation in Mishneh Torah, Hilkhot teshuvah, 2:4, regarding the penitent's total change of character—the penitent's becoming as if a new person—may also inform de León's thinking, which, in turn, anticipates, significantly, Joseph Soloveitchik's celebrated conception of repentance as "self-creation" (an idea articulated by the latter in conversation with both Maimonides and Max Scheler. See, for example, Dov Schwartz, *Religion or Halakha: The Philosophy of Rabbi Joseph B. Soloveitchik*, trans. Batya Stein (Leiden: Brill, 2007), 1: 291–308). On "soul-making" in analytical psychology and the question of its relevance to kabbalah studies, see Jeremy Phillip Brown, "Review of Jonathan Garb's *Yearnings of the Soul: Psychological Thought in Modern Kabbalah*," *Aries: Journal for the Study of Western Esotericism* 18 (2018): 131–136.

[11] See the discussion below of the phrase "by the attribute with which a person conducts himself so will he be conducted"; MS Munich, Bayerische Staatsbibliothek, Cod. hebr. 47, fol. 347b.

[12] Elliot R. Wolfson, ed., *The Book of the Pomegranate: Moses de Leon's* Sefer ha-Rimmon (Atlanta, GA: Scholars Press, 2020) = Moses de León, *Sefer ha-Rimmon*, 172.

the precise penitential regimen to which *Sefer ha-Rimmon* alludes cannot be found in what survives of *Or zarua'* or in the remnants of the composition he adduced directly—that is, 1286's *Shushan ha-'edut.*

Some paragraphs later, the text again mentions a specific "how-to" discussion of repentance that appeared in *Shushan ha-'edut.*

> And we already clarified in *Sefer Shushan ha-'edut* concerning the saying of the sages: "The place where penitents abide, not even the perfectly righteous may abide therein."[13] For their level is great, and their praise is exalted. . . . The righteous cannot abide [in the place where the penitents abide] because their stature is greater than [the righteous]. Therefore, the matter of repentance for humans is to turn before their Creator and examine the regimens of repentance (*le-'ayyen be-tiqqune ha-teshuvah*). . . . We see how many were the sinners who sinned with their souls and did evil things before Him. But when they returned, [He] extended His right hand to them and received them with His mercy (*be-ḥasdo*). . . . Therefore, every sinner who returns to his Maker is beloved from above and adored from below. And He, be He blessed, praises him, and He loves repentance because it is nearer to Him than all other gradations, and He calls [out] to him [the penitent], "peace!" . . . And behold, we exposited the matters of repentance and its procedures and secrets and all of its structures in *Sefer Shushan ha-'edut.*[14]

How to account for the riddle of *Sefer ha-Rimmon*'s allusions to penitential instruction contained in *Shushan ha-'edut*? The phrases "instructions concerning the proper [way of] repentance," "those matters that [constitute] the correct regimen of repentance," and "the matters of repentance and its procedures and secrets and all of its structures" seem to describe a penitential regimen similar to the "Order of Penitents" preserved in the Munich fragment. But, again, no such material appears in the extant parts of *Shushan ha-'edut.*

A probable scenario is that the lost portion of the latter composition did indeed contain instructions for penitents, and possibly a didactic set of instructions very similar in character to those found in the "Order of

[13] Paraphrasing b. Berakhot 34b; b. Sanhedrin 99a; compare Ṭodros ben Joseph ha-Levi Abulafia, *Oṣar ha-kavod*, fol. 21a. Ṭodros Abulafia, *Sha'ar ha-razim*, ed. Michal Oron (Jerusalem: Mossad Bialik, 1989), 108; MS Munich, Bayerische Staatsbibliothek, Cod. hebr. 47, fol. 348b; Zohar 3:16b.

[14] De León, *Sefer ha-Rimmon*, 174–175.

Penitents" (and perhaps also *Or zarua'*). Such a regimen may have figured in the lost fifth and final chapter of *Shushan ha-'edut.* The extant table of contents tells us that this chapter discussed "the secret of the worship of the enlightened and their conduct (*sod 'avodat ha-maskilim ve-hanhagatam*)" and "the secret of the worship of awe and the worship of love (*sod 'avodat ha-yirah ve-'avodat ha-ahavah*), which are the substance of the perfection of the worship of the enlightened."[15] Though this remains a hypothesis, we may conclude with confidence that, when writing *Sefer ha-Rimmon*, de León actively promoted at least one of the penitential regimens he had composed before 1287. If one assumes, only somewhat more tentatively, that both *Or zarua'* and *Shushan ha-'edut* originally included unique penitential programs distinct from the "Order of Penitents," then one may posit the composition of no fewer than three such regimens before the end of 1286.

A fourth treatise on repentance appears at the latest datable phase of de León's activity. *Mishkan ha-'edut*, composed in 1293, contains a treatise about thirteen *middot* of *teshuvah*—thirteen penitential attributes (not the classical thirteen attributes of *raḥamim* (compassion) associated with Exodus 34:6–7 [and sometimes Micah 7:18–20]).[16] As in the "Nameless Composition," the thirteen attributes are founded upon a theosophic paradigm. But in the later work, the correspondences between the sefirot and the thirteen attributes of *teshuvah* are more clearly delineated.[17] Another notable difference between the two treatments is the discrepancy between their respective accounts of the thirteen elements of repentance. In *Mishkan ha-'edut*, the thirteen principles of *teshuvah* are primarily a means of expiating different kinds of sin—in other words, penances;[18] whereas, in the "Order of Penitents," the thirteen

[15] Gershom Scholem, "Shene quntresim le-R. Moshe de León," *Kobez al Yad* 8, no. 18 (1976): 325–384, here 330–370 = Moses de León, *Shushan ha-'edut*, 330–331; these two subjects are the first and last of the seven subjects listed for Chapter Five. Another scenario, albeit one less probable, is that de León intended to refer, however imprecisely, to an earlier treatment of repentance and inadvertently provided a false reference.

[16] For a locus classicus, see the reading attributed to R. Yoḥanan in b. Rosh HaShanah 17b: "'And the Lord passed before him [Moses], and proclaimed' [His thirteen attributes] (Exodus 34:6). R. Yoḥanan said, 'Were it not written in scripture, it would be impossible to say this: it teaches that the Blessed Holy One wrapped Himself like a prayer leader [in a prayer shawl] and he showed Moses the order of the [penitential] prayer. He said to him: Whenever Israel transgresses, may they act before Me according to this order (*ka-seder ha-zeh*), and I shall forgive them."

[17] See n 109 below.

[18] On the multiple meanings of the term *teshuvah* in the writings of the Rhineland pietists, see Ivan Marcus, *Piety and Society: The Jewish Pietists of Medieval Germany* (Leiden: Brill, 1981), 144–146. And see Haym Soloveitchik, "Piety, Pietism and German Pietism: 'Sefer Hasidim I' and the Influence of 'Hasidei Ashkenaz,'" *Jewish Quarterly Review* 92 (2002): 455–493, esp. 458, where the author argues for a firm distinction between *teshuvah* as penance versus *teshuvah* as repentance. On the one hand, de León plays upon the multiple significations of the term in a manner that blurs some of the semantic distinctions delineated by Soloveitchik. On the other hand, the treatise on *teshuvah*

middot of *teshuvah* correspond to thirteen aspirational mandates for penitential behavior.[19] It is also noteworthy that in some places in the treatise on repentance in *Mishkan ha-ʿedut*, de León appropriates language directly from the penitential writings attributed to the renowned Ashkenazi pietist Eleazar ben Judah ben Qalonymos of Worms (the Roqeaḥ).[20]

Additionally, there are two examples from zoharic texts that, if they may be established as the editorial handiwork of de León, would demonstrate further instances of the author's familiarity with, and adoption of, the penitential literature of Ashkenazi pietists.[21] The verbatim use of language from Ashkenazi penitential material occurs, without attribution, in two places in both the Mantua and Cremona editions of the Zohar, in textual units from the anthology's homiletical stratum. In two instances—one brief (2:199b), and one lengthy (3:126b–127a)—whole excerpts from Eleazar of Worms's composition *Yoreh ḥaṭṭaʾim* are rendered into zoharic Aramaic and restructured.[22] A significant quantity of additional material from the Zohar relevant to the project of assessing de León's penitential pietism requires an independent analysis.[23]

Taken together, the evidence adduced here is more than sufficient to show that de León attempted during multiple phases of his career to construct a penitential program based on his speculation, and that he elaborated at least three such programs, if not four. One of these programs—the latest, it appears—sourced material from the penitential discourse of Ashkenaz.[24]

in *Mishkan ha-ʿedut* prescribes penances for individual sins, but in a way commensurate with theosophical knowledge.

[19] Avishai Bar-Asher, "Penance and Fasting in the Writings of Rabbi Moses de León and the Zoharic Polemic with Contemporary Christian Monasticism" [in Hebrew], *Kabbalah* 25 (2011): 293–319, here 304. See Bar-Asher, ed., *R. Moses de León's* Sefer Mishkan ha-ʿedut [in Hebrew] (Los Angeles, CA: Cherub Press, 2013), 62–64 = Moses de León, *Mishkan ha-ʿedut*, 62–64.

[20] This poses a problem for Haym Soloveitchik's conclusion regarding the triviality of Rhineland pietism's influence in Iberia; see his "Piety, Pietism and German Pietism," 472–477.

[21] Jeremy Phillip Brown, "Distilling Depths from Darkness: Forgiveness and Repentance in Medieval Iberian Jewish Mysticism" (PhD diss., New York University, 2015), 214–215.

[22] See Yehuda Liebes, ed., *Gershom Scholem's Annotated Zohar (Jozefow 1873)* [in Hebrew] (Jerusalem: Magnes Press, 1992), 4:1871 and 5:2668; Simeon bar Yohai [attr.], *The Zohar: Pritzker Edition*, trans. Daniel Matt, Joel Hecker, and Nathan Wolski (Stanford, CA: Stanford University Press, 2011, 2014), 6:6:136n.86, 8:306n.56, and 311n.67.

[23] See Jeremy Phillip Brown, *A World of Piety: The Aims of Castilian Kabbalah* (Stanford, CA: Stanford University Press, 2025), esp. Chapter 4 ("Making Other People: The Formative Aspirations of Zoharic Piety").

[24] This militates against Isaiah Tishby's summary assertion that the Zohar has "no direct link with the development of the concept [of *teshuvah*] in Spain and Germany." See Tishby, ed., *The Wisdom of the Zohar: An Anthology of Texts* (Portland, OR: Littman Library of Jewish Civilization; Oxford: Oxford University Press, 2002), 3:1501. See, too, Hillel Ben-Sasson, "The Concept of Repentance in the Zohar," *Jerusalem Studies in Jewish Thought* 26 (2021): 97–125.

As noted, examples of direct appropriation are found in 1293's *Mishkan ha-'edut* (however, the additional material from Ashkenaz embedded in the zoharic homilies attests to a related usage of writings attributed to Eleazar of Worms). The earlier approach to pietism developed in our "Nameless Composition" offers a model of repentance aimed at a vision of holy living through the refinement of one's character in harmony with the truths of kabbalah. Our review of the evidence clarifies that, even before the emergence of theosophical speculation in de León's oeuvre, the author sought to inculcate penitential praxes—which involved, inter alia, prevailing over the evil inclination and the emulation of God's example—as a function of his efforts to impart a prelapsarian knowledge.

2.3 Kabbalah as a Penitential Movement Within Judaism

Having thus characterized the broad context of de León's penitential writings, we are now prepared to analyze the specific construction of repentance in his earliest theosophical work. Generally speaking, the text does not seek to redress its readership's neglect of the commandments. Instead, it promotes a way of living that is faithfully attuned to the contemplation of God's attributes. Put simply, de León tells his reader how to *live in accord with the truth.* In this case, the truth is the theosophical doctrine of a singular divinity comprising sefirot—the signature doctrine, which, again, appears here for the first time in any of de León's extant Hebrew writings. In other words, the pietism, or *ḥasidut,* promulgated by our text is one that facilitates a rigorous agreement of life with the truths of theosophic speculation. The text envisions a life that emulates the merciful and graceful character of the divinity and thus testifies to the truth of the divine attributes within the human realm. When truth and life are thus paired, life bears witness to a single ethico-theosophical totality. Though this paradigm is foreshadowed in de León's pretheosophical writings, the "Nameless Composition" has the historical distinction of being the earliest extant work to develop an organized program of a "kabbalized" *ḥasidut.* This distinction applies not only to de León's oeuvre, but, truly, to the entire history of kabbalah and ḥasidism.

An axiomatic correspondence that guides our text's construction of pietism is that which obtains between *teshuvah,* or repentance, and *'olam ha-ba*—that is, the eschatological notion of the coming world. From a theological perspective, it is perfectly sensible to underscore the link between repentance and the coming world, both in terms of the long-standing rabbinic conception of the otherworldly boon awaiting the penitent, but also in terms of the kabbalists' esoteric schema of correspondences. According to the latter schema, both terms, *teshuvah* and *'olam ha-ba*, correspond to the sefirah *binah*.[25] It is this correspondence that our text brings to bear when it invokes the discussion in Mishnah Sanhedrin concerning Israel's portion in the coming world, which stipulates that all of Israel will inherit a portion of *'olam ha-ba*, save for those who adopt heretical beliefs and practices. This rabbinic discussion serves as the *locus classicus* in Jewish theology for delimiting the parameters of belief. Maimonides, for example, affirmed his thirteen articles of rabbinic faith on its authority.[26]

According to our text's anachronistic reading of rabbinic heresiology, when the ancient sages taught that such persons would have no reward in the coming world, they were referring to those who deny the theosophical truths of kabbalah. Accordingly, "the path of repentance, which is the secret of the coming world, would be withheld from them."[27] The language of withholding the path of repentance recalls de León's pretheosophical account of Adam's postlapsarian bind. According to the present text, those from whom repentance is withheld regard the world as if it had no divine arbiter. "They deny the supernal world, saying: 'There is neither judgment nor judge.'"[28] In this statement, repudiating the supernal world—the world of divinity—is tantamount to committing the heresy of disavowing God's just providence. The text goes on to clarify that such heretics, who repudiate the theosophical divinity, are categorically incapable of heeding the "purifying afflictions" that the divine Judge dispatches as occasions to expiate their sins. Thus, they spurn the ways of "the exalted ancient pietists" (*ḥaside 'elyon ha-rishonim*), who, "when stricken with such afflictions, would search their deeds,[29] and

[25] See, for example, Daniel Abrams, *R. Asher ben David: His Complete Works and Studies in His Kabbalistic Thought* [in Hebrew] (Los Angeles, CA: Cherub Press, 1996), 107–108: "and the custodians of the tradition (*ba'ale ha-qabbalah*) say that this sefirah is called *binah* and likewise called *teshuvah* . . . and about her the sages of blessed memory said, 'great is *teshuvah*, which reaches to the Throne of Glory' (b. Yoma 86b)"; on this motif, see Brown, "Distilling Depths from Darkness," 102–113.

[26] Maimonides, *Commentary to the Mishnah* (= *Haqdamot ha-Rambam la-Mishnah*, trans. Yitzhak Shailat [Jerusalem: Hoṣa'at Ma'aliyot, 1992]), introduction to m. *Sanhedrin*, chap. 10, 369–374.

[27] MS Munich, Bayerische Staatsbibliothek, Cod. hebr. 47, fol. 343a.

[28] MS Munich, Bayerische Staatsbibliothek, Cod. hebr. 47, fol. 343a. Referring to the classical rabbinic notion that disavowal of divine justice is equal to heresy; y. Sanhedrin 10:2, 28d; Genesis Rabbah, 26:6; Leviticus Rabbah, 30:3; Pesiqta de-R. Kahana, 24:11; Zohar 1:72a, 1:87b, 2:91a, 3:99a (*Piqqudin* [ascr. *Ra'ya mehemna*]).

[29] B. Berakhot 5a; compare adaptations of this rabbinic teaching in *Sefer Ḥasidim*, MS Parma, §§. 1, 221, 256, 281, 993, 1512.

examine them meticulously, in order to repent of their wicked ways, making their afflictions an atonement for all of their sins, and being released therefrom into freedom."[30] Our text's construction of *teshuvah* presupposes, again, the ultimate truth value of kabbalistic doctrine: "And truly, their words [i.e., the ancient pietists' account of the liberating effects of self-examination] are sweeter than honeycomb when they are scrutinized according to the matters of Torah by way of truth (*'inyane ha-torah 'al derekh ha-emet*)."[31] Freedom (*ḥerut*) is yet another name for the sefirah of *binah*, a teaching the text imparts, by goading the reader to scrutinize the expiatory knowledge of the ancients "by the way of truth" (a phrase signaling the author's allusion to a theosophical reality), and by urging the reader to understand the notion of emancipation hyperliterally—"he is *literally* released to freedom (*ki be-vaddai yoṣe le-ḥerut*)."[32] On the other hand, the heretic has no share in the coming world, and no expiatory means of emancipation, precisely because he denies the truth, which is to say, the veracity of the Godhead unfolding from the sefirah of *binah/teshuvah*. If one repudiates the reality of *teshuvah*, how, then may the truth of *teshuvah* emancipate his life? This is the question prompted by the text's theosophical adoption of the rabbinic heresiology.[33] Its logic is analogous to the reasoning underlying a dictum attributed to Jesus of Nazareth: "People will be forgiven for every sin and blasphemy, but blasphemy against the Spirit will not be forgiven" (Matthew 12:31). Put positively, a requisite condition for release from sin is belief in an emancipating divine reality.

Who is the penitent that our text contrasts to the heretical antitype? It follows that the penitent—the "broken vessel" who discerns the merciful comportment of the divine attributes flowing from *binah* and strives to emulate their conduct—is the exemplary Jew who merits blessing. Since our text is not simply interested in belief but also in a penitential form of life that testifies to the truth of the divine realities, it is clear that its adaptation of

[30] MS Munich, Bayerische Staatsbibliothek, Cod. hebr. 47, fols. 343a–b.

[31] MS Munich, Bayerische Staatsbibliothek, Cod. hebr. 47, fol. 343b; for the use of this characteristically Naḥmanidean phrase, see also fols. 358b, 376b—perhaps another feature of the text that suggested to a copyist its attribution to Naḥmanides (see the discussion in Chapter One); on this locution, see Elliot R. Wolfson, "By Way of Truth: Aspects of Naḥmanides' Kabbalistic Hermeneutic," *AJS Review* 14, no. 2 (1989): 103–178; and Moshe Halbertal, *Nahmanides: Law and Mysticism*, trans. Daniel Tabak (New Haven, CT: Yale University Press, 2020), s.v. "Nahmanides's biblical commentary; exoteric and esoteric ('the way of truth')."

[32] The text's denial of freedom to the heretic means that he will not be emancipated from his sin or his punishment.

[33] For related statements regarding the consequences for those who neglect the study of kabbalah, see Tishby, *Wisdom of the Zohar*, 3:1086–1087.

rabbinic heresiology aims to inculcate an orthopraxy corresponding to its theosophical orthodoxy. This orthopraxy, however, is a pious path of supererogation that exceeds the righteous standard of justification vis-à-vis the commandments.

This pious form of life entails a receptivity to experiencing physical suffering as a token of God's affection. If a person who is physically afflicted searches their deeds and finds an error, that person should repent of the error, wherewith God will forgive. If, however, an afflicted person searches their deeds and finds no error, then that righteous person may be assured that God has bestowed afflictions of love.[34] Such love-stricken people, the text teaches, manifest divinity in the world:

> The people to whom afflictions of love belong are the vessels of the Blessed Holy One, those in which He dwells. Thus, it says: "[I dwell] with him that is of a contrite and humble spirit."[35] This is because the vessels of the Blessed Holy One are broken, and not perfect vessels. And such is the secret of the continuation of the verse: "to enliven the spirit of the humble, and to enliven the heart of the contrite ones." And it is inevitable that those are the people in whose midst the Exalted One dwells when they are His vessels. And certainly, such is the reason for there being afflictions of love—as it says: "the one whom the Lord loves, he chastises" (Proverbs 3:12)—in order to purify them for the coming world and to increase their reward.[36]

This passage reinforces our text's construction of pietism by contrasting the way of God's broken vessels with its antitype, the wayward life—that is, the way of the heretics who "are deceitful concerning the King Himself."[37] These persons will gain no share of the life of the coming world, no access to

[34] MS Munich, Bayerische Staatsbibliothek, Cod. hebr. 47, fol. 343b. In *Sefer ha-Rimmon*, 43—building upon b. Berakhot 5a—de León names the love that causes the pious to rejoice in their afflictions a "perfect love"; compare Zohar 1:11b–12a, 3:68a; on afflictions of love, also see *Sefer Ḥasidim* MS Parma, §§. 1291, 1950; and Naḥmanides, *Sha'ar ha-Gemul*, chap. 3, in Charles Chavel, ed., *Kitve ha-Ramban* (Jerusalem: Mossad ha-Rav Kook, 1963), 2:269–271.

[35] Isaiah 57:15. On the broken vessel, see Psalms 31:13; Leviticus Rabbah 7:2; Pesiqta de-R. Kahana, 24:5; compare Zohar 1:10b; and esp. 2:86b, where the poor, and the *shekhinah* are identified as "broken vessels": "because the King dwells in those broken vessels" (*mishum de-di'ureh de-malka be-hane mane tevire*); 2:158b, 218a; 233a, esp. 3:9a, referring to "the King's vessels" (*mane de-malka*); and esp. 90b–1a: "The Blessed Holy One dwells not but in a broken place, in a broken vessel (*la shari ela ba-'atar tevira be-mana tevira*) . . . such a place is more complete than all, for he humbles himself so that the glory (*ga'uta*) of all may rest upon him, a supernal glory that is complete."

[36] MS Munich, Bayerische Staatsbibliothek, Cod. hebr. 47, fol. 343b.

[37] MS Munich, Bayerische Staatsbibliothek, Cod. hebr. 47, fol. 343b.

repentance, and no way to freedom, because they deny the truth. In their deceit, "they cause a separation and disavow the Oral Torah."[38]

Our text's charge against the heretics who disavow the Oral Torah is not merely an inculpation of Karaites or others who contested the authority of rabbinic tradition but a general polemic against those who contest theosophical doctrine.[39]

> For the written Torah and the oral Torah are a single matter and a single secret. And there is no division between them. And whosoever differentiates between the two cuts the shoots (*qoṣeṣ ba-neti'ot*).[40] But even this is not enough for the heretics and apostates who not only differentiate between the two, but also disavow Torah completely. They do not heed its words, but rather mock it. And since the matter is bound by the secret of faith (*sod ha-emunah*), they [the heretics and apostates] have no faith at all. And by no means do they have any share in the coming world, but rather, they are barred from the path of *teshuvah*.[41]

In de León's theosophical writings, it is conventional that the unity of the Written Torah and Oral Torah is bound up with the union of *tif'eret* and *malkhut*.[42] The codependency of the oral tradition and the written text is already articulated in terms of the relationship between these sefirot in the "Nameless Composition,"[43] where it is described as a "secret of faith."[44]

[38] MS Munich, Bayerische Staatsbibliothek, Cod. hebr. 47, fol. 344a.

[39] MS Munich, Bayerische Staatsbibliothek, Cod. hebr. 47, fol. 344a. On the presence of Karaites and the incidence of rabbinic anti-Karaite polemic in medieval Iberia, see Daniel J. Lasker, *From Judah Hadassi to Elijah Bashyatchi: Studies in Late Medieval Karaite Philosophy* (Leiden: Brill, 2008), 125–140.

[40] Compare, for example, de León, *Shushan ha-'edut*, 343, 345, 365. On this motif in early kabbalah, see Tzahi Weiss, *Cutting the Shoots: The Worship of the Shekhinah in the World of Early Kabbalistic Literature* [in Hebrew] (Jerusalem: Magnes Press, 2015). On de León's ideology of Oral Torah generally, see Brown, *World of Piety*, esp. Chapter 1 ("Revival of Ancient Piety").

[41] MS Munich, Bayerische Staatsbibliothek, Cod. hebr. 47, fol. 344a. The apostate polemicist Alfonso de Valladolid (ex. Abner of Burgos) claimed that de León had composed an anti-Karaite letter against the "Saducees." See Isadore Loeb, "Polémistes chrétiens et juifs en France et en Espagne," *Revue des études juives* 18 (1889): 43–70, 62; Carlos Sainz de la Maza, "Alfonso de Valladolid y los caraítas: Sobre el aprovechamiento de los textos históricos en la literatura antijudía del siglo XIV," *El Olivo* 14 (1990): 15–32; Ryan Szpiech, "L'hérésie absente: Karaïsme et karaïtes dans les œuvres polémiques d'Alfonso de Valladolid (m. V. 1347)," *Archives de sciences sociales des religions* 182 (2018): 191–206.

[42] On the Written Torah and Oral Torah, see, for example, de León, *Shushan ha-'edut*, 335–337, 367–369; and Tishby, *Wisdom of the Zohar*, 3:1088–1089.

[43] MS Munich, Bayerische Staatsbibliothek, Cod. hebr. 47, fols. 337a, 340a ("For the secret of the truth [i.e., *tif'eret*] is the Written Torah. And the Oral Torah is comprised within it, but all is one matter, and an apt secret for one who understands."), fol. 359b.

[44] Compare, for example, de León, *Shushan ha-'edut*, 340, 360, 370.

Our text's iteration of this term in the present heresiological context may be its earliest known use by de León. The characteristic phrase refers to foundations of theosophical doctrine (the corresponding Aramaic term *raza di-mehemanuta* appears often in the Zohar).[45] This passage drives home the point that kabbalah represents the essence of rabbinic oral tradition, whose mysterious bond to Hebrew Bible constitutes a fundamental "secret of faith." With this assertion, de León strategically reconstituted the profile of antirabbinic heresy to include any Jew who would equivocate regarding the doctrine of the sefirot. One of the legitimating claims of the early kabbalists of Girona—a claim upheld by Ṭodros ben Joseph ha-Levi Abulafia of Toledo and avowed by de León throughout the theosophical compositions underwritten, in large part, by Ṭodros's son—is, indeed, the assertion of kabbalah's identification with the Oral Torah.[46] Kabbalah is, according to this claim, an ancient, albeit hidden, wisdom revealed to Israel at Sinai. By underscoring the essential unity of scripture and the oral tradition, our text avows the identity of Torah and kabbalah. This position implies that any Jew who disavows kabbalah is no less heretical than a Karaite. Insofar as the "Nameless Composition" is the first work by de León to articulate his theosophical doctrine, it is remarkable to observe the boldly adversarial rhetoric its author assumed as a zealous partisan of the doctrine's orthodoxy. Because penitents are precisely those "broken vessels" who humbly adopt the correct belief, and because kabbalah, per our text, is the scriptural-cum-rabbinic theology of Israel par excellence, one can appreciate that de León framed kabbalah as a penitential movement within Judaism—a movement that would redeem Israel from ostensibly heretical forms of would-be rabbanism.

In the course of articulating its heresiology, our text elaborates on the ontic separation of *tif'eret* and *malkhut*—the severing of shoots (*qoṣeṣ ba-neti'ot*) referred to above. What causes this separation? Only the cardinal violation of the heretics? Or also lesser sins? After all, the text states that "all

[45] On this lemma in the Zohar, see *Book of the Pomegranate*, 68; Elliot R. Wolfson, *Luminal Darkness: Imaginal Gleanings from Zoharic Literature* (New York: Oxford University Press, 2007), 16, 22, 37, 40, 42, 191. On related terms concerning faith in the Zohar, see Yehuda Liebes, "Sections of the Zohar Lexicon" [in Hebrew] (PhD diss., Hebrew University of Jerusalem, 1976), 439–442. The phrase "secret of faith" became a signpost for the subsequent discourse of kabbalistic theosophy and, ironically, that of the heretical Sabbatean theology of the seventeenth century. See Liebes, *Studies in Jewish Myth and Messianism* (Albany: State University of New York, 1993), 107–113; and Avraham Elqayam, "The Mystery of Faith in the Writings of Nathan of Gaza" [in Hebrew] (M.A. thesis, The Hebrew University of Jerusalem, 1993).

[46] Oded Yisraeli, "Jewish Medieval Traditions concerning the Origin of Kabbalah," *Jewish Quarterly Review* 106, no. 1 (2016): 21–41.

transgressions are gripped and bound by the supernal world."[47] But the text is quick to clarify that the effects of individual sins are distinct from the comprehensive sin of heresy insofar as ordinary transgressions impact only some part of the divine structure, whereas the heretic's disavowal threatens to void the reality of the Godhead altogether: "Be it known to you that the King's decree is not comparable to the King Himself. And one who spurns one is not like one who spurns the other." Unlike other sinners who still have a way to repent, the punishment reserved for the heretic is *karet*. Such a person is "cut off" from the divine reality, severed from the domain of God's compassionate attributes.[48] Adopting the terminology of Ezra of Girona, de León indicates that heretical souls will be "cut off" from "the image that contains all images."[49] Those souls will not find respite in the sheltering garden of divinity, but rather, will be exposed to the ordeal of spiritual indigence. Such a soul "finds no rest because it has strayed from its place, like a bird which strays from its nest"; it is excluded "from the pleasure and satisfaction of the coming world."[50]

[47] MS Munich, Bayerische Staatsbibliothek, Cod. hebr. 47, fol. 345a.

[48] Numbers 15:31. See Zohar 3:159b, where *karet* refers to the exclusion of the extirpated soul from the divine realm in death. On the theosophical interpretation of this punishment, see Leore Sachs-Shmueli, "The Rationale of the Negative Commandments by R. Joseph Hamadan: A Critical Edition and Study of Taboo in the Time of the Composition of the Zohar" [in Hebrew] (PhD diss., Bar Ilan University, 2019), 2:237–239; and Sharon Koren, *Forsaken: The Menstruant in Medieval Jewish Mysticism* (Waltham, MA: Brandeis University Press, 2011), 110–111.

[49] Compare, for example, de León, *Shushan ha-'edut*, 353–355, where de León also uses the phrase "form of all forms"; and see Shilo Pachter, "'A Sin without Repentance': On a Disagreement between Moses de León and the Zohar" [in Hebrew], in *And This Is for Yehuda*, ed. Maren Niehoff, Ronit Meroz, and Jonathan Garb (Jerusalem: Mandel and Bialik Institutes, 2012), 144–163; Ezra's commentary to the Song of Songs in Chavel, Kitve ha-Ramban, 2:537. Yakov M. Travis ("Kabbalistic Foundations of Jewish Spiritual Practice: Rabbi Ezra of Gerona— On the Kabbalistic Meaning of the Mitzvot" [PhD diss., Brandeis University, 2002], 254–255) claims that observing the commandment of levirate marriage prevents "the image that contains all images" from being destroyed. Compare similar terminology in Ezra's letters, in Gershom Scholem, "A New Document Concerning the History of the Beginning of the Kabbalah" [in Hebrew], in *Sefer Bialik*, ed. Jacob Fichman (Tel Aviv: Omanut, 1934), 141–162, here 156 and n. 71. Ezra appears, in turn, to develop his language from the neoplatonic conception of Ibn Ezra on Exodus 33:21. On "the image that contains all images" and the secret of levirate marriage, also see the "sod" text attributed to Moses of Burgos, MS Munich, Bayerische Staatsbibliothek, Cod. hebr. 54, fol. 281a; Tishby, *Wisdom of the Zohar*, 3:375n.63; Liebes, "Sections of the Zohar Lexicon," §. 123, pp. 61–62. Compare Zohar 1:19a; *Zohar ḥadash*, 59a (*Midrash ha-Ne'lam*); Isaiah Tishby, "Responsa of R. Moses de León in Matters of Kabbalah" [in Hebrew], *Studies of Kabbalah and Its Branches* (Jerusalem: Magnes Press, 1982), 58n.183; de León, *Sefer ha-Rimmon*, 241 (specifies a place from which one will be cut off if one does not marry and procreate). See the responsum of de León cited in Isaac of Acre, *Sefer Me'irat 'enayim* (Amos Goldreich, "*Sefer Me'irat 'Einayim* by Isaac of Acre" [PhD diss., the Hebrew University of Jerusalem, 1981]), 32–33. On levirate marriage in de León, also see de León, *Sefer ha-Mishqal*, 88; and now Avishai Bar-Asher, "The Earliest *Sefer ha-Zohar* in Jerusalem: Early Manuscripts of Zoharic Homilies and an Unknown Homily from the *Midrash ha-Ne'elam* (?)" [in Hebrew], *Tarbiz* 84, no. 4 (2016): 575–614, esp. 595–596, 602–603, 609.

[50] On the imagery of the wayward bird, see also Biti Roi, *Love of the Shekhina: Mysticism and Poetics in* Tiqqune ha-Zohar [in Hebrew] (Ramat-Gan: Bar Ilan University Press, 2017), 168–207.

Accordingly, the punishment of *karet* is enjoined upon the childless, who disregard the obligation to be fruitful and multiply, just as it is upon the heretic, whose beliefs bear no fruit. One scholar has explained that in de León's Hebrew writings, the expression "image which contains all images," the archetypal image par excellence, refers to "the [divine] source of the souls of Israel, which is like a single great soul, within which all of the individuated souls, or likenesses, are contained."[51] This rationale underlies the Jewish obligation to procreate. "A person transmits the individuated part of the [supernal] soul to their child. And only when [the individuated soul] is actualized on the earth does it also sustain the supernal [realm]."[52] Just as Ezra of Girona had earlier discussed being cut off from this archetypal image as a punishment for failing to fulfill the obligation of levirate marriage, de León deployed a similar rationale to admonish those who fail to have children generally. "Therefore, the soul of one who dies childless is cut off from the image which contains all images, which is like a [universal] human which contains all [particular] humans below."[53]

How does childlessness typify the antithesis of kabbalistic pietism? The answer lies precisely in the text's positive construction of pietistic sexuality, which is the next "secret" to which it alludes.[54] The kabbalists developed a rich theosophical and exegetical lore around the ancient view that rabbinic scholars (*talmide ḥakhamim*) might limit the satisfaction of their wives' conjugal rights (*'onah*) to the time of the Sabbath eve.[55] In the Castilian kabbalah literature of the thirteenth century, this custom takes on an ascetic character. How so? By heroizing sexual abstinence without jettisoning the obligation to procreate. And by viewing the practice of abstaining from intercourse on weekdays while fulfilling one's obligation on the Sabbath as the most efficacious way to engender blessed children. In signaling their commitment

[51] Liebes, "Sections of the Zohar Lexicon," §. 123, p. 61.

[52] Liebes, "Sections of the Zohar Lexicon," §. 123, p. 61.

[53] Liebes, "Sections of the Zohar Lexicon," §. 123, p. 61.

[54] MS Munich, Bayerische Staatsbibliothek, Cod. hebr. 47, fols. 345b–346a.

[55] See the detailed treatment of this aspect of kabbalistic sexuality in Elliot R. Wolfson, *Language, Eros, Being: Kabbalistic Hermeneutics and Poetic Imagination* (New York: Fordham University Press, 2005), 307–332, esp. 302 for a discussion of the alternate exegetical basis of Christian male abstinence. See also Jeremy Phillip Brown, "The Reason a Woman is Obligated: Women's Ritual Efficacy in Medieval Kabbalah," *Harvard Theological Review* 116, no. 3 (2023): 422–446; Daniel Abrams, *The Female Body of God in Kabbalistic Literature: Embodied Forms of Love and Sexuality in the Divine Feminine* [in Hebrew] (Jerusalem: Magnes Press, 2004), 165–166; David Biale, *Eros and the Jews* (Berkeley, CA: University of California Press, 1992), 111–115; and Elliot Ginsburg, *The Sabbath in Classical Kabbalah* (Albany: State University of New York Press, 1989), 101–121, 289–296.

to this practice, the kabbalists even imagined themselves as the "eunuchs" mentioned in Isaiah 56:4–5:

> For thus saith the Lord concerning the eunuchs that keep My sabbaths, and choose the things that please Me, and hold fast by My covenant. Even unto them will I give in My house and within My walls a monument and a memorial better than sons and daughters; I will give them an everlasting name, *that shall not be cut off.*[56]

Interpreted in light of the verse, the kabbalists regarded their practice as the proper way of perpetuating God's covenant with Israel—the very antithesis of being "cut off."

Because *tiferet* and *malkhut* often personify the divine groom and bride who consummate their marriage on the Sabbath, kabbalists deemed the Sabbath the most opportune time to conceive children in partnership with the divinity. This abstemious approach to sexuality is an important aspect of de León's kabbalistic construction of pietism. The theosophical and exegetical lore surrounding this practice became conventional among kabbalists in de León's generation and after. Though we cannot recover a more detailed exegesis of the key verses from Isaiah that was, by all indications, present in the lost portion of our nameless text, we can, nonetheless, ascertain that this composition is, in all likelihood, the earliest testament to its "kabbalization" in terms of a pietistic sexual ethic.[57] If this is correct, then it may be appreciated that de León presented the earliest kabbalistic interpretation of the key verses in expressly penitential terms. Here, the aim of the sexual ethic is to "replenish the site" (*lemallo't et ha-maqom*)—namely, the site from which the childless souls are torn, to compensate, it seems, for the weakening of the "image of all images" caused by those who neglect the commandment of procreation. In contrast to those pious individuals who will replenish the archetypal image of the Godhead, those wicked ones who spurn such teachings find themselves "cut off," without recourse to repentance.

[56] On the use of these verses from Isaiah by Patristic authors to elicit the teaching of asceticism and chastity from the Hebrew Bible, see Elizabeth A. Clark, *Reading Renunciation: Asceticism and Scripture in Early Christianity* (Princeton, NJ: Princeton University Press, 1999), 89, 105–106, 125, 179, 195; our emphasis.

[57] MS Munich, Bayerische Staatsbibliothek, Cod. hebr. 47, fols. 345b–346a. This source may be collated with the other Castilian interpretations of Isaiah 56:4–5 discussed in Wolfson's *Language, Eros, Being*; so, too, may a (para-)zoharic Hebrew-Aramaic exegesis of the verse from a Vatican MS adduced in Avishai Bar-Asher, "The Zohar and Its Aramaic: The Dynamic Development of the Aramaic Dialect[s] of the Zoharic Canon" [in Hebrew], *Leshonenu* 83 (2021): 221–287, esp. 256–257.

Thus they become wayward birds, who neglect this practice as a result of their disavowal of the sefirot, whose patterns, in turn, model the sanctioned rhythms of human sexuality.

To review, the text's vision of pietism requires, at a most basic level, avowing the truth of kabbalistic doctrine, according to which the attributes of divinity constellate an archetypal model for emulation by the pious. Other mandates include repentance, self-examination, discerning afflictions of love, making oneself a broken vessel, and, in particular, foregoing sexual relations six days of the week. Inversely, the two cardinal offenses barring individuals from the way of repentance are disavowal of the Oral Torah and childlessness—two sins that are tantamount to denying theosophical doctrine. Further examples of how the text links human behavior to the operations of the divine world focus on the proper alignment of the right and left "sides" of the divinity. The ideal relationship between these sides is characterized by balance. But counterintuitively, the text represents the balancing of left and right in terms of the subordination of the left side by the right.[58] With respect to human action, the operation of balancing is exemplified by a principle of rabbinic pedagogy that comes as the moral to a story about Joshua ben Peraḥiah, who fails to rebuke his student with due tact. Though de León does not mention the student's infamous name, it bears mentioning that within the story's talmudic context, the student is none other than Jesus of Nazareth; it is Rabbi Joshua's painful rebuke that leads Jesus to stray into idolatry.[59] This cautionary tale conveys the lesson that a teacher should never rebuke with both hands, but rather push away with the left, while drawing the student near with the right.[60] Even so, this balancing should be accomplished in such a way that the right side predominates, "so that the power of love will subjugate the power of hate."[61]

According to the text, it is God's own *ḥasidut*—the archetype of piety modeled by the divinity—that establishes the predominance of the right side

[58] On our text in connection with the kabbalistic ethic of containing the left within the right—a thread running through the ethical discourse of the zoharic homilies— see Wolfson, *Luminal Darkness*, 1–28 (and esp. 26–27nn.88, 90, and 98).

[59] B. Sanhedrin 107b; b. Sotah 47a; Peter Schäfer, *Jesus in the Talmud* (Princeton, NJ: Princeton University Press, 2007), 34–40; and Jeffrey Rubenstein, *Stories of the Babylonian Talmud* (Baltimore, MD: Johns Hopkins University Press, 2010), 116–149. Also, in MS Munich, Bayerische Staatsbibliothek, Cod. hebr. 47, see fol. 348b; and compare Zohar 2:106b, 3:177b; de León, *Sefer ha-Rimmon*, 63, 308; and Charles Mopsik, ed., *R. Moses De Leon's* Sefer Sheqel ha-Qodesh (Los Angeles, CA: Cherub Press, 1996) = Moses de León, *Sheqel ha-qodesh*, 33.

[60] On this dictum, see also MS Munich, Bayerische Staatsbibliothek, Cod. hebr. 47, fol. 346a, and 348b.

[61] MS Munich, Bayerische Staatsbibliothek, Cod. hebr. 47, fol. 348a.

and the power of *ḥesed*. With this teaching, the entanglement of theosophy and piety is once again on full display:

> Thus Torah warns: "Thou shalt not take vengeance, nor bear any grudge against the children of thy people, but thou shalt love thy neighbor as thyself: I am the Lord" (Leviticus 19:18). And the sages teach [that the declaration] "I am the Lord" [on the heels of the commandment to love one's fellow indicates that the Lord is] . . . the one who conducts Himself by those attributes, [as if to say], that I am not always fixed on the attribute of hate and hostility.[62] Rather, I arise from the seat of judgment and establish myself upon the seat of compassion. I cannot alight upon the seat of judgment in order to act compassionately with people. I therefore sit upon the seat of compassion.[63] And this is the meaning of [the central *piyyut* of the Seliḥot liturgy, which invokes God's covenant with Israel of thirteen attributes of compassion (*raḥamim*)—the covenant of the thirteen[64]]: "God! The King sits upon the mercy seat and conducts himself with *ḥasidut*, merciful piety"—*ḥasidut* is the secret of the right side,[65] which shows that the Exalted One clings to the secret of the right side in order to do *ḥesed*, to act mercifully with His creatures.[66]

The divine model of *ḥasidut* exemplifies the prudent negotiation of right and left.[67] Curiously, our text employs the phrase "the median way" (*ha-derekh ha-memuṣa'at*)—the Maimonidean rendering of Aristotle's "golden mean"—when elaborating this facet of its theosophical piety. This observation points to the novel conclusion that Moses de León attempted to reconcile, however cursorily, his ontology of penitential attributes with the classical tradition of virtue ethics.[68]

[62] The reference to the teaching of the sages probably alludes to Avot. R. Natan, 16:4, although in that context, the rabbis read the appearance of the phrase "I am the Lord" that follows the commandment of fellow-love as an indication that the latter is justified because God created one's fellow.

[63] See Pesiqta de-R. Kahana, 23:8, 11; Leviticus Rabbah, 29:3, 4, 6, 9, 10; b. Avodah Zarah 3b.

[64] Based on b. Rosh HaShanah 17b and b. Berakhot 7a. See Yehuda Liebes, *Studies in Jewish Myth and Jewish Messianism*, trans. Batya Stein (Albany: State University of New York Press, 1992), 1–64.

[65] On *ḥasidut*, see de León, *Shushan ha-'edut*, 331; de León, *Sefer ha-Rimmon*, 47, 325.

[66] MS Munich, Bayerische Staatsbibliothek, Cod. hebr. 47, fol. 346a.

[67] This approach may be compared with that of Ṭodros Abulafia, who, when commenting on b. Berakhot 7a, interpreted God's prayer that mercy prevail over His other attributes as God's longing to "make the left right." See Abulafia, *Oṣar ha-kavod* (Satmar: M. L. Hirsch, 1926), 5b.

[68] The Tibbonide usage of *middah memuṣ'at* appears, for example, in the classic Hebrew translations of Maimonides's Judeo-Arabic commentary on tractate Avot (in its introduction—i.e., *Eight Chapters*, ch. 4—and again in his commentary on m. Avot 4:4). But while the Aristotelian ethos of the "golden mean" involves *avoiding* both extremes (or sometimes inclining slightly toward the virtuous extreme), our text's middle way *encompasses* both extremes, but in a manner that subjugates

> Thus, God conducts His world according to the attribute of compassion (*raḥamim*). And this is the median way (*ha-derekh ha-memuṣa'at*), that a person chooses the good rung, and the straight path, so that that person may emulate the ways of his Creator. But verily the attribute of the left, which is the attribute of might (*middat ha-gevurah*), should not be [left] by itself. For the Blessed and Exalted One dwells not in the midst of the world but with an even temperament (*mezeg ha-shavveh*),[69] from both sides. And this is the secret of the attribute of compassion (*raḥamim*).[70]

The median way of compassion does not entail the abandonment of the left. By the same token, it should not involve deserting the right side. For if "in pursuit of the left one abandons the right, the left side will arouse him [to sin] and the [attribute of] judgment will stand before him."[71] The text teaches how one should relate to the left side through the example of the Levites, who sing joyfully while clinging to the power of the left side with which they are identified. The Levites "draw forth their attribute, drawing it near to the right side, drawing joy to it in order to bring it closer to the right."[72] They bring joy to the left side precisely because "one cannot allay anger and sadness but with joy."[73] Here, we see how our text includes the tempering of emotions as a facet of its pietistic vision.

the judgmental extreme to the compassionate one. When accounting for this accommodation of virtue ethics to a theosophical paradigm, it is necessary to substitute "compassionate" for virtuous and "judgmental" for vicious because, even for the purposes of comparison, it is equivocal to attribute the distinction between vice and virtue to a divinity who is not given to vice. To be sure, it may be argued that Maimonides had already equivocated in this regard by identifying his virtue ethics of the "golden mean" with *imitatio Dei*. Another equivocation is our text's use of the Maimonidean phrase "median way" to designate the way of piety (*ḥasidut*), because Maimonides had instead aligned the "median way" with the path of the righteous person, while characterizing the way of piety as a diversion from righteousness toward excessive virtue (for an overview, see, for example, Lawrence Kaplan, "An Introduction to Maimonides' 'Eight Chapters,'" *Edah Journal* 2, no. 2 [2002]: 2–23).

69 The even temperament (*mezeg ha-shavveh*) mentioned here, modeled by God for human emulation, may be contrasted to the ideal of equanimity developed in the writings of Baḥya Ibn Paquda, Ashkenazi pietism, Safedian kabbalah, and Beshtian ḥasidism, insofar as the latter sources stress indifference to praise or blame and to good or ill fortune. See Gershom Scholem, *Major Trends in Jewish Mysticism* (New York: Schocken Books, 1995), 96; Haym Soloveitchik, "Three Themes in Sefer Hasidim," *Association for Jewish Studies Review* 1 (1976): 311–358, here 328–329; Moshe Idel, *Studies in Ecstatic Kabbalah* (Albany: State University of New York Press, 1988), 113; Louis Jacobs, *Holy Living: Saints and Saintliness in Judaism* (Northvale, NJ: Jason Aronson Press, 1990), 64.

70 MS Munich, Bayerische Staatsbibliothek, Cod. hebr. 47, fol. 346b.

71 MS Munich, Bayerische Staatsbibliothek, Cod. hebr. 47, fol. 346b.

72 MS Munich, Bayerische Staatsbibliothek, Cod. hebr. 47, fol. 346b.

73 MS Munich, Bayerische Staatsbibliothek, Cod. hebr. 47, fol. 346b.

Another facet of the pietism promoted by our text is moral psychology. The delineation of the divinity into right and left sides corresponds to the psychological division of the heart into good and evil inclinations. The "Nameless Composition" ushers de León's speculation on this facet of rabbinic psychology—which, as discussed earlier, was critical to the discourse of repentance already in the author's pretheosophical writings—into a theosophical domain. The subordination of left to right in the divinity—the prevailing of mercy over judgment—provides the model for the human's conquest of the evil inclination with the good.[74] In turn, supererogatory action on the part of humans manifests the corresponding divine attributes. Precisely because "all things cling to that which is above, and you find nothing in the world that does not cling to the supernal pattern," the text suggests inclining toward *ḥesed*, to examine one's transgressions, to do repentance, "and [to] whisper to one's heart to take hold of the good way."[75] In so doing, one will summon the divine attribute of *ḥesed*, which receives penitents graciously. All of this follows a clear theosophical rationale: "By the attribute with which a person conducts himself, so will he be conducted."[76] In fact, this rationale is a kabbalistic reworking of an old rabbinic principle of commensurability in punishment: "[B]y the measure that a person measures [his deeds], by that he is measured."[77] However, in its kabbalistic revision, the matter does not simply concern justifying the proportionality of God's punishments to human errors. Rather, it pertains to the notion that human action draws divine influence into the world. Such influence may be judgmental or gracious, depending on which divine attribute one's action emulates. Or, as the text elaborates, "that attribute with which a person conducts himself emanates upon him the power of that attribute."[78] It is according to such providential

[74] MS Munich, Bayerische Staatsbibliothek, Cod. hebr. 47, fol. 347a. Compare de León, *Sefer ha-Rimmon*, 42. On the good and evil inclinations in the early kabbalah of Catalonia, see Ezra of Girona, "Perush Shir ha-Shirim," in Chavel, *Kitve Ramban*, 2:496–497; Georges Vajda, *Le Commentaire d'Ezra de Gérone sur le Cantique des cantiques, traduction et notes annexes* (Paris: A. Montaigne, 1969), 376; Vajda, *L'Amour de dieu dans la théologie juive du moyen age* (Paris: J. Vrin, 1957), 196–197. In the writings of Moses of Burgos, see Gershom Scholem, "An Inquiry in the Kabbala of R. Isaac ben Jacob Hacohen, III: R. Moses of Burgos, the Disciple of R. Isaac (Continued)," *Tarbiz* 4, nos. 2–3 (1932): 207–225, here 209; Ṭodros Abulafia, *Oṣar ha-kavod*, fols. 41a and 54b (which explains Jacob's immortality in terms of his resolve to resist the rule of the evil inclination). On the two inclinations in the *Zohar* and some representative texts, see Tishby, *Wisdom of the Zohar*, 2:761–770, 795–807. See also the discussion of penitential attributes below.

[75] MS Munich, Bayerische Staatsbibliothek, Cod. hebr. 47, fol. 347b.

[76] MS Munich, Bayerische Staatsbibliothek, Cod. hebr. 47, fol. 347b.

[77] M. Sotah 1:7; Sifre Numbers, 106:1; Numbers Rabbah, 9:24.

[78] MS Munich, Bayerische Staatsbibliothek, Cod. hebr. 47, fol. 347b. Also see Azriel of Girona, *Commentarius in Aggadoth auctore R. Azriel Geronensi* [in Hebrew], ed. Isaiah Tishby (Jerusalem: Mekize Nirdamim, 1945), 31 (concerning the attribute of Jacob the Patriarch); similarly,

mechanics that our text explains Deuteronomy's rousing charge to individual responsibility: "See, I set before you this day life and goodness, death and evil; . . . Choose life, that you may live."[79] Readers are not only vested with the moral agency to decide their own lots, but, more radically, the agency to determine the role that God's attributes play in this world and the world to come.

2.4 Homeward Birds: Penitents on the Thirteenfold Path

On the heels of our text's account of the wayward birds—that is, the souls who disavow the sefirot—the text offers a poetic bricolage of biblical verses to illustrate the blessed repose of homeward birds.[80] In contrast to the wayward birds, to whom the text denies a way to repentance and a portion of the coming world, the homeward birds are the kabbalist-penitents, whose regimen secures their place within the paradisiacal garden corresponding to the eighth attribute—that is, *binah*. Here, this sefirah is called "the secret of the penitents' rightful portion of the coming world,"[81] by virtue of which the penitents reside in the presence of the King. In keeping with de León's pretheosophical positioning of repentance at the threshold of prelapsarian knowledge, the birds find their repose within an Edenic garden. But in contrast to the author's earliest discourse of repentance, the text elaborates a distinctive thirteenfold delineation of the divinity. God is arrayed in thirteen attributes of repentance (*middot shel teshuvah*), which, here, are ordered according to the pattern of Solomon's Sea,[82] a thirteenfold template that organizes much of the theosophical (and angelological, cosmological, etc.) speculation in our text. In the present context, this motif encapsulates an order of mimetic knowledge concerning God's thirteen exemplary

Menaḥem Recanati's Torah commentary frequently applies this rabbinic principle to the divine attributes (for example, see Recanati, *Perush Recanati*, ed. Amnon Gross [Tel Aviv: Aharon Barzani, 2003], 2:55 [on Deut. 14:22]). This rabbinic principle is also adapted in the negative theurgical discourse of R. Joseph Hamadan, where, understood theosophically, it provides a rationale for punishment; see Sachs-Shmueli, "Rationale of the Negative Commandments," 2:136–140.

[79] Deuteronomy 30:15, 19.

[80] On bird imagery in the Zohar, see Avishai Bar-Asher, "The Soul Bird: Ornithomancy and Theory of the Soul in the Homilies of Zohar Pericope Balak" [in Hebrew], in *The Zoharic Story—Studies of Zoharic Narrative*, ed. Jonatan M. Benarroch, Yehuda Liebes, and Melilla Hellner-Eshed (Jerusalem: Ben-Zvi Institute, 2017), 354–392.

[81] MS Munich, Bayerische Staatsbibliothek, Cod. hebr. 47, fol. 347b.

[82] This motif is absent from the discussion of thirteen penitential attributes in *Mishkan ha-'edut*.

attributes—that is, the thirteenfold regimen our text presents as the right way of repentance.

> May the Lord keep you, "valiant hero" (Judges 6:12), at your place among . . . the portions of the supernal gradations in the King's "nut grove" (Song of Songs 6:11), "browsing among the roses" (Song 6:3) and the fronds of its palms, and luxuriating upon the wine carefully distilled from the nectar of pomegranates. There is the fountain that [like Solomon's Sea] flows out upon the twelve channels in the four splendid directions, "three arrayed to each side" (1 Kings 7:23–26, 2 Chronicles 4:2–5), to establish a regimen according to the order of His habitation.[83] Each bird of the heavens longs to delight from the fronds and opens its mouth there, chirping upon the myrtle branches, each according to its kind,[84] standing in its shade . . . . There, each division of the heavens and the winds ascends and descends before the palaces and halls, each one by the attributes of He who sustains life with compassion and resurrects the dead. There the King is at His table, and [His] "chariots are myriads" (Psalms 68:18), ascending and descending. He is sublime, for His unity is unique. And a crown is in His hand. But no one enters into His palace a person stricken and afflicted . . . save any to whom the "King extends His golden scepter" (Esther 8:4),[85] that he may live.[86]

At the center of this rich description of the penitent's beatific portion stands the life-giving fountain, corresponding to *binah*,[87] that irrigates twelve channels, which, in turn, correspond to a doubling of the six sefirot from *ḥesed* to *yesod*. This 1 + 12 configuration typifies the thirteenfold Solomon's Sea pattern pervading the "Nameless Composition" (see Figure 4.2 in Chapter 4). In the present context, the structure of the overflowing fountain of divinity corresponds to the thirteenfold way of repentance. The text

[83] The term "His habitation," recalls Sefer Yeṣirah 1:12, which describes God as founding His abode out of the elements.

[84] This may refer to the different classes of souls who merit entry to paradise. See Bar-Asher, *Journeys*, 315–376.

[85] See b. Sanhedrin 22a. On the royal scepter as a theurgical figure in related kabbalistic literature and its midrashic sources, see Iris Felix, "Theurgy, Magic and Mysticism in the Kabbalah of R. Joseph of Shushan" [in Hebrew] (PhD diss., Hebrew University, Jerusalem, 2005), 145–179; and Sachs-Shmueli, "Rationale of the Negative Commandments," 2:12, 44, 146, 155, 172, 217, 219, 233–234, 239–243, 250–256.

[86] MS Munich, Bayerische Staatsbibliothek, Cod. hebr. 47, fols. 347b–348a.

[87] See secs. 2.6, 4.3, and 4.8 for discussion of *binah* as life-giving (*toṣe'ot ḥayyim*), and uterine stream (*yuval*).

goes on to identify the penitential regimen with "the scepter of the King." The latter is the very instrument that God extends to the aspiring penitent as would a sovereign to his vicegerent. This scepter—namely, the thirteenfold program—holds the promise of empowering the penitent, "a person stricken and afflicted," who seeks entry to God's palace, with the means of potentiating his own vitality. This empowerment by means of the scepter, namely, the thirteenfold regimen, recalls *Sefer ha-Rimmon*'s description of the penitent's soul-making. There, in the 1287 text, the penitent is said to make his own soul by assimilating the norms of penitential conduct (*tiqqun ha-teshuvah ha-nekhonah*) that were outlined in *Shushan ha-'edut* (1286), apparently in a portion that has been lost.

After enticing the reader with the bold promise of returning to paradise, the text proceeds to describe the stations of the penitents' divine itinerary. Initially, the King brings those "near to Him to behold a vision of the face of the King, those who dwell first in the kingdom (*malkhut*). They are the penitents who ascend toward the summit, which preceded the creation of the world."[88] This summit that preexisted creation is none other than the divine gradation of *teshuvah* (i.e., *binah*), the eighth sefirah counting from below. This two-tiered process of ascent, first to *malkhut*, and subsequently to *binah/teshuvah* may be interpreted in two different ways. One possibility is that the text distinguishes between (1) the place where penitents dwell during their lives, which is *malkhut*, and (2) the place to which their souls ascend after death, namely, *teshuvah/gan 'eden*. Another possibility is that this two-tiered process refers to the recursive ascent of *malkhut* to *teshuvah/binah* that is coordinated with human repentance elsewhere in de León's writings and the Zohar.[89] In either case, the high station of *teshuvah* facilitates the penitents' ascent "to the chariot, into the presence of 'the men of war,'[90] who are in the midst of the supernal vision, sitting, drawing near, and standing to behold the supernal light and made to shine as the radiance of the firmament (*ke-zohar ha-raqia'*)[91]—irradiating; and thus these supernal ones behold the brilliant goodness, the illuminating light whose sight no eye can master."[92]

[88] On *teshuvah* preexisting the creation of the world, see Genesis Rabbah, 1:4; b. Pesaḥim 54a; Nedarim 39b; Tanḥuma, Naso 11; Pirqe R. Eliezer, 3; Azriel of Gerona, *Commentarius in Aggadoth*, 2–3, 95–96, 98–99, 102–103, 116; Abrams, *R. Asher ben David*, 107–108; Zohar 1:90a (*Sitre Torah*), 1:134b; 3:34b, 69b; *Zohar ḥadash*, fols. 5a and 85a (both in *Midrash ha-Ne'lam*).

[89] See de León, *Sefer ha-Rimmon*, 162–163; Brown, "Distilling Depths from Darkness," 241–247.

[90] Numbers 31:21 and 31:53, alluding here to the heavenly hosts.

[91] Daniel 12:3.

[92] MS Munich, Bayerische Staatsbibliothek, Cod. hebr. 47, fol. 348a.

The invisibility to the physical eye of the penitents' sublime vision may support the interpretive possibility that their ascent to the eighth sefirah occurs at death.[93] If, on the other hand, the author meant that the thirteenfold regimen facilitates the penitent's acquisition of a luminous body, then one might read the text's colorful phenomenology of the penitents' vision as describing a lived experience. The latter reading is emboldened by the text's rhetoric of resurrection (e.g., "that he may live") and its description of the penitents' reunion with the angelic ranks, where the subjects come to bask in and irradiate the divine light. This recalls not only the ancient apocalyptic motif of angelification,[94] but, more specifically, de León's pretheosophical account of the penitent who acquires an immaterial body by prevailing over his materiality and beautifying his deeds in light of God's model.

The text turns next to describe the form of living that wins this cherished lot for the penitent. Again, de León returns to the basic assumption that emulating God's own *ḥasidut* is the surest way to concretize divine mercy within the world.

> He . . . does everything to sustain His world, to conduct [it] with His attribute of merciful piety (*ḥasidut*), and since he is abundantly merciful (*rav ḥesed*), he conducts his world according to mercy (*ḥesed*). And he brings forth reality mercifully (*be-ḥesed*), according to the verse: "a world of *ḥesed* is built" (Psalms 89:3).[95] . . . And generally speaking, the matter teaches that the entire sustenance of all worlds is mercy (*ha-ḥesed*), since He, may he be exalted, comports himself with merciful piety (*ḥasidut*) and thus is it written: "For I am merciful (*ki ḥasid ani*), declares the Lord; I do not bear a grudge for all time. (Jeremiah 3:12)[96]

A parallel reading of the Psalmist's phrase "a world of *ḥesed* is built"[97] from a later work by de León clarifies that the upbuilding of mercy is not a process that has already been completed.[98] Rather, the verse employs the imperfect

[93] On beholding divinity at death in related material, see Elliot R. Wolfson, *Through a Speculum: Vision and Imagination in Medieval Jewish Mysticism* (Princeton, NJ: Princeton University Press, 1994), 44–45, 333–336.

[94] See, e.g., Peter Schäfer, *The Origins of Jewish Mysticism* (Princeton, NJ: Princeton University Press, 2011), s.v. "angelification."

[95] On this verse, see de León, *Sefer Or zarua'*, 296; de León, *Sefer ha-Rimmon*, 291, 346; and de León, *Sheqel ha-qodesh*, 32.

[96] MS Munich, Bayerische Staatsbibliothek, Cod. hebr. 47, fol. 348a.

[97] Psalms 89:3; contextually, "forever shall mercy be built."

[98] De León, *Sheqel ha-qodesh*, 32.

tense to indicate an ongoing process by which human emulation of the divine model actively contributes to the establishment of a merciful world. Such a process may be seen to exemplify the kind of discourse that scholars have classified in terms of "theurgy"—that is, a coaxing down of divine substance into the world through the performance of action sympathetic to God.[99] But, whereas scholarship has generally represented theosophical kabbalah as a performative discourse that views the commandments in particular as "Les rites qui font Dieu,"[100] here it is the penitents' supererogatory regimen, rather than the commandments per se, that causes the divine substance to suffuse lower levels of being.[101]

As throughout, the matter of repentance is calibrated to the hierarchy of divine gradations. This is accomplished, again, by reading the ancient rabbinic dicta kabbalistically: "When one turns in repentance, in all cases the right hand draws him near,[102] that he shall be close to his Creator, for in all cases, the rung of penitents is superior to all [other] rungs. And the sages of blessed memory taught,[103] 'in the place where penitents stand, there not even the perfectly righteous can dwell.' "[104] The penitents derive their higher merit from the fact that "they withdraw themselves from all desires of this world to which they were once accustomed, being uprooted from this world, from the iniquities of its desires; and truly each penitent abstains (*poresh*) from those ways to which he was once accustomed."[105] Such an abstemious regimen—and here the text embraces the expressly ascetic language of abstinence (*perishut*)—may not be predicated of the merely righteous.

[99] See Moshe Idel, *Kabbalah: New Perspectives* (New Haven, CT: Yale University Press, 1988), 173–199; Seth Lance Brody, "Human Hands Dwell in Heavenly Heights: Worship and Mystical Experience in Thirteenth. Century Kabbalah" (PhD diss., University of Pennsylvania, 1991); Charles Mopsik, *Les grands textes de la Cabale: Les rites qui font Dieu* (Lagrasse Verdier: Paris, 1993); and Brown, "Reason a Woman Is Obligated," 422–446.

[100] To use Charles Mopsik's provocative phrase.

[101] On the contribution to a putatively theurgical discourse of repentance on the part of the figure known as "Joseph of Hamadan," see Sachs-Shmueli, "Rationale of the Negative Commandments," 2:175–183. On theurgy in early modern kabbalistic ethics, see Patrick B. Koch, "Approaching the Divine by *Imitatio Dei*: *Tzelem* and *Demut* in R. Moshe Cordovero's *Tomer Devorah*," in *Visualizing Jews through the Ages: Literary and Material Representations of Jewishness and Judaism*, ed. Hannah Ewence and Helen Spurling (New York: Routledge, 2015), 48–61. To Koch's exposition may be added that the moralistic presentation of *keter* in *Tomer Devorah* exemplifies the sixteenth-century currency of the thirteenfold conception of *keter*—a conception originally advanced by Gikatilla in medieval Castile that reached broader audiences by means of similar speculation in the Zohar's *Idra* literature.

[102] B. Sanhedrin 107b; b. Sotah 47a.

[103] B. Berakhot 34b; b. Sanhedrin 99a; Maimonides, Mishneh Torah, Hilkhot teshuvah, 7:4; Zohar 1:39a (*Hekhalot*), 29b, 2:106a–b, 13b, 202b, 16b. See de León, *Sefer ha-Rimmon*, 174–175.

[104] MS Munich, Bayerische Staatsbibliothek, Cod. hebr. 47, fol. 348b.

[105] MS Munich, Bayerische Staatsbibliothek, Cod. hebr. 47, fol. 348b.

Having so primed the reader to enter the path of piety, the eighth chapter of the "Nameless Composition" presents its "Order of Penitents" (*Siddur ba'ale teshuvah*). This didactic treatise outlines a thirteen-step program for pietistic living. It contains thirteen short chapters, each detailing one penitential attribute. The "Order" presents these sanctioned forms of living as ontologized attributes (*middot*), which, taken collectively, recapitulate the divine pattern. Nonetheless, the text of the "Order" itself is relatively unencumbered by the kinds of theosophical correspondences that characterize the pietistic discourse contained earlier in the text.

The individual attributes of repentance are thus outlined in the thirteen chapters of the "Order":

1. Turning away from sin
2. Subduing the evil inclination
3. Praying, supplicating, confessing, weeping
4. Abandoning sinful thoughts and slaying the evil inclination.
5. Guarding the eyes[106]
6. Guarding the tongue[107]
7. Making oneself wretched and being gracious towards enemies
8. Forgiving and outwardly reconciling with others
9. Seeking forgiveness and outward reconciliation with others
10. Discerning one's own shame and avoiding the shaming of others
11. Submissiveness
12. Defeating anger[108]
13. Speaking honestly and avoiding deceit

[106] The text claims that the eyes sell the body into sin, characterizing them as "prostitutes." On averting one's gaze in the pietistic discourse of Ashkenaz, note the prohibition against looking at women discussed in Elliot R. Wolfson, "Martyrdom, Eroticism and Asceticism in Twelfth-Century Ashkenazi Piety," in *Jews and Christians in Twelfth-Century Europe*, ed. John Van Engen and Michael Signer (Notre Dame, IN: University of Notre Dame Press, 2001), 171–220, here 191–193; Wolfson, "The Face of Jacob in the Moon: Mystical Transformations of an Aggadic Myth," in *The Seduction of Myth in Judaism: Challenge or Response?*, ed. S. Daniel Breslauer (Albany: State University of New York Press, 1997), 235–270, here 243–244; and Wolfson, "Sacred Space and Mental Iconography: *Imago Templi* and Contemplation in Rhineland Jewish Pietism," in *Ki Baruch Hu: Ancient Near Eastern, Biblical, and Judaic Studies in Honor of Baruch A. Levine*, ed. Robert Chazan, William Hallo, and Lawrence Schiffman, 593–634 (Winona Lake, IN: Eisenbrauns, 1999), esp. 627–628; Judith Baskin, "From Separation to Displacement: The Problem of Women in *Sefer Hasidim*," *AJS Review* 19 (1994): 1–18, here 5–6; Baskin, "Images of Women in Sefer Hasidim," in *Mysticism, Magic and Kabbalah in Ashkenazi Judaism*, ed. Karl Erich Grözinger and Joseph Dan (Berlin: Walter de Gruyter, 1995), 93–105.

[107] Compare de León, *Sefer ha-Rimmon*, 93–94.

[108] On the control of one's anger as a condition for accessing theosophic secrets in Ashkenazi piety, see Joseph Dan, *The Esoteric Theology of Ashkenazi Hasidism* [in Hebrew] (Jerusalem: Bialik

Prima facie, there is nothing inherently kabbalistic about this order of behavioral norms. Included are elements of ancient rabbinic piety and the pietism typified by *Sefer Ḥasidim*. The precise calibration of the sefirot to each of the thirteen individual penitential attributes is not clear in the present treatise; at least, there is little basis for recovering a one-to-one system of correspondence for each and every value. In fact, other than *binah*/*teshuvah* and *malkhut*, the only specific gradations named in connection with the ontologized modes of conduct are the following: (a) the seventh *middah* (making oneself wretched and gracious toward enemies), which is the gradation called *shalom* (peace)—*tif'eret* or *yesod*); (b) the eighth *middah* (forgiving others), which is linked to *ḥesed*; and (c) the thirteenth *middah* (speaking honestly and disparaging mendacity), which is the gradation of *emet* (truth)—that is, again, *tif'eret*. Even the thirteenfold treatise on repentance in *Mishkan ha-'edut* (1293) is not without ambiguity with respect to such correspondences.[109]

Although taken individually, the theosophical coordinates of the individual *middot* are uncertain, their collective correlation to the graduated Godhead is evident. The text returns to the theme of the penitent's coordination with the divine world at the very conclusion of the "Order," precisely where it rejoins the larger composition. There, the thirteen penitential attributes are assigned to the gradations descending from, and including *teshuvah*, which is the eighth gradation counting from below to above. These seven or thirteen gradations, depending on how they are delineated (1 + 6, or 1 + [6 x 2])—*binah* through *yesod*—are accessible to the penitent through his bond with the last sefirah, *malkhut*, or here *ṣedeq*, which is the eighth power when one counts from *teshuvah* downward.[110]

> [Although] we have alluded to the matters of repentance in the secret of the eighth attribute [*teshuvah*], it is certain that the last attribute, which is the attribute of *ṣedeq* [i.e., *malkhut*], likewise comprises those matters. Even

Institute, 1968), 74; and Gershom Scholem, *On the Kabbalah and Its Symbolism*, trans. Ralph Mannheim (New York: Schocken, 1965), 135–136.

[109] Brown, "Distilling Depths from Darkness," 228–230.

[110] Here, this union of the eighth with the eighth may be compared with the speculative motif of the union of the seventh with the seventh, attested in Zohar 1:45b (*Hekhalot*) and 2:260b–261a (*Hekhalot*); see Tishby, *Wisdom of the Zohar*, 2:613n.183.

> though the great supernal one [i.e., *teshuvah*] is the eighth, the small one which is last [= *malkhut*] is likewise eighth—this one patterned after that. And thus, the secret of the penitent (*ba'al ha-teshuvah*) is to conduct oneself by those thirteen attributes in order that he will bring forth redemption and that his forgiveness will be found before his Creator.[111]

By living in conformity with the "Order of Penitents," the penitent hastens redemption by actualizing the affinity between the great eighth gradation (*binah*) and the small eighth gradation (*malkhut*), that is, by living in such a way that recapitulates something of *binah*'s transcendent character within the rung of the divinity that dwells below.

2.5 Inducement from the Mendicants

The penitential program adduced in de León's "Nameless Composition" provides important testimony concerning the sociohistorical aspirations of Castilian kabbalah. This testimony urges scholars to coordinate kabbalah with other discourses of rabbinic pietism that appeared during the thirteenth century, especially those that arose in competition with the penitential cultures of western Christendom.[112] In fact, we know from *Mishkan ha-'edut* that de León's own efforts to bolster Israel's penitential profile placed Judaism in direct competition with the flourishing penitential cultures of mendicant Christianity. This phenomenon parallels well-studied discourses of rabbinic pietism in medieval Western Europe. To characterize the broader historical circumstances in which such competition contributed to the formation of rabbinic piety, we will adduce three roughly contemporaneous examples of

[111] MS Munich, Bayerische Staatsbibliothek, Cod. hebr. 47, fols. 358b–359a. Compare de León, *Mishkan ha-'edut*, 73–75. While *ṣedeq* is a term here for *malkhut*, *ṣedeq 'elyon* refers to *binah* in writings attributed to Moses of Burgos; Scholem, "An Inquiry in the Kabbala of R. Isaac ben Jacob Hacohen: III. R. Moses of Burgos, the disciple of R. Isaac (continued)" [in Hebrew], *Tarbiz* 5, no. 2 (1934): 180–198, see 181.

[112] Some of these circumstances have been studied closely with respect to the practices of confession, fasting, and penance. On confession, see Ivan Marcus, *"Sefer Hasidim" and the Ashkenazic Book in Medieval Europe* (Philadelphia: University of Pennsylvania Press, 2018), 41–43, which complicates his original argument in *Piety and Society*, 121. On fasting, see Elisheva Baumgarten, "Appropriation and Differentiation: Jewish Identity in Medieval Ashkenaz," *AJS Review* 42 (2018): 39–63. On penance, Yaakov Elbaum, *Repentance of the Heart and the Acceptance of Suffering* [in Hebrew] (Jerusalem: Magnes, 1993); Talya Fishman, "The Penitential System of Hasidei Ashkenaz and the Problem of Cultural Boundaries," *Journal of Jewish Thought and Philosophy* 8 (1999): 201–229; and Emese Kozma, "The Practice of Teshuvah (Penance) in the Medieval Ashkenazi Jewish Communities" (PhD diss., Eötvös Loránd University, 2012), esp. 308–415.

Jews placing Christian piety on a precarious pedestal for the emulation of their correligionists.

The first comes from the *Sefer ha-Yashar*, traditionally attributed to Jacob ben Meir Tam, but which some scholars have placed in northern Iberia during the second half of the thirteenth century. According to some, it is a work containing allusions to the nascent kabbalah.[113] The work exemplifies a posture of both admiration and revulsion in relation to the piety of Christians[114] and, in this case, Franciscan mendicants.

> One ought to envy the poor who have not a moment's sustenance, and who, despite all their deprivation and poverty, do not shirk their worship of God, blessed be He. One ought also to envy the nations of the world and the worshippers of vanity who afflict their souls with all types of torment, who . . . roam to the ends of the earth, a month's journey, in the drought of the day and the frost of the night . . . . And this is what the fools, and idiots—the worshippers of stone—do! All the more ought one who worships the Master of Universe behave this way! Though he ought not to envy them, but [rather] do twice as much as he [i.e., the mendicant] is able.[115]

The exemplarity of the poor, and especially that of the mendicant, points to a shortcoming in the devotion of Israel, who, while possessed of the correct doctrine, falls short of the arduous standard modeled by Christian piety.

Similarly, writing around 1270, in the Languedoc, Menaḥem ben Solomon ha-Meiri, in a striking instance of Jewish self-criticism, pointed to the deficiency of Israel's penitential culture in comparison to the Christianity of his day. His *Ḥibbur ha-teshuvah* begins by reporting the view of an unnamed Christian contemporary that the historical travails of the Jews are the result of their laxity in matters of penance and confession.[116] Echoing a statement

[113] Gershom Scholem suggested the year 1260 in On the Kabbalah and Its Symbolism, 147. Shimon Shokek gave Girona as the provenance; see Shimon Shokek, "The Relationship between 'Sefer ha-Yashar' and the Gerona Circle" [in Hebrew], *Jerusalem Studies in Jewish Thought* 6, nos. 3–4 (1987): 337–366; though one of the arguments adumbrated to support this view is based upon false premises, Girona may nonetheless be a feasible setting for some of the text; see Brown, "Distilling Depths from Darkness," 25–26.

[114] On similarly complex attitudes on the part of thirteenth-century Spanish kabbalists regarding Christian theology, see Jeremy Phillip Brown, "What Does the Messiah Know? A Prelude to Kabbalah's Trinity Complex," *Maimonides Review of Philosophy and Religion* 2 (2023): 1–49.

[115] *Sefer ha-Yashar* (Jerusalem: Eshkol, 1978), 43; Shimon Shokek, *Jewish Ethics and Jewish Mysticism in Sefer ha-Yashar*, trans. Roslyn Weiss (Lewiston, ME: Edwin Mellon Press, 1991), 25.

[116] See Gregg Stern, *Philosophy and Rabbinic Culture: Jewish Interpretation and Controversy in Medieval Languedoc* (London: Routledge, 2014), 57–58; and Fishman, "Penitential System of Hasidei Ashkenaz," 220–221 (also there, note the case of Jacob Anatoli).

of Naḥmanides, the text attributes to the unnamed Christian the view that "we do not have among us a single book containing all of the ways of repentance (*sefer meyuḥad kollel le-khol darkhe ha-teshuvah*), apart from words here and there in scattered instances."[117] It is this alleged desideratum that ha-Meiri's big book on repentance set out to fill.[118]

The third statement comes from de León himself, which exhibits a spirit of penitential competition between Jews and Christians, or, more specifically, between kabbalists and Franciscans.[119] The Castilian author penned this statement in 1293's *Mishkan ha-'edut*:

> And He [God] will blot out the names and the remembrance of those haters of Israel, for such will be done to those who are called "penitenciados," who go about without robes, flagellating themselves and drawing blood from their flesh. For they take [this practice] from our holy Torah [!] and likewise from our tradition. And what if they, of impure seed, who hate the Blessed Holy One, act this way? Then all the more so must those of the Lord's portion who do repentance many times over so that their souls will not be lost.[120]

On the face of it, one might assume that this characterization of mendicant penance bears some resemblance to intra-Christian polemics against Minorites. Such condemnation is preserved even in Franciscan hagiography, where the citizens of Assisi, upon beholding the public nudity of the brothers, say that too much penance has made them insane![121] However, the

117 Menaḥem ben Solomon ha-Meiri, *Ḥibbur ha-teshuvah*, ed. Abraham Sofer (New York: Hotza'at Talpiyot, 1950), 2. In his "Epistle to the French Rabbis," Naḥmanides wrote that prior to the Mishneh Torah of Maimonides (i.e., Hilkhot teshuvah), "we found no words of repentance (*divre teshuvah*) in the Talmud except for isolated statements scattered among the laws and the lore without clarification. And in all of the writings of the early and latter geonim we found no such things" (Chavel, *Kitve Ramban* 1:343). It is curious that Naḥmanides made no reference to the discussions of repentance preceding Maimonides, such as those by Saadia Gaon, Baḥya Ibn Paquda, and, in particular, Abraham Bar Ḥiyya.

118 If Naḥmanides ignored pre-Maimonidean treatises on repentance, the Meiri's failure to mention post-Maimonidean penitential works is noteworthy.

119 On this startling passage, which has been omitted from several manuscripts due in all likelihood to its polemical quality, see Bar-Asher, "Penance and Fasting," 307–308.

120 The Castilian term "penitenciados" is transliterated in Hebrew letters; see de León, *Mishkan ha-'edut*, 69. See Bar-Asher, "Penance and Fasting," 307–308; and Brown, "Distilling Depths from Darkness," 233; Brown, *World of Piety*, Chapter 4.

121 See *Actus beati Francisci et sociorum ejus*, ed. Paul Sabatier (Paris: Fischbacher, 1902), sect. 32, pp. 113–114 (while recounting events that transpired prior to the period of de León's activity, the text was likely anthologized a few decades after de León's death in the early fourteenth century. See Antonio Montefusco, "The History as a Pendulum: The 'Actus' and the 'Fioretti,'" *Franciscan Studies* 71 [2013]: 361–373, esp. 363, which dates the text to the 1330s); and Jacques Dalarun, *A l'origine des Fioretti: Les Actes du bienheureux François et de ses compagnons*, trans. Armelle Le Huërou

focus of de León's critique is not that these "penitenciados" have erred in the intensity of their austerities. Rather, they offend by claiming such practices as their own, that they have, in de León's view, misappropriated such practices from Israel. And yet, as seen in the *Sefer ha-Yashar*, the Jewish author cannot condemn the penitential culture of the mendicants without, on the other hand, goading Israel to surpass their example.[122]

These statements help to flesh out, so to speak, the competitive drive behind the formation of novel pietistic discourses by rabbinic authors in the thirteenth century, especially in relation to the mendicant orders then flourishing throughout Western Europe. This will aid readers in assessing the appearance of kabbalah as a penitential discourse in medieval Castile in relationship to the broad diffusion of mendicant cultures throughout Western Europe[123]—and, more specifically, the challenges posed to Judaism by the "penitents from Assisi."[124]

(Paris: Cerf, 2008), esp. 7–27. On Christological dimensions of Franciscan nudity in the account of the *Fioretti* and the Franciscan rule conceived as a means of emulating the "new fool," see John Saward, *Perfect Fools: Folly for Christ's Sake in Catholic and Orthodox Spirituality* (Oxford: Oxford University Press, 2000), 85–86.

[122] Compare the rhetorical turn of mutual admiration and polemic in the following statement concerning the self-sacrificial temperament of Christian cavalry preserved in *Sefer Ḥasidim*, MS Parma, §. 985: "Pay attention to how some people risk their very lives for the sake of personal honor. For example, [Christian] knights go into the thick of battle and even sacrifice themselves to enhance their reputations and to avoid being humiliated. . . . How much more should [a Jew] be resourceful for the sake of his Creator's honor?" See Ivan Marcus, "A Jewish-Christian Symbiosis: The Culture of Early Ashkenaz," in *Cultures of the Jews*, vol. 2, *Diversities of Diaspora*, ed. David Biale (New York: Schocken, 2002), 146–214, here 183. Using the same strategy, *Sefer Ḥasidim* and, later, R. Isaac of Corbeil hold up the example of Christians in silent prayer to inveigh against frivolous behavior during synagogue worship (*Sefer Ḥasidim* MS Parma, §§. 1589 and 224; and Isaac of Corbeil, *Sefer Miṣvot ha-qatan*, §. 11). See Ivan Marcus, "Jews and Christians Imagining the Other in Medieval Europe," *Prooftexts* 15 (1995): 209–226, here 220–221; and Ephraim Kanarfogel, *Peering through the Lattices: Mystical, Magical, and Pietistic Dimensions in the Tosafist Period* (Detroit, MI: Wayne State University Press, 2000), 83.

[123] Yitzhak Baer, "Religious Social Tendency of the Sefer Hasidism" [in Hebrew], *Zion* 3 (1938): 1–50; Baer, "The Historical Background of the Raya Mehemna" [in Hebrew], *Zion* 5 (1940): 1–44, here 10, 18–19, 30; and Baer, *A History* of *the Jews in Christian Spain*, trans. Louis Schoffman (Philadelphia: Jewish Publication Society, 1978), 1:261–277. Also see Scholem, *Major Trends in Jewish Mysticism*, 234, and 83–84 on the Ashkenazi pietists); Pinchas Giller, *The Enlightened Will Shine: Symbolization and Theurgy in the Later Strata of the Zohar* (Albany: State University of New York Press, 1993), 27–32; Harvey Hames, *Like Angels on Jacob's Ladder: Abraham Abulafia, the Franciscans and Joachimism* (Albany: State University of New York Press, 2007); see Bar-Asher, "Penance and Fasting"; Eitan P. Fishbane, *The Art of Mystical Narrative: A Poetics of the Zohar* (Oxford: Oxford University Press, 2018), 28–30, 134, 286–314. On Jewish-mendicant relations, in this context and more broadly, see Jeremy Cohen, *The Friars and the Jews: The Evolution of Medieval Anti-Judaism* (Ithaca, NY: Cornell University Press, 1982), 33–102; and Larry Simon, "Intimate Enemies: Mendicant-Jewish Interaction in Thirteenth-Century Mediterranean Spain," in *Friars and Jews in the Middle Ages and Renaissance*, ed. Steven McMichael (Leiden: Brill, 2004), 53–80.

[124] On this epithet for the Franciscans, see the *Anonymous of Perugia*, in *Francis of Assisi: Early Documents* (Hyde Park, NY: New City Press, 2000), 2:43. On the penitential character of the early

2.6 A Social Vision for Kabbalah

Taken at face value, one may regard the penitential program preserved in the "Nameless Composition" as little more than a subterranean curiosity for the history of Judaism. However, de León's subsequent writings reprise many of the theosophico-moralistic teachings contained within this early text. More consequentially for the broader history of Jewish pietism and kabbalah, one finds such teachings interspersed throughout the Zohar. In fact, the theosophico-moralistic teachings of the Zohar, which provide some of the richest and most frequently cited source material for early modern kabbalistic *musar*,[125] found their original articulation in this pivotal composition. Our text's didactic account of the way of repentance—the pious form of life that testifies to the knowledge of God's attributes—contains the moralistic teachings scattered throughout the Zohar in a single extensive and thematically organized framework. If our text is de León's first work to espouse a theosophic doctrine—a supposition that is strengthened by the text's use of penitential discourse to champion the orthodoxy of kabbalah—then it would appear that the author originally imagined his kabbalah of the sefirot as a form of penitential pietism.[126] Moreover, the composition's "Order of Penitents" is unique in the history of medieval kabbalah for its *regula*-type style, this being several centuries before the development of the theosophically inflected Hanhagot or conduct literature,[127] and earlier than the kinds

Franciscan movement, see Raffaele Pazzelli, *St. Francis and the Third Order: The Franciscan and Pre-Franciscan Penitential Movement* (Chicago: Franciscan Herald Press, 1989); Robert M. Stewart, "The Rule of the Secular Franciscan Order: Origins, Development, Interpretation," (PhD diss., Graduate Theological Union, Berkeley, CA, 1990); Bert Roest, *Franciscan Literature of Religious Instruction before the Council of Trent* (Leiden: Brill, 2004), 191–205; and Michael F. Cusato, "To Do Penance / *Facere poenitentiam*," *The Cord* 57 (2007): 3–24; also printed in Cusato, *The Early Franciscan Movement (1205–1239): History, Sources and Hermeneutics* (Spoleto: Centro Italiano di Studi Sull'alto Medioevo, 2009), 49–68.

[125] See Patrick B. Koch, *Human Self-Perfection: A Re-assessment of Kabbalistic Musar-Literature of Sixteenth-Century Safed* (Los Angeles: Cherub Press, 2015). One can even view the copious literature of kabbalistic *musar* (esp. *Reshit ḥokhmah* of Elijah de Vidas) as an effort to anthologize many of the scattered zoharic ethical teachings, which, unbeknownst to its authors, had been among the original contents of a single neglected document. Nonetheless, the early modern kabbalistic *musar* drew upon many other sources and integrated elements that lay beyond those zoharic ethical traditions owing their patrimony to this text alone.

[126] See the fuller development of this argument in Brown, *World of Piety*.

[127] See Zeev Gries, "The Fashioning of Conduct Literature at the turn of the Sixteenth Century and in the Seventeenth Century and its Historical Significance" [in Hebrew], *Tarbiz* 56, no. 4 (1987): 527–581; and Gries, *Conduct Literature (Regimen Vitae): Its History and Place in the Life of the Beshtian Hasidism* [in Hebrew] (Jerusalem: Bialik Institute, 1989).

of social charter documents and regulations of kabbalistic fellowships known from the sixteenth century onward.[128]

Our study of de León's penitential writings suggests that a theosophical regimen similar to the "Order of Penitents" may have also appeared in the missing portion of 1286's *Shushan ha-ʿedut*, and a regimen from a lost chapter of *Or zaruaʿ* may have even preceded the author's theosophical turn. It is impossible to determine whether, in their historical moment, such penitential writings served the social function their author had envisioned.[129] But there is little doubt that the "Nameless Composition" gives voice to de León's socio-historical ambitions for kabbalah. Whether it remained aspirational or served a normative function for a living community, the penitential pietism promulgated in this text should factor into future scholarship on the social background in which the Zohar was produced.[130] When reading the Zohar's statements of praise for the pious who gaze into their hearts and do perfect repentance every day,[131] its accounts of saintly acts of self-denial, and the like, one is struck, especially after studying our text's penitential discourse, that such material epitomizes at least the values—if not also the practices—of its Castilian authorship.

To shed additional light on de León's social agenda, it is instructive to consider our topic alongside the contemporaneous pietistic culture of Ashkenaz. Scholars have studied the latter as a function of both *Piety* and *Society*, per the title of Ivan Marcus's classic study of Ashkenazi pietism. What are the results of comparing de León's "Order of Penitents" with developments in Ashkenaz? Unlike 1293's *Mishkan ha-ʿedut*, one finds no texts from Ashkenaz embedded within the "Order." Still, the "Order" is characterized by many features it has in common with a particular thread of moralistic instruction

[128] Such as the charter of Ḥayyim ben Joseph Vital's fellowship, the regulations of Moses Ḥayyim Luzzatto's circle, or the four charters produced by the Bet El community associated with Shalom Sharʿabi (written in the hand of Ḥayyim Joseph David Azulai); see, for example, Gershom Scholem, "A Charter of the Students of R. Isaac Luria" [in Hebrew], *Zion* 5 (1940): 133–160; Isaiah Tishby, *Messianic Mysticism: Moses Hayim Luzzatto and the Padua School* (London: Littman Library of Jewish Civilization; Liverpool: University of Liverpool Press, 2008), 289–336; and Pinchas Giller, *Shalom Sharʿabi and the Kabbalists of Beit El* (New York: Oxford University Press, 2008), 8–9.

[129] On the supposition that de León convened a fraternity of fellows, see Daniel Abrams, "Divine Yearning for *Shekhinah*—'The Secret of the Exodus from Egypt': R. Moses de León's *Questions and Answers* from Unpublished Manuscripts and their Zoharic Parallels," *Kabbalah* 32 (2014): 7–34, esp. 18–19; and above, sec. 1.2.

[130] On the social organization of the Castilian kabbalists whom scholars have identified as "the circle of the Zohar," see Hartley Lachter, "Charity and Kabbalah in Medieval Spain: Possible Evidence from Isaac ibn Sahula's *Meshal ha-Kadmoni*," *Iberia Judaica* 6 (2014): 119–126.

[131] For example, Zohar 1:220a.

found in the *Sefer Ḥasidim* corpus.[132] This may be seen in the text's construction of a supererogatory way of living on the basis of behavioral principles, many of which de León derived from rabbinic literature. But unlike the material from Ashkenaz, the "Order" does not adumbrate penances for specific sins. By contrast, de León's 1293 penitential treatise stipulates penances for individual transgressions, drawing directly, as mentioned, from the private penitentials of Eleazar of Worms. It seems that the use of private penitentials competed with the older practice (associated with Judah of Regensburg) of receiving penances directly from a rabbinic confessor-figure (*ḥakham*).[133]

The "Nameless Composition," on the other hand, is not concerned with *teshuvah* in the sense of prescribing penances—that is, satisfying the temporal punishments due for sin. It is primarily interested in the initiation of Jews to a way of living that exceeds the explicit requirements of the law, a regimen for leading a holy life according to God's pious example. Yet there is an ideational tension at play—one that may typify all forms of penitential pietism (including medieval Ashkenazi models)[134]—which is produced by communicating a pious way of living in the name of a discursive rubric (i.e., repentance) designed to ensure a religious means of expiation for those who stumble in the law. We have seen how the "Nameless Composition," in its pietistic approach to penance, makes *teshuvah* into a supererogatory category—where the penitent represents the consummate paragon of virtue, rather than a type of reformed sinner. The grievous sinners invoked by the text are

[132] Particularly relevant is the material that Haym Soloveitchik, based on the work of Jacob Reifmann and Ivan Marcus, isolated as *SḤ I*, or the so-called *Sefer ha-Ḥasidut*. According to Marcus, this material may not be divorced in a radical way from the broader corpus of *Sefer Ḥasidim*; important too is Soloveitchik's early assessment that one may distinguish its ideational content in terms of "a presentation of the principles of the [pietist] movement" (Soloveitchik, "Three Themes," 335n74), rather than an elucidation of the compensatory "penitential system" with which scholars have come to associate *Ḥaside Ashkenaz*. See Ivan Marcus, "*Sefer Hasidim" and the Ashkenazic Book*, 36–44; Marcus, "The Recensions and Structure of *Sefer Hasidim*," *Proceedings of the American Academy for Jewish Research* 45 (1978): 131–153, here 152–153; and Soloveitchik, "Piety, Pietism and German Pietism," 455–466.

[133] Marcus, *Piety and Society*, 121–129; and Marcus, "*Hasidei Ashkenaz* Private Penitentials: An Introduction and Descriptive Catalogue of Their Manuscripts and Early Editions," in *Studies in Jewish Mysticism*, ed. Joseph Dan and Frank Talmage (Cambridge, MA: Association for Jewish Studies, 1982), 57–83, and his reappraisal in Marcus, "*Sefer Hasidim" and the Ashkenazic Book*, 41–43.

[134] This tension also features in the philosophical and Sufi-inflected models of repentance expressed in Maimonides, Mishneh Torah, Hilkhot teshuvah, and in Baḥya Ibn Paquda's *Kitāb al-Hidāyā ila farā'iḍ al-qulūb* respectively. Alternately, another tension introduced vis-à-vis the more traditional juridical economy of repentance is the construction of *teshuvah* as the hyperbolic inflation of transgression promoted by Jonah Gerondi. On this, see Hillel Ben-Sasson, "Transgressions and Punishments: The Special Contribution of Rabenu Yonah Gerondi's *Sha'arei Teshuvah*" [in Hebrew], *Tarbiz* 86, no. 1 (2018): 63–106. For evidence of de León's familiarity with Jonah, see his *Sefer ha-Rimmon*, 215, where Jonah's interpretation of Proverbs 27:5 is acknowledged, perhaps in reference to a portion of Jonah's commentary on Proverbs that is no longer extant.

heretical types that are "cut off" from repentance because they disavow kabbalah. Inversely, penitents testify to God's attributes through their behavior as a function of their right belief, exemplifying not only pious character but also orthodoxy.

As instructive as it is to coordinate the kabbalistic material with developments from Ashkenaz, it is not sufficient to explain the appearance of de León's penitential pietism alongside intra-Judaic developments alone. The testimony provided by de León himself regarding the example of contemporary Franciscans serves to index the author's recognition of the impressive social traction of Franciscan penitential culture. Jews should do better than Christians, thought de León, and he viewed kabbalah as the most effective theological agenda for lifting Jews above the competition.

With respect to the competition, there is ample evidence for the development of Franciscan infrastructure in Castile during the period of de León's activity.[135] The popular image of Francis of Assisi as the leader of a penitential movement within the church was canonized in 1289 with the Papal endorsement of the *tertius ordo Fratrum Minorum*, also known as the (!) "Order of Penitents"[136] (when Pope Nicholas IV issued the bull titled, "Supra montem"). This document—produced four years before de León's statement in *Mishkan ha-'edut* and roughly four years after the "Nameless Composition"—fixed a definitive *regula* for the tertiaries and recognized Francis as its "auctor intellectualis."[137] The rule, just as earlier rules followed by the first and second orders, refers to itself as a form of living (*forma vivendi*, or *forma vitae*); its didactic short-chapter form very much resembles

[135] The dispersion of Minorite communities throughout Iberia had already begun in the days of Francis, and at least fifteen houses were established prior to his death. By the end of the thirteenth century, the movement had founded no fewer than sixty houses throughout the peninsula. See John Moorman, *A History of the Franciscan Order from Its Origins to the Year 1517* (Oxford: Clarendon Press, 1968), 71. On early convents in de León and Castile, see Atanasio López, *La Provincia de España de los Frailes Menores: Apuntes histórico-críticos sobre los orígenes de la Orden Franciscana en España* (Santiago, Chile: El Eco Franciscano, 1915), 148ff; and Francisco Javier Rojo Alique, "Para el estudio de conventos franciscanos en Castilla y León: San Francisco de Valladolid en la Edad Media," in *El Franciscanismo en la Península Ibérica: Balance y Perspectivas, Congreso Internacional*, ed. Maria del Mar Graña Cid (Barcelona: Griselda Bonet Girabet, 2005), 419–428. According to López, early accounts describe the sponsorship of mendicants on the part of Fernando III (son of Alfonso IX), as a strategic aspect of his efforts to stoke the *Reconquista* among mendicants; he also notes (p. 149) that it was in Burgos in 1221 that Francis's disciple and successor Friar Giovanni Parenti first presented the Franciscan Rule to Fernando III, on the recommendation of Bishop Don Mauricio. Moreover, the Franciscans claim Fernando III as a member of the *Ordo Tertium*, the "Order of Penitents," by whom he is still venerated as a saint.

[136] Although here "Order" (*ordo*) refers to a community, and de León's "Order" (*siddur*) refers to a regulatory composition, the former refers to a penitential community founded on the basis of a *regula*, and the latter refers to a composition intented for the use of a community of penitents.

[137] Roest, Franciscan Literature of Religious Instruction, 197–198.

de León's "Order of Penitents." Similarly, Francis's 1223 rule, the *Regula Bullata*, which became the official *forma vitae* of the *Ordo Fratrum Minorum*, contains twelve chapters, which de León's thirteen approximates.[138]

But beyond the matter of the treatise's formal characteristics lies a more compelling question. What are the theological implications of aligning these confessionally antagonistic corpora? For the Franciscans, the *forma vitae* rules encapsulated the divine life exemplified by Jesus of Nazareth. The rules are communally circumscribed means of approaching evangelical perfection, primarily through the emulation of the attributes of poverty, chastity, and obedience.[139] In the "Order," the sefirah of *teshuvah* (or *binah*), the divine reality that encompasses the thirteen penitential attributes, is similarly characterized in terms of life. In fact, upon concluding the "Order," its author divulged the "secret" of *binah*'s anthropomorphic, or better, gynomorphic form; the text alludes to her uterine quality as the place from which life issues: "The secret of this gradation is her being the one who issues life, 'for life issues (*toṣe 'ot ḥayyim*) from her' (Proverbs 4:23)." Here, the text draws upon an older Catalonian tradition for the generic identification of *teshuvah*/*binah* as the source of life. But, as we will explore at greater length in Chapter Four, our author personified *binah* in specifically maternal terms, on the basis of her parturitive function with respect to the seven sefirot that issue from her.[140] As the womb of the lower sefirot, she engenders the attributes of the divine life that the ideal penitent will exemplify. Moses de León anticipated that penitents would relate to such symbolism in a concrete manner, by seizing hold of the life issuing from *binah*—that is, the life of *teshuvah*—and

[138] On the Franciscan rule literature, see Roest, *Franciscan Literature of Religious Instruction*, 197–198, and David Flood, *Francis of Assisi and the Franciscan Movement* (St. Bonaventure, NY: Franciscan Institute Publications, 2017).

[139] Malcolm Lambert, *Franciscan Poverty: The Doctrine of the Absolute Poverty of Christ and the Apostles in the Franciscan Order, 1210–1323* (London: Society for Promoting Christian Knowledge, 1961), 31–67; Duane Lapanski, *Evangelical Perfection: An Historical Examination of the Concept in the Early Franciscan Sources* (St. Bonaventure, NY: Franciscan Institute, 1977).

[140] Ezra ben Solomon of Girona, *Perush ha-Aggadot* = Abraham ben Judah Elmalik. *Liqquṭe shikheḥah u-fe'ah* (Ferrara: Abraham Ibn Usque, 1556), 1b; Azriel of Girona, *Commentarius in Aggadoth*, 3. See MS Munich, Bayerische Staatsbibliothek, Cod. hebr. 47, fols. 359a–359b, 366a, 372b, 382b, 384a; see our discussion in Chapter Four; and see de León, *Shushan 'edut*, 361; de León, *Sefer ha-Rimmon*, 6, 148, 222; de León, *Sefer ha-Mishqal*, 72; and Elliot R. Wolfson, "Hai Gaon's Letter and Commentary to *'Aleynu*: Further Evidence of De Leon's Pseudepigraphic Activity," *Jewish Quarterly Review* 81, nos. 3–4 (1991): 365–410, esp. 386; Mark Sendor notes that in Proclus, the hypostasis associated with the process of *reversio* is called "Life" (ζωή), and that in Christian adaptations of the neoplatonic doctrine of *reversio*—for example, in Eriugena—the regressive movement takes on an added penitential "dimension as an individual and collective process: reversion represents the return of the sinner, and of humanity, to God." Mark Sendor, "The Emergence of Provençal Kabbalah" (PhD diss., Harvard University, 1994), 1:369.

that they would commit themselves to the "Order." In the cases of de León and the Franciscans alike, the way of life assigned to penitents is set into motion by a vitalistic concept of divine exemplarity, which requires, in the first instance, contemplating the formal qualities of divine life, and in the second, emulating their perfection. In the case of de León, that involves embodying mimetic knowledge of the sefirot. In the case of the Franciscans, *imitatio Christi*.[141] In both cases, contemplation of the divine form of life undergirds the aspirational norms of the pietistic community.

141 See Denise L. Despres, "Exemplary Penance: The Franciscan 'Meditations on the Supper of Our Lord,'" *Franciscan Studies* 47 (1987): 123–137.

3
Secrets of the Hebrew Language

3.1 From Catalonia to Castile

The previous chapter showed how Moses de León articulated his first sustained foray into the Zohar's signature theosophical doctrine on the basis of a practical program of pietistic living. This chapter will explore the role of gender in shaping de León's unique conception of the divinity. We examine the function of language in the formation of Castilian kabbalah. It is evident that de León's adoption and adaptation of the theosophical doctrine of the ten sefirot, evidence of which is first attested in our "Nameless Composition," owed a significant debt to earlier developments in Iberian kabbalah, including the far-reaching idea that the stratified divinity somehow comprised subtle primordial letters. Nonetheless, the particular linguistic lore of earlier kabbalists had but a limited impact on de León, whose earliest writings are characterized by their independence from previous theosophical discourse on the Hebrew language and, in fact, demonstrate an intensive engagement with letter speculation prior to the adoption of any theosophical conception of the Godhead into his Hebrew corpus. The present chapter will show that de León's earliest pretheosophical discourse on language remained an important source for his thinking long after his theological sea change.

Pre-zoharic speculation on the divine character of the Hebrew alphabet coalesced in a host of sources. It seems that no single text did more to prompt speculation on the ontological status of the Hebrew alphabet than *Sefer Yeṣirah*. The work is also the earliest to feature the terminology of "ten sefirot." This term initially referred to the numerical principles of quantity and sequence with which God created the world. Read contextually, there is little justification for the view, adopted variously by virtually all kabbalistic interpreters, that the sefirot signify a hierarchy of attributes stratifying the divine order. Even so, a variety of early kabbalistic thinkers poured their theosophical speculation into the terminological mold of the "ten sefirot *belimah*" mentioned repeatedly in that book. Indeed, *Sefer Yeṣirah* speaks of

Light is Sown. Avishai Bar-Asher and Jeremy Phillip Brown, Oxford University Press.
© Oxford University Press 2025. DOI: 10.1093/oso/9780197744819.003.0003

"thirty-two paths of wisdom," which is the sum of the "ten sefirot *belimah*" and the twenty-two letters of the Hebrew alphabet. One of the earliest kabbalistic texts to adopt *Sefer Yeṣirah*'s terminology of "thirty-two paths of wisdom" as a springboard for theosophical speculation on the Hebrew letters is the anonymous *Sefer ha-Bahir*. Like *Sefer Yeṣirah*, the enigmatic homilies of the latter work wielded significant authority during kabbalah's formative period, some of which contained musings on the forms of the Hebrew letters. The shapes of the letters, per the Bahir, intimate details about the nature of the divinity.[1] The thirteenth-century readers of the Bahir showed special interest in its unprecedented approach to language.[2] Taking a cue from the text, the early kabbalists developed an eclectic curriculum of rabbinic teachings on the Hebrew letters, including traditions sourced from classical midrashim on letters in the Torah, talmudic lore about the alphabet, Hekhalot and Merkavah literature, the "Alphabet of Rabbi Aqiba" (*Otiyyot de-Rabbi ʿAqiba*),[3] and the writings of Abraham Ibn Ezra.[4]

The earliest kabbalists of Catalonia, in particular, breathed new life into several ancient traditions about the creation of the universe through the medium of letters (especially the four letters of the Tetragrammaton: YHVH) by investing them with theosophical significance.[5] In some cases, these authors attributed their readings of ancient cosmogonic traditions to pious purveyors of wisdom from Provence, most famously "the *Ḥasid*," Isaac "the Blind," the

[1] See esp. O. H. Lehmann, "The Theology of the Mystical Book Bahir and Its Sources," *Studia Patristica* 1 (1957): 477–483; Elliot R. Wolfson, "Hebraic and Hellenic Conceptions of Wisdom in *Sefer ha-Bahir*," *Poetics Today* 19 (1998): 147–176, here 151–156; Jonathan Dauber, *Knowledge of God and the Development of Early Kabbalah* (Leiden: Brill, 2012), 191–216; Avishai Bar-Asher, "The *Bahir* and Its Historiography: A Reassessment," *Journal of Religion* 103, no. 2 (2023): 115–144.

[2] See, for example, Steven T. Katz, "Mysticism and the Interpretation of Sacred Scripture," in *Mysticism and Sacred Scripture*, ed. Steven T. Katz (Oxford: Oxford University Press, 2000), 21–32; Moshe Idel, *Absorbing Perfections: Kabbalah and Interpretation* (New Haven, CT: Yale University Press, 2002); and Elliot R. Wolfson, *Language, Eros, Being: Kabbalistic Hermeneutics and Poetic Imagination* (New York: Fordham University Press, 2005).

[3] Karl E. Grözinger, "The Names of God and the Celestial Powers: Their Function and Meaning in the *Hekhalot* Literature," in *Early Jewish Mysticism: Proceedings of the First International Conference on the History of Jewish Mysticism*, ed. Joseph Dan (Jerusalem: Hebrew University of Jerusalem, 1987), 53–70; Elliot R. Wolfson, *Alef, Mem, Tau: Kabbalistic Musings on Time, Truth, and Death* (Berkeley: University of California Press, 2005), 145–166.

[4] On the importance of Ibn Ezra's writings, such as *Sefer Ṣaḥut*, for the development of kabbalistic letter speculation, see David Neumark, *Geschichte der jüdischen Philosophie des Mittelalters* (Berlin: Verlag von Georg Reimer, 1910), 2:371–373; Elliot R. Wolfson, "Anthropomorphic Imagery and Letter Symbolism in the Zohar" [in Hebrew], *Jerusalem Studies in Jewish Thought* 8 (1989): 147–180, here 150–152.

[5] See, esp., Haviva Pedaya, *Name and Sanctuary in the Teaching of R. Isaac the Blind* [in Hebrew] (Jerusalem: Magnes Press, 2001), 103–147; and Hillel Ben-Sasson, *Y-HWH: Its Meanings in Biblical, Rabbinic, and Medieval Jewish Thought* [in Hebrew] (Jerusalem: Magnes Press, 2019), 171–230.

son of Abraham ben David (the Rabad) of Posquières.[6] At the same time, the Catalonian kabbalists also revised the exegetical traditions of *Sefer Yeṣirah* by advancing an alternative reading of the text. Rather than glossing the sefirot as primordial numbers or celestial spheres, they advanced the view that they refer to archetypal realities of a substantially divine nature. But a perusal of the kabbalistic literature produced in Catalonia during the first two-thirds of the thirteenth century reveals minimal investment in the numerological value of the letters or in the sefirot as numerical ciphers. Similarly, cosmogonic accounts of the Catalonian kabbalists, which stress the role of the sefirot and/or primordial letters in the creation of the world, show little interest in the mathematical and neo-Pythagorean speculations associated with *Sefer Yeṣirah* and its commentarial tradition.

Contemporaneous speculation about the secrets of the Hebrew language flourished in non-kabbalistic contexts, too. A few generations of scholars active in the Franco-German cultural orbit left behind a rich body of alphabetical speculation about the divinity and the cosmic order. Compositions written by members of the Qalonymide family of Ashkenaz stand out in this regard,[7] as do works associated with Neḥemiah of Erfurt (especially texts that have only recently come to light).[8] Other regions witnessed the itinerant activities in the latter half of the thirteenth century of Abraham Abulafia, whom scholarship has hailed as the main exponent of a "prophetic kabbalah." This eccentric figure produced a sprawling corpus throughout the course of his travels around the Mediterranean basin.[9] His writings promote a prophetic discipline of Hebrew letter combination—based on an arcane reading of

[6] See, for example, Pedaya, *Name and Sanctuary*, 1–102; Eitan P. Fishbane, "The Speech of Being, the Voice of God: Phonetic Mysticism in the Kabbalah of Asher ben David and His Contemporaries," *Jewish Quarterly Review* 98 (2008): 485–521.

[7] See Joseph Dan, *The History of Jewish Mysticism and Esotericism* [in Hebrew] (Jerusalem: Shazar Center, 2011), 6:493–525; and Daniel Abrams, "'The Secret of Secrets': The Concept of the Divine Glory and the Intention of Prayer in the Writings of R. Eleazar of Worms" [in Hebrew], *Daat* 34 (1994): 61–81.

[8] Moshe Idel, "Between Ashkenaz and Castile: Incantations, Lists, and 'Gates of Sermons' in the Circle of Rabbi Neḥemiah ben Shlomo the Prophet, and Their Influences" [in Hebrew], *Tarbiz* 77, nos. 3–4 (2008): 475–554; Idel, "On R. Neḥemiah ben Shlomo the Prophet's 'Commentaries on the Name of Forty-Two' and *Sefer ha-Ḥokhmah* Attributed to R. Eleazar of Worms" [in Hebrew], *Kabbalah* 14 (2006): 157–261; Idel, "On the Genre of Commentaries on the Forty-Two Letter Divine Name and Its Later History" [in Hebrew], *Kabbalah* 42 (2018): 131–191.

[9] For general surveys, see, for example, Gershom Scholem, "The Name of God and the Linguistic Theory of the Kabbala," *Diogenes* 20, no. 79 (1972): 59–80; and Scholem, "The Name of God and the Linguistic Theory of the Kabbala (Part 2)," *Diogenes* 20, no. 80 (1972): 164–194; Moshe Idel, "Reification of Language in Jewish Mysticism," in *Mysticism and Language*, ed. Steven T. Katz (Oxford: Oxford University Press, 1992), 42–79; Idel, "Defining Kabbalah: The Kabbalah of the Divine Names," in *Mystics of the Book: Themes, Topics, and Typologies*, ed. Robert A. Herrera (New York: Peter Lang, 1993), 97–122.

Maimonidean epistemology—with the intended purpose of awakening the holy spirit among the people of Israel.[10]

Around the same time, several cities of Castile were home to kabbalists cultivating diverse conceptions of the Hebrew language. Segovia is one city in which scholars have placed a concise treatise, ascribed to the obscure Castilian figure Jacob ha-Kohen, on the theosophical meaning embedded in the letters of the Hebrew alphabet.[11] Ṭodros ben Joseph ha-Levi Abulafia of Toledo, a disciple of Isaac ha-Kohen of Soria, was familiar with interpretations of the letterforms and cantillation marks, which he included in one of his two known works.[12] A younger contemporary of Ṭodros ben Joseph active in the same milieu was Joseph Gikatilla of Medinaceli. Though renowned for his late theosophic works like *Sha'are orah*, his first major composition, *Ginnat egoz* (1274), exemplifies speculation on various aspects of the Hebrew language. The surprising fact that this work betrays no hint of the theosophical doctrine of the sefirot led scholars to assume that at some point in the late 1270s, Gikatilla broke sharply with "letter mysticism" and saw the light, as it were, of a new theosophical creed.[13] Scholars

[10] Moshe Idel, "The Writings of Abraham Abulafia and His Teaching" [in Hebrew] (PhD diss., Hebrew University, 1976), 1:142–166; Idel, *The Mystical Experience in Abraham Abulafia*, trans. Jonathan Chipman (Albany: State University of New York Press, 1988), 13–54; Idel, *Language, Torah, and Hermeneutics in Abraham Abulafia* (Albany: State University of New York Press, 1989), 1–28; Elliot R. Wolfson, *Abraham Abulafia—Kabbalist and Prophet: Hermeneutics, Theosophy and Theurgy* (Los Angeles, CA: Cherub Press, 2000).

[11] See his commentary on the letterforms printed in Gershom Scholem, "Qabbalot R. Yiṣḥaq ve-R. Ya'aqov bene R. Ya'aqov ha-Kohen: Meqorot le-toledot ha-qabbalah lifne hitgallut ha-Zohar," *Madda'e ha-Yahadut* 2 (1927): 201–219; thereon, see Asi Farber, "Jacob ben Jacob ha-Kohen's Commentary to Ezekiel's Chariot" [in Hebrew] (MA thesis, Hebrew University of Jerusalem, 1978); Daniel Abrams, "'The Book of Illumination' of R. Jacob ben Jacob ha-Kohen: A Synoptic Edition from Various Manuscripts" [in Hebrew] (PhD diss., New York University, 1993), 9–48; Orna R. Wiener, "The Mysteries of the Vocalization of the Spanish-Castilla Kabbalah in the 13th Century" [in Hebrew] (PhD diss., Bar-Ilan University, 2009), 52–175.

[12] See Ṭodros ben Joseph ha-Levi Abulafia, *Sha'ar ha-razim*, ed. Michal Kushnir-Oron (Jerusalem: Mossad Bialik, 1989), 73–74.

[13] Gershom Scholem, *Major Trends in Jewish Mysticism* (New York: Schocken Books, 1954), 194 with nn. 132–133. See, further, Asi Farber, "Traces of the Zohar in the Writings of R. Joseph Gikatilla" [in Hebrew], *'Alei Sefer* 9 (1981): 70–83, here 70 (repr. with slight variations in Asi Farber, ed., *R. Joseph Gikatilla's Commentary to Ezekiel's Chariot* [in Hebrew] [Los Angeles, CA: Cherub Press, 1998], 28–41); Farber, "Qeṭa' ḥadash me-haqdamat R. Yosef Gikatilla le-Sefer Ginnat egoz," *Jerusalem Studies in Jewish Thought* 1 (1981): 158–176, esp. 158–163; Shlomo Blickstein, "Between Philosophy and Mysticism: A Study of the Philosophical-Kabbalistic Writings of Joseph Giqatila (1248–ca. 1322)" (PhD diss., Jewish Theological Seminary of America, 1983), 115–123; Elke Morlok, *Rabbi Joseph Gikatilla's Hermeneutics* (Tübingen: Mohr Siebeck, 2011), 23–35; Annett Martini, ed., *Yosef Gikatilla: The Book of Punctuation; Flavius Mithridates' Latin Translation, the Hebrew Text, and an English Version* (Turin, Italy: Nino Aragno Editore, 2010). See also Hartley Lachter, "Kabbalah, Philosophy, and the Jewish-Christian Debate: Reconsidering the Early Works of Joseph Gikatilla," *Journal of Jewish Thought and Philosophy* 16, no. 1 (2008): 1–58; Federico Dal Bo, *Emanation and Philosophy of Language: An Introduction to Joseph ben Abraham Giqatilla* (Los Angeles, CA: Cherub Press, 2019), 1–96.

thus hypothesized an impasse in Gikatilla's intellectual life precipitating an abrupt about-face and a turning away from an Abulafian "prophetic kabbalah," at which time Gikatilla began absorbing theosophical kabbalah from an unidentified source. Scholarship first advanced the narrative of a sort of theosophical "conversion" decades ago, and, in the absence of contravening evidence, this story has gone unquestioned.

In connection with this narrative, scholars posited a nearly identical transformation for Moses de León, Gikatilla's contemporary, treating the trajectories of authors as evidence of a rapid and significant reorientation in the region. Scholem and others in his wake applied this conversion-type narrative to explain a broader and more central conundrum—namely, the appearance of disparate discursive tendencies within the zoharic anthology. How is one to account for the juxtaposition within the same corpus of the chiefly cosmological *Midrash ha-Ne'lam*, on the one hand, with the theosophical style of the Zohar's homilies on the Torah, on the other? Scholem supposed that these incommensurable tendencies reflected the intellectual paradigms prevailing before and after the "conversion" of de León—the author that Scholem deemed responsible for both these strata within the Zohar. Scholars have assumed that the cosmogony and theology of *Midrash ha-Ne'lam* on Genesis (among other lections) represents a pretheosophic worldview that was, as yet, unschooled in the kabbalistic doctrine of the sefirot. Scholars aligned the worldview of the latter zoharic composition with the pretheosophical orientation of Gikatilla and de León's earliest writings.[14] In addition to Gikatilla and de León, it is now possible to count a third Castilian figure who appears to have undergone a comparable transition. With the recent identification of a kabbalistic explanation of the ten sefirot by their contemporary Isaac ben Solomon Ibn Sahula, we have additional evidence of an author whose writing demonstrates a comparable

[14] See, in particular, the formulation of Alexander Altmann, "*Sefer Or Zarua'* by R. Moses de Leon: Introduction, Critical Text, and Notes" [in Hebrew], *Kobez al Yad* 9, no. 19 (1980): 219–293, here 243, apparently following Scholem, *Major Trends in Jewish Mysticism*, 194–195, which is mostly about Gikatilla; Altmann, *Zohar: The Book of Splendor: Basic Readings from the Kabbalah* (New York: Schocken Books, 1949), xiv. See, too, Ephraim Gottlieb, *Kabbalah at the End of the Thirteenth Century* [in Hebrew], ed. Yehuda Liebes (Jerusalem: Akademon, 1969), 6–7; Gottlieb, *Studies in the Kabbalah Literature* [in Hebrew], ed. Joseph Hacker (Tel Aviv: Tel Aviv University Press, 1976), 101 (Altmann's formulation is based on Gottlieb's descriptions). Compare Moshe C. Weiler, "Issues in the Kabbalistic Terminology of Joseph Gikatilla and in His Relationship to Maimonides" [in Hebrew], *Hebrew Union College Annual* 37 (1966): 13–44, and Weiler, "The Kabbalistic Doctrine of R. Joseph Gikatilla in His Works" [in Hebrew], *Ṭemirin* 1 (1972): 157–186. See, further, Yehuda Liebes, "How the Zohar Was Written," in *Studies in the Zohar* (Albany: State University of New York Press, 1993), 99 with nn. 78–79.

transition to a theosophical outlook. Although the writings of Ibn Sahula from the early 1280s contain the earliest citations from the pretheosophical *Midrash ha-Ne'lam*, his newly discovered commentary on Psalms espouses a theology based upon the doctrine of the sefirot expressed in the writings of Naḥmanides and Asher ben David.[15]

The fact that the writings of several Castilian figures from the same period lend themselves to a convenient "before and after" division has contributed to the historical image of a clean break along a chronological fault line that bisects the late thirteenth century. However the historical catalyst for this supposedly sharp conceptual turn remains unknown. This chapter will show that de León's "Nameless Composition" complicates the supposition of a neat division in ways that are instructive for understanding the history of Castilian kabbalah and the earliest cultivation of the zoharic literature. As we have argued throughout, this pivotal composition points to a transitional phase within a gradually shifting paradigm. In what follows, we offer an analysis of the treatise's language speculation, its doctrine of the "noetic point," its relationship to de León's other known works and the early writings of Joseph ben Abraham Gikatilla, as well as the author's avowed knowledge of the Islamic discourse of lettrism (*'ilm al-ḥurūf*). Our analysis sifts through the conceptual humus from which the Zohar's foundational ideas germinated. It also shows the critical importance of de León's recently discovered early compositions—some of which have not appeared in any printed medium—for discerning the prehistory of the zoharic homilies on the Torah.

3.2 The *Sefer ha-Ne'lam* Corpus

The early phase of de León's kabbalistic activity first came into focus following the discovery of links between works bearing his signature and anonymous texts bearing his signature style. Foremost among these is a large fragment from *Or zarua'*,[16] an unsigned commentary on the pericope of Genesis that de León mentions in one of his later, signed works—1290's

[15] See Avishai Bar-Asher, "Isaac ben Solomon Ibn Sahula's Commentary on Psalms" [in Hebrew], *Kobez al Yad* 26, no. 36 (2018): 1–45, esp. nn. 21–26. On the relationship between Rabad and Asher ben David, see Jeremy Phillip Brown, "God as an Androgyne in Medieval Kabbalah," forthcoming in *Traditio* 80 (2025).

[16] See Scholem, *Major Trends in Jewish Mysticism*, 194 with nn. 132–133, and Altmann, "*Or Zarua'*," 243–244.

Sefer ha-Mishqal / Sefer ha-Nefesh ha-ḥakhamah.[17] An array of evidence, including connections with Gikatilla's *Ginnat egoz*, helped prove that this work had been written by de León many years before 1290, when he first referred to it. For whatever reason, however, the author left the text unsigned. Once scholars identified de León as the author of *Or zarua'*, a work radically different in its subject matter and concept from the rest of his then-known oeuvre, the attribution gave rise to a fundamental disagreement about the formation of de León's putative masterpiece, the Zohar.[18] The disagreement specifically concerned the part of the Zohar called *Midrash ha-Ne'lam*, because *Or zarua'* is one of the earliest sources—if not the earliest—to include citations from and adaptations of that part of the Zohar.[19]

Research has established critical connections between fragments of other anonymous works and the fragment from *Or zarua'*, based on their similar language, style, and subject matter. Such connections have, in turn, clarified de León's authorship of the anonymous texts as well.[20] Although they are not accompanied by explicit dates of composition, a number of factors indicate that these texts belong to de León's pretheosophic period. These texts typically engage in linguistic speculation on the meaning of letterforms, vowel points, divine names, et cetera, which correlates with the structures and functions of the celestial spheres, angelology, cosmogony, the secrets of the chariot, and more.[21] One of these unsigned works survives in more

[17] De León, *Sefer ha-Mishqal*, 42.

[18] See Gershom Scholem, *Kabbalah* (Jerusalem: Keter, 1974), 433; Altmann, "*Or zarua'*," 243–244. For the disagreement between Scholem and Altmann, see Elliot R. Wolfson, *The Book of the Pomegranate: Moses de León's* Sefer ha-Rimmon (Atlanta, GA: Scholars Press, 1988), 4–5 (introduction); Daniel Abrams, "The Secret of the Upper and Lower Waters: An Unknown Work from Early Castilian Kabbalah" [in Hebrew], in *And This Is for Yehuda: Studies Presented to Our Friend, Professor Yehuda Liebes on the Occasion of His Sixty-Fifth Birthday*, ed. Maren Niehoff, Ronit Meroz, and Jonathan Garb (Jerusalem: Mossad Bialik, 2012), 311–324, here 313; Joseph Dan, *The History of Jewish Mysticism and Esotericism* [in Hebrew] (Jerusalem: Shazar Center, 2014), 10:266–267n.25.

[19] See Altmann, "*Or zarua'*," 221, 235–240. See also Nathan Wolski, "Metatron and the Mysteries of the Night in *Midrash ha-Ne'lam*: Jacob ha-Kohen's *Sefer ha-Orah* and the Transformation of a Motif in the Early Writings of Moses de León," *Kabbalah* 23 (2010): 69–94.

[20] Gershom Scholem, "Review of Carlo Bernheimer, *Codices Hebraici Bybliothecae Ambrosianae*" [in Hebrew], *Kiryat Sefer* 11 (1934): 188; Scholem, "Qabbalot," 30; Scholem, *Kabbalah*, 60; Asi Farber, "On the Sources of Rabbi Moses de León's Early Kabbalistic System" [in Hebrew], *Jerusalem Studies in Jewish Thought* 3, nos. 1–2 (1984): 67–96. See, further, Abrams, "Book of Illumination" 53–56.

[21] See Avishai Bar-Asher, "*Sefer ha-Ne'lam*, New Parts of *Sefer Or Zarua'*, and Clarifications Regarding the Early Writings of R. Moses de León: Studies and Critical Editions" [in Hebrew], *Tarbiz* 83, nos. 1–2 (2014–2015): 197–329. Compare Scholem's characterization of *Or zarua'* with his emphasis on its philosophical dimension: Gerhard [Gershom] Scholem, "Eine unbekannte mystische Schrift des Mose de Leon," *Monatschrift für Geschichte und Wissenschaft des Judentums* 71, nos. 3–4 (1927): 109–123, here 121; Elliot R. Wolfson, "Left Contained in the Right: A Study in Zoharic Hermeneutics," *AJS Review* 11, no. 1 (1986): 27–52, here 49n.98; Wolfson, "Moisés de León y el Zohar," in *Pensamiento y mística hispano judía y sefardí*, ed. Judit Targarona Borrás, Angel

manuscripts than all of the others combined—*Sod Darkhe ha-otiyyot ve-ha-nequddot* (*Secret of the Paths of the Letters and the Vowels*).[22] Another is extant in only two manuscripts and has no title; it is divided into chapters named after the Hebrew vowels.[23] Recent research has yielded the discovery of fragments of a third work called *Sefer ha-Ne'lam*, which appears to be the first work composed by León.[24] These mysterious compositions share the basic approach of *Or zarua'*, but they are distinguished from the latter by their pseudepigraphic character.[25] The discovery of *Sefer ha-Ne'lam* and its abundance of clues pointing to de León's handiwork not only helped to clarify the authorship of the large corpus of early unsigned works but also showed that, long before he embarked on his zoharic writing, de León adopted the

Sáenz-Badillos, and Ricardo Izquierdo Benito (Cuenca, Ecuador: Ediciones de la Universidad Castilla-La Mancha, 2001), 167–192, here 167–168; Jeremy Phillip Brown, "Distilling Depths from Darkness: Forgiveness and Repentance in Medieval Iberian Jewish Mysticism" (PhD diss., New York University, 2015), 197–205, 212–218.

[22] See Gershom Scholem, *Reshit ha-qabbalah* (Jerusalem: Schocken Books, 1948), 124 with n. 1; Scholem, *The Origins of Kabbalah* (Princeton, NJ: Princeton University Press, 1992), 362n.317. Compare Moritz Steinschneider, "Hebräische Handschriften in Parma," *Hebräische Bibliographie* 10, no. 58 (1870): 96–104, here 99n.3; Steinschneider, "Zur kabbalistischen Literatur: III. Jakob und Isak Kohen," *Hebräische Bibliographie* 17, no. 98 (1877): 36–38, here 37; Elliot R. Wolfson, "Letter Symbolism and *Merkavah* Imagery in the Zohar," in *Alei Shefer: Studies in the Literature of Jewish Thought; Presented to Dr. Alexander Safran*, ed. Moshe Hallamish (Ramat-Gan: Bar Ilan University, 1990), 195–236, here 204n.31 [English pagination]; Daniel Abrams, "From Germany to Spain: Numerology as a Mystical Technique," *Journal of Jewish Studies* 47 (1996): 85–101, here 86–87n.9; Moses de León, *Sefer ha-Ne'lam*, 221–227; Avishai Bar-Asher, "From the Vaults of Thebes: Moses de León's Pseudepigraphic Writings on the Letters, Vowel Signs, Theonyms, and Magical Practices and the Origin of Zoharic Fiction" [in Hebrew], *Kabbalah* 51 (2022): 157–248, where the edition of the text appears on 200–248 = Moses de León, *Sod Darkhe ha-otiyyot*; cited are 164–165. For printings of the work misattributed to Jacob ha-Kohen, see "Sefer Sod darkhe ha-niqqud ve-ha-otiyyot," in *Yalqut ha-Ro'im ha-gadol*, ed. Shraga Bauer and Shraga Eisenbach (Jerusalem: Nezer Shraga, 2000), 1–58 [seventh pagination]; and Wiener, "Mysteries," 377–449.

[23] MS Paris, Bibliothèque nationale de France, héb. 817, fols. 55a–91b, and MS New York, Jewish Theological Seminary of America, 1886, fols. 1a–24b. See Gershom Scholem and Bernhard I. Joel, eds., *Catalogus Codicum Cabbalisticorum Hebraicorum* [in Hebrew] (Jerusalem: Hebrew University, 1930), 58; Scholem, "An Inquiry in the Kabbala of R. Isaac ben Jacob Hacohen: III. R. Moses of Burgos, the Disciple of R. Isaac (Continued)" [in Hebrew], *Tarbiz* 5, no. 2 (1934): 180–198, here 195–196n.11; Scholem, "An Inquiry in the Kabbala of R. Isaac ben Jacob ha-Kohen: III. R. Moses of Burgos, the disciple of R. Isaac (Concluded)" [in Hebrew], *Tarbiz* 5, no. 3/4 (1934): 305–323, here 305n.1; Scholem, "A Key to Commentaries on the Ten Sefirot" [in Hebrew], *Kiryat Sefer* 10 (1933–1934): 498–515, here 506; Farber, "Sources," 68n.2; Moses de León, *Sefer ha-Ne'lam*, 221–227; Avishai Bar-Asher, "The Earliest Citation from *Sefer ha-Zohar* and from Whence the Book of *Zohar* Received Its Name" [in Hebrew], *Kabbalah* 39 (2017): 95–109. Also see Elliot R. Wolfson, "Biblical Accentuation in a Mystical Key: Kabbalistic Interpretations of the *Te'amim*," *Journal of Jewish Music and Liturgy* 12 (1989–1990): 1–16, here 1–4; Moshe Idel, "On the Meanings of the Term 'Kabbalah'" [in Hebrew], *Pe'amim* 93 (2003): 38–76, here 53n.62.

[24] Bar-Asher, "*Sefer ha-Ne'lam*"; Bar-Asher, "New Fragments from *Sefer Or zarua'* and *Sefer ha-Ne'lam*" [in Hebrew], *Tarbiz* 83, no. 4 (2016): 635–642; Bar-Asher, "*Sefer ha-Nequddah*, the Short *Sefer ha-Yiḥud*, and Fragments from *Sefer Or zarua'* and *Sefer Toledot Adam*" [in Hebrew], *Kabbalah* 35 (2016): 307–321.

[25] See Farber's conjecture in "Sources," 92–96 with notes.

compositional technique of ascribing wisdom to fictive purveyors of secret knowledge, a practice that anticipated the pseudepigraphic conceit of the Zohar. The traditions and worldview of this imagined intelligentsia constitute the esoteric knowledge developed throughout de León's earliest works. This literary feature points to an important shift in genre that, together with other conceptual transitions we chart in our analyses, characterizes de León's larger oeuvre.

Unlike de León's signed works, which exemplify the mode of theosophical speculation associated with the kabbalah of the Zohar, the earliest unsigned compositions do not conceive of a graduated order of attributes suffused by a divine substance (whether by an unknowable ether or by a substance comprised of primordial letters), nor do they speak of sefirot or potencies manifested outwardly by God. Their metaphysics concerns the hierarchy of all created entities (intellects qua angels, spheres), which issue from the creative action of God as *causa prima*. The speculation typical of this corpus turns on the investigation of graphemic, phonological, and numerological aspects of the Hebrew consonants and vowels. It aims to demonstrate how the basic components of language corroborate the ontological/ cosmological expanse encompassing the spheres, the angels, and the divine chariot. In these writings, God is referred to as "the supernal Gradation, may He be blessed" (an epithet adapted from Maimonides),[26] "the Master," "the supernal Charioteer," "the Sovereign of All," "the Ancient One," and more. The order of being descends causally from God to three worlds, which span from the upper world of the intellects—the realm of form unadulterated by matter—to the middle world of celestial spheres in which incorruptible celestial matter receives form to the lower, sublunar world, where form commingles with corruptible matter.[27] Mediating between "the supernal Gradation," that is, the divinity, and these three worlds is the active intellect, which de León considered the first created entity. The active intellect is also personified as an archangel, "the Prince of the Countenance" (*Sar ha-Panim*) or Metatron, a quasi-demiurgical entity from which all creations beneath it are "emanated" (*nishpa'im*).[28] In the fifth section of *Or zarua'*, de

[26] See Moses Maimonides, Mishneh Torah, Hilkhot yesode ha-Torah, 2:8, where the term refers not to the deity but rather to the first order of created being.

[27] On these schemata and their possible sources in medieval thought, see Wolfson, "Letter Symbolism," 196–197n.5; Bar-Asher, "Earliest Citation," 103–109.

[28] On the identification of Metatron with the Active Intellect in different kabbalistic circles in the thirteenth century, see Idel, "Writings of Abraham Abulafia," 1:87–88; Farber, "Sources," 84–87; Elliot R. Wolfson, "God, the Demiurge and the Intellect: On the Usage of the Word *Kol* in Abraham ibn Ezra," *Revue des études juives* 149 (1990): 77–111.

León therefore describes the active intellect as a supernal chariot located above the chariot of the "living creatures" (*ḥayyot*) that Ezekiel beheld, a notion elaborated in all of these early unsigned works.[29]

Nearly all the known texts comprising de León's corpus can be assigned with relative ease to one or another intellectual period: either to the author's pretheosophical period or to the period in which de León took up the characteristically theosophical doctrine of the sefirot. But one work—the "Nameless Composition"—straddles both worldviews to a unique degree.[30] As Asi Farber has pointed out, some of its alphabetical speculations are clearly lifted from earlier works, a move she interpreted as part of an attempt to square the older material with the spirit of theosophical kabbalah.[31] At the same time, the composition reworks the earlier speculations into a new conception of the Godhead and the cosmos rooted in the kabbalistic theosophy of the sefirot. As such, the fragment of the composition before us offers a glimpse into the formation of a unique strain of theosophic kabbalah. The composition, again, complicates the conventional narrative of a sharp break. It suggests, instead, that the Castilian kabbalists negotiated a more gradual and complex process of reorientation in the final quarter of the thirteenth century. Studying the adaptation and repurposing of de León's earliest pretheosophical exegesis of the Hebrew language allows us to track the gradual evolution of the Castilian discourse with a considerable degree of nuance. It thus becomes possible to chart, by tracing the developmental course of de León's linguistic speculation, a main intellectual tributary flowing into the Zohar.

The "Nameless Composition" concentrates on mysteries of the Hebrew letters and vowel points in the penultimate and final chapters, where they figure within the text's account of the uppermost sefirot; the secrets discussed here relate primarily to the sefirah of *ḥokhmah*, and the relation of the latter to the domain of ultimate transcendence surpassing it (referred to as *ayin* and *keter*), and the emergence of all existence therefrom. Accordingly, these chapters contain interesting disquisitions on the first two letters of the Tetragrammaton, *yod* and *heh*, which the author consistently

[29] See Farber's thorough treatment in "Sources," 79–87.

[30] See Farber, "Sources," 70; and Moses de León, *Sefer ha-Ne'lam*, 213–214, 253–254. For the conception of the sefirot in the Munich treatise, see Yehuda Liebes, *Ars Poetica in Sefer Yetsira* [in Hebrew] (Jerusalem: Schocken Books, 2000), 283n.13.

[31] Compare the account in Farber, "Sources," 87–91.

associates with *ḥokhmah* and the sefirah that is conjoined to it, namely, *binah*.[32]

Thanks to the discoveries of the complete versions of *Or zarua'* and *Sefer ha-Ne'lam*, and related scholarly advances, one can now properly assess the full scope of de León's thought, with the "Nameless Composition" constituting the missing link connecting the earliest material to de León's signed works. In light of this, we offer a comparative analysis of de León's early writings (especially *Or zarua'*) and the latter text. Our analysis is divided into three parts. The first deals with speculations on the letter *alef* and their theological ramifications, the angelology of the "two chariots," and the cosmology of the three worlds. The second part focuses on speculative lore concerning the letters of God's names, which the text attributes to "custodians of the secret of the letters," and which is based on a novel intellectualist theosophy. The third section explores techniques of letter pairing (*megalgelim ha-otiyyot*), which the text attributes to "custodians of the secret of arithmetic," and the construction of a realm of purely intellectual existence.

3.3 *Alef*: One, Two, Three, and Four

In *Or zarua'*, de León clusters the main alphabetical speculations into the sixth chapter. There three separate discussions are set within the framework of "three secrets." Each of these "mysteries" comprises interpretations of the morphology, phonology, and numerology of Hebrew letters, with a particular focus on the tenth letter, *yod*. The recently located missing portion of *Or zarua'* yields additional material dealing with alphabetical speculation (i.e., a subsection of "the first mystery"). This additional discussion deploys various structural elements in the Hebrew language to interpret the biblical description of the four banners of the Israelite tribes in Numbers 10.[33]

A careful comparison of each of these discussions in *Or zarua'* with the large extant portion of our text reveals deliberate changes de León made when transposing the linguistic hermeneutic from one conceptual framework to

[32] The extant fragment indicates that the first part of the work, now lost, originally included homilies on the last two letters of the Tetragrammaton, *vav* and *heh*, which were associated with the lower sefirot, including the female *malkhut*.

[33] See de León, *Sefer ha-Ne'lam*, 213. This passage is absent from all manuscript witnesses except for the recently discovered manuscript containing the full work; see there, 301–304. Compare Scholem's proposed identification of the "custodians of the secret of arithmetic" with the German Pietists: Scholem, "Eine unbekannte mystische Schrift," 116–117n.4.

another. Investigation of other pretheosophical works in the *Sefer ha-Ne'lam* corpus shows even more extensive evidence of such reworking. Additionally, throughout our nameless fragment, de León attributes a number of these earlier speculations to obscure groups of unspecified adepts, such as the "custodians of the secret of the letters" (*ba'ale sod ha-otiyyot*) and "custodians of the secret of arithmetic" (*ba'ale sod ha-ḥeshbon*). What can we make of the fact that such attributions are in fact veiled allusions to de León's own earlier compositions? On the one hand, it seems that the author resorted to fictional references to suffuse his treatise with an air of authority. On the other, such references have the rhetorical function of establishing distance from the author's earlier thinking while demonstrating its enduring relevance for subsequent projects.

The "first secret" in *Or zarua'* includes a series of alphabetical speculations, only some of which are reprised in modified form by our fragment. An interesting example of an idea that did not survive the shift to the new conceptual framework is the numerological equation between the four letters of the Tetragrammaton and the first five letters of the Hebrew alphabet. The numerical equivalence of the entire Tetragrammaton is 26: Y (10) + H (5) + V (6) + H (5). The same operation performed on the first four letters of the alphabet yields 10: ' (1) + B (2) + G (3) + D (4). Now, 10 is the numerical value of the tenth letter, *yod*, and, when *yod* is written in full (YVD), it equals 20: Y (10) + V (6) + D (4). If one adds to the sum the fifth letter of the Hebrew alphabet, *heh*, also spelled out in full (H'), then one arrives at 26: 20 (YVD) + 5 (H) + 1 (').[34] One scholar explained that this string of numerological equivalences is intended to demonstrate, through letter symbolism, that "the divine name . . . comprises the totality of existence, or, alternatively expressed, the chariot and the charioteer."[35] This exegesis thus encapsulates the metaphysics of *Or zarua'* and kindred pretheosophic works,[36] in which God is identified with the lofty "supernal gradation" (symbolized by the letter *heh*), namely, the divine Charioteer riding upon the two chariots, one atop the other. The first chariot is "the tenth intellect," "the lesser charioteer," also identified with the archangel Metatron (corresponding to the tenth letter *yod*), and beneath him are the four angelic bearers of the second

[34] Avishai Bar-Asher, "*Sefer ha-Ne'lam*, New Parts of Sefer Or Zarua and Clarifications Regarding the Early Writings of R. Moses de León: Studies and Critical Editions" [in Hebrew], *Tarbiz* 83, nos. 1–2 (2015): 256–318 = Moses de León, *Or zarua'*, here 300, 306.

[35] Wolfson, "Letter Symbolism," 202.

[36] For parallel exegeses in other works in the *Sefer ha-Ne'lam* corpus, see the sources in Wolfson, "Letter Symbolism," 204, near n. 32; and Bar-Asher, "Earliest Citation," 106n.96.

chariot: Michael, Raphael, Gabriel, and Nuriel (symbolized by the letters *alef* through *dalet*).[37]

Although de León did not migrate this entire set of numerological correspondences into our text, its traces factor into the latter's speculation about the relationship between the Tetragrammaton and the first letters of the alphabet.[38] In lieu of the correspondence between the letter *yod* and "the tenth intellect," which appears in *Or zarua'* and related works, our text posits a correspondence between the letter *yod* and the sefirah of *ḥokhmah*.[39] Consequently, the exposition in *Or zarua'* (with its focus on the four archangels upon which the tenth intellect "rides") did not survive the transposition to a new conceptual register. The other alphabetical "secrets" of *Or zarua'* that linked the Tetragrammaton and the first four letters of the alphabet suffered the same fate.[40] By disconnecting the letter *yod* from the tenth intellect (i.e., Metatron) and connecting it to the sefirah of *ḥokhmah*, de León methodically erased any hint of the previous model in which the angels of the chariot populated the divine realm (as arithmetically encoded in the letters of the Tetragrammaton). At most, the status of these angels—entities of real substance—is diminished to that of mere cognomina or symbols. In other words, our nameless text reduces the angels to indices for different aspects of the divine order.

3.4 The Four Israelite Banners

While de León omitted some of his earliest speculation from our nameless text, most likely because it did not square with the author's newly adopted theosophy, he carefully reworked several motifs to fit the new paradigm. This is exemplified by the author's treatment of the continuation of the "first secret" in *Or zarua'*. In the last chapter of the work,[41] there appears an extensive

[37] On this, see Altmann, "*Or zarua'*," 270. But see the discussion about the "double chariot" in Farber, "Sources," 83–84. As noted by Farber, de León ascribed this double-chariot conception to "the wisdom of the kabbalah" and affirmed it several times in *Or zarua'* to express his disagreement with the doctrine of a single chariot. The notion is also presented in the recently discovered introduction to *Sefer ha-Ne'lam*, where de León distinguishes between the "great Charioteer," meaning God or "the highest gradation," and the "lesser charioteer," beneath whom lies the lower chariot of the four archangels and the four "living creatures (*ḥayyot*). See Bar-Asher, "*Sefer ha-Ne'lam*," 236–237. Also see Wolfson, "Letter Symbolism," 204.

[38] MS Munich, Bayerische Staatsbibliothek, Cod. hebr. 47, fol. 370b.

[39] Wolfson, "Letter Symbolism," 204–205 and n. 33.

[40] Compare Wolfson, "Letter Symbolism," 204–205 and n. 33.

[41] MS Munich, Bayerische Staatsbibliothek, Cod. hebr. 47, fols. 366a–370b.

interpretation of the four standards of the Israelite encampment, and their connection to various fourfold structures in cosmology (the four elements, the four "ends of the earth"), the Hebrew language (the first four letters of the alphabet, four of the Hebrew vowels [*qamaṣ*, *ḥiriq*, *pataḥ*, and *sheva*]), and angelology (the four angels of the Countenance).[42] The text describes the arrangement of the angelic camps on high that mirror the Israelite camps below, discussing the banners of Reuben and Judah as follows:

> "On the south: the banner of the camp of Reuben" (Numbers 10:2)—it is below Judah on the right side, but unlike Judah because Judah is above, at the head, and Reuben is below. You should be aware of the fact that the beginning of Judah is on the left side and comes to the right and remains on the right, whereas Reuben begins on the right side and comes to the left and remains on the left. . . . On account of this, the waters—which are from the right side and are cold and wet—went to the north, which is cold and wet; just as you find originally that the fire became bound to the south, since fire is hot and dry, and the south is hot and dry. In this way, the corners are interlinked and [causally] emerge from one another.[43]

In this passage, one can see how the two triads of north-left-water and south-right-fire allude to a pair of theosophical correspondences in which the various gradations extend from and are, in turn, linked to one another. A comparison of this interpretation with similar ones provided by de León in his *Sefer ha-Ne'lam* corpus reveals a few discrepancies. Our text gestures only vaguely at the connection between the four angels and various elements of the Hebrew language but recasts the angelological and cosmological features to express new ideas.[44] In the other early works, one encounters a highly detailed explication of the midrash on the banners that presents an utterly different theology and cosmology.[45]

[42] For these fourfold correspondences, see Farber, "Sources," 88n.50; and Farber, "Commentary," 104–105n.18. Ronit Meroz also discussed the correspondence between the four elements and the four cardinal directions in de León's thought in her treatment of his "Commentary on the Thirteen Attributes [by Which the Torah Is Expounded]" (see Figure 1.3 in Chapter 1), which is in fact part of the "Nameless Composition." See Ronit Meroz, "Kabbalah, Science and Pseudo-Science in Ramdal's Commentary on the Thirteen Attributes," in *And This Is for Yehuda: Studies Presented to Our Friend, Professor Yehuda Liebes, on the Occasion of His Sixty-Fifth Birthday*, ed. Maren R. Niehoff, Ronit Meroz, and Jonathan Garb (Jerusalem: Mossad Bialik, 2012), 123–143. See, too, Wolfson, "Anthropomorphic Imagery," 160n.58.

[43] MS Munich, Bayerische Staatsbibliothek, Cod. hebr. 47, fol. 366a–b.

[44] See Farber, "Sources," 88 with n. 50.

[45] For a comprehensive treatment, see Avishai Bar-Asher, *Journeys of the Soul: Concepts and Imageries of Paradise in Medieval Kabbalah* [in Hebrew] (Jerusalem: Magnes Press, 2019), 269–273.

Consider the following example. In de León's earlier description of the four banners in *Or zarua'*, he presents an elaborate parallelism between the middle and lower worlds, between the four archangels bearing the chariot above and the four Israelite encampments below.[46] He is in fact expanding upon Numbers Rabbah (2:10), which asserts that the banners are arranged according to the four cardinal directions and that each angel of the chariot corresponds to a particular tribal banner. Our author interprets this midrash through the alphabetical wisdom characteristic of his earlier writings, adding a set of correspondences between the four banners and four vowel points. According to the ontology in *Or zarua'*, the four angels of the chariot are stationed beneath the "supernal Gradation" and are identical to the separate intellects (with the "tenth intellect" on top) from which the world of the spheres and the lower world unfold.[47] A similar and consistent picture emerges from the other unsigned works in the *Sefer ha-Ne'lam* corpus. At the center of the angelological order are the four "living creatures" (*ḥayyot*) bearing the chariot, or the angels of the Countenance upon which Metatron, "Prince of the Countenance," rides (the latter, in turn, constitutes a supernal chariot ridden by the supernal Charioteer, i.e., "the Master," the transcendent God).[48]

The sources for the cosmology in these works and in the rest of the *Sefer ha-Ne'lam* corpus have yet to be identified.[49] Nevertheless, it is

[46] This appears in the full version of *Or zarua'*.

[47] On the question of the ontological ambivalence of the tenth intellect, which also plays a special role in de León's other unsigned writings, see Farber, "Sources," 79–80 with n. 28, and Wolfson, "Letter Symbolism," 196–197n.5 and 203n.27.

[48] See the unsigned *Sha'ar ḥeleq ha-nequddah* in MS Paris, Bibliothèque nationale de France, héb. 817, fol. 81a (and see fol. 82b). In fragments of *Sefer ha-Ne'lam* only a rough version of this two-tiered structure is found, and without any connection to the Israelite standards of the lower world; see Moses de León, *Sefer ha-Ne'lam*, 322. But another work from this corpus contains a lengthy discourse on the standards that has nearly the same wording as found in the recently discovered full edition of *Or zarua'*, which attests to intertextuality or a shared source. See further Avishai Bar-Asher, "Concepts and Imageries of Paradise in Medieval Kabbalah" [in Hebrew] (PhD diss., Hebrew University, 2014), 214–218; and compare Farber, "Sources," 67. For example, Reuben's order of travel (Numbers 10:18) alludes to the southern position of the archangel Nuriel, who is appointed over fire: "Nuriel is appointed over fire, and there he is to the southern side, for there is no warmth in the heat of a flame except [in the] south, and there is no cold in the frigidity of the world except [in the] north, and for this reason he is appointed there" (MS Paris, Bibliothèque nationale de France, héb. 817, fol. 87a).

[49] In these compositions, we find, at most, pseudepigraphic attributions to fabricated figures or works, which can thwart the search for real sources. In this case, one possible candidate is the appendix to Baruch Togarmi's *Mafteḥot ha-qabbalah*, which transmits a tradition in Togarmi's name about the twin encampments—angelic and Israelite—and the three worlds; see MS Paris, Bibliothèque nationale de France, héb. 770, fols. 7r–8r. R. Isaac of Acre also copied this tradition: Amos Goldreich, "*Sefer Me'irat 'Einayim* by Isaac of Acre" (PhD diss., Hebrew University of Jerusalem, 1981), 186–187. See Ephraim Gottlieb, *Kabbalah in the Writings of R. Baḥya ben Asher Ibn Halawa* [in Hebrew] (Jerusalem: Kiryat Sepher, 1970), 55–57; Israel Weinstock, *Perush Sefer Yeṣirah*

significant that in our nameless text de León began to adumbrate concepts and structures stemming from the theosophic doctrine of the sefirot. For instance, the detailed description of the Israelite banners concludes with a fourfold scheme: *alef*-Michael-*qamaṣ*; *bet*-Gabriel-*ḥiriq*; *gimel*-Raphael-*pataḥ*; *dalet*-Uriel-*sheva*. Our author aligns these groupings with different gradations of the divinity: *alef*-Michael-*qamaṣ* corresponds to the "right side" or side of *ḥesed*, symbolized by the High Priest; *bet*-Gabriel-*ḥiriq* corresponds to the "left side," the female, the supernal *gevurah*; *gimel*-Raphael-*pataḥ* corresponds to the "Tree of Life," the "median line"; *dalet*-Uriel-*sheva* alludes to "the mystery of the fire."[50] For the first time in de León's writings, the angelic realm is mapped onto the sefirot of *hesed* and *gevurah*, the middle sefirah between them (apparently *yesod* rather than *tiferet*), and the lowest sefirah (*malkhut*). This is accompanied by an isomorphic principle: "the four below are bound to, and emerge from the secret of the four above."[51] It is not beyond the realm of possibility that de León was familiar with theosophical interpretations given to the midrash in Numbers Rabbah by Catalonian kabbalists a generation or two earlier.[52]

Scrutiny of de León's manifestly theosophic, later compositions shows that he expanded the connection between these four triads and four gradations of the divinity,[53] describing the four elements and the four banners along theosophic lines. In his *Sheqel ha-qodesh* (1292),[54] the presentation closely

almoni mi-yesodo shel R. Avraham Abulafia (Jerusalem: Mossad ha-Rav Kook, 1984), 51–53; Moshe Idel, "The World of Angels in Human Form" [in Hebrew], *Jerusalem Studies in Jewish Thought* 3 (1984): 1–66, here 61n.264; Idan Pinto, "Universe—Sanctuary—Man: On a Threefold Analogy in Two Anonymous Texts and Their Traces in Thirteenth-Century Kabbalah" [in Hebrew], *Tarbiz* 88, no. 3 (2022): 400–406.

[50] MS Munich, Bayerische Staatsbibliothek, Cod. Hebr. 47, fols. 368a–370b.

[51] MS Munich, Bayerische Staatsbibliothek, Cod. Hebr. 47, fol. 370a.

[52] See Ezra ben Solomon of Girona, "Perush le-Shir ha-Shirim," in *Kitve Ramban*, ed. Charles H. Chavel (Jerusalem: Mossad ha-Rav Kook, 1964), 2:489–490; Moses Naḥmanides, *Commentary on the Torah*, on Numbers 2:2; Azriel of Girona, *Commentarius in Aggadoth auctore R. Azriel Geronensi* [in Hebrew], ed. Isaiah Tishby (Jerusalem: Mekize Nirdamim, 1945), 72–73.

[53] See, for example, Charles Mopsik, ed., *R. Moses de León's Sefer Sheqel ha-Qodesh* (Los Angeles, CA: Cherub Press, 1996) = Moses de León, *Sheqel ha-qodesh*, 33; Isaiah Tishby, "She'elot u-teshuvot le-Rabbi Moshe de León be-'inyene qabbalah" [in Hebrew], in *Studies in Kabbalah and Its Branches: Research and Sources* (Jerusalem: Magnes, 1982), 1:36–75 (repr. from *Kobez al Yad* 5, no. 15 [1950]: 9–38), and 40–41; and Avishai Bar-Asher, "R. Moses de León's *Sefer haPaRDeS* and the Zoharic Commentaries on Biblical Narratives," *JSIS* 24 (2024): 1–71, there 52–53; the responsum by de León about the fringed garment (*ṣiṣit*) printed in Michal Oron, *Window to the Stories of the Zohar: Studies in the Exegetical and Narrative Methods of the Zohar* [in Hebrew] (Los Angeles, CA: Cherub Press, 2011), 193; Avishai Bar-Asher, ed., *R. Moses de León's* Sefer Mishkan ha-'edut [in Hebrew] (Los Angeles, CA: Cherub Press, 2013) 158 = Moses de León, *Mishkan ha-'edut*, 158.

[54] Moses de León, *Sheqel ha-qodesh*, 96.

matches its Aramaic zoharic parallel, where "the secret of the holy supernal chariot" is recorded in the name of Rabbi Simeon bar Yoḥai.[55] Both the Hebrew and the Aramaic versions include a metallurgical theory of the four material elements based on Aristotelian physics (water, fire, air, earth), under which they correspond to the four cardinal directions (south, north, east, west), and from which are cast the four elemental metals (copper, gold, silver, and iron) and the four lesser metals ("inferior copper" [tin], yellow dross, lead, and iron).[56] In addition, these groupings of four appear in the later works as means of characterizing the seven lower sefirot, with *ḥesed*, *gevurah*, *raḥamim*/*tiferet* (rather than *yesod*), and *malkhut* forming the trunk. In the previous chapter, we observed how de León integrated an Aristotelian motif into a vast lexicon of terms corresponding to the divine order; here we see another instance of the same phenomenon attested in *Sheqel ha-qodesh* and the Zohar. Furthermore, these schematic interpretations underscore the influence of the divine realm on the lower domains and, reciprocally, the isomorphic character of the lower domains vis-à-vis the supernal ones. They also set up an important distinction between the first three gradations and the fourth attribute (corresponding to *malkhut*), in which the divine process of individuation is complete, and whence the individuation of created entities ("world of separate [intellects]"; *'olam ha-nifradim*) concatenates."[57]

3.5 *Alef*: Three Worlds

Like the "secret of the banners," de León's earliest theosophical work similarly retools the speculation from *Or zarua'* on the form of the *alef* (which appears in the final section of the "first mystery"). The Masoretic grapheme of Hebrew *alef* is א, which is formed by three strokes: a long line slanting right in the middle, one short ascender on the right extending leftward at the top, and one short descender on the left, extending rightward at the bottom. *Or zarua'* identifies the three strokes of the *alef* (א) with three individual letters. The diagonal middle stroke he identified as a *vav* (ו), the short ascending stroke appears as a *yod* (י), and the descending stroke is seen as an inverted

[55] Zohar, 2:24a–b.

[56] The translation of the Aramaic terms for the metals is based on *The Zohar: Pritzker Edition*, trans. Daniel Matt (Stanford, CA: Stanford University Press, 2007), 4:87.

[57] See at length in Bar-Asher, *Journeys of the Soul*, 102–104; for the possible sources of this conception, the likes of which Abraham Abulafia mentioned, see there, 96n.382.

dalet (ᒪ).[58] The first letter of the Hebrew alphabet, then, comprises the three letters that spell the name of the tenth letter: *yod* (יוד). This threefold structure of the *alef*, according to de León, denotes the three worlds at the heart of his pretheosophic cosmology: the upper, spiritual world of the intellects, signified by the *yod* on top of the *alef*; the middle, material world of the celestial spheres, signified by the central *vav*; and the sublunar world whose mundane character is signified by the *dalet* at the bottom. In *Or zarua'* and the other works in de León's *Sefer ha-Ne'lam* corpus, this threefold scheme frames a threefold cosmovision.

Our nameless text reproduces the speculation of the *alef* in full, together with its dissection into the three letters of *yod* corresponding to three worlds (see Figure 3.1). Conspicuously missing, however, is any conceptual linkage between these three worlds and their cosmological/ angelological significance in *Or zarua'*. In this context, our author transposed the three-worlds account of the *alef* into a new theosophical register. He did so by drawing lines from these three rungs of created being to three orders of the divinity. The upper world (symbolized by *yod*) corresponds to the concealed recesses of the "hidden world" (*ḥokhmah* and *binah*); the middle world (symbolized by the linear *vav*, the sixth letter) corresponds to the "medial line" that functions as the axis of the "six extremities" mentioned in *Sefer Yeṣirah*, that is, the six sefirot from *ḥesed* through *yesod*; and the lower world (symbolized by *dalet*) is identified throughout this composition with the lower female sefirah (*malkhut*). Our text replaces the early corpus's Aristotelian depiction of each world's causal movement of the existents directly below it with an account in which the unified divine substance extends through the relative individuation of three intradivine worlds. Interestingly, when de León lines up the three worlds with the intradivine structures, he breaks the tripartite mold by inserting a fourth element, *binah*, which conjoins with *ḥokhmah*:

> When the form א stands in its secret, the secret of its unity denotes the three worlds visible within it: the upper world, which is the concealed world (= *ḥokhmah*), [and] which is joined with [the letter] *ṭet* (= *binah*), since it is a world unto itself. And from there the secret of the middle world goes forth and spreads out. When it is joined with it (= the upper world), it makes it

[58] Moses de León, *Or zarua'*, 304–305. Compare the speculations on the letterform of *alef* in R. Jacob ha-Kohen's commentary on the letterforms in Scholem, "Qabbalot," 202.

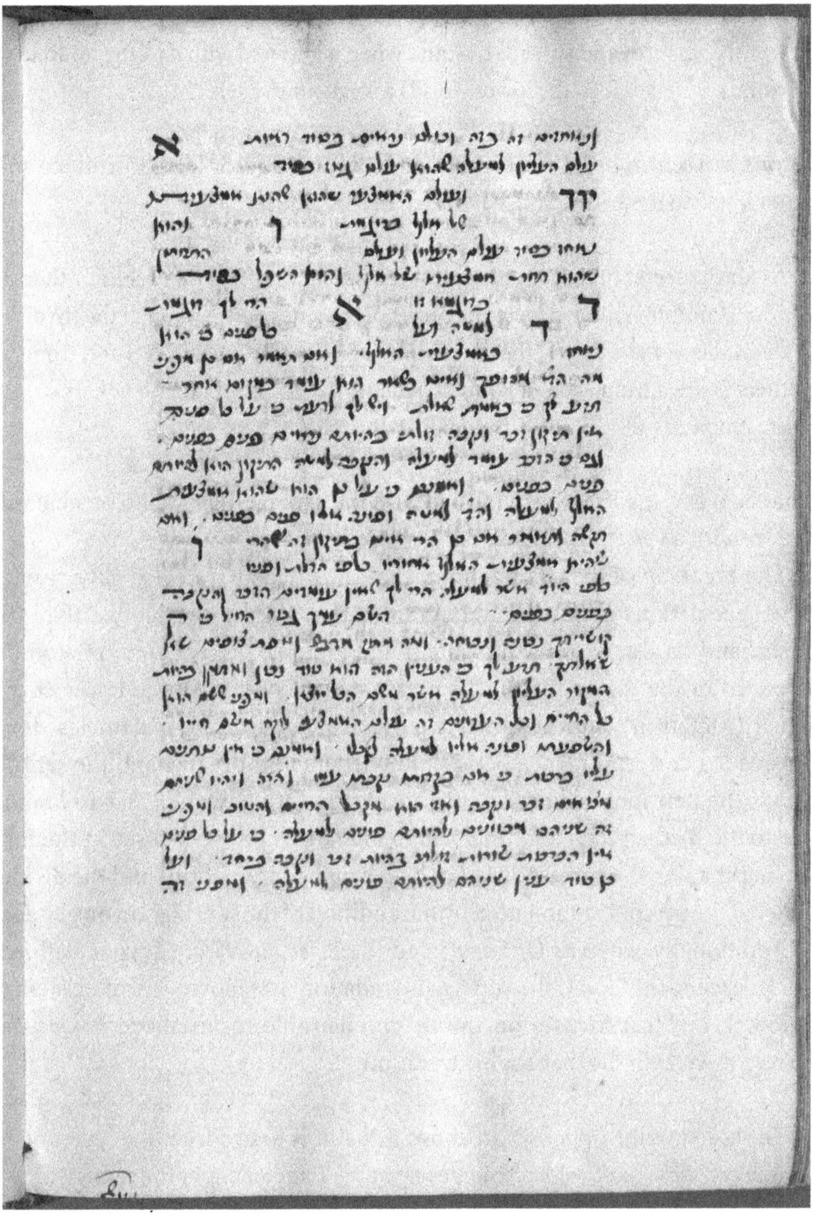

Figure 3.1 Secret of the *alef*, comprising three worlds: *yod*, *vav*, and *dalet*; MS Munich, Bayerische Staatsbibliothek, Cod. hebr. 47, fol. 361b.

> (= the middle world) a world unto itself. Thence the mystery of the lower world goes forth and spreads out, and when it is joined with it (= the middle world), it makes it (= the lower world) a world unto itself.[59]

As one can see, in order to account for *binah*, the author must introduce another letter to the triune *yod-vav-dalet*, in this case *ṭet*:

> As for the secret of the letter *ṭet*, it is the semblance of a closed exedra[60] that admits nothing into it except the secret of the letter *yod*. Although the tip of the *yod* is not visible . . . , the idea is that it (= *yod*) enters it (= *ṭet*) and from there is filled from each of its sides, since it (= *yod*, symbolizing *ḥokhmah*) encompasses all.[61]

That is to say, the letterform of the ט has the semicircular shape of a closed exedra with a *yod* (י) resting atop its left ascender.[62]

The breaking of the triadic mold to fit the divine tetrad also gave rise to new speculations about the Tetragrammaton. We showed above that *Or zarua*ʿ and its associated works attempted to relate the Tetragrammaton to the triad of the divine realm: the great Charioteer (God), the lesser charioteer (Metatron), and the angelic chariot. By contrast, our nameless text advances a correspondence between the letters of the Name and the sefirot due to the new fourfold model: *yod* corresponds to *ḥokhmah*, *heh* to *binah*, *vav* to the median line, and final *heh* to *malkhut*.[63] As we will see in the following chapter, the correspondence between the three worlds and the divine order of the sefirot is augmented by the addition of the speculation on gender.

Additionally, whereas *Or zarua*ʿ and the *Sefer ha-Neʿlam* corpus defined the transcendent God ("the supernal Gradation") as moving all of existence below it, our text focuses on the inapprehensible realm above *ḥokhmah*, known as *keter* in the theosophic tradition:

> The secret of the upper world above is that it is drawn from the secret of supernal *ḥokhmah*, which emerges from the Fundament of fundaments,[64]

[59] MS Munich, Bayerische Staatsbibliothek, Cod. hebr. 47, fol. 361ª.

[60] *Akhsadra* (derived from the Greek: ἐξέδρα).

[61] MS Munich, Bayerische Staatsbibliothek, Cod. hebr. 47, fol. 361ª.

[62] In his discussion, de León relates the fact that the tenth letter, *yod*, actually represents the ninth sefirah, and the ninth letter, *ṭet*, represents the eighth sefirah (when counting upward from below). See MS Munich, Bayerische Staatsbibliothek, Cod. hebr. 47, fol. 361ª.

[63] See MS Munich, Bayerische Staatsbibliothek, Cod. hebr. 47, fol. 374a–b.

[64] Or "Essence of essences" (*me-ʿiqqar kol ha-ʿiqqarim*).

> from the Cause of causes. And this is the supernal Gradation, the pure, rarefied ether that can never be apprehended, whence all the *devarim* (= the sefirot) are emanated and emerge through the secret of *ḥokhmah*, which is "the beginning of God's paths" (Job 40:19). It is therefore the primordial ether, most ancient of all, most concealed of all, inapprehensible to all.[65]

This paragraph illustrates yet again the transition from de León's earlier theology and angelology to the theosophical paradigm. The "supernal Gradation," which the earlier corpus identified with the transcendent God and the first Cause, is henceforth identified with *keter*, the transcendent aspect of the Godhead, the uppermost crown of the divine order, which admits only of apophatic descriptions.[66]

The "Nameless Composition" aligns the three worlds with yet another trio—the three gradations of the human soul. The latter are, in turn, linked to different strata of the divinity, and here too we observe how older cosmological notions accommodate the novel theosophical structures:

> The *ruaḥ* is always intermediate, sustaining the *nefesh*, which is the lowest. This *ruaḥ* only exists through the *neshamah*, which is supernal [and] sustains the *ruaḥ*. As to the *neshamah*, it is the mystery of the upper world [that] sustains the *ruaḥ*, and based on it the *ruaḥ* sustains the *nefesh*. Thus, the three are bound together.[67]

The necessary causality that governs the threefold cosmology and the assertion of essential differences between the different planes of being is carried over into this discussion of psychology. The maintenance of such a distinction is critical for discriminating between the most recondite aspect of the soul and its source, namely, the "primordial ether" that is "never apprehended; it encompasses them all and apprehends them, but it is not apprehended through them."[68]

[65] MS Munich, Bayerische Staatsbibliothek, Cod. hebr. 47, fol. 365b.

[66] On the ether in de León's thought, see George Margoliouth, "The Doctrine of the Ether in the Kabbalah," *Jewish Quarterly Review* 20 (1908): 825–861; Jeremy Phillip Brown, "Glimmers of the World Soul in Kabbalah," in *World Soul: A History*, ed. James Wilberding (New York: Oxford University Press, 2021), 124–150, here 135–142.

[67] MS Munich, Bayerische Staatsbibliothek, Cod. hebr. 47, fol. 381a.

[68] MS Munich, Bayerische Staatsbibliothek, Cod. hebr. 47, fol. 381a.

Finally, we do well to note references to the three worlds that recur in de León's later writings.[69] Surprisingly, in his later theosophical works, the author returned to the secrets of the letterforms and vowel points. In *Maskiyyot kesef*, for instance, the author quotes a cosmological discussion of this nature in the name of anonymous "custodians of the wisdom of the explicit [divine] names" (*ba'ale ḥokhmat shemot ha-meforashim*).[70] The linkage between gradations within the soul and the three worlds is similarly prominent in virtually all of de León's subsequent treatments of psychology.[71] But more than merely reviewing the lines of correspondence established by our text between degrees of the soul and the three worlds of a divine being—which de León continued to develop throughout his later works[72]—our analysis suggests that de León coordinated the "theosophization," so to speak, of his early cosmovision with another discursive development to which the author subjected his pretheosophical ideation, namely, psychologization. Indeed, the close coordination of these developments first exhibited by our text had significant implications for the merging of divine ontology and psychology

[69] See esp. Wolfson, *Book of the Pomegranate* = Moses de León, *Sefer ha-Rimmon*, 94–95; Moses de León, *Sheqel ha-qodesh*, 104–106; Moses de León, *Mishkan ha-'edut*, 12–15; MS Oxford, Bodleian Oppenheim Add. 4° 4 (Neubauer 1565), fols. 47b–48a.

[70] Jochanan H. A. Wijnhoven, "*Sefer Maskiyyot Kesef*: Text and Translation with Introduction and Notes" (MA thesis, Brandeis University, 1961), 14–15. Compare Moses de León, *Sefer ha-Rimmon*, 329–330, 333. See Moses de León, *Sefer ha-Ne'lam*, 247–248.

[71] The same is true of his central idea of the *neshamot* flying from "the river that issues from Eden"—namely, the sefirah of *yesod*. De León describes how *malkhut* receives the efflux of *binah* from *yesod*: "'The *ḥayyah* beneath the God of Israel' (Ezekiel 10:20) is the known *ḥayyah* that rules at night. It encompasses the appropriate efflux from the 'river that issues from Eden' (cf. Genesis 2:10) and 'produces the *nefesh* of [the] *ḥayyah*' (cf. Genesis 1:24) certainly through the power of emanation of the *ḥayya* that is above. This is when the river that issues from Eden is in its normal state and the *neshamot* fly from it, as we have [already] discussed" (MS Munich, Bayerische Staatsbibliothek, Cod. hebr. 47, fol. 338°). For the source of this idea, see *Sefer ha-Bahir*, §§. IX:1 (14), 174–175; and XVI:7:1 (39), 181. For the motif of the flying souls in early kabbalistic literature, see, inter alia, Ezra of Girona, "Perush Shir ha-Shirim," 497–498, and compare Azriel of Girona, *Commentarius in Aggadoth*, 13. The tree from which the *neshamot* (souls) fly is also mentioned in *Sefer ha-Bahir*, §. IX:1 (14), 174–175, in a discussion of the tree called *kol*. For an extensive analysis of this paragraph in the Bahir, see Elliot R. Wolfson, "The Tree That Is All: Jewish-Christian Roots of a Kabbalistic Symbol in *Sefer ha-Bahir*," *Journal of Jewish Thought and Philosophy* 3 (1994): 31–76; Avishai Bar-Asher, "The Bahir as It Once Was: Transmission History as a Tool for Reconstructing and Reassessing the Text, Format, and Ideas of the Original Composition" [in Hebrew], *Tarbiz* 89, no. 1 (2022): 73–225 = *Sefer ha-Bahir*, esp. 137–139 and n. 274.

[72] Gershom Scholem addressed the doctrine of three worlds in de León's *Sheqel ha-qodesh* and *Mishkan ha-'edut* in his article "An Inquiry in the Kabbala of R. Isaac ben Jacob Hacohen: II. The Evolution of the Doctrine of the Worlds in the Early Kabbala (Conclusion)" [in Hebrew], *Tarbiz* 3, no. 1 (1932): 33–66, here 42–43. For further use of the division into three worlds, see de León's commentary on the thirteen attributes at the end of the fragment of the Munich treatise, printed in Meroz, "R. Moshe de León's Commentary," 136–138. For a comprehensive treatment of de León's doctrine of the soul, see Bar-Asher, *Journeys of the Soul*, 192–251.

that would become, by dint of the formative impact of the Zohar, a pervasive feature of rabbinic-cum-kabbalistic discourse on the soul through the ages.

3.6 *Ḥokhmah*: Nine and Ten

There is one extract from the early letter speculation in *Or zarua'* that de León transplanted almost entirely intact to his earliest theosophical composition: the alphabetical segment of the "second secret" in the sixth chapter of the former work. The source in *Or zarua'* includes speculations about the fifth letter, *heh*, which is said to symbolize the transcendent God, or "the supernal Gradation."[73] The two possible spellings of the fifth letter *heh*, HY and H', are then interpreted as alluding to the incomplete divine name YH (i.e., Yah) and to the complete Tetragrammaton, YHVH. First, "HY is YH, which is half of the Name (= YH[VH]), and half of the Name is like the whole."[74] Second, as demonstrated earlier in the chapter, when the *yod* and *heh* of the incomplete name YH are written out in full, they have a numerical value of 26, which is also the value of the whole Tetragrammaton.[75] The next speculation concerns the phonetics of the consonant *heh*. As a voiceless glottal fricative, the letter is articulated "effortlessly," so it symbolizes the transcendent God who emanates all of existence effortlessly. In the same way that the *heh* is the sound of sighing, of "rest and repose"—"whoever toils in his work and desires to rest from strenuous labor opens with *heh*"[76]—so "*heh* sustains all existents and from it they are all emitted."[77] The transcendent God is said to be the source of the divine overflow and of providence; elsewhere, the text represents *heh* as "the captain of the whole boat," propelling all of reality by the force of His spiritual wind.[78]

In keeping with the phenomenon we have observed throughout, de León's earliest theosophical work updates the old speculative topos in a manner

[73] Moses de León, *Or zarua'*, 306–310.
[74] De León, *Or zarua'*, 306. Compare the Talmud commentary of Rabbenu Ḥananel ben Ḥushiel to b. Eruvin 18b: "Since the Temple was destroyed, we exalt the Holy One outside the Land with half of the Name, which is tantamount to its entirety."
[75] De León, *Or zarua'*, 306.
[76] De León, *Or zarua'*, 308.
[77] De León, *Or zarua'*, 309.
[78] De León, *Or zarua'*, 309. See Scholem, "Schrift," 117 with n. 1; Altmann, "*Or Zarua'*," 282n.248; Farber, "Sources," 79–80n.28; Wolfson, "Letter Symbolism," 202n.26; Bar-Asher, "*Or Zarua'*," 237n.210. See, too, *Sod darkhe ha-shemot*, MS St. Petersburg, Institute of Oriental Manuscripts, Russian Academy of Sciences D 21 (Guenzburg 606), fol. 30a.

befitting the new paradigm. The letter *heh* no longer alludes to the transcendent deity but to the sefirah beneath *ḥokhmah/binah* (these two sefirot are symbolized by YH, the first two letters of the Tetragrammaton). Our text takes the two earlier interpretations of YH, the numerological and the phonological, and weds them under the canopy of theosophy:

> [The letter] *heh* is the spirit (*ruaḥ*) that sustains and gives life to all spirits. . . . Therefore, you find that because *heh* sustains everything and is rest and repose, everyone in the world according to their suffering and privation returns only to this letter *heh*. . . . As for the secret of *heh*, it encompasses the secret of the Name, for in it *yod* and *heh* are joined together. Therefore, the custodians of the secret of the letters say that *heh* causes the boat to move, because the boat cannot move without wind (*ruaḥ*). Verily, the letter *heh* is the secret of the Name. And they said that since *heh* comprises all of the first letters ' B G D H, so you have the secret of YH, since ' B G D is ten through the secret of *yod*, and *heh* remains.[79]

In light of the parallels presented above, it is more than likely that de León's invocation of sources like the "custodians of the secret of the letters" referred however surreptitiously to his own authorship. With references to these adepts of yore, it seems that the author referred, more specifically, to past iterations of his own writing—precisely in the context of reworking his own earlier speculation.[80]

On the heels of his account of the *heh*, de León introduces a novel idea about the first eight letters of the Hebrew alphabet. The letter *vav* is considered a dividing line between two groups of letters that each have a numerical value of 15, which is also the sum of the letters of the incomplete name of God, YH (Y [10] + H [5] = 15):

> As for 'BGDHVZḤ, you find YH (= 15) on the one side (' [1] + B [2] + D [3] + G [4] + H [5]) and YH (= 15) on the other (Z [7] + Ḥ [8]). *Vav* is in the middle to govern through the secret of YH. Concerning our statement

[79] MS Munich, Bayerische Staatsbibliothek, Cod. hebr. 47, fols. 372b–373a.

[80] MS Munich, Bayerische Staatsbibliothek, Cod. hebr. 47, fol. 378a, cites, in the name of "some sages," an idea about the word "*eḥad* according to the secrets of its letters"; this, too, can be traced to *Or zarua'*, 264–267.

> that *heh* is the secret of the Name, it is so with respect to its articulation and its [numerological] secret.[81]

This division of the first eight letters into two groups contains a hint of the double use of the code in the name YH. That is to say, the focus here is both on its articulation in the vocal tract, and on its hidden significance of its numerical value. Here, again, we observe the richness of the linguistic foundations of the early theosophical work, as displayed by the variety of speculations produced by a host of arcane techniques.[82]

The second group of anonymous sages to whom our text ascribes alphabetical lore is "our rabbis of blessed memory," who "plumbed the depths" of the numerological significance of the initial letters of the alphabet. The text attributes the following numerological explanation to such figures:

> 'B GD HV ZḤ Ṭ. These nine letters are the secret of the number of His essence. . . . Because you find that the secret number of the nine letters (= 45) amounts to the secret of the complete Name with its letters [written

[81] MS Munich, Bayerische Staatsbibliothek, Cod. hebr. 47, fol. 373a. See discussion of this passage below in Chapter 5.

[82] The lengthy appendix to the "Nameless Composition" on the ten names that may not be erased delineates how the respective theonyms align with various levels of the divine order: Ehyeh refers to *ayin*, "the inapprehensible ether"; the incomplete name Yah (its letters [YH] deriving from Ehyeh ['HYH]) refers to *ḥokhmah*, "the Beginning of existence"; and Eloah refers to *binah*, the female aspect on the left that is the source of the human *neshamah*. The next two names are viewed as encoding general principles: The Tetragrammaton expresses the unity of all the sefirot, and Ṣeva'ot—meaning "hosts"— denotes their all-encompassing nature. The sixth name, Elohim, corresponds to the Attribute of Judgment. The seventh, El, is not linked to a particular sefirah and so can refer to any level within the divine order. The eighth name, *Shaddai*, signifies the sefirah that corresponds to the penis (*yesod*); on this, see Elliot R. Wolfson, "Circumcision and the Divine Name: A Study in the Transmission of Esoteric Doctrine," *Jewish Quarterly Review* 78 (1987): 77–112. The ninth, *Adonai*, signifies the last, female sefirah known as "the Matron" (*maṭronita*), based on a Hebrew-Aramaic exegesis ascribed to "our rabbis of blessed memory," the likes of which we find word for word in the Zohar, 3:21b (see Yehuda Liebes, "Review of Charles Mopsik, *Moses de León's Sefer Sheqel ha-Qodesh*, with an introduction by Moshe Idel, Los Angeles, 1996" [in Hebrew], *Kabbalah* 2 [1997]: 275). The ten—or, more precisely, nine—names that may not be erased therefore constitute a system that enciphers the entire emanative structure, and the interconnection and unity of its sefirot. De León's resolute refusal to fully coordinate the ten names with the ten sefirot is rooted in his principled misgivings about enumerating all ten sefirot ("the tenth is not part of the enumeration"). It is also worth noting that this list, which effectively summarizes many of the theosophic-kabbalistic innovations about the letters and names in this entire composition, was later re-edited by de León, and that this revamped version has been preserved as an appendix to Moses de León, *Sheqel ha-qodesh*, 98–102. Whenever de León deviated in the later text from the older unnamed work, he introduced the changes with "some say" or "some explain." For a similar ambivalence concerning two theosophical interpretations of the ten names that may not be erased, see Zohar, 3:10b–11b, where the opinion found in the book of the elder *Rav Hamnuna* is contrasted with that of the ostensibly younger Rabbi Eleazar. On the latter text, and the ascription of wisdom to Hamnuna, refer to Chapter 5.

> out] in full, like so: YVD H' V'V H' (= 45). They are ten letters that correspond to the ten sefirot *belimah*. This secret is revealed through nine letters of the alphabet, which correspond to the nine sefirot, through which the secret of His Name, may He be blessed, is revealed. . . . These nine letters amount to the secret of the ten, since the secret of the Name is ten letters, and the number of its secret is *mah* (what) (= M [40] + H [5] = 45). That is why the secret of 'B GD HV ZḤ Ṭ is *mah*—all yield the sum of the same matter. For this reason, you find that the secret of *ḥokhmah*, which is in the secret of *mah*, is the potentiality of the essence (*mahut*) that can show the secret, for everything proceeds from within it.[83]

In this instance, too, the words ascribed to ancients can be pinpointed in *Or zarua'*, in the "third secret" of the sixth chapter.[84] There de León noted that the numerological value of the Tetragrammaton spelled out in full is 45, and thus equal to the sum of the first nine letters. This equivalence accords with his approach in *Or zarua'*, in that it reveals something about the inapprehensible "supernal Gradation," the transcendent God, and His relationship to the "lower gradation," the tenth intellect that is God's chariot.[85] But in the nameless theosophical work, the number 45 is the numerological value of the word *mah* (what), which is included within *ḥokhmah*. The continuation then explains that *ḥokhmah* consists, as it were, of the two short words *koaḥ* (potentiality; a word produced by reversing the first two letters of *ḥokhmah*) and *mah* (what), because it is the nature of the sefirah of *ḥokhmah* to be the "potentiality of the essence," "because the potentiality (*koaḥ*) of His essence (*mahuto*), may He be blessed and elevated, exists within *ḥokhmah*."[86] As with the previous cases, we see again how de León transforms an exegesis originally about the transcendent God into one about the uppermost reaches of the divinity (in this case, *ḥokhmah*). This is buttressed by other explanations brought by the author in his treatment of the letters, in which the letter *yod*, which comes right after the aforementioned nine and completes the series of the first ten letters, graphically signifies *ḥokhmah* through its form.

This numerological account also highlights the tension between the tenfold structure of *Sefer Yeṣirah*'s "ten sefirot *belimah*" and the nine discernible

[83] MS Munich, Bayerische Staatsbibliothek, Cod. hebr. 47, fol. 364a.
[84] De León, *Or zarua'*, 310.
[85] De León, *Or zarua'*, 310.
[86] MS Munich, Bayerische Staatsbibliothek, Cod. hebr. 47, fol. 364a.

sefirot stretching from *ḥokhmah* to *malkhut*. It underscores the transcendence of the gradation above *ḥokhmah*, namely *ayin* (i.e., "nothing"), which our text refuses to count in its enumeration of the sefirot. Indeed, de León tried to thread this needle in his subsequent writings. Minding the gap between the ninefold and the tenfold is critical for tracking the encroachment of de León's distinctive apophatic theology into the inherited patterns of tenfold speculation, a development that is typified also by the Zohar's homilies on the Ten Commandments.[87]

3.7 *Yod*: The Noetic Point

A third group of anonymous sages mentioned in de León's earliest theosophical work is "the custodians of the secret of arithmetic." Our text notes their proficiency in techniques of letter pairing, that is, methods that generate ordered lists of letter pairs from predetermined sets.[88] The *atbash* cipher (א"ת ב"ש) is one of the ancient systems of encryption that anticipates such methods. With *atbash*, it is possible to encode one's writing by substituting individual letters with letters that are equidistant from the middle of the alphabet; for example, the first letter may be substituted for the last, and the second letter for the penultimate, the third for the antepenultimate and so on. Nonetheless, the specific techniques de León had in mind are methods that, again, couple letters in ordered sequences rather than encrypt language per se.

Our text presents two different methods of pairing the first nine or ten letters of the alphabet. The first method produces five pairs from the ten letters (ʾY BṬ GḤ DZ HV; א"י ב"ט ג"ח ד"ז ה"ו), the numerical value of each being 11 (ʾ [1] + Y [10] = 11; B [2] + Ṭ [9] = 11; etc.). According to this operation, "the number is not lost."[89] That is, the sum of each pair equals the number of letters in the entire set—ten—plus one, which teaches that "the One transcends them all, because He is the reality of oneness."[90] The second letter technique,

[87] See Avishai Bar-Asher, "Decoding the Decalogue: Theosophical Re-Engraving of the Ten Commandments in Thirteenth-Century Kabbalah," in *Accounting for the Commandments in Medieval Judaism: New Studies in Law, Philosophy, Pietism, and Mysticism*, ed. Jeremy Phillip Brown and Marc Herman (Leiden: Brill, 2021), 156–175.

[88] MS Munich, Bayerische Staatsbibliothek, Cod. hebr. 47, fol. 371a.

[89] MS Munich, Bayerische Staatsbibliothek, Cod. hebr. 47, fol. 362a–b.

[90] MS Munich, Bayerische Staatsbibliothek, Cod. hebr. 47, fol. 362b.

known as ʾṬ BḤ (א"ט ב"ח),[91] takes the first nine letters as its set and yields four pairs plus one unpaired letter (ʾṬ BḤ GZ DW H; ג"ז ד"ו ה א"ט ב"ח).[92] Here "The number exists but the one is absent," that is, each of the four pairs has a numerical value of 10 (ʾ [1] + Ṭ [9] = 10; B [2] + Ḥ [8] = 10; etc.), but there is no remainder of one to signify the underlying unity.[93] Only the initial sequence of the first ten letters bears witness to the complete unity, for it includes and pairs together the first and tenth letters, namely *alef* and *yod*. When *alef* and *yod* are combined, they call to mind multiple facets of divine unity—oneness, primordiality, superiority, completion, and uniqueness:

> You shall find that the unity is the beginning and the first, the unique One. As for the mystery of primordial *ḥokhmah*, it is both on this side and on that side. It is first since everything is in perfect unity. ʾY (א"י): These are the letters whose pairing [expresses] the secret of His unity, may He be elevated and blessed, since *yod* is the beginning, *alef* is the head, middle, and end. And yet *ḥokhmah* is above everything, since He . . . is revealed through the secret of *ḥokhmah*, which is the means by which His true reality comes into being. . . . Therefore, you may know that the *yod* alone is the secret of His unity . . . because the *yod* is the concealment of thought (*maḥshavah*) that is hidden in the secret of His being.[94]

This passage builds upon the parsing of the grapheme *alef* into three component letters (*yod*, *vav*, *dalet*), which presupposes that the *alef* encompasses the unity of divine existence. The letter *yod* here represents *ḥokhmah*, whose aspect is the concentrated potentiality of God's thought and being and the primordial core of His unity. Moreover, the promotion of the letter *yod* from the tenth and final position in the alphabetic set to the first letter pairing (ʾY) alludes to *ḥokhmah*'s dual standing within the divine order: "*ḥokhmah* is first and *ḥokhmah* is last."[95] Alongside the "primordial *ḥokhmah*" identified with the highest sefirah and the beginning of all that is, there is a second *ḥokhmah*, at the lower boundary of the divine ontology, which derives from

[91] On the ʾṬ BḤ technique see Yakir Paz and Tzahi Weiss, "From Encoding to Decoding: The AṬBḤ of R. Hiyya in Light of a Syriac, Greek, and Coptic Cipher," *Journal of Near Eastern Studies* 74 (2015): 45–65.

[92] MS Munich, Bayerische Staatsbibliothek, Cod. hebr. 47, fol. 362b.

[93] "When the *yod* is not joined with the *heh* the matter is absent, even though the secret of the matter is complete with respect to the decadic aspect" (MS Munich, Bayerische Staatsbibliothek, Cod. hebr. 47, fol. 362b).

[94] MS Munich, Bayerische Staatsbibliothek, Cod. hebr. 47, fols. 362b–363a.

[95] MS Munich, Bayerische Staatsbibliothek, Cod. hebr. 47, fol. 362b.

the first. While the first *ḥokhmah* stands at the head of the sefirot, the second is identified with the final sefirah (*malkhut*), which interacts with the sensible world of individual existents below the sefirot. The primordial *ḥokhmah* belongs to the purely intellectual realm of the "intelligible." By contrast, the lower *ḥokhmah* is entwined with the sensible world and humans may apprehend it through a process of intellectual refinement that is likened to the removal of dross.[96] In this context, our text embarks on a lengthy discussion about the gender of the two divine wisdoms. Focusing primarily on the lower *ḥokhmah* identified with "the female world," the text speculates about the letterforms of *dalet* and *heh*. Here again we observe how our nameless work synthesizes speculation on the sefirot, in this case elaborating upon an idea found in *Sefer ha-Bahir* about the light of *ḥokhmah* that "causes everything" (this idea is part of the Bahir's notion of a doubled *shekhinah*—"There is a *shekhinah* below as there is a *shekhinah* above").[97] De León would go on to develop the doctrine of two wisdoms throughout his subsequent writings, with the teaching becoming a focus of zoharic speculation in its repeated disambiguations of "supernal *ḥokhmah*" vis-à-vis "lower *ḥokhmah*."

The composition develops its identification of the supernal divine wisdom with the punctiform grapheme of the letter *yod*, which it regards as the inception point of being. As such, *ḥokhmah* appears in the image of the Hebrew letter indicated by a minuscule point, the slightest marking from which "the formation of the letters" extends, an image that captures the concentrated potentiality of the letters, the sefirot, and hence, all existence.[98] Our text also understands the potentiality of *ḥokhmah* in terms of the "noetic point," which is to say, the initial condensation of nothingness from which language, thought, and being unfold.

[96] MS Munich, Bayerische Staatsbibliothek, Cod. hebr. 47, fols. 364b–365a. Such a process of apprehending the lower divine wisdom may be notionally analogous to the mental operation of stripping form from matter posited by Aristotelian epistemology, albeit applied to a higher order of existence and knowledge.

[97] *Sefer ha-Bahir*, §. XXX:21 (116), 207. See Gershom Scholem, *Das Buch Bahir: Ein Text aus der Frühzeit der Kabbala* (Berlin: Arthur Scholem, 1923), 123–125 with n. 4. This notion should not be confused with the idea of a second intellectual realm at the top of the sefirot. The cause for this confusion lies with a number of Scholem's writings on the beginning of kabbalah in Provence and Catalonia, particularly Scholem, *Origins*, 91–97, 270–276. For a critical history of this confusion, see Avishai Bar-Asher, "Illusion Versus Reality in the Study of Early Kabbalah: The *Commentary on Sefer Yetzirah* Attributed to Isaac the Blind and Its History in Kabbalah and Scholarship" [in Hebrew], *Tarbiz* 86, nos. 2–3 (2019): 340–349.

[98] MS Munich, Bayerische Staatsbibliothek, Cod. hebr. 47, fol. 359b.

> *yod* is one tiny point—a child can write it; it is the first of all thought, since it is the beginning of everything. . . . *yod* is a noetic point (*nequddah maḥshavit*), . . . the beginning of all thought, since it is small and hidden, and nothing is smaller than a single point. Therefore, you find that the secret of the letter of this point has nothing above it save complete nothingness (*ayin*).[99]

This passage portrays the concentrated potentiality of divine wisdom as a kernel yielding the actualization of all. The phrase "first of all thought" recalls an adage often attributed to Aristotle in medieval wisdom that claims "the first in thought is last in action." Fittingly, the classical sources demonstrating the authentically Aristotelian roots of this dictum express what is "first in thought" in terms of a "point of inception," or "starting point" (ἀρχὴ).[100] De León not only translated a locus of classical idealism into a theosophical framework, which is noteworthy in its own right, but also subjected it to a linguistic turn, wherein the utmost potentiality is not that of action within thought, nor even the potentiality of thought within language, but rather the potentiality of language within the minuscule point anterior to even the formation of letters in which all being is coiled in a superlative state of focused potential.

It is our text that employs the figure of the "noetic point" for the first time in the present sense as a function of the transition from the angelology of the *Sefer ha-Ne'lam* corpus, which identified the letter *yod* with Metatron—namely, the active intellect, to de León's prodigious theosophical writing.[101] This transition is a crucial development within the evolution of punctiform speculation in kabbalistic theology.[102] In its elaboration

[99] MS Munich, Bayerische Staatsbibliothek, Cod. hebr. 47, fol. 371a.

[100] S. M. Stern, "'The First in Thought Is the Last in Action': The History of a Saying Attributed to Aristotle," *Journal of Semitic Studies* 7, no. 2 (1962): 234–252, esp. 235: "The end aimed at is, then, the starting-point of our thought, the end of our thought the starting-point of action"; "that which proceeds from the starting-point and the form is thinking, and that which proceeds from the final step of the thinking is making."

[101] For its most sophisticated usage in de León's theosophical writings, see de León, *Sheqel ha-qodesh*, 87–88, and, at greater length in the French translation at 255–257, esp. n. 898. On this matter, see further, Isaiah Tishby, ed., *The Wisdom of the Zohar: An Anthology of Texts*, trans. David Goldstein (Portland, OR: Littman Library of Jewish Civilization; Oxford: Oxford University Press, 1989, repr. 2002), 1:281.

[102] For its appearance in Isaac ha-Kohen's works, see Scholem, "Qabbalot," 114, and Scholem, "An Inquiry in the Kabbalah of R. Isaac ben Jacob" [in Hebrew], *Tarbiz* 2, no. 2 (1931), 195, esp. the sources in 206n.16. It bears mentioning that Isaac ha-Kohen's *Perush ha-merkavah* has survived only as an interlude within a long work written by none other than de León; see Bar-Asher, ed., *Mishkan ha-'edut*, lxvi–lxxi. For its appearance in Gikatilla's writings, see esp. Joseph ben Abraham Gikatilla, *Sha'are orah*, ed. Joseph Ben-Shlomo (Jerusalem: Mossad Bialik, 1981), 1:119; see also the discussions in Blickstein, "Between Philosophy and Mysticism," 67–68, 92–112; and in Shem Ṭov Ibn

by subsequent authors, the "noetic point" becomes the limit toward which human consciousness aspires, as if the concentration of consciousness into this single point could encompass all being. Offshoots of this idea take center stage in later theological developments, such as the doctrine of divine self-contraction (*ṣimṣum*).[103] To support the suggestion that de León's writings anticipate the Lurianic theology of *ṣimṣum*, it is possible to adduce several passages in de León's theosophic writings that present *ḥokhmah* as the primordial point from which stems "the unfolding of the [divine] structure" and of all existence. In a 1290 account penned by de León, *ḥokhmah* is the point of inception for a circular divine structure that radiates outward in a concentric fashion:

> The secret of the central point is the beginning of the [divine] structure within the circle, because the circle does not curve properly except by means of the central point within the circle's emptiness, from which the whole [of the circle] is properly constructed. The point located within its space is the main element . . . , and it is the beginning of the [divine] structure.[104]

The geometrical premise of de León's later thinking about the concentricity of the divinity is an important source for the conventional idea that the sefirot radiate concentrically.

Rather than attributing all such innovations to his own authorial ingenuity, the "Nameless Composition" sometimes attributes them to nameless numerologists, supposed stewards of arcane wisdom. The secrets attributed

Shem Ṭov's works, see Gershom Scholem, "Seride sifro shel R. Shem Ṭov ibn Gaon al yesodot torat ha-sefirot" [in Hebrew], *Kiryat Sefer* 8, no. 4 (1932): 534–542, here 538; and Moshe Idel, "Kabbalistic Materials from the School of Rabbi David ben Yehudah he-Ḥasid" [in Hebrew], *Jerusalem Studies in Jewish Thought* 2 (1983): 169–207, here 189–190 (see Idel's proposal for the origin of this term in the writings of David ben Judah).

103 These considerations are relevant to the scholarly inquiry into the medieval roots of the theosophical notion of *ṣimṣum* that is associated with Isaac Luria and his disciples in the sixteenth century and beyond. See Mopsik's introduction to Moses de León, *Sheqel ha-qodesh*, 68; and, in particular, Moshe Idel, "On the Concept of Ẓimẓum in Kabbalah and Its Research" [in Hebrew], *Jerusalem Studies in Jewish Thought* 10 (1992): 59–112; Idel, "The Mud and the Water: Towards a History of a Simile in Kabbalah," *Zutot* 14 (2017): 64–72; Bracha Sack, "R. Moses of Cordovero's Doctrine of Ẓimẓum" [in Hebrew], *Tarbiz* 58, no. 2 (1989): 207–237; Paul Franks, "The Midrashic Background of the Doctrine of Divine Contraction: Against Gershom Scholem on Tsimtsum," in *Tsimtsum and Modernity*, ed. Daniel Weiss and Agata Bielik-Robson (Berlin: de Gruyter, 2020), 39–60.

104 De León, *Sefer ha-Mishqal*, 110–111. Compare Ronit Meroz, "An Anonymous Commentary on Idra Raba by a Member of the Saruq School," *Jerusalem Studies in Jewish Thought* 12 (1996): 307–378, here 317–318 and n. 49.

to these apparently fictive sages pertain chiefly to the uppermost intellectual strata of the divinity.[105] It is productive to compare the speculations about the inception of being that debut in our work with their analogues in de León's earlier, unsigned works. In the latter, we find that the causal order descending from the transcendent God ("the supernal Gradation") to the three worlds below Him (intellects, spheres, and lower world) has its origins in an initial outburst of creative emanation—usually imagined as a flash of brilliant light engendering multiplicity.[106] The *Sefer ha-Ne'lam* corpus identifies this primordial emanation with the overflow of the active intellect (i.e., the first creation that mediates between the supernal Gradation and the three worlds, personified as "the Prince of the Countenance," that is, Metatron). The pretheosophical texts discern clues about these sublime matters by studying the graphic representation of the Hebrew vowel points and cantillation signs. The vowel points, which are said to "move" the consonantal letters, represent patterns of causal motion, whereas the cantillation signs animate both the letters and the vowel points through musical melody, which may correspond to the subtle music of the cosmos associated with the movement of the spheres—a classical motif attested in the Maimonidean tradition.[107] Prominent in this context is the correspondence of "the Prince of the Countenance" to the superscript vowel *ḥolem* (or *ḥolam*). The latter is placed

[105] To the list of formative ideas attested in de León's nameless work that shaped the course of subsequent discourse, one may add the noteworthy fact that our text characterizes the emergence of *ḥokhmah* from *ayin* in terms of the rabbinic notion of "the God who builds worlds and lays them waste." MS Munich, Bayerische Staatsbibliothek, Cod. hebr. 47, fol. 372a. For the loci classici, see Genesis Rabbah 3:7 and 9:2. Farber suggested that this idiosyncratic characterization may perhaps be considered a parallel to the mythical creation and destruction of primordial worlds depicted in the Zohar's *Idra* literature. See Asi Farber, "'The Husks Precede the Fruit': On the Question of the Origin of Evil in the Early Kabbalah" [in Hebrew], *Eshel Beer Sheva* 4 (1996): 118–142, here 133–134.

[106] See, for example, MS Paris, Bibliothèque nationale de France, héb. 817, fol. 83a.

[107] Moses Maimonides, *Guide of the Perplexed*, trans. Shlomo Pines (Chicago: University of Chicago Press, 1963), 267 (2:8),; and compare to Joseph ben Abraham Gikatilla, *Ginnat egoz* (Jerusalem: Yeshivat ha-Ḥayim ve-ha-Shalom, 1989), 436–437; and see Elke Morlok, "Visual and Acoustic Symbols in Gikatilla, Neoplatonic and Pythagorean Thought," in *Lux in Tenebris: The Visual and the Symbolic in Western Esotericism*, ed. Peter Forshaw (Leiden: Brill, 2016), 21–49. The idea of the vowels moving the letters connects to the notion of vowel points as "the soul (*neshamah*) of the letters," which was adopted by kabbalists under the influence of the Bahir; see *Sefer ha-Bahir*, §. XXVI:2 (83), 195. The first lines of the Munich treatise (MS Munich, Bayerische Staatsbibliothek, Cod. hebr. 47, fol. 335b) suggest that such a discussion was originally located in the lost part of the composition. Compare, for example, Wijnhoven, "Maskiyyot Kesef," 14–15. Ṭodros Abulafia cited this idea in combination with a tradition about the letters and vowels: "I have received profound matters and innermost ideas about the form of the vowel points and the letters" (Ṭodros ben Joseph ha-Levi Abulafia, *Sha'ar ha-razim*, 73–74). Shem Ṭov Ibn Gaon copied this in his *Sefer Badde ha-aron u-migdal Ḥananel*, written in Safed in 1325; see the facsimile edition edited by D. S. Loewinger (Jerusalem: Mizraḥ u-ma'arav, 1977), 168. Another author who sourced this motif from Ṭodros was David ben Judah he-Ḥasid; see *The Book of Mirrors: Sefer Mar'ot ha-Ẓove'ot*, ed. Daniel C. Matt (Chico, CA: Scholars Press, 1982), 161–162.

above the letter, just as the active intellect is superordinate to the rest of creation, and the cascading of emanation from the active intellect is further associated with the medial and subscript vowel points (the vowel *shureq*—or *shuruq*—and the vowel *ḥiriq*).[108] Throughout de León's earliest theosophical work, on the other hand, one can discern how the early thinking about the vowel points prefigures patently theosophical formulations, where, for example, the superscript *ḥolem* no longer alludes to the Prince of the Countenance but now to the sefirah of *ḥokhmah*.[109]

Our author even went on to incorporate these ideas into his signed theosophic writings. For instance, *Sheqel ha-qodesh* describes the divinity, who "out of His great concealment . . . brought into existence the secret of His existence from Himself, and brought into existence from Himself the secret of the light of the essential radiance, according to the secret of a single point, which is greatly concealed,"[110] that is, "the noetic point."[111] The divinity brings forth existence from that luminous point of primordial radiance, identified with "the supernal thought which is the first cause," in other words, with the sefirah of *ḥokhmah*.[112]

What is more, the notion of a luminous point that radiates the brilliant concatenation of divine gradations is familiar to readers of the Zohar. It appears in a much-studied discourse at the very beginning of the Zohar on Genesis,[113] which consists of a series of brief meditations on the very first verse of the Torah. The latter takes the glow of the primal radiance as its point

[108] Compare *Sod Darkhe ha-shemot ve-sod ha-otiyyot*, MS Paris, Bibliothèque nationale de France, héb. 770, fol. 212a.

[109] "The three [vowel] points are positioned one above the other, three of them in one pattern: *ḥolem, ḥiriq, shuruq*—upper, middle, lower. For you find that *ḥolem* is supernal, above everything, and moves the letters below it according to its desire and will" (MS Munich, Bayerische Staatsbibliothek, Cod. hebr. 47, fol. 369a).

[110] Moses de León, *Sheqel ha-qodesh*, 92; Moses de León, *Sefer ha-Rimmon*, 106–107 (compare Gershom Scholem, "Shene quntresim le-R. Moshe de León," *Kobez al Yad* 8, no. 18 (1976): 325–384, esp. 330–370 = Moses de León, *Shushan ha-'edut*, 331). See Tishby, *Wisdom of the Zohar*, 2:552–553; Haviva Pedaya, *Vision and Speech: Models of Revelatory Experience in Jewish Mysticism* [in Hebrew] (Los Angeles, CA: Cherub Press, 2002), 134–135; Michal Oron, *Sefer ha-Shem Attributed to R. Moses de León* [in Hebrew] (Los Angeles, CA: Cherub Press, 2010), 72. Compare Moses de León, *Sheqel ha-qodesh*, 22: "He, may He be blessed, from the sealed and concealed *davar* brought into existence the radiance of a single, greatly concealed point at the beginning, from which He extended His existence through *the radiances of the mysteries* from a greatly concealed emanation."

[111] Moses de León, *Sheqel ha-qodesh*, 16–17.

[112] See Roland Goetschel, "The Conception of Prophecy in the Works of R. Moses de León and R. Joseph Gikatilla" [in Hebrew], *Jerusalem Studies in Jewish Thought* 8 (1989): 217–237, here 234; Melila Hellner-Eshed, *A River Flows from Eden: The Language of Mystical Experience in the Zohar*, trans. Nathan Wolski (Stanford, CA: Stanford University Press, 2009), 36–37, 257.

[113] This homily on "the enlightened ones will be radiant like the radiance of the firmament" (Daniel 12:3) has been printed at the beginning of the Zohar on the Torah since its very first printing: *Sefer ha-Zohar* (Mantua, 1558), vol. 1, fol. 15a–b; *Sefer ha-Zohar* (Cremona, 1559–1660), cols. 9–10. On this literary unit within the broader context of the zoharic homilies on the first verses

of departure,[114] much like other zoharic homilies on the phrase "the radiance of the firmament" (Daniel 12:3).[115] Here one finds a description of a "blinding spark" and the perforation of "a high and hidden point" described as the "beginning" of being, quite similar to the description of *ḥokhmah*.[116] Woven like a thread throughout these homilies is this notion of a primal point from which existence proceeds—from the "creation" of Elohim by wisdom (i.e., the individuation of *binah* from out of *ḥokhmah*) to the propagation of everything through divine speech.[117] There is a clear resemblance between the imagery of the unfolding divinity in the familiar Aramaic homily in the Zohar, and the formulations of de León's Hebrew writings. The account of the "noetic point" in our nameless composition displays an intermediate character, when positioned midway between the two conceptual extremes of de León's pretheosophical emanationism, on the one hand, and the theogonic renderings of Genesis, on the other, found in the Zohar.

3.8 The Andalusi Legacy of Arabic Lettrism

Without trivializing our efforts to situate the letter speculation of our nameless fragment within de León's variegated Hebrew corpus and the zoharic anthology, it will be helpful to highlight two broader cultural contexts for

in Genesis, see Michal Oron, "Three Commentaries to the Story of Genesis and Their Significance for the Study of the 'Zohar'" [in Hebrew], *Daat* 50–52 (2003): 183–189 (repr. in Oron, *Window*, 134–140).

[114] Zohar, 1:15b–16a. A number of scholars have noted the link between the term "radiance" and its appearance in Daniel 12:3 in *Sefer ha-Zohar*; see Yehuda Liebes, "Zohar ve-Eros" [in Hebrew], *Alpayyim* 9 (1994): 73–74 with n. 45; Elliot R. Wolfson, *Through a Speculum That Shines: Vision and Imagination in Medieval Jewish Mysticism* (Princeton, NJ: Princeton University Press, 1994), 355–357, 377–380; Boaz Huss, *The Zohar: Reception and Impact*, trans. Y. Nave (Oxford: Littman Library of Jewish Civilization, 2016), 47–48, 51–57; Pinchas Giller, *Reading the Zohar, the Sacred Text of the Kabbalah* (Oxford: Oxford University Press, 2001), 69–87; Daniel Abrams, "The 'Zohar' as Palimpsest: Dismantling the Literary Constructs of a Kabbalistic Classic and the Turn of the Hermeneutics of Textual Archeology," *Kabbalah* 29 (2013): 7–60, here 30–32.

[115] For example, the short homily on this verse printed in *Tiqqune ha-Zohar*, ed. Reuben Margaliyot (Jerusalem: Mossad ha-Rav Kook, 1978), fol. 1a; compare *Zohar ḥadash*, ed. Reuben Margaliyot (Jerusalem: Mossad ha-Rav Kook, 1953), 104 col. b (*tiqqunim*).

[116] For a brief discussion of this passage's textual history, see, for example, Ronit Meroz, *The Spiritual Biography of Rabbi Simeon bar Yochay: An Analysis of the Zohar's Textual Components* [in Hebrew] (Jerusalem: Mossad Bialik, 2018), 27–28.

[117] Zohar, 1:15a. In this discourse, one also finds a description of the splitting of the point of radiance into "the mystery of the three [vowel] points: *ḥolem*, *shuruq*, and *ḥiriq*" (1:15b), an idea also repeated in de León's signed works, as we have said. See, for example, Moses de León, *Sefer ha-Rimmon*, 329; and compare the general point made in Scholem, *Major Trends in Jewish Mysticism*, 395n.132.

interpreting the contents of this chapter. The first suggestion is based on an observation by the late Parisian scholar Charles Mopsik (1956–2003). With a modicum of hesitation, Mopsik suggested de León's "noetic point" (as attested in both the "Nameless Composition" and *Sheqel ha-qodesh*, dated to 1292) may be considered a rough equivalent to the scholastic notion of the "punctus scientificus." To corroborate this equivalence, Mopsik adduced the following statements concerning the "punctus scientificus" from a student of Albert the Great (ca. 1200–1280) named Ulrich (Engelbert) of Strasbourg (Ulricus de Argentina; ca. 1225–1278): "There is a point that knows what is"; "a point endowed with knowledge"; and "Suppose that a luminous point emits an infinity of rays and that each of them, coming from the same point, has the same species and cause. Suppose further that this point will be endowed with knowledge: It will know the diversity of all its rays at this one unique point."[118] Mopsik, however, failed to adduce an explicit reference in de León's corpus to a Dominican source for his terminology. Alluring as the parallels may be, their comparison underscores marked contrasts with de León's thinking. Perhaps most critically, they yield nothing comparable to de León's account of a linguistic substance extending from the hyper-condensed source of thought. Moreover, the scholastic formulations furnished by Mopsik do not identify the "punctus scientificus" with a single punctiform grapheme, which, furthermore, functions as an abbreviation of the explicit name of God.

Another discourse that merits exploration in comparison with de León is that of the Islamic science of lettrism, or *'ilm al-hurūf*, which found rich expression in thirteenth-century al-Andalus. Albeit tentatively, and without sufficient local evidence, scholarship has suggested this discourse, and especially its amplifications of the slightest diacritical markings, as another context for understanding de León's interest in the primordial point.[119] This suggestion is justified not only because the science of lettrism is attested in historico-geographical proximity to medieval Castile and exhibits generic resemblances to his letter speculation, but because de León made express reference to it, a fact overlooked in previous research. The author's remarkable reference to a Muslim tradition of alphabetical speculation is located in *Sod Darkhe ha-otiyyot ve-ha-nequddot*, which belongs to de León's early *Sefer*

[118] Rendered into English from Mopsik's introduction to Moïse [= Moses] de León, *Le Sicle du sanctuaire: Chéqel ha-Qodech*, trans. Charles Mopsik (Lagrasse: Éditions Verdier, 1996), 65–70.

[119] Annemarie Schimmel, "The Primordial Dot: Some Thoughts About Sufi Letter Mysticism," *Jerusalem Studies in Arabic and Islam* 9 (1987): 350–356.

ha-Ne'lam corpus. It is there that we read about "sages of the Ishmaelites" who construct Arabic letters by means of the same secret knowledge de León himself promoted, that is to say, knowledge of an originary alphabet constructed out of vowel points.

What is the basis for de León's claims to such knowledge? In a number of places, he invoked his knowledge of archaic letterforms, which he identified with the original Hebrew orthography sanctioned by God. In a fragment from a chapter of an early work (titled *Sha'ar yesod ha-otiyyot*), preserved in only one manuscript, de León claimed that such knowledge is lost on contemporaneous scribes, whose fanciful conventions nonetheless stimulate the soul.

> When a person beholds the letterforms [fashioned by scribes], his intellective soul may delight in the forms and consider them to be the proper ones [i.e., forms] chosen by God. But it is not so. The [true] letterforms do not conform to the artistry nor the ornamentation by which the scribes, of their own whim, see fit to fashion them. Rather, they are the forms from which the secrets and fundamentals proceed.[120]

Such appeals to an authentic, archaic form of the Hebrew letters appear in a few places within our author's oeuvre. In one case, de León proposed that the letter ג (*gimel*) might be constructed by propping the נ (*nun*) atop the subscript *ḥiriq* vowel point (נִ). Similarly, the ד (dalet) may be constructed by resting a *pataḥ* (-) on top of a *sheva* (thus ַ‎ְ).[121] The letter ב (*bet*) may be formed by placing the double point of the *ṣere* vowel on top of an inverted *dalet*: thus, ב. It is in the context of such speculation that de León remarks: "And the sages of the Ishmaelites employ [the Arabic letter] ذ in the place of *dalet* (ד), for it is all one secret."[122] The intent of this claim is that the written form of the Arabic language corroborates de León's vocalic construction of the Hebrew consonants, that is, the composition of the letters out of

[120] MS New York, Jewish Theological Seminary of America, 1886, fol. 24b.

[121] He claims that scribes active to the north of Iberia, that is in "northern France (*Ṣarfat*) and Germany (*Ashkenaz*)," formed the *dalet* in this way; compare *Sha'ar ḥeleq ha-nequddah*, MS New York, Jewish Theological Seminary of America, 1886, fol. 3b. De León contended that the Hebrew orthography in Castile ought to adopt the latter conventions to more effectively express the cosmological secrets encoded in the letters; this contention dovetails with the literary conceit of *Sod Darkhe ha-otiyyot ve-ha-nequddot*, a text conceived by its author as a kind of (fictitious) proceedings volume produced by a "great Sanhedrin" of Jewish esotericists from West to East, after a conclave about the mysteries of the Hebrew language. See Bar-Asher, "From the Vaults of Thebes," 164–165.

[122] MS Ramat Gan, 1038, fol. 25a; MS Paris, Bibliothèque nationale de France, héb. 770, fol. 212b.

vowel points, because the image of the Arabic grapheme *dhāl* with the diacritic resting above it (ذ) reflects the archaic construction as the Hebrew letter *bet* (ב). The inverted *dalet* comprising all but the canopy of the *bet* resembles the form of the Arabic *dhāl*, whereas the pointing atop the inverted *dalet* with a *ṣere* corresponds to the Arabic diacritic; thus ב̈ = ذ.

What kind of awareness of Islamic lettrism does this reflect on de León's part? His pointed reference to the sages of the Muslims (*ḥakhme ha-Yishme'elim*), as opposed to any individual learned in Arabic, suggests that he ascribed to such sages a wisdom (*ḥokhmah*) associated specifically with Islam concerning the secrets of written Arabic. Moreover, it shows that de León deemed such wisdom to be continuous with his own Hebrew letter speculation. The assertion that "it is all one secret" would appear to convey de León's confidence that the Muslim sages somehow preserved vestiges of the secret knowledge concerning the primordial nature of written language that he presumed to possess. Awareness on de León's part of Arabic lettrism, whether casual or informed, might be explained by its written proliferation in al-Andalus from an earlier period.[123] Readers of such literature will encounter cosmological explanations of the three graphic strata of Arabic writing—the letters, the vowels, and the diacritics—that are wholly comparable to the kinds of correspondences delineated by de León between the three strata of Hebrew script and the threefold theo-cosmic order, namely, the early speculation prefiguring the author's theosophical turn.

[123] The Andalusi sage Muḥammad ibn 'Ali Ibn al-'Arabī (d. 1240) collected and developed many traditions of such cosmological interpretation in his *Al-Futūḥāt al-makkiyya*. See, for example, the fifth chapter of *Al-Futūḥāt al-makkiyya* (Cairo: Bulaq Press, 1911), 1:130, on the mystery of the *Basmala* (which opens almost all of the ṣuras of the Qur'ān) and of the letters and vowel points that constitute it. On Ibn al-'Arabī's cosmological interpretation of the letters, see Claude Abbas, "Andalusī Mysticism and the Rise of Ibn 'Arabī," in *The Legacy of Muslim Spain*, ed. Salma Khadra Jayyusi (Leiden: Brill, 1992), 2:909–933; Wolfson, "Letter Symbolism," 202n.26; Michael McGaha, "The *Sefer ha-Bahir* and Andalusian Sufism," *Medieval Encounters* 3 (1997): 20–57, esp. 48–57; Michael Ebstein, *Mysticism and Philosophy in al-Andalus: Ibn Masarra, Ibn al-'Arabī and the Ismā'īlī Tradition* (Leiden: Brill, 2014). Ibn Masarra offered many interpretations of the Arabic letters in *Kitāb Jawāṣṣ al-ḥurūf*, which served as a source for Ibn al-'Arabī. See Pilar Garrido Clemente, "Edición crítica del *K. jawāṣṣ al-ḥurūf* de Ibn Masarra," *Al-Andalus Magreb* 14 (2007): 51–89. For lettrism in the thought of Aḥmad al-Būnī (12th–13th c.), see Noah D. Gardiner, "Esotericism in a Manuscript Culture: Aḥmad al-Būnī and His Readers Through the Mamlūk Period" (PhD diss., University of Michigan, 2014), 88–103; Yousef Casewit, *The Mystics of Al-Andalus: Ibn Barrajān and Islamic Thought in the Twelfth Century* (Cambridge, UK: Cambridge University Press, 2017), esp. 128–170.

3.9 An Early Dispute with Joseph Gikatilla

In his nameless theosophical work, de León stressed that the primordial point—whether signaled by the letter *yod* or the vowel *ḥolem*—denotes *ḥokhmah*, the positive inception point of the divine being, which is nonetheless rooted within the absolute transcendence of *ayin*; the point of *ḥokhmah* does not encompass the imperceptible depth of the divinity but rather constitutes the potentiation of divine substance; when fully actualized, the substance breaches the threshold of divinity and overflows into the realm of creation, stimulating the activity of intellects, the motion of the spheres, and so forth. This theosophic understanding of the *ḥolem* thus builds, again, upon speculation from de León's earlier works, which posits the point as the source of emanation and causal motion stemming from God.

Scrutiny of de León's earliest writings reveals that his distinctive speculations about the letters and vowel points resulted, in part, from a disagreement with the interpretive schema for the Tiberian vowel points articulated by Joseph Gikatilla in the early 1270s.[124] Gikatilla interpreted the vowel points within the framework of a conception of the Godhead that borrowed heavily from Aristotelian cosmology and metaphysics. He assumed that the vocalic phonemes of the Hebrew language, embodied graphically in the vowel points, represent variations within the causal motion by which the *causa causorum* moves the intellects, which, in turn, move the spheres and the other existents beneath them. Some of Gikatilla's ideas received stimulus from the writings of Jewish thinkers active in al-Andalus during the eleventh and twelfth centuries, such as Solomon Ibn Gabirol, Abraham Bar Ḥiyya, Abraham Ibn Ezra, and the thirteenth-century Toledan figure Isaac ben Abraham Ibn Latif.[125]

[124] Alexander Altmann ("*Sefer Or zarua*'," 235–240) presented many parallels between de León's *Or zarua*' and Gikatilla's *Ginnat egoz*, and he accepted Gershom Scholem's explanation (*Major Trends in Jewish Mysticism*, 194) that the former was influenced by the latter. See also Farber, "Traces of the Zohar," 70 with n. 2. Asi Farber ("New Fragment," 161n.6) initially raised the possibility of reversed directionality, with de León influencing Gikatilla. She subsequently expanded upon this in a study of what she called "the circle of *Sefer Or zarua*'," with which she associated the works discussed in this chapter and that she walled off hermetically from the adepts who spread Gikatilla's early kabbalah. See Farber, "Sources," 67–70, 84–85, 93–96, and compare Joseph ben Abraham Gikatilla, *David et Bethsabée: Le secret du marriage*, ed. Charles Mopsik (Paris: Éditions de l'Éclat, 2003), 15–16. With the discovery of *Sefer ha-Ne'lam* and the interconnected corpus of associated works, recent scholarship has argued that they contain direct responses to Gikatilla, rather than the other way around. See Bar-Asher, "Earliest Citation," 92–97; and Bar-Asher, "Vaults of Thebes," 167–178.

[125] See Karl E. Grözinger, *Jüdisches Denken: Theologie, Philosophie, Mystik* (Frankfurt am Main: Campus, 2004), 2:303–333 (esp. 309–304 on Ibn Gabirol and Maimonides). The centrality of Ibn Ezra's writings, esp. *Sefer Ṣaḥut* and *Sefer ha-Shem*, is treated at length in Martini, *Yosef Gikatilla: Book of Punctuation*, 61–65, 97–117. For other references to Ibn Ezra's work,

Comparative analysis of the many parallel passages on the Hebrew vowels in the early writings of Gikatilla and de León suggests that de León reworked Gikatilla's material to produce his own distinctive teachings on the vowels. One literary conceit adopted by de León for articulating disagreements with his contemporaries is the creative attribution of dissenting opinions to fictive personages, like "Ezra," or to apparently invented works.[126] In *Sod Darkhe ha-otiyyot ve-ha-nequddot*, a scholarly persona named Rabbi Isaac the Ascetic (*ha-parush*) voices adamant opposition to signifying God by means of the *ḥolem*. Among other arguments, the character notes that the form of the *ḥolem* resembles other vowel signs. In fact, Gikatilla dealt with this objection in detail in his own writings, particularly in a response to a question posed by his teacher, one Rabbi Abraham.[127] It seems that de León responded to this challenge through the use of pseudepigraphy, identifying Rabbi Isaac as an authoritative source for his dissenting view.[128]

In place of the *ḥolem*, de León proposed the more formally distinctive *qamaṣ*, arguing that the latter is not subject to the theological shortcomings of the *ḥolem*:

> Other [vowel points] are similar to the *ḥolem* in form and image, which is not true of the *qamaṣ*; it encompasses (*qomeṣ*) everything in its grasp (*qumṣo*), and all are encompassed (*niqmaṣim*) in its hand, as we will explain. For nothing resembles it, neither in form, nor image, nor character.[129]

Instead of Gikatilla's choice of the *ḥolem*, the superscript point intended by Gikatilla to signal God's exaltedness above all description, de León chose the *qamaṣ* to express God's all-encompassing nature, His containment of all reality in potentia.

see Blickstein, "Between Philosophy and Mysticism," 53n.53 and 101n.29. On Ibn Latif as a possible source for Gikatilla's early writings, see Farber, "New Fragment," 160–161n.5; and Blickstein, "Between Philosophy and Mysticism," 97–101.

[126] On this issue, see Bar-Asher, "Earliest Citation"; and Bar-Asher, "Vaults of Thebes."

[127] Earlier scholarship identified this figure with Abraham Abulafia, who praises Gikatilla in one of his works; see Gottlieb, *Studies*, 103–105; Moshe Idel, "*Sefer Yetzirah*: Twelve Commentaries on *Sefer Yetzirah* and the Extant Remnants of R. Isaac of Bedresh's Commentary" [in Hebrew], *Tarbiz* 79, nos. 3–4 (2010): 471–556, here 556n.538. Gikatilla, however, may have referred to another Abraham; see more recently Bar-Asher, "The Punctiform Deity: Theological Debates Among the Masters of *Niqqud* in the Works of R. Joseph Gikatilla's 'Disciples'" [in Hebrew], *Kabbalah* 53 (2022): 103–236.

[128] "Verily, in the kabbalah of our R. Isaac the Ascetic, may he rest in peace, we find the secret" (Moses de León, *Sod Darkhe ha-otiyyot*, 217).

[129] Bar-Asher, "Vaults of Thebes," 216–217.

This attempt to improve upon Gikatilla's vowel theory culminated in an anonymous work associated with de León's early writings that is preserved (seemingly only in part) in two manuscripts.[130] This composition, which we will call *Sha'ar ḥeleq ha-nequddah*, includes metaphysical, cosmological, and angelological interpretations of the vowel points and of their connections to the letters of the Tetragrammaton.[131] In this presentation, the letters and vowels of the divine name stand at the top of the metaphysical and cosmological chain of being. The details indicate that de León further developed his vowel theory into a full-fledged alternative to Gikatilla's thinking.[132] In this work, too, de León compared God to the *qamaṣ*, to which he subordinated the *ḥolem*. Demoted from the realm of divinity as such, the *ḥolem* would now symbolize the principle of causation that moves the first intelligible existent (the active intellect associated with the letter *yod*) and thenceforth the rest of the intellects, spheres, and so on.[133] In this well-developed system, the causal movement and hierarchy descending from "the supernal Gradation," down through the created gradations of being below (the intellects, spheres, and lower world), originate, as we have seen in other texts, in an initial outburst of emanation through which multiplicity emerges. De León identified this outpouring with form and intellect, describing it as a burst of radiance overflowing from God, which clothes the causal energy in a sheath of luminosity.[134]

The text compares the causal movement flowing into "the tenth intellect," the uppermost tip of the *yod*. The latter is identified with the divine efflux emerging from God, but not with the divinity per se. Instead, de León chose the *qamaṣ* and the letter *heh* to represent the transcendent deity who both encompasses and surpasses the fullness of creation. The programmatic shift

[130] MS New York, Jewish Theological Seminary of America, 1886, fols. 1a–24b (folios missing from the beginning), and with slight differences MS Paris, Bibliothèque nationale de France, héb. 817, fols. 81–89b.

[131] Bar-Asher, "Earliest Citation," 88–97.

[132] This was recently published in Bar-Asher, "Punctiform Deity," 190–207 (appendix 3). For another instance of disagreement between this work and Gikatilla's *Ginnat egoz*, see Farber, "Sources," 84–87.

[133] Asi Farber ("Sources," 78n.28) identified the entity signified by the *yod* with that represented by the *ḥolem*. But there are scattered references across the length of *Sha'ar ḥeleq ha-nequddah* that distinguish between the referent of the *yod*, that is, the "tenth intellect," and what the *ḥolem* indicates—namely, "the activity that issues from the supernal gradation" that articulates the *yod*. See Wolfson, "Biblical Accentuation," 1–4. Other expressions of this concept appear in *Sod darkhe ha-otiyyot ve-ha-nequddot*; see Moses de León, *Sod Darkhe ha-otiyyot*, 213.

[134] In this context, the *ḥolem* is repeatedly compared to a "light of brilliance" that overflows from the transcendent God down onto the tenth intellect; see, for example, MS New York, Jewish Theological Seminary of America, 1886, fol. 17a–b.

exhibited by this text shows that de León aligned himself with those who opposed to the identification of divine transcendence with a singular point. Like the proverbial pearl produced from an irritating grain of sand, de León's early schematization of the vowels grew, at least in part, out of his discomfort with Gikatilla's theology of the punctiform *ḥolem*.

In view of de León's repeated comparisons of God to the *qamaṣ* in his pseudonymous and pseudepigraphic works, arising from a reasoned departure from Gikatilla's theological speculations on the vowel points, one can better appreciate the significance of his later works of kabbalistic theosophy, especially the "Nameless Composition." There, when de León treats the vowels, he mentions "those who say about the secret of the sublimity of the vowel points that the secret of the *qamaṣ* is the supernal One, since it encompasses (*qomeṣet*) and includes the rest of the vowel points."[135] In the past, some thought this an insubstantial and trivial view that de León opposed.[136] Besides the fact that our author reiterated aspects of his theory of the *qamaṣ* from the works of the *Sefer ha-Ne'lam* corpus, one can even discern his sympathetic regard to this position: "The secret of this matter is the true secret, given that the *qamaṣ* encompasses the secret of all the vowel points in the world and is therefore called *qamaṣ*."[137] The opinion of "those who say" in the "Nameless Composition" is none other than de León's own early dissenting opinion. Evidence of de León's running dispute with Gikatilla, the crux of which is the *ḥolem*-versus-*qamaṣ* debate, found its way into a treatise on theosophical kabbalah.[138]

Strikingly, it is through de León's reworking of Gikatilla's vowel theory that he comes to advance a schema that is comparable to the Islamic lettrism discussed above—a schema based on the correspondences between the theo-cosmic order and the written forms of the Hebrew language. Findings of this nature strongly suggest that Castilian kabbalists interested in alphabetical secrets possessed knowledge of comparable speculations espoused by Muslim authors writing in de León's Iberian milieu.[139]

[135] Munich, Bayerische Staatsbibliothek, Cod. hebr. 47, fol. 369a.

[136] See Gershom Scholem, "Eine unbekannte mystische Schrift des Mose de Leon," *Monatschrift für Geschichte und Wissenschaft des Judentums* 71 (1927): 109–123, here 117n.3, and following him Farber, "Sources," 88–89 with n. 51.

[137] MS Munich, Bayerische Staatsbibliothek, Cod. hebr. 47, fol. 369a.

[138] For a review of Gikatilla's adaptation of his own theory of the vowel signs for theosophic Kabbalah, see Bar-Asher, "Punctiform Deity," 150–156 with the literature cited therein.

[139] Ibn al-ʿArabī reports in his *Al-Futūḥāt al-makkiyya* (6:105) that he had a discussion with a Jewish scholar about the secrets of the letter *bā*. For the unlikely treatment of this anecdote as evidence that Ibn al-ʿArabī had a familiarity with kabbalah, see Claude Addas, *Ibn ʿArabī, ou, La quête du soufre rouge* (Paris: Gallimard, 1989), 138–139. See also Wolfson, "Letter Symbolism,"

3.10 A Generative Reconciliation of Paradigms

The foregoing analysis of de León's letter speculation demonstrates that our nameless composition is a rare witness to the transition from de León's early period, during which the author produced an extensive portfolio of unsigned compositions, to a later period reflected in the signed theosophical treatises that are closely linked to the zoharic project. In this transitional phase, de León continued to engage in speculation on divine names, letters, and vowel points, which he attributed to enigmatic groups of adepts. Signs of this intermediate stage are also evident in de León's later theosophical works,[140] a factor that complicates the oversimplified description of a sharp, decisive break ascribed to de León and his contemporaries. The scholarly consensus of a general desertion of alphabetical mysticism by Castilian kabbalists in the thirteenth century and a sudden rallying to theosophical kabbalah may be discarded in favor of a more nuanced and complex narrative. The transition entailed not only the accommodation of an older speculative system to the avant-garde, but also the forging of new conceptual models through the tentative merging of disparate projects. Our text exhibits a deliberate migration of speculative topoi from one conceptual framework to another. As a result, the text does not so much dispense with the earlier angelological and cosmological concepts but rather reduces them to instantiations within the created realm of a higher-order pattern embodied first and foremost by the divinity. The notion of the dual chariot is superseded by a different duality, one that consists of the exemplary divinity, on the one hand, and the theophanic universe, on the other. This duality is bridged by a set of correspondences between the two isomorphic realms. We have shown how de León repurposed the three-tiered cosmology for the task of delineating three worlds internal to

202n.26; and Michael McGaha, "The *Sefer ha-Bahir* and Andalusian Sufism," *Medieval Encounters* 3 (1997): 20–57, esp. 48–57.

[140] Moses de León's obvious appreciation of the kabbalah of divine names comes across in his theosophic discussions of the reasons for commandments and customs ("mysteries"), in which he mentions the custodians of the divine names. See Jochanan H. A. Wijnhoven, "Sefer ha-Mishkal: Text and Study" (PhD diss., Brandeis University, 1964), 116, 136; Wijnhoven, "Maskiyyot Kesef," 14–15. Reference is made to these attributions in Scholem, "Qabbalot," 92n.4; Farber, "Sources," 87n.47; Moses de León, *Sefer ha-Rimmon*, 70 (with notes); Michal Oron, *Samuel Falk: The Baal Shem of London* [in Hebrew] (Jerusalem: Mossad Bialik, 2003), 17n.25; Moses de León, *Mishkan ha-'edut*, 88–89; Avishai Bar-Asher, "*Kabbalah* and *Minhag*: Geonic Responsa and the Kabbalist Polemic on *Minhagim* in the Zohar and Related Texts" [in Hebrew], *Tarbiz* 84, no. 1 (2016): 195–263, here 214–223.

the singular Godhead and redeployed the fourfold array of the chariot angels as the fourfold structure to the Godhead.

To review, Moses de León's early alphabetical speculations disclosed mysteries about the transcendent God, the active intellect (or Metatron), as well as the angels and celestial spheres. In our text, the Hebrew letters intimate secrets about the inner substance of divine wisdom. The text likewise recasts the Aristotelian model of causation as a function of the potentiating character of *ḥokhmah*. In this connection, de León deployed different letter combinations to demonstrate the graphemic and phonological expression of *ḥokhmah* as the "noetic point" into which all language, all knowledge, and all existence are hyper-compressed. Our text also posits a lower *ḥokhmah* at the most immanent extent of the divine "world of unity" (*'olam ha-yiḥud*), functioning as a lower condescension of the divine intellect into the realm of the sensible. Considered broadly, the accommodation of early speculation to theosophy engendered the conceptual shifts embodied in our transitional text, a fertile reconciliation of paradigms yielding speculative patterns that shaped de León's zoharic writings.

4
The Rose of Testimony

4.1 The Transition to Gender in Castilian Kabbalah

Compared to the Zohar, whose representations of the divinity as simultaneously male and female have generated substantial interest,[1] the Hebrew

[1] See, for example, Gershom Scholem, *On the Mystical Shape of the Godhead*, trans. Joachim Neugroschel, ed. Jonathan Chipman (New York: Schocken, 1991), 88–196; Isaiah Tishby, ed., *The Wisdom of the Zohar: An Anthology of Texts*, trans. David Goldstein (London: Littman Library, 1991), 1:371–422, 3:355–1406; Daniel Matt, "David ben Yehudah Heḥasid and His Book of Mirrors," *Hebrew Union College Annual* 51 (1980): 129–172, esp. 162–166; Elliot R. Wolfson, "Woman—the Feminine as Other in Theosophic Kabbalah: Some Philosophical Observations on the Divine Androgyne," in *The Other in Jewish Thought and Identity*, ed. Laurence Silberstein and Robert Cohn (New York: New York University Press, 1994), 166–204; Wolfson, *Through a Speculum That Shines: Vision and Imagination in Medieval Jewish Mysticism* (Princeton, NJ: Princeton University Press, 1994); Wolfson, *Circle in the Square: Studies in the Use of Gender in Kabbalistic Symbolism* (Albany: State University of New York Press, 1995); Wolfson, *Language, Eros, Being: Kabbalistic Hermeneutics and Poetic Imagination* (New York: Fordham University Press, 2005). See, too, the critical essays collected in Wolfson, *Luminal Darkness: Gleanings from Zoharic Literature* (Oxford: Oneworld, 2007); Wolfson, "Bifurcating the Androgyne and Engendering Sin: A Zoharic Reading of Gen. 1–3," in *Hidden Truths from Eden: Esoteric Readings of Genesis 1–3*, ed. Caroline Vander Stichele and Susanne Scholz (Atlanta, GA: Society for Biblical Literature, 2014), 83–115; Charles Mopsik, *Sex of the Soul: The Vicissitudes of Sexual Difference in Kabbalah*, ed. Daniel Abrams (Los Angeles, CA: Cherub Press, 2005); Daniel Abrams, *The Female Body of God in Kabbalistic Literature: Embodied Forms of Love and Sexuality in the Divine Feminine* [in Hebrew] (Jerusalem: Magnes, 2004); Abrams, "'A Light of Her Own': Minor Kabbalistic Traditions on the Ontology of the Divine Feminine," *Kabbalah* 23 (2006): 7–29; Abrams, *Kabbalistic Manuscripts and Textual Theory: Methodologies of Textual Scholarship and Editorial Practice in the Study of Jewish Mysticism* (Jerusalem: Magnes, 2010), 149–157; Abrams, "Divine Jealousy: Kabbalistic Traditions of Triangulation," *Kabbalah* 35 (2016): 7–54; Moshe Idel, "The Feminine Aspect of Divinity in Early Kabbalah" [in Hebrew], in *Tov Elem: Memory, Community and Gender in Medieval and Early Modern Jewish Societies*, ed. Roni Weinstein, Elisheva Baumgarten, and Amnon Raz-Krakotzkin (Jerusalem: Bialik Institute, Mandel Institute of Jewish Studies, 2001), 91–110; Idel, "Androgyny and Equality in the Theosophical-Theurgical Kabbalah," *Diogenes* 208 (2005): 27–38; Idel, *Kabbalah and Eros* (New Haven, CT: Yale University Press, 2005); Idel, "The Divine Female and the Mystique of the Moon: Three-Phases Gender-Theory in Theosophical Kabbalah," *Studia Archaeus* 19–20 (2015–2016): 151–182; Idel, *The Privileged Divine Feminine in Kabbalah* (Berlin: de Gruyter, 2018); Arthur Green, "Kabbalistic Re-Vision," *History of Religions* 36 (1997): 265–274; Green, "Shekhinah, the Virgin Mary, and the Song of Songs: Reflections on a Kabbalistic Symbol in Its Historical Context," *AJS Review* 26 (2002): 1–52; Peter Schäfer, *Mirror of His Beauty: Feminine Images of God from the Bible to the Early Kabbalah* (Princeton, NJ: Princeton University Press, 2004), 118–136; Shifra Asulin, "The Stature of the *Shekhina*: The Place of the Feminine Divine Countenance (*Parzuf*) in *Idra Rabba* and *Idra Zuta*" [in Hebrew], in *Spiritual Authority: Struggles over Cultural Power in Jewish Thought*, ed. Howard Kreisel, Boaz Huss, and Uri Ehrlich (Beer Sheva: Ben-Gurion University Press, 2009), 103–183; Ellen Davina Haskell, *Suckling at My Mother's Breasts: The Image of a Nursing God in Jewish Mysticism* (Albany: State University of New York Press, 2012); Leore

Light is Sown. Avishai Bar-Asher and Jeremy Phillip Brown, Oxford University Press.
© Oxford University Press 2025. DOI: 10.1093/oso/9780197744819.003.0004

writings of Moses de León have garnered significantly less attention—especially as they concern the construction of God's gender.[2] To the extent that this topic has been studied in de León's signed corpus, scholarship has not advanced any analysis that might leverage a critical distinction between the intertwined corpora of the Zohar, on the one hand, and de León's Hebrew writings, on the other, in terms of their respective discourses on gender. Similarly, researchers have yet to identify critical distinctions among the various individual works composed by de León or to chart the course of the author's thinking about gender in terms of its development over time.

At least four factors have waylaid such analyses. The first is a reductionism in how some have construed the hypothesis of "de León as author of the Zohar."[3] We are referring to the supposition of a basic doctrinal identity permeating both corpora that rarely proceeds beyond the identification of their mutual agreement.[4] Second is an opposing tendency—spurred by group-authorship hypotheses of the Zohar's composition,[5] as well as a growing consensus concerning the Zohar's belated appearance as a "book"[6]—to pursue connections between the Zohar and other

Sachs-Shmueli, "The Image of the Prophetess Miriam as a Feminine Model in Zoharic Literature" [in Hebrew], *Kabbalah* 33 (2015): 183–210; Sachs-Shmueli, "'I Arouse the Shekhina': A Psychoanalytic Study of Anxiety and Desire of the Kabbalah in Relation to the Object of Taboo," *Kabbalah* 35 (2016): 227–266; Biti Roi, *Love of the Shekhina: Mysticism and Poetics in* Tiqqunei ha-Zohar [Hebrew] (Ramat Gan: Bar Ilan University Press, 2017); Ruth Kara-Kaniel, "King David and Jerusalem from Psalms to the Zohar," in *Psalms in/on Jerusalem*, ed. Ophir Münz-Manor and Ilana Pardes (Berlin: de Gruyter, 2019), 67–107; Jeremy Phillip Brown, "Espousal of the Impoverished Bride in Early Franciscan Hagiography and the Kabbalah of Gerona," *History of Religions* 61, no. 3 (2022): 279–305; Brown, "The Reason a Woman Is Obligated: Women's Ritual Efficacy in Medieval Kabbalah," *Harvard Theological Review* 116, no. 3 (2023): 422–446.

[2] On isolating the study of the Zohar from that of de León's Hebrew writings, see Daniel Abrams, "Divine Yearning for *Shekhinah*: 'The Secret of the Exodus from Egypt'— R. Moses de León's Questions and Answers from Unpublished Manuscripts and Their Zoharic Parallels," *Kabbalah* 32 (2014): 7–34.

[3] One exception to this paradigm is Shilo Pachter, "'A Sin Without Repentance': On a Disagreement Between Moses de León and the Zohar," in *And This Is for Yehuda: Studies Presented to Our Friend, Professor Yehuda Liebes, on the Occasion of His Sixty-Fifth Birthday*, ed. Maren Niehoff, Ronit Meroz, and Jonathan Garb (Jerusalem: Mossad Bialik, 2022), 144–163. On the question of de León as author of the Zohar, and its evolution through scholarship, see Avishai Bar-Asher, ed., *R. Moses de León:* Sefer Mishkan ha-'edut [Hebrew] (Los Angeles, CA: Cherub, 2013), 26–51.

[4] Gershom Scholem, *Major Trends in Jewish Mysticism* (New York: Schocken, 1946), 156–204; Tishby, *Wisdom of the Zohar*, 1:1–6; Daniel Abrams, "Gershom Scholem's Methodologies of Research on the Zohar," in *Scholar and Kabbalist: The Life and Work of Gershom Scholem*, ed. Mirjam Zadoff and Noam Zadoff (Leiden: Brill, 2018), 3–16.

[5] Yehuda Liebes, *Studies in the Zohar* (Albany: State University of New York Press, 1993), 85–138.

[6] Boaz Huss, *The Zohar: Reception and Impact*, trans. Yudith Nave (Oxford: Littman Library of Jewish Civilization, 2016), 36–66 ("The Zohar as an Imagined Book"); Daniel Abrams, "The 'Zohar' as Palimpsest: Dismantling the Literary Constructs of a Kabbalistic Classic and the Turn to the Hermeneutics of Textual Archaeology," *Kabbalah* 29 (2013): 7–60; and the expanded presentation in Abrams, *Kabbalistic Manuscripts*, 3–16.

kabbalistic authors active in and after de León's generation. Productive as these developments have been for discerning networks of authorial activity surrounding the Zohar, they have left the figure of de León and his voluminous corpus somewhat stranded. The third factor is that some scholars have abandoned the project of delineating a chronology of texts authored by de León—a figure who, ironically, did more than any other medieval kabbalist to mark the date of his compositions.[7] Related to the absence of a cogent sequence of the author's works is a fourth factor, on which we will elaborate momentarily, namely, the default of scholars to synchronic analyses, which tend to essentialize some frameworks at the expense of others. As preliminary as text-critical and historical-critical modes of analysis may seem at this late phase, nearly eighty-five years after the appearance of Scholem's *Major Trends in Jewish Mysticism*, it is a testament to the still-nascent stage of kabbalah studies that scholars have not yet applied diachronic analyses to a topic as compelling as gender to a thinker as central as de León.[8]

This chapter will examine the speculation on gender preserved in de León's "Nameless Composition." In addition to the many eye-opening attributes of this work profiled in the previous chapters of this book, the text preserves de León's first effort to develop a speculative framework of divine androgyny. We turn now to analyze these efforts and to coordinate them with other works by de León and relevant passages from the Zohar. We will employ the neologism "androgynology" as a shorthand way of referring to language concerning God's possession of both male and female attributes—*zakhar u-neqevah* in the scriptural language assumed by de León.[9] Perhaps the only scholar to address this subject in de León's writings specifically, Elliot R. Wolfson has argued that the *hieros gamos* motif, that is, the divine marriage of the male and female poles of the Godhead, constitutes the "single thought" mooring de León's "essential teaching."[10] There is indeed ample evidence that this motif plays a significant role in de León's speculation, as it does in much subsequent kabbalistic wisdom. It surfaces with unique frequency throughout *Sefer ha-Rimmon* (1287). This is, in part, because that

[7] Abrams, "Divine Yearning," 18–19.

[8] In defense of a similar archaeological approach for charting the evolution of Castilian kabbalah, but with respect to the topic of eschatology, see Avishai Bar-Asher, *Journeys of the Soul: Concepts and Imageries of Paradise in Medieval Kabbalah* (Jerusalem: Magnes, 2019), 11–21.

[9] Genesis 1:27. See Alexander Altmann, "*Homo Imago Dei* in Jewish and Christian Theology," *Journal of Religion* 48 (1968): 235–259; Idel, *Kabbalah and Eros*, 53–103; Jeremy Phillip Brown, "God as Androgyne in Medieval Kabbalah: Toward a History of the Doctrine" (forthcoming).

[10] Elliot R. Wolfson, *The Book of the Pomegranate: Moses De Leon's* Sefer Ha-Rimmon (Atlanta, GA: Scholars Press, 1988), 67.

composition deals extensively with kabbalistic rationales of the commandments (*ṭaʿame ha-miṣvot*),[11] and de León's rationales appeal to the performative capacity of the commandments to reconcile the male and female facets of divinity.[12] According to some such rationales, the harmonization of the male and female attributes reconstitutes their primordial unity.[13]

There is clear evidence that de León's interest in the efficacy of the commandments is prefigured in the "Nameless Composition," although the conjugal character of their performance is muted in comparison to later works. For example, the text's account of the commandment of almsgiving (*ṣedaqah*), which draws clearly from the language of Ezra of Girona,[14] directly informs the treatment of almsgiving in *Sefer ha-Rimmon*.[15] Nonetheless, explicitly gendered speculation does not surface in our text's account, nor does it figure conspicuously in the text's accounts of other commandments, which, as we noted in Chapter 1, occupy only a minor part of what remains of our text.[16] Nonetheless, the text demonstrates a marked concern with the

[11] For an overview of the rationales of the commandments in medieval Judaism, see Marc Herman and Jeremy Phillip Brown, "The Commandments as a Discursive Nexus of Medieval Judaism," in *Accounting for the Commandments in Medieval Judaism: Studies in Law, Philosophy, Pietism, and Kabbalah*, ed. Jeremy Phillip Brown and Marc Herman (Leiden: Brill, 2021), 3–24.

[12] On this and other functions of performing the commandments, see Gershom Scholem, *On the Kabbalah and Its Symbolism*, trans. Ralph Manheim (New York: Schocken, 1965), 130; Elliot R. Wolfson, "Mystical Rationalization of the Commandments in *Sefer ha-Rimmon*," *Hebrew Union College Annual* 59 (1988): 217–251; and Jeremy Phillip Brown, "Of Sound and Vision: The Ram's Horn in Medieval Kabbalistic Rituology," in *Qol Tamid: The Shofar in Ritual, History and Culture*, ed. Jonathan Friedman and Joel Gereboff (Claremont, CA: Claremont Press, 2017), 83–113; and Brown, "Reason a Woman Is Obligated."

[13] For the characterization of the divine unity in terms of a specifically *male* androgyny, with "one [male] gender with two sexuated instantiations," see Wolfson, *Language, Eros, Being*, 147. For the initial study advancing this characterization, see Wolfson, "Woman—the Feminine as Other."

[14] Azriel of Girona, *Commentarius in Aggadoth auctore R. Azriel Geronensi* [in Hebrew], ed. Isaiah Tishby (Jerusalem: Mekize Nirdamim, 1945), 6, 38–39; Abraham ben Judah Elmalik, *Liqqute Shikheḥah u-Fe'ah* (Ferrara, Italy: Abraham Ibn Usque, 1556), 7b. For the reception of Ezra's account of almsgiving, see, too, Ṭodros Abulafia, *Oṣar ha-kavod*, 54b–55a; and Baḥya ben Asher on Genesis 49:33; Yosef Caro, *Beit Yosef, Hoshen Mishpat* §. 1. On the commandments in Ezra, see Yakov M. Travis, "Kabbalistic Foundations of Jewish Spiritual Practice: Rabbi Ezra of Gerona—on the Kabbalistic Meaning of the Mitzvot" (PhD diss., Brandeis University, 2002). On almsgiving, see Brown, "Espousal of the Impoverished Bride."

[15] MS Munich, Bayerische Staatsbibliothek, Cod. hebr. 47, fols. 337b–338a; Wolfson, Book of the Pomegranate = Moses de León, *Sefer ha-Rimmon*, 111–117. On almsgiving in the Zohar, see Joel Hecker, *Mystical Bodies, Mystical Meals: Eating and Embodiment in Medieval Kabbalah* (Detroit, MI: Wayne State University Press, 2005), 173–178.

[16] Pace Scholem's judgment that the text contains no such material: "Identität mit dem halachamystischen S. ha-rimmon ist ausgeschlossen, unser Fragment enthält auf 100 Seiten keine einzige Halachadeutung!" See Gerhard [Gershom] Scholem, "Eine unbekannte mystische Schrift des Mose de Leon," *Monatsschrift für Geschichte und Wissenschaft des Judentums* 71, nos. 3–4 (1927): 109–123, esp. 121. However, his inclination to disambiguate the work from *Sefer ha-Rimmon* is sound.

divine ontology of gender. In fact, its fascination with the topic is without parallel in earlier known kabbalistic writings.[17]

This chapter will profile the most representative themes of our text's distinctive treatment of gender, as well as themes that are ignored or insufficiently addressed in previous scholarship.[18] With this, we aim to demonstrate the uniqueness of our text within the broader oeuvre of works ascribed in some fashion to de León—including the Zohar. The composition's distinction lies in communicating a broader range of positionings and dynamics for the female attributes of divinity than any other known work attributable to de León. This relative diversity of the text's androgynology arises as a function of its three-world framework,[19] its thirteenfold paradigm, and, especially, its repeated assertions—more than five centuries before the "Ewig-Weibliche" of Goethe—of the divine female's "eternal femininity" (*neqevut 'olamit*). We will even have the occasion to observe the tendency of the Venetian scribe responsible for copying the text—in contrast to the more faithful work of our text's Moroccan copyist—to reduce the greater breadth of its gender speculation into the narrower mold of discourse that had gained prominence by the sixteenth century. Additionally, we will uncover vestiges of de León's early androgynology in his later work and in the Zohar's homilies on the Torah. Our analysis focuses on five motifs that illustrate de León's initial foray into gendering the divinity: (1) the form of the letter *alef*, to which we return from the previous chapter; (2) the prophetic phrase "female shall compass male"; (3) the positioning of the female world between two males; (4) the thirteenfold pattern of Solomon's Sea; and (5) the shifting indices of the female world (i.e., *dalet* and *heh*).

The material we will examine here challenges essentializing interpretations. But perhaps more significantly, our review of the early discourse on gender highlights the developmental trajectory of a most contentious theme of kabbalistic wisdom that has divided modern scholars. The chapter will explore the deep intellectual background of such central motifs as, for example, the thirteen-petaled rose, the much-studied symbol that graced the first folio of the Mantua Zohar. We will not therefore limit our treatment to isolating a curious station on de León's journey, but will instead

[17] A proper historical account of the kabbalistic discourse of androgyny remains a desideratum; for a prolegomenon, see Brown, "God as Androgyne."

[18] For the preliminary account, which we develop here extensively, see Jeremy Phillip Brown and Avishai Bar-Asher, "The Enduring Female: Differentiating Moses de León's Early Androgynology," *Jewish Studies Quarterly* 28, no. 1 (2021): 21–53.

[19] On this three-world framework, see above, and Bar-Asher, *Journeys of the Soul*, 198–213.

go further to demonstrate the endurance of de León's early androgynology in both his subsequent compositions and the Zohar.

4.2 *Alef*: Three Worlds (Again)

Theosophical speculation on the form of the *alef*, the first letter of the Hebrew alphabet, appeared already in *Sefer ha-Bahir*, which likens the letter's form to both the brain and the ear.[20] As we saw in Chapter 3, from the earliest phase of Moses de León's writing, the threefold form of the *alef* had already given rise to speculation concerning the tripartite structure of the cosmos.[21] In the *Sefer ha-Neʿlam* corpus, the letter's three strokes refer to the three domains of the cosmic order from top to bottom: the separate intellects, the celestial spheres, and the sublunary realm. Our text, however, recasts this speculation (see Figure 3.1). Here the three strokes of the single letter call to mind the divine order. The threefold singularity of the letterform helps de León evoke the divinity in triune terms—though in a vocabulary distinct from Trinitarian Christology.[22] The pattern of the *alef* allows one to discern a threefold divine order that is recapitulated by the three worlds of the cosmic order.

In de León's Hebrew writings, then, the topic of the *alef* marks a site of transition between an older three-worlds framework that is chiefly cosmological and a later delineation of three worlds that is theosophical in nature.[23]

[20] Avishai Bar-Asher, "The Bahir as It Once Was: Transmission History as a Tool for Reconstructing and Reassessing the Text, Format, and Ideas of the Original Composition," *Tarbiz* 89, no. 1 (2022): 73–225, esp. 183, 185. See Elliot R. Wolfson, *Alef, Mem, Tau* (Berkeley: University of California Press, 2006), 140–142. On the form of the *alef* in the *Sefer ha-Orah* attributed to Jacob ben Jacob ha-Kohen, see Elliot R. Wolfson, "Letter Symbolism and *Merkavah* Imagery in the Zohar," in *Alei Shefer: Studies in the Literature of Jewish Thought Presented to Rabbi Dr. Alexandre Safran*, ed. Moshe Hallamish (Ramat Gan: Bar Ilan Press, 1990), 195–236, here 200. On the commentary on the Hebrew alphabet attributed to Isaac ben Jacob ha-Kohen, see Gershom Scholem, "Qabbalot R. Yiṣḥaq ve-R. Yaʿaqov bene R. Yaʿaqov ha-Kohen: Meqorot le-toledot ha-qabbalah lifne hitgallut ha-Zohar," *Maddaʿe ha-Yahadut* 2 (1927): 201–219, here 202–203.

[21] On de León's pretheosophical speculation on the *alef*, see Chapter 3.

[22] At one place in its meditation on the form of the *alef* (MS Munich, Bayerische Staatsbibliothek, Cod. hebr. 47, fols. 361a), our text alludes to an earlier treatment of this topic in the same composition that presumably belongs to its lost portion. For a close parallel, see Charles Mopsik, ed., *R. Moses De Leon's Sefer Sheqel ha-Qodesh* (Los Angeles, CA: Cherub Press, 1996) = Moses de León, *Sheqel ha-qodesh*, 87–89 (where the three-worlds speculation on the *alef* is related to the doctrine of the *yod* as the *nequddah maḥshavit* or noetic point). On trinitarian speculation vis-à-vis unity, see the appendix to *Sheqel ha-qodesh*, 103–106, discussed in Liebes, *Studies in the Zohar*, 140–145; and Jeremy Phillip Brown, "What Does the Messiah Know? A Prelude to Kabbalah's Trinity Complex," *Maimonides Review of Philosophy and Religion* 2 (2023): 1–49, esp. 2–8.

[23] See Gershom Scholem, "An Inquiry in the Kabbala of R. Isaac ben Jacob Hacohen, II: Evolution of the Doctrine of the Worlds in the Early Kabbala" [in Hebrew], *Tarbiz* 2, no. 4 (1931): 415–442; and

The later framework appears in our text for the first time and is well attested in de León's subsequent teachings.[24] With respect to the Zohar, an outlook paralleling the pretheosophical phase of de León's speculation can be found in the *Midrash ha-Ne'lam* stratum, whereas the later three-world theosophy informs the zoharic homilies.[25] Most important for our purposes is that the turn to theosophical speculation involves a gendering of the discourse.[26] As one might expect, it is within this transitional context that de León's thinking about "male and female" exhibits a high degree of novelty and dynamism.[27]

We return, as in the previous chapter, to the technical details of our text's account of the three worlds. The supernal or hidden world is contained by the sefirah *binah*, and its cipher is the letter *yod*; the middle world includes the six intermediate sefirot (from *ḥesed* to *yesod*); and the lower world is identical to the female sefirah *malkhut*, that is, the *shekhinah*. The text identifies the middle world with the letter *vav*, the sixth letter of the alphabet, and the lower world with *dalet*. This letter, which is the fourth in the alphabet, is already associated with the poor and dispossessed (*dal*) in ancient rabbinic abecedary lore, an association that is developed in *Sefer ha-Bahir*.[28] For this reason, the identification of the lower world with the *dalet* suggests its dependency upon the worlds above.[29] As the fourth letter, *dalet* may refer to the four angelic encampments surrounding *malkhut*, which is the most proximate of the ten sefirot to the angels.[30]

Scholem, "An Inquiry in the Kabbala of R. Isaac ben Jacob Hacohen, II: Evolution of the Doctrine of the Worlds in the Early Kabbala" [in Hebrew], *Tarbiz* 3, no. 1 (1931): 33–66.

[24] On the sustained use of the three-world framework in de León's later theosophical speculation, and, especially, his correlation of this framework with a threefold psychology, see Bar-Asher, *Journeys of the Soul*, 209.

[25] See above, sec. 3.1.

[26] See Avishai Bar-Asher, "*Sefer ha-Ne'lam*, New Parts of *Sefer Or Zarua* and Clarifications regarding the Early Writings of R. Moses de León: Studies and Critical Editions" [in Hebrew], *Tarbiz* 83, nos. 1–2 (2015): 197–329, here 214. On the gendering of letter speculation as characteristic of the zoharic corpus, see Wolfson, "Letter Symbolism," 217.

[27] On the anthropomorphism of letter mysticism in de León and the Zohar, and its relationship to the question of gender, see Elliot R. Wolfson, "Anthropomorphic Imagery and Letter Symbolism in the Zohar" [in Hebrew], *Jerusalem Studies in Jewish Thought* 8 (1989): 147–181; and Wolfson, "Letter Symbolism."

[28] B. Shabbat 104a. See the discussion of the *dalet* in Brown, "Espousal of the Impoverished Bride," 287–291.

[29] See, for example, fol. 375a, where the dispossession of *malkhut* (*dalutah*) is explained in terms of her poverty of light vis-à-vis the sun (which corresponds to *tiferet*).

[30] On the four angelic encampments of the *shekhinah*, see Ezra ben Solomon of Girona, "Perush Shir ha-Shirim," in *Kitve Ramban*, ed. Charles B. Chavel (Jerusalem: Mossad Rav Kook, 1986), 2:510; Zohar 2:256b (*Hekhalot*); and see both Baḥya ben Asher and Menaḥem Recanati on Genesis 1:21.

> The form of the *alef* stands in its secret; its unity intimates the matter of the three worlds that appear in its midst: the supernal world, which is the hidden world conjoined with [the letter] *ṭet*, [i.e., *binah* is conjoined with *ḥokhmah*][31] becoming a world within itself; from there emerges and extends . . . the intermediate world. And when it conjoins with it [the upper world], it [the intermediate world] makes a world within itself. And from there emerges and extends . . . the lower world. And when it conjoins with it [the intermediate world], it [the lower world] makes a world within itself. And, in fact, all of them are bound up, this one with that, and gripped, this one by that, and all of them appear in the image of the *alef* [א]—the supernal world is above, for it is a hidden world, in the secret of [the letter] *yod*; and the intermediate world is the middle [stroke] of [the letter] *alef*, patterned upon [the letter] *vav*, and it is grasped by . . . the supernal world; and the lower world, which is below the middle of *alef*, is the subordinate world [*ha-shafel*], in the secret of [the letter] *dalet*—according to this pattern: א. Behold, the pattern of the *dalet* below is truly grasped by the middle of the *alef*.[32]

In plumbing the theosophical depths of the *alef*, de León engages in speculation that is at one and the same time (a) unitive, (b) threefold, and (c) tenfold. The text emphasizes the three worlds and their subtle unity by articulating the complex decomposition of (a) the singular *alef* into (b) the three letters, which spell out the name of the letter (c) *yod* (ד + ו + י), the tenth letter of the alphabet. This inscription of the tenth letter within the *alef*—the very emblem of transcendental oneness—calls to mind a tenfold unity that circumscribes the ten sefirot. This alone, however, does not exhaust the dynamism of the unitive theology exhibited by this passage, wherein the tenfold unity is distributed across three intradivine worlds.

On the one hand, the relationship between the three worlds is one of continuity. Each successive world extends as a continuation of the world above it, just as each successive stroke of the *alef* flows from the previous. On the other hand, the process of extension yields a mode of conjunction from below, an active bonding on the part of the extended reality to its source. This action, in turn, transforms the extended reality into "a world within itself." We make special note of the fact that our text utilizes the vocabulary of

[31] See the text immediately preceding this passage on MS Munich, Bayerische Staatsbibliothek, Cod. hebr. 47, fol. 361a, concerning the bond of *ḥokhmah* and *binah*.

[32] MS Munich, Bayerische Staatsbibliothek, Cod. hebr. 47, fols. 361a–b.

extension (*hitpashṭut*), perhaps to distinguish this intradivine process from the extroverted processes of emanation into the created realm.[33] Through this process of extension, each extended world individuates in relation to its source precisely by reinforcing its unity therewith. The extension, then, realizes its autonomy, becoming "a world within itself," when clinging to the world from which it extends and reifying its dependency thereon. The dynamic paradigm of unity propounded by this text is thus predicated upon a reciprocal assertion of autonomy and dependency, which obtains through the conjunction of intradivine worlds.

What is the significance of gender within this paradigm? The grasping and bonding that characterize such conjunction bespeak the eroticism of the male-female encounter. But the interaction of male and female may not be reduced to its erotic dimension; their coordination also involves, as we will see, procreative, birth-giving, nutritive, and distributive capacities. The gendered character of the text's unitive dynamism is further illustrated by the movement of *dalet*, a cipher for the lower world of the female. When the *dalet* embodies the lower stroke of the *alef*, the letter does not appear in its typical form. Instead of its usual upright position (ד), the *dalet* appears in a rotated position ┘. The female letterform faces upward toward the source of her extension, to conjoin with the *vav*, the intermediate world of the male, in an embrace of the male by the female. Referring to this gesture, de León writes, "There is no adornment of male and female (*tiqqun zakhar u-neqevah*) unless they appear face to face." On the one hand, the intimacy of this bond requires the subordination of the *dalet* to the *vav*, such that "the male stands above and the female below."[34] On the other hand, the bond depends upon the autonomous turning of the female toward the male: "The middle [stroke] of the *alef* is above, and the *dalet* is below but turning toward him, face to face."[35]

Nonetheless, the text goes on to indicate that when the *vav* appears as the middle stroke of the *alef*, it turns away from the *dalet*. In this instance,

[33] It is conventional for scholars to conflate these processes by referring to them with one and the same emanationist language, leaving the theologies developed by likes of de León susceptible to the now-hackneyed criticism of pantheism. On this criticism, see Joseph Ben Shlomo, "On Pantheism in Jewish Mysticism According to Gershom Scholem and His Critics" [in Hebrew], *Da'at* 50–52 (2003): 461–482; Ben Shlomo, "Gershom Scholem on Pantheism in the Kabbala," in *Gershom Scholem: The Man and His Work*, ed. Paul Mendes-Flohr (Albany: State University of New York Press, 1993), 56–72; Jeremy Phillip Brown, "La Perversión de la Cábala Judía: Gershom Scholem and Anti-Kabbalistic Polemic in the Argentine Catholic Nationalism of Julio Meinvielle," *All Religion Is Inter-Religion: Engaging the Work of Steven M. Wasserstrom*, ed. Kambiz GhaneaBassiri and Paul Robertson (London: Bloomsbury, 2019), 65–73, here 71–72.

[34] MS Munich, Bayerische Staatsbibliothek, Cod. hebr. 47, fol. 361b.

[35] MS Munich, Bayerische Staatsbibliothek, Cod. hebr. 47, fol. 361b.

the male and female are not united in a face-to-face embrace (*en 'omdim ha-zakhar ve-ha-neqevah panim be-fanim*).[36] Instead, the *vav* faces the *yod*. While this embrace is similarly male-female in nature, the male stands in a subordinate relationship to the upper world, which is gendered as female. How should this be understood? The text describes the upper world with the same kind of maternal language that characterized *binah* in the text's penitential discourse: "The supernal source [is] above, from which everything arises, since all life and all refinements are there."[37] The *vav* clings to the upper female as a son would to his mother: "That intermediate world obtains his life and his substance from there, and turns upward toward it, to receive it."[38] But this vitalization of the male world, of the *vav* by the *yod* (through the mediation of a *ṭet* posited between them),[39] is contingent upon the male's conjugal union with *dalet*, the lower female or bride: "There is no bestowal of blessings upon him unless he takes his female [i.e., the *dalet*] with him [i.e., in marriage], and the two of them are found [to be] 'male and female (*zakhar u-neqevah*),' and then he will receive life and goodness."[40] This contingency illustrates well the coordination of generative (i.e., the bestowal of life and blessings) and conjugal processes between two generations and among at least three personae within the divine family represented by the three letters contained within the unifying *alef*.[41] It is noteworthy that no father persona figures overtly within this threefold family framework.

The text goes on to explain the oscillations of the two lower letters, sometimes positioning themselves to receive blessings and nourishment from the upper world, at other times turning to embrace one another in marital intimacy.

> And for this reason, both of them [i.e., *dalet* and *vav*] intend to turn themselves upward, for, really, no blessings are bestowed save when male and

[36] MS Munich, Bayerische Staatsbibliothek, Cod. hebr. 47, fol. 361b.
[37] MS Munich, Bayerische Staatsbibliothek, Cod. hebr. 47, fol. 361b.
[38] MS Munich, Bayerische Staatsbibliothek, Cod. hebr. 47, fol. 361b.
[39] On MS Munich, Bayerische Staatsbibliothek, Cod. hebr. 47, fol. 361a, the same verse (Proverbs 4:23) that defined the birth-giving function of *binah* in our text's penitential discourse ("for life issues from her"; see herein, secs. 2.6, 4.3, 5.3) is adduced as the esoteric significance of the womb-like letter *ṭet*: "the secret of the letter *ṭet* is that 'life issues from her' to all of the rest [of the sefirot] through the potency of the letter that conjoins with her [i.e., *yod*] and thus is the secret of the eighth and ninth [i.e., the conjunction of *binah* with *ḥokhmah*]." On the *yod* appearing within the form of letter *ṭet*, see Chapter 3.
[40] MS Munich, Bayerische Staatsbibliothek, Cod. hebr. 47, fol. 361b.
[41] The threefold pattern brings the upper female to the fore, deemphasizing the role of *ḥokhmah*; per the statement adduced above in n. 39, *ḥokhmah* plays a key role in these processes, though within the configuration of divine personae, it is not personified to the same degree as *binah*.

> female are together, and this is the secret . . . of the two [letters] being turned upward. And for this reason, the *vav*, which is the middle of the *alef*, is rotated upward and away from his female, in order to receive nurture for both of them. And after he receives, he reverses to appear face to face with his female [i.e., the *dalet*].[42]

It is a commonplace of kabbalistic speculation to assign masculinity or femininity to the structures of the Godhead based upon their function as benefactors or beneficiaries, respectively, within the economic distribution of the divine substance.[43] But in the passage just adduced, the gender of the intradivine worlds is not determined by such binary functions. Though the male world serves to channel blessings to the lower feminine, his role is likewise receptive vis-à-vis *binah* above. This posture of receptivity, in which the male orients himself alongside the female in the upward-facing expectation of a disbursement, does not compromise his masculinity.[44] Though *binah*, the uterine sefirah, is bound to *ḥokhmah* in constituting the upper world, there is no indication in our text that her femininity is eclipsed, or that she herself becomes male through her bestowal of vitality to the male world (nor does our text personify *ḥokhmah* as a paternal benefactor). Moreover, the text does not depict *binah* in terms of a "phallic womb," an image some have claimed depicts *binah* throughout the Castilian discourse. Nor does the text reduce the attribute of generativity to a symbolic function of the male, or, more specifically, to the phallus.[45] The expectations created by previous scholarship fail to capture the dynamic personifications of gender at play.

Furthermore, the dynamic paradigm of unity outlined here, in contrast to what we encounter in other texts by de León, does not provide a basis for assuming that the femininity of the lower world is somehow effaced, or incorporated into the male, as a function of their embrace.[46] Although she

[42] MS Munich, Bayerische Staatsbibliothek, Cod. hebr. 47, fol. 361b–362a.

[43] For a classic discussion of the correlation of gender with differentiated economic functions, see Ṭodros Abulafia, *Sha'ar ha-razim*, ed. Michal [Kushnir-]Oron (Jerusalem: Mossad Bialik, 1989), 86; for a programmatic discussion, see Wolfson, "Woman— the Feminine as Other," 188; on the gendering of economic functions within the Godhead, see Brown, "Espousal of the Impoverished Bride."

[44] For early modern traditions concerning the feminization of the male, see Wolfson, *Circle in the Square*, 110–111.

[45] Consider, by contrast, the perspective discussed in Wolfson, *Circle in the Square*, 98–106. Also see Abrams, *Female Body of God*, 92–123, which interprets the alleged depictions of *binah*'s phallic motherhood as a critique of masculinity.

[46] This is in contrast, for example, to the perspective expressed in Wolfson, "Woman— the Feminine as Other," 175–176, and *Circle in the Square*, 92–98.

is, apparently, dependent on the male world above her for the disbursement of divine substance—which may suggest a patriarchal distribution of life, blessings, and nurture—such resources enter the divine economy through the upper female, who serves as a maternal benefactor. The determination of gender in terms of binary economic functions does not serve as an absolute principle governing our text's outlook.

4.3 Female Shall Compass Male: *Binah* as the Mother of a Son

Previous scholarship has noted the importance to kabbalah of Jeremiah's prophecy that "female shall compass male" (Jeremiah 31:22). Some have interpreted these words as heralding an inversion of the gender hierarchy that will transpire at the time of Israel's redemption—an ascent of the lower female to the upper echelons of the divinity.[47] Our text, however, interprets the language differently. Like the language "for life issues from her," the biblical phrase "female shall compass male" describes *binah*. It expresses a process of intradivine extension by which *binah*—as the female principle of the hidden, supernal world—projects her femininity into the intermediate world, which, only upon completion, becomes male. This process is linked, in particular, to the gradation of *binah*, which is personified as a mother (here, she is identified with the uterine "stream"; *yuval*).[48] Thus, rather than limiting the scriptural phrase "female shall compass male" to its contextual meaning (*peshaṭ*)—that a woman will come to woo a man—our text renders the phrase in terms of the female *becoming* male. This interpretation follows one that Rashi reported having heard from Judah ben Moses ha-Darshan (eleventh century): "Woman will turn to become male."[49] According to our text, *binah* gives rise to the intermediate world through a process that ultimately crosses over the gender threshold from female to male. In other

[47] Wolfson, *Language, Eros, Being*, 110, 187, 491; Wolfson, "Bifurcating the Androgyne," 109; and Elliot R. Wolfson, *Open Secret: Postmessianic Messianism and the Mystical Revision of Menaḥem Mendel Schneerson* (New York: Columbia University Press, 2012), 201; Idel, *Privileged Divine Feminine*, 38, 69, 113–114, 142.

[48] Based on Jeremiah 17:8, "spreading its roots by a stream (*yuval*)"; see discussion of this cognomen in Chapter 5.

[49] See Rashi on Jeremiah 31:22. See, too, Ṭodros Abulafia, *Sha'ar ha-razim*, 86, where the verse is presented at a secret understood by the enlightened, a secret is related to the identification of the divine structure (*binyan*) with the human likeness—comprising both male and female—seated upon the throne of Ezekiel's vision (Ezekiel 1:26).

words, the phrase "female shall compass male" calls to mind the gender instability of the maternal *binah* as a female who gives birth to a male, a process that mitigates the absolute terms of her femininity.[50] Such an interpretation may suggest de León's familiarity with Christian readings of Jeremiah's prophecy in reference to the womb of Mary encompassing the fetal Jesus.[51]

The description of this transition from female to male is couched in an account of the dissemination of divine substance from the uppermost reaches of the Godhead. In describing how the primordial ether (*avir ha-qadmon*) brings forth the lower gradations,[52] the text explains that the inapprehensible substance of *keter* cannot be revealed in itself, but only by means of its concealment within the lower gradations, wherein the divinity assumes a nexus of gendered personifications.[53]

> [The ether] is elevated through the elevation of the levels and becomes elevated through the elevation of everything. . . . And it is completely fortified by means of its elevation [of the gradations] and its concealment of everything, for its gradation and height are not revealed in any respect. And truly the secret of its existence from *ḥokhmah* and downward is not known and revealed except by means of the elevation of existence from the supernal world, the "stream" [*ha-yuval*, i.e., *binah*]. And [this] is the secret of "female shall compass male."[54]

The subtle ether becomes apprehensible as it, paradoxically, conceals itself within increasingly determinate rungs of divine being, beginning with *binah*.

[50] Later (MS Munich, Bayerische Staatsbibliothek, Cod. hebr. 47, fol. 384a) in the appendix to our text that furnishes a theosophical commentary on the divine names (fols. 381a–385a; which also appears in a revised form as an appendix to de León, *Sheqel ha-qodesh*, 98–102), the phrase "female shall compass male" pertains to de León's assertion that *binah*, in contrast to the gradations subordinate to her, does not contain any judgment despite her apparent location on the left side (see fol. 383a). Also compare Gershom Scholem, "Shene quntresim le-R. Moshe de León," *Kobez al Yad* 8, no. 18 (1976): 325–384, esp. 330–370 = de León, *Shushan ha-'edut*, 332, where Jeremiah 31:22 is applied to a two-world framework, as well as other discussions of scriptural phrase in Moses de León, *Sefer ha-Rimmon*, 143; and Moses de León, *Sheqel ha-qodesh*, 49, which are discussed below.

[51] See, for example, Athanasius, *Expositio fidei*, 3; and Jerome on Jeremiah 31:22.

[52] On the primordial ether in de León, see George Margoliouth, "The Doctrine of the Ether in the Kabbalah," *Jewish Quarterly Review* 20 (1908): 825–861.

[53] On the femininity of the primordial ether in *'iyyun* traditions, see Mark Verman, *Book of Contemplation: Medieval Jewish Mystical Sources* (Albany: State University of New York Press, 1992), 202–204; Wolfson, *Circle in the Square*, 65–66, 184n.145. The *'iyyun* text adduced there preserves a tradition fancifully ascribed to Naḥmanides that identifies the primordial ether with *binah*, as a further specification of its femininity. While the primordial ether is linked, in our text, to *binah*, it is, in turn, channeled via *ḥokhmah*, and ultimately rooted in *ayin*, i.e., *keter*. See MS Munich, Bayerische Staatsbibliothek, Cod. hebr. 47, fols. 365b–366a. On the transition of the ether from inapprehensible to apprehensible at the threshold of *binah*, see fol. 382b; compare de León, *Sheqel ha-qodesh*, 100.

[54] MS Munich, Bayerische Staatsbibliothek, Cod. hebr. 47, fol. 366a.

In an arresting passage, likely the first of its kind in de León's corpus, the author portrays the dialectic of concealment and revelation as a process of divine self-parturition (as we will see further on, a close Aramaic parallel to this passage appears in the zoharic homilies).[55] In expressing the imperceptible inflow from *keter*, the upper female gives birth to the intermediate world. The eventually male world of the six medial sefirot, however, remains female, sexually indistinguishable from the mother, until it is fully birthed. Accordingly, the differentiation and corresponding gender determination of the intermediate world takes effect at the moment its penis emerges from the womb.

> This supernal world is [the] "issue of life" to all (*toṣe'ot ḥayyim la-kol*);[56] it is the source of all the outgoing streams in the female who brings forth fruit (*meqor kol ha-neḥalim ha-yoṣe'im ba-neqevah ha-moṣi peri le-ma'asehu*).[57] And truly, she "shall compass male," on account of one righteous [male] (*ṣaddiq*) who stands below her. For you find that all of the limbs of the body are counted as female, until the covenant [of circumcision] arrives [i.e., the penis],[58] which is one limb by itself. But it [its arrival] changes all of the [other] limbs, making them male (*ve-hu ha-ḥozer le-khol ha-'evarim heyotam zakhar*). And by this secret, the supernal world is "female shall compass male" [that is, female shall become male]. But the lower world is female, standing in eternal femininity (*ve-'olam ha-taḥton hi neqevah ha-'omedet be-neqevut 'olamit*). And she never becomes male (*enah ḥozeret le-'olam zakhar*). And for her adornments (*tiqquneha*) are daughters who act valiantly.[59] And how pleasing is this subject for every enlightened person, that the lower world is female, standing in eternal femininity (*'olam shel maṭah neqevah ha-'omedet be-neqevut 'olamit*).[60]

[55] On birth in kabbalah generally, see Elliot R. Wolfson, "Patriarchy and the Motherhood of God in Zoharic Kabbalah and Meister Eckhart," *Envisioning Judaism: Studies in Honor of Peter Schäfer on the Occasion of His Seventieth Birthday*, ed. Ra'anan S. Boustan, Klaus Herrmann, Reimund Leicht, Annette Yoshiko Reed, and Giuseppe Veltri (Tübingen: Mohr Siebeck, 2013), 1049–1088; and Ruth Kara-Ivanov Kaniel, *Human Throes: Birth in Kabbalah and Psychoanalysis* [in Hebrew] (Jerusalem: Shalom Hartman Institute, 2018).

[56] According to Proverbs 4:23.

[57] Based partially on Isaiah 54:16.

[58] The text seems to understand that the divine newborn bears the sign of the covenant without having undergone circumcision, along the lines of an early rabbinic tradition about thirteen biblical figures born in this way. On the latter motif, see Isaac Kalimi, "He Was Born Circumcised: Some Midrashic Sources, Their Concept, Roots and Presumably Historical Context," *Zeitschrift für die Neutestamentliche Wissenschaft und die Kunde der älteren Kirche* 93, nos. 1–2 (2002): 1–12. For a broad treatment of circumcision in Jewish esotericism, see Wolfson, "Circumcision and the Divine Name: A Study in the Transmission of Esoteric Doctrine," *Jewish Quarterly Review* 78, nos. 1–2 (1987): 77–112.

[59] Based on Proverbs 31:29.

[60] MS Munich, Bayerische Staatsbibliothek, Cod. hebr. 47, fol. 366a.

Let us make two primary points about this remarkable passage and what it conveys about the relative permeability of gender boundaries within the Godhead. First, in explaining how the primordial ether is incorporated into the sefirot, the text specifies that the five successively extended limbs of the divine body (= *ḥesed, din, tif'eret, neṣaḥ,* and *hod*) are linked to the upper female, oriented toward her womb. This remains the case until the sexually specific limb of the righteous newborn emerges: the circumcised penis (*yesod*; or as it is called above, *ṣaddiq* and *berit*). At this point, all of the initially female limbs—*ḥesed, din, tif'eret, neṣaḥ, hod,* and *yesod*—become male retroactively. In other words, the upper female world produces the sexual differentiation of the intermediate world as a male body that testifies to the truth of the covenant. This process causes the newborn body, which began as an extension of the female body, to individuate into a male and thenceforth to relinquish its gendered identification with the mother.[61] Thus, the description of the upper world as "female shall compass male" refers specifically to the transitional process of *binah* as the female who comes to mother a male child. The novelty of this account becomes clear when viewed against the backdrop of earlier kabbalistic speculation on the gendered attributes of the divinity. Notwithstanding the claim that the first five limbs to emerge from the womb lose their femininity once the penis appears, the very premise that these five (= *ḥesed, din, tif'eret, neṣaḥ,* and *hod*) begin as female is a bold recasting of the medial sefirot, which seldom, if ever, appear as female in the earlier material. In contrast to these permeable gender boundaries within the intermediate world, the lower female world stands resolutely in her femininity.[62] In fact, the text underscores the eternality of her female character.[63] This is a

[61] The text describes a process by which the womb's generativity does not in principle render it phallic, belying scholarly interpretations of *binah* as a "phallic womb" that ostensibly becomes male by virtue of its generative function. It is the belated appearance of the penis that breaks the gendered identification with *binah* and, in fact, underscores a binary distinction between the womb, in the first instance, and the penis, in the second. For a close parallel to this exegesis of "female shall compass male," replete with the narrative of all limbs being considered female until the appearance of the penis, see de León, *Sheqel ha-qodesh*, 49. See also Moses de León, *Sefer ha-Rimmon*, 191–192, for a related exegesis of "female shall compass male," where the verse similarly refers to *binah* initiating the process that engenders the intermediate male world; this text, moreover, depicts the relationship of the hidden world, emphasizing the uterine *binah*, to the revealed male world in terms of Solomon's Sea resting atop the twelve oxen, namely, in terms of the superordination of the female above the male world. For another reading of Jeremiah 31:22 in terms of the hidden world's manifestation of the revealed world, see de León, *Sefer ha-Rimmon*, 143.

[62] Compare this account of the androgyny of the three worlds with the zoharic account of the sexual differentiation of two worlds, male and female, respectively, discussed in Wolfson, *Circle in the Square*, 89.

[63] We have not located other instances where de León refers to the female world as eternal (*'olamit*) or perpetual (*temidit*) as we see in this text, though it will be shown below that both de León and

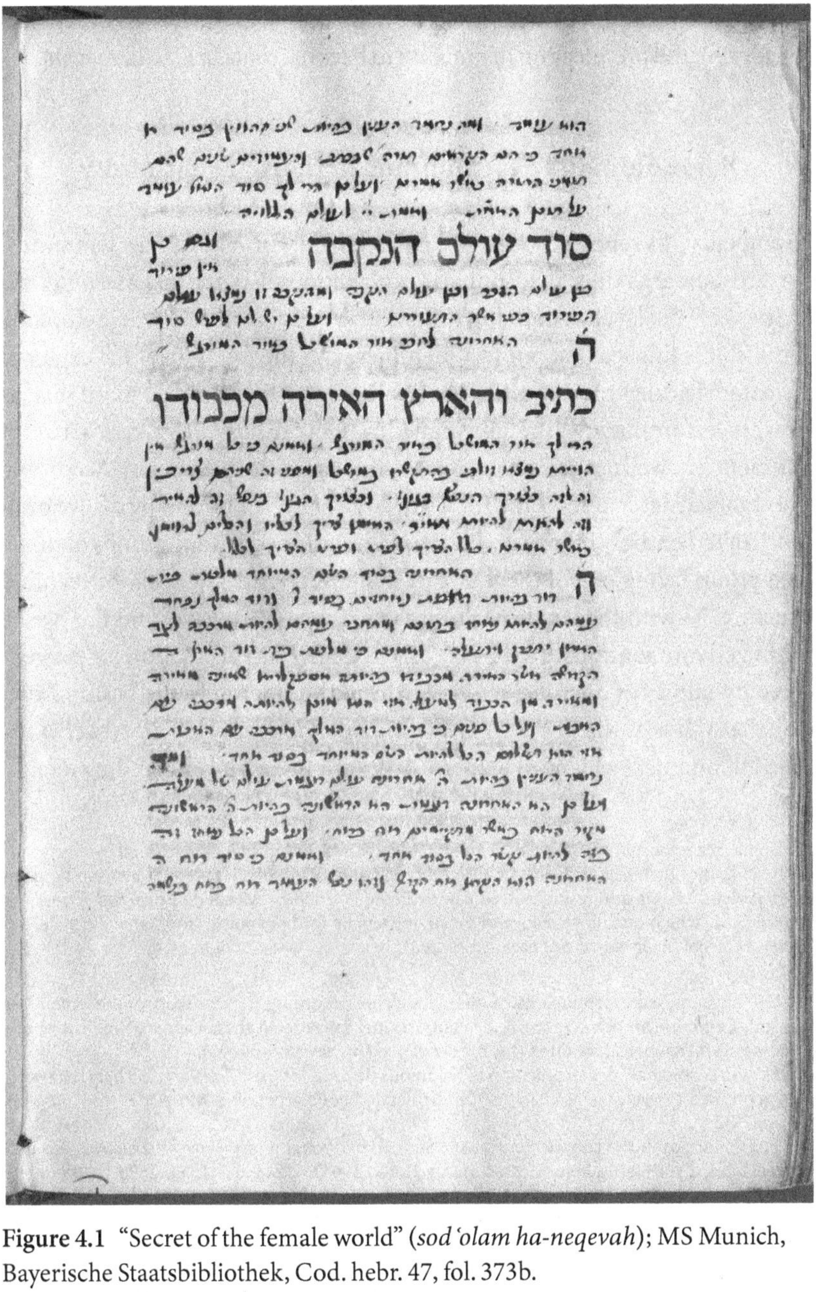
סוד עולם הנקבה
כתיב והארץ האירה מכבודו

Figure 4.1 "Secret of the female world" (*sod 'olam ha-neqevah*); MS Munich, Bayerische Staatsbibliothek, Cod. hebr. 47, fol. 373b.

paradigm that cannot be reconciled with the dogmatic assertions of scholars concerning the predilection of *malkhut* to become male in Castilian texts.[64]

4.4 Solomon's Sea: Standing in Eternal Femininity

To embellish its repeated assertion of the female world's steadfast femininity, our text embarks on a theosophical explanation of (*yam shel Shelomo*; see Figure 4.2), the laver containing water for priestly purification in Solomon's Temple. It is this sea that our text identifies with the fountain at the center of the paradisiacal garden awaiting the penitent. It is likewise this motif that, as we will see, foreshadows the appearance in 1286 of *Shushan ha-'edut*'s "rose of testimony," as well as the Zohar's celebrated rose of thirteen petals. According to its biblical descriptions, the sea was a large basin supported by twelve oxen constructed entirely of brass, with the oxen stationed in four groups of three, each group facing one of the four cardinal directions. The sea's thirteenfold structure[65]—with the single basin situated above the twelve, and the twelve organized into four quadrants—occasions de León's speculation on the gendered dynamics of divinity.[66] Initially, the author identifies the basin resting atop the twelve as the lower female world, *malkhut*, situated atop twelve angelic attendants, "valiant daughters," who are likewise gendered as female.

the Zohar read the phrase *neqevah temimah* (i.e., a "female without blemish"; Leviticus 4:28, 32) in a manner that is equivalent to our text's affirmations of *malkhut*'s abiding femininity; compare Scholem, "Shene quntresim le-R. Moshe de León," 371–384 = Moses de León, *Sod 'Eser sefirot belimah*, 381, which qualifies the love of the divine female for her spouse (the righteous male, i.e., *yesod*) as eternal (*neqevato ohevet tamid la-ṣaddiq*).

[64] On the supposed exceptionality of our text's claims regarding the eternality of the female, see Wolfson, *Luminal Darkness*, 7–8n.80. By contrast, Idel interpreted these claims as indicative of a broad-based theosophical tradition (see his *Privileged Divine Feminine*, 93).

[65] For the cosmological interpretation of Solomon's Sea, see *Midrash Tadshe* §. 2. There the twelve oxen are linked to twelve constellations, paralleling de León's account in Moses de León, *Shushan ha-'edut*, 332.

[66] For this topos in the zoharic corpus, see Simeon bar Yoḥai [attr.], *Sefer ha-Zohar*, 3 vols., ed. Reuven Margaliyot (Jerusalem: Mossad Harav Kook, 1964) = Zohar 1:155a, 259b (*Hashmaṭot*), and 251b (*Hashmaṭot*), which appears also in Simeon bar Yoḥai [attr.], *Zohar ḥadash*, ed. Reuven Margaliyot (Jerusalem: Mossad ha-Rav Kook, 1953), 8b. In the printed text, this discussion is collated with *Sitre otiyyot*, though Ronit Meroz has ascribed the fragment to which the discussion belongs to the Castilian kabbalist Joseph Angelet, based on parallel material in that author's *Kupat ha-rokhelin* (MS Oxford, Bodleian Library, Opp. 228 [Neubauer 1618], fol. 188a–b). See Ronit Meroz, "R. Joseph Angelet and His Zoharic Writings" [in Hebrew], in *Ḥiddushe Zohar: Meḥqarim ḥadashim be-sifrut ha-Zohar*, ed. Ronit Meroz (Tel Aviv: Tel Aviv University Press, 2007), 334–340, esp. 305; see also *Zohar ḥadash*, 51b (where the twelve oxen are assigned to the female world) and compare 55a. These zoharic iterations of this motif agree that the oxen correspond to the female world, whereas the sea, sometimes identified as the sea of *ḥokhmah*, is male.

Figure 4.2 Early eighteenth-century rendering of Solomon's Sea resting upon twelve oxen; Conrad Mel, הים מוצק, *dissertatio theologico-philologica, de Mari Aeneo, seu labro magno templi Salomonis, 1 Reg. VII. & II. Chron. IV.* (Regiomontum [=Königsberg]: Reusnerus, 1702), 2–3 (interleaf).

The twelve attendants correspond to the twelve tribes of Israel, oriented toward the four corners of the world, and rallying around four banners.

> There is a secret about [Solomon's] Sea, which stands upon twelve oxen. As it says, "It stands upon twelve oxen, three facing north, three facing west, three facing south, and three facing east, and the sea is upon them from above" (2 Chronicles 4:4; 1 Kings 7:25). And truly all of these twelve oxen are female in their adornment of the female who stands over them <the male [*sic*]> from above.[67]

Somewhere along its path of transmission, it seems, a copyist corrupted the text, imposing the female's subordination to the male, where it is evidently alien to the flow of the passage. Either an earlier copyist of our text or, more likely, Meir ben Isaac ha-Levi, the sixteenth-century scribe responsible for producing the single witness to this portion of our text, inserted the infelicitous word "the male" (*ha-zakhar*) into this sentence, thus bringing our text into artificial agreement with conventions of gendered speculation known from other sources.[68] Indicative of the workshop in which it was produced, our manuscript bears many corruptions. But such corruptions multiply where the text's bolder pronouncements on gender appear and thus merit careful scrutiny.[69] We can emend the text, to read much more clearly: "And truly all of these twelve oxen are female in their beautification of the female who stands over them . . . from above."[70] Our emendation is consistent with what is explicated in the continuation of the text:

> And since we are clarifying this, we must explain a secret concerning the subject of the four banners that stand as "a standard to nations" (Isaiah 11:10). You may know that they are adornments of the female standing over them (*tiqqune ha-neqevah ha-'omedet 'alehem*), and all of them are in the

[67] MS Munich, Bayerische Staatsbibliothek, Cod. hebr. 47, fol. 366a.

[68] MS Munich, Bayerische Staatsbibliothek, Cod. hebr. 47, fol. 366a. On the harried conditions in which the scribes of Adelkind's Venice workshop labored, see annotations to sec 1.7, in Chapter 1.

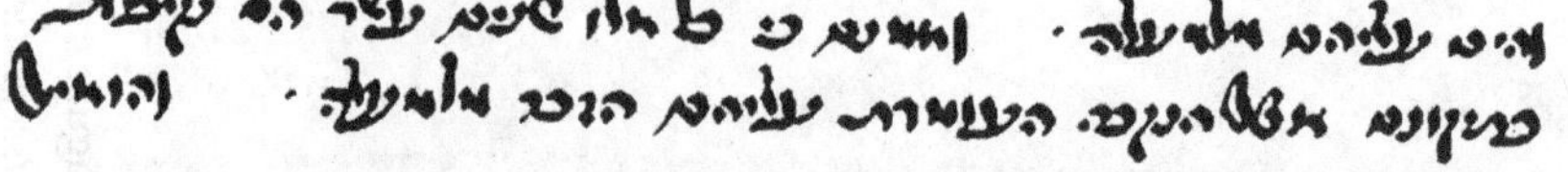

[69] These observations are reinforced by the comparison of the Munich fragment with the portion of our text preserved in MS New York, Jewish Theological Seminary of America, 1777; see annotations to sec. 4.7 below.

[70] MS Munich, Bayerische Staatsbibliothek, Cod. hebr. 47, fol. 366a.

> secret of femininity (*be-sod ha-neqevut*),[71] caused by the female standing over them; and they are the twelve "tribes, tribes of Yah, testimony for Israel" (Psalms 2:4).[72] And the secret of this subject is that the four banners [correlate with] the secret of the four corners of the earth: east and west, north and south, [corresponding to the banners of] Judah, Ephraim, Dan, and Reuben, three tribes in each corner.[73]

This passage illustrates well how the scribal miscorrection of texts amounts to a form of quasi-censorship in the transmission of kabbalistic androgynology. Additionally, it posits a female-female relationship between the lowest sefirah (*malkhut*) and the angelic throngs, and the twelve tribes of Israel who support her (both of which are gendered as female). Insofar as the female world of angels issues from the female hypostasis of the Godhead, we find another instance where the differential assignment of gender on the basis of benefactor versus beneficiary roles is not absolute. In her emanatory posture toward the angelic world, the divine bride does not become male. But in terms of the broader archive of medieval kabbalah, this paradigm is less exceptional than it might at first blush appear. In fact, the female personification of angels as bridesmaids to the divine bride is a common component of the marriage lore attested in the zoharic corpus.[74]

Going further, our text does not limit its exegesis of Solomon's Sea to subordinating the female attendants to the lower female. It describes a supernal thirteenfold structure from which the lower female extends. The supernal thirteenfold structure follows the same pattern as that below, but with an alternately gendered hierarchy. Instead of a single female gradation atop twelve female entities, this higher-order thirteenfold consists of the hidden world

[71] Later, MS Munich, Bayerische Staatsbibliothek, Cod. hebr. 47, fol. 367b, we read, regarding the lower female world, that "this world has a beautification [as] the foundation of the separate entities (*tiqqun yesod ha-nifradim*) as in the sublunary world, according to the secret of the twelve oxen."

[72] On the banners of the tribes, see Numbers Rabbah 2:10. On the banners in the kabbalah of Girona, see Ezra of Girona, "Perush Shir ha-Shirim," 489–490; Naḥmanides, *Commentary on the Torah*, on Numbers 2:2; Azriel of Girona, *Commentarius in Aggadoth*, 72–73. On this topos in de León's earlier writings, see Bar-Asher, "*Sefer ha-Ne'lam*," 213 ff.; and Bar-Asher, "The Earliest Citation from *Sefer ha-Zohar* and from Whence the *Book of Zohar* Received Its Name" [in Hebrew], *Kabbalah* 39 (2017): 79–156, here 150–156. In de León's theosophical writings, see his *Responsa*, printed in Isaiah Tishby, *Studies in Kabbalah and Its Branches: Researches and Sources* [in Hebrew] (Jerusalem: Magnes, 1982), 36–63, here 40–41. On early esoteric speculation concerning the twelve tribes, see Gershom Scholem, *The Origins of the Kabbalah*, trans. Allan Arkush (Princeton, NJ: Princeton University Press, 1987), 64–65. On the identification of the twelve tribes with the oxen of Solomon's Sea, see de León, *Shushan ha-'edut*, 332; and Zohar 1:155a, 240b–241a, 2:164b, 244a–b.

[73] MS Munich, Bayerische Staatsbibliothek, Cod. hebr. 47, fol. 366a.

[74] See, for example, Zohar 2:133b–134a.

(already gendered as female) resting upon twelve male gradations—the spiritual entities comprising the intermediate world.[75] Just as we saw in our text's penitential theosophy, the figure of twelve results from a commonplace of kabbalistic speculation involving a doubling of the sefirot. Accordingly, the twelve male attributes are equal to the six sefirot comprising the intermediate world. Both ontologically, then, and in terms of gender, the text distinguishes this set of twelve, which is positioned squarely within the domain of divinity, by virtue of its masculinity. This stands in contrast to the femininity assigned by our text to the twelve mundane tribes of Israel.

> The female [i.e., *malkhut*] stands over the twelve oxen, for she receives from . . . the twelve above. For the supernal world stands above the twelve pillars, which are spiritual entities (*ruḥaniyyim*) above.[76] And the lower world stands above the twelve "tribes, tribes of Yah, testimony for Israel" (Psalms 2:4). But those supernal ones above are males. And the lower ones below are females. And the female standing over them never becomes male.[77] And truly, because the lower world is female, never reverting [to male], this is the secret of [the verse:] "Many daughters have acted valiantly, but you rise above all of them" (Proverbs 31:29).

Readers of the manuscript witness this passage confront another case where the scribe has, consciously or not, introduced extraneous ideation into the text. Here again he has obfuscated a paradigmatic feature of our text's speculation, in this case, by distorting an additional affirmation of the divine female's enduring femininity. It is evident, however, even amid the textual corruptions, that the intention of the composition is to once again affirm that *malkhut*, in her superordinate stature above the twelve angelic throngs, does not become male.

As we will observe when returning to the topic of Solomon's Sea (see sec. 4.6 below), our text goes on to allude to yet a third thirteenfold structure.

[75] This figure is also attested in Moses de León, *Sefer ha-Rimmon*, 191–192.

[76] On the identification of the twelve tribes with the lower sefirot, see, for example, Zohar 1:155a, 158a, 241a.

[77] On the errors characteristic of Adelkind's scriptorium, see, again, sec. 1.7, in Chapter 1. We emend the text to read ואין הנקבה העומדת עליהם חוזרת זכר לעולם. See fol. 366b:

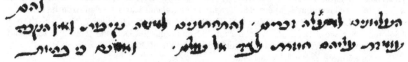

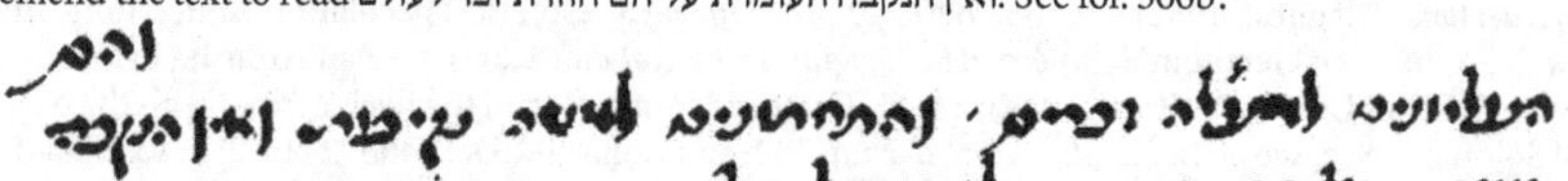

But with respect to the two thirteenfolds already delineated, let us visualize how de León coordinates these patterns with his three-worlds speculation. If we step back to bring the fuller panorama into view, it becomes clear that the two sets of thirteen reduce to a threefold female-male-female chain. In this sequence, the upper female, *binah*, as representative of the hidden world, stands above the twelve male tiers comprising the intermediate world. These twelve, in turn, give rise to the eternally female lower world of *malkhut* (which, in turn, manifests the twelve female angelic throngs). This pattern, which underscores the perennial character of the female world, is a rather complex way of calling to mind the simpler premise that within the divinity, the male is situated between two females.

4.5 Male Between Two Females, Female Between Two Males

Scholars have observed that, in Castilian kabbalah, the "love triangle" positioning of the human male between two females provides the basis of a conjugal ethic, which charges the male subject with the mandate of making himself androgynous, that is, becoming "male and female."[78] He accomplishes this goal by binding himself to two females at once—his human wife and the *shekhinah* who alights upon him because, through his marriage, he reproduces the supernal pattern of androgyny. In contrast to the situation in which the male facet of the Godhead is bound between two divine female worlds, this mimetic rationale for marriage positions a human male between one female who is divine and one who is human.

Still, another triangle involves the positioning of a divine female between two males, one divine, one human.[79] By triangulating gender in this way, our text shifts its focus from the female-male-female triangle that is fully circumscribed within the bounds of divine ontology (i.e., the three-worlds triad of *binah*, the medial sefirot, and *malkhut*), to an overlapping male-female-male triangle, which comprises both divine and human personae. In fact, our text subordinates this male-female-male triad, below, to the female-male-female triad, above. But in contrast to the angelological tradition that affirmed the femininity of the created world of angelic throngs

[78] See, for example, Tishby, *Wisdom of the Zohar*, 3:1355.

[79] On the triangulation of the divine family, see Sachs-Shmueli, "'I Arouse the Shekhina'"; Abrams, "Divine Jealousy," 7–54; Idel, "Feminine Aspect," 91–110.

vis-à-vis *malkhut*, here our text posits masculinity within the created world. The behavior of the righteous human male below imitates that of the male attribute of righteousness in the divine world, identified with King Solomon, whereas the lower world, *malkhut*, mediates between above and below. Here, again, notwithstanding the embrace by males on both sides, the perpetual femininity of the lower world endures.

> For the secret of that [i.e., lower] world is grasped above, and grasped below; and all of its qualities consist in [its] standing between above and below. And it is necessary to inform you concerning the secret of King Solomon, peace upon him, whom the sages called "a king to whom peace belongs."[80] He is a secret of the male world. And, truly, the "righteous foundation of the world" (Proverbs 10:25) stands between two females of the world;[81] he takes from one and gives to another. Likewise, in the secret of the lower world, which is the perpetual female (*ha-neqevah temidit*) standing between two males—the "righteous life of the world" is above [her],[82] and she receives from him; and the righteous below, to whom she bestows below. And then she stands between two righteous men, as the sages taught; the moon only shines during such a time when there is a righteous man [found] in that generation. And this is because she stands between two righteous [males], a righteous [male] above, and a righteous [man] below. . . . And therefore this is the secret of the aforementioned lower world, whose motion pertains to that which is above and below.[83]

It is, again, a touchstone of de León's kabbalah, especially of his teachings about the commandments in *Sefer ha-Rimmon*, to stress the sacramental efficacy of righteous deeds, that is, how performing the commandments yields an outpouring of blessing from the divine world. The efficacy of the commandments is such that, symbolically speaking, their performance stimulates moonlight.[84] The righteous behavior of men influences the female world,

[80] See b. Shevu'ot, 35b; and *Sefer ha-Bahir*, §. XVI:13–14 (44), 182; Elliot R. Wolfson, *Along the Path: Studies in Kabbalistic Myth, Symbolism, and Hermeneutics* (Albany: State University of New York, 1995), 205n71; and Wolfson, *Language, Eros, Being*, 163.

[81] See b. Ḥagigah, 12b; *Sefer ha-Bahir*, §. XX:2 (71), 190; Azriel of Girona, *Commentarius in Aggadoth*, 34.

[82] Based on Daniel 12:7. See Genesis Rabbah, 1:5; Zohar 1:4b, 132a, 135b, 164a, 167b.

[83] MS Munich, Bayerische Staatsbibliothek, Cod. hebr. 47, fol. 367b.

[84] In the present case, the masculinity of the righteous is intended. On the efficacy of women in medieval kabbalah, however, see Sachs-Shmueli, "Image of the Prophetess"; Idel, *Kabbalah and Eros*, 122–125, 247–250; Idel, *Privileged Divine Feminine*, 16, 182–183 and 213; and Brown, "Reason a Woman Is Obligated."

identified with the moon, to bestow divine substance to humans. The moon shines, in turn, because it is illuminated by the sun, that is, the male world above her.[85] But again, neither the illumination of the lower female world by the male above her, nor her function as a benefactor vis-à-vis the human male, undoes her femininity, the perpetuity of which is stated explicitly and repeatedly. Nor, moreover, does the receptive function of the human male render him female. Rather, in receiving from the lower female, the human male recapitulates the receptive function of the divine male, who, "standing between two females,"[86] is, in turn, the beneficiary of a higher female benefactor situated in the hidden world. Though the lower female is unwavering in her femininity, she, like the male, vacillates in her orientation, insofar as her "motion pertains to that which is above and below" her. Such vacillation may relate to the upturning of the *dalet*, the letter that represented the "female world" in the aforementioned account of the *alef*. It also anticipates our text's account of the lower female's shifting indices, which we will examine below (sec. 4.7).

In surveying these overlapping triads, we see once again that the differentiated economic functions of receptivity and bestowal do not determine gender in any rigid sense. With respect to *malkhut*, specifically, who is situated at the intersection of the two triads, her female perpetuity is not qualified by the fluctuations of her role within the distribution of divine resources.

4.6 Solomon's Sea (Again): The Pattern of Female Superordination

Returning to the speculative topos of Solomon's Sea, we recall that one particular feature of this thirteenfold pattern is that it facilitates a binary subdivision of the thirteen into one basin, above, and twelve supports below.

[85] In reference to the Hebrew writings of Moses de León, Scholem noted the connection between the conventional association of *shekhinah* with the moon, on the one hand, and the astrological notion, on the other hand, that the moon has "no light of her own" but merely refracts the light of the masculine sun. See Moses de León, *Shushan ha-'edut*, 338n.60; and Moses de León, *Sod 'Eser sefirot belimah*, 381 and n. 79, where the patriarchal economic dynamic is clear: "And understand that the sun is the matter of the male who gives nourishment and resources to the female, for, in her being the moon above, it is known that she has no splendor of her own whatsoever."

[86] On the situation of the male *tiferet* between the two females, *binah* and *malkhut*, reflected in Jacob's marriage to two sisters, see de León, *Responsa*, 40–45; de León, *Shushan ha-'edut*, 343; and compare Zohar 1:153b; 2:6b.

The binary facet of this thirteenfold pattern helps the text depict ontological relationships obtaining between worlds, such that the basin corresponds to a source structure and the twelve oxen indicate elements receiving their substance from that source. This pattern applies to the lower female world as the reservoir for the thirteen angelic throngs below her. It applies also to the upper female world as the font of the twelve male gradations of the intermediate world.[87] Here we pick up the thread of our text's articulation of a fourfold isomorphism that correlates the angelic throngs to the divine realm. The text emphasizes a correspondence between the angels and the divinity on the basis of their mutual identification with the four sublunary elements and four corners of the earth. Again, the fourfold structure is a feature of the Solomon's Sea pattern, insofar as the twelve oxen face the four cardinal directions (in four groups of three oxen each).

> And this is the secret of the four [tribal encampments] below that are bound and emerge according to the secret of the four [archangels] that are above. And those are bound to the four principal elements, and yet both above and below they are twelve [i.e., 4 × 3]. And the females stand atop their backs, and everything is one pattern, and they are thirteen above, and thirteen in the middle, and thirteen below.[88]

What this terse passage reports concerning the divine pattern that is reproduced by the angelic, elemental, and political realms is consistent with what we found earlier in the text. At every iteration of the Solomon's Sea pattern, a fourfold functions as a factor of the twelvefold. Yet here the text applies this isomorphism to yet a third ontological realm, namely, the sublunary realm. To the domain below the moon belong the four cardinal directions, the four elements, and the mundane twelve tribes that constitute the twelvefold political body of Israel. In both the case of the angelic twelvefold and the divine twelvefold, each twelvefold stands in a situation of ontological dependency upon a female. And this is precisely how we interpret the text's reference to "the females"—in the plural (i.e., both *binah* and *malkhut*)—that stand on the backs of the two fourfold (= twelvefold) structures, respectively. Here, again, the text posits that in each thirteenfold, the basin is female, resting upon twelve supports.

[87] These twelve reduce to six, namely, the six intermediate sefirot, from *ḥesed* to *yesod*.
[88] MS Munich, Bayerische Staatsbibliothek, Cod. hebr. 47, fol. 370a.

Once more, it is compelling that the thirteenfold pattern is one that privileges the female. In the first instance, a female (*binah*) rests atop males (the six medial sefirot). In the second instance, a female (*malkhut*) rests atop females (the angelic throngs). In the case of the sublunary realm, our text does not explicate precisely which female entity embodies the basin, nor does it specify the gender of the mundane entities that correspond to its supports. Each thirteenfold, while repeating a basic pattern, has different characteristics. Still, it appears from the continuation of the text that just as the twelvefold angelic realm arrays itself in relation to *malkhut*, so too Israel, which comprises the twelve tribes, should orient itself toward the *shekhinah*. This suggests that *malkhut* too functions as the ontological reservoir for the twelvefold mundane realm, perhaps mediated by her indwelling within the angelic world.[89]

> And you will find that the way all the worlds [are composed is that] they exist by the secret of thirteen. And thus, you may know that there is one matter and one pattern for all. And so you may understand that the secret of the twelve below is the twelve "tribes of Yah, testimony for Israel" (Psalms 2:4), three toward each side, as it says, "three facing north, three facing west, three facing south, three facing east—and the sea is upon them from above" (2 Chronicles 4:4; 1 Kings 7:25). There you have twelve, and [with] the sea standing above them, there are thirteen, as it says, and "the sea is upon them from above." And truly, "All of their hind parts were inward" (ibid.); you will find the reason that "all of their hind parts were inward"; you may know how the four corners [of the earth] are the supernal elements, from which everything emerges. And therefore "their hind parts were inward" out of respect for the four corners of the world, so that they would not turn their backs toward them. And this is a warning below that a person should not turn his back toward the *shekhinah*.[90] All the more so [does this warning apply to] those above who draw their "hind parts inward" [out of respect] for the glory of the four corners. And their faces were turned toward each side so that they would be influenced by that abundance overflowing therefrom (*nishpa'im me-ha-shefa' ha-hu ha-shofe'a me-hem*).[91] . . . And truly, you may know that this matter pertains [also] to

[89] While de León presents the archetypal twelve tribes of the divinity as male, the historical twelve tribes belong to the world of separation that connotes femininity (as do the twelve angelic throngs); see MS Munich, Bayerische Staatsbibliothek, Cod. hebr. 47, fol. 367b.

[90] Loosely based on b. Berakhot 6b; also see b. Yoma 53a.

[91] We have emended *nishpa'im* from the corrupted *nishpat*.

above, insofar as the supernal world stands over twelve—and the sea [i.e., *binah*] above them, and they are thirteen above, so all the worlds are in the secret of thirteen.[92]

Let us parse the details of this highly technical passage. Its author's point about each thirteenfold reproducing the same pattern is exemplified by the fourfold organization of each twelvefold, with a superordinate female comprising a thirteenth unit above. But the fact that each thirteenfold has different features, in terms of both gender and ontological status, adds complexity to the deceptively simple pattern they share. On the one hand, each twelvefold manifests its reverence for the female above it by orienting itself toward the four cardinal points. On the other hand, both the mundane and angelic twelvefolds act from outside of the divinity toward the lower divine female, whereas the orientation of the supernal twelvefold constitutes a connection to the upper female from within the ontological boundaries of divinity. Notwithstanding the variations accommodated by this paradigm, Solomon's Sea is a speculative topos that privileges the female in terms of rank in each of its iterations. This thoroughgoing paradigm of female superordination did not achieve prominence within the long history of kabbalistic speculation on gender. On the contrary, this particular topos, like many others in our text, only persists, as we will see below (sec. 4.8), in dislocated vestiges in later writings of Moses de León and the Zohar. Though the topos largely disappears from the tradition of commentary on the Zohar, its recovery demonstrates a more supple discourse on gender at the root of de León's theosophical project.

4.7 *Dalet/Heh*: Shifting Index of the Female

We turn now to traverse another intersection of our text's understanding of "male and female" with its discourse on the Hebrew letters. In this case, we encounter the shifting index of the lower female, *malkhut*, who is alternatingly signified by two Hebrew letters. Sometimes she is indicated by *dalet* and sometimes by *heh*, depending on the status of her conjunction with the gradations above her. The *heh* of this index is none other than the final

[92] MS Munich, Bayerische Staatsbibliothek, Cod. hebr. 47, fol. 370a–b.

letter of the Tetragrammaton, YHVH.[93] Like the first *heh* of YHVH, which corresponds to the female *binah*,[94] the Name's final *heh* corresponds to the lower female attribute of divinity, namely, *malkhut*. The text calls this letter the "secret of the female world" (Figure 4.1). In his discussion of this "secret," Moses de León stitches together a dazzling patchwork of correspondences related to the conjunction of male and female worlds, that is, *tiferet* and *malkhut*. Though the two would ideally remain conjoined to ensure the unity of the Godhead, the female—as the foundation of the separate entities (*yesod ha-nifradim*)[95] and the source of the world of separation (*'olam ha-perud*)—is positioned at the ontological boundary separating divinity from creation.[96] We have already established our text's lunisolar characterization of *malkhut* to convey the idea that, when she bestows light on the created world, she depends upon the male world as the source of her radiance. In the speculation adduced here, we encounter a variation on this idea. But in this case, the text translates the lunisolar motif into the register of prophetology. When Israel's prophets beheld their visions, the phenomenon resulted from the convergence of two gradations of divine light shining in tandem.[97] The two gradations of light are the intelligible light, which is imperceptible as such, and the sensible light. The former is radiated from the male, and the latter is emitted by the female. Only by clothing the intelligible light within the sensible light do prophetic images become perceptible as phenomena.

[93] On the letter *heh* in our text and in the early writings of de León, see Scholem, "Eine unbekannte mystische Schrift," 117n.1; Alexander Altmann, "*Sefer Or Zarua'* by R. Moses de Leon: Introduction, Critical Text, and Notes" [in Hebrew], *Kobez al Yad* 9, no. 19 (1980): 219–293, here 282, esp. n. 248; Asi Farber, "On the Sources of Rabbi Moses de León's Early Kabbalistic System" [in Hebrew], *Jerusalem Studies in Jewish Thought* 3, nos. 1–2 (1984): 67–96, here 80n.28; and the extensive note in Wolfson, "Letter Symbolism," 202n.26.

[94] For an excursus on *binah* as the initial *heh* of the Tetragrammaton, "the great *heh*," see MS Munich, Bayerische Staatsbibliothek, Cod. hebr. 47, fol. 372b.

[95] MS Munich, Bayerische Staatsbibliothek, Cod. hebr. 47, fol. 367b.

[96] Compare the discussion of "secret of the female world," in Moses de León, *Shushan ha-'edut*, 332.

[97] Other discussions in de León include an additional gradation of light, "the brilliant light" (*or ha-bahir*), which may be equivalent to the intelligible light. See Elliot R. Wolfson, "Hai Gaon's Letter and Commentary to 'Aleynu': Further Evidence of De Leon's Pseudepigraphic Activity," *Jewish Quarterly Review* 81, nos. 3–4 (1991): 365–410, here 387nn.87–92. This terminology, which belongs already to the speculation of Ezra of Girona, is closely related to Neoplatonic classifications of graduated light, which developed in conversation with and translation from medieval Arabic sources; see Azriel of Girona, *Commentarius in Aggadoth*, 34n.15; Scholem, *Origins of Kabbalah*, 224; Y. Tzvi Langermann, "Gradations of Light and Pairs of Opposites: Two Theories and Their Role in Abraham Bar Ḥiyya's *Scroll of the Revealer*," in *Texts in Transit in the Medieval Mediterranean*, ed. Y. Tzvi Langermann and Robert G. Morrison (University Park: Pennsylvania State University Press, 2016), 47–66. On light speculation in Bar Ḥiyya and Pseudo-Dionysius, see Adeena Krentzman-Ossi, "The Implications of the Metaphysics of Light of Abraham Bar Ḥiyya," *Granot* 2 (2002): i–xvii; Avishai Bar-Asher, "The *Kuzari* and Early Kabbalah: Between Integration and Interpretation Regarding the Secrets of the Sacrificial Rite," *Harvard Theological Review* 116, no. 2 (2023): 228–253, esp. 236–237.

But while our text has thus far represented the relationship of the female world to the male in terms of the former's dependency upon the latter, this passage relies, to a greater extent than elsewhere, on a rhetoric of male-female reciprocity. This reciprocity may result from the fact that here, in contrast to the lunisolar paradigm wherein the female merely transmits the male's light, our text endows the female with a positive quality of light all her own.[98]

> And . . .[99] there should be no separation between the male world and the female world; but from that female exists the world of separation (*'olam ha-perud*). . . . And therefore we must explain the secret of the final *heh* [of the Tetragrammaṭon], to bind intelligible light with sensible light. . . . For no sensible thing would have any essence were it not bound with something intelligible; and, for this reason, the two of them need one another, just as a soul requires a body and as a body requires a soul—one making the other to shine, and this makes it illuminate. The artisan needs his utensils, and the utensils the artisan, as we have said. The general necessitates the particular and the particular necessitates the general.[100]

But immediately after emphasizing the mutual reciprocity of male and female,[101] the text returns to accentuate an asymmetrical dependency of the female upon the male. Here de León introduces the notion that the final letter of the divine name remains incomplete—in the sign of the *dalet*, an emblem of poverty.[102] It remains incomplete, that is, unless it unites with the male to establish the *heh*, thus completing the Tetragrammaton.[103] Such a union obtains between the sovereign House of David, corresponding to the female world (i.e., *malkhut*, sovereignty), and the supernal patriarchs, who symbolically populate the world of the medial sefirot. We have already seen how the

[98] See Abrams, "Light of Her Own."

[99] Here the Munich text lacks a phrase that appears in MS New York, Jewish Theological Seminary of America 1777, fol. 23a: "And from thenceforth is the female world."

[100] MS Munich, Bayerische Staatsbibliothek, Cod. hebr. 47, fol. 374b. See de León's discussion of Rabbi Ishmael's thirteen hermeneutical principles concerning the reciprocal dependency that obtains between the general and the particular (see Figure 1.3); printed in Ronit Meroz, "Kabbalah, Science and Pseudo-Science in Ramdal's Commentary on the Thirteen Attributes," in Niehoff, Meroz, and Garb, *And This Is for Yehuda*, 123–143, here §. 19, p. 142, and see the discussion on p. 136.

[101] Compare the parallel discussion of the reciprocal dependency in Jochanan H. A. Wijnhoven, ed., "Sefer ha-Mishkal: Text and Study" (PhD diss., Brandeis University, 1964) = Moses de León, *Sefer ha-Mishqal*, 45.

[102] For earlier speculation concerning the letter *dalet* in the pre-sefirotic writings of de León, see Bar-Asher, "*Sefer ha-Ne'lam*," 223, 308.

[103] See Jeremy Phillip Brown, *A World of Piety: The Aims of Castilian Kabbalah* (Stanford, CA: Stanford University Press, 2025), esp. chap. 4 ("Making Other People: The Formative Aspirations of Zoharic Piety").

dalet, as an emblem of the female world, depends on the *vav*, which signifies the male, in our text's speculation on the three letters that are discernible within the form of the *alef*. Here it is perhaps implied that the *heh*—which looks like a *dalet* with an added stroke descending vertically along its left side—is an apt pictograph for the conjunction of the *dalet* (ד) with the linear *vav* (ו): ה.

In keeping with its exploration of prophetology,[104] the text adduces another motif that, like the symbolism of the sun's conjunction with the moon, accentuates the female's dispossession. It identifies the female with "the mirror that does not shine" by itself, but rather receives her light from *tif'eret*, "the shining mirror," that is, the male.[105]

> The final *heh* is the secret of the unified name, which is the Kingdom of the House of David, when the Patriarchs cling to the secret of *dalet*. And King David is appointed with them, becoming grasped in their midst, and conjoined with them to become a chariot for the Lord, may He be blessed and exalted.[106] And truly, the Kingdom of the House of David is the Holy "Land which is enlightened from His glory" (Ezekiel 43:2), being a mirror that does not shine [in itself], but illuminates from the glory above. Then, he [David] is prepared to become a chariot with the Patriarchs. And truly, when King David becomes a chariot with the Patriarchs, then he is the perfection of everything, being the unified name in the secret of one. And how pleasant is this subject, when the final *heh* [of the Tetragrammaton] is a world patterned upon the upper world (*'olam dugmat 'olam shel ma'lah*).[107]

When the lower female world appears as *heh*, as the culmination of the unified name, she recapitulates the pattern of the upper world. The above-below correspondence underscored in this passage might appear to suggest that the binding of the lower female to the intermediate world reproduces

[104] B. Yevamot 49b. For earlier speculation on these categories of ancient rabbinic prophetology, see Azriel of Girona, *Commentarius in Aggadoth*, 33–34; Roland Goetschel, "The Conception of Prophecy in the Writings of Moses de León and Joseph Gikatilla" [in Hebrew], *Jerusalem Studies in Jewish Thought* 8 (1989): 217–238, esp. 222–224; and sources adduced in Wolfson, *Through a Speculum*, 351n.86. See also the text of de León, printed in Abrams, "Divine Yearning," 21.

[105] For a zoharic passage linking the lunar character of the *shekhinah* with her poverty, see Zohar 1:249b.

[106] Compare a similar discussion in Moses de León, *Shushan ha-'edut*, 334, concerning the completion of the chariot with *dalet*.

[107] MS Munich, Bayerische Staatsbibliothek, Cod. hebr. 47, fol. 374b.

the male-female pattern of the hidden world—where *binah* is bound to *ḥokhmah.*[108] But, curiously, the text does not in this case identify *binah* with the upper *heh*, as one might anticipate, nor does any male-female polarity between *ḥokhmah* and *binah* dictate the isomorphism.

Rather, the lower world matches the upper because, like the upper world, the lower *heh* yields an outpouring of spirit. Ultimately, then, the text's speculation on prophetic inspiration gives rise to pneumatology.[109] The holy spirit, the very source of prophetic inspiration, springs, per our text, from the lower *heh*. In fact, the discharge of the holy spirit proceeding from the letter *heh* is a motif known already from de León's pretheosophical writings.[110] But here the exhalation of spirit from the lower *heh* is but the final outpouring of a continuous stream of spirit rooted in *ḥokhmah* (and not *binah*, which is typically signified by the upper *heh*). The sefirah *ḥokhmah* is identified here as "the holy" (*ha-qodesh*), which the female draws down through her bond to the male world.

> And how pleasant it is when the final *heh* is a world [that is] patterned after the supernal world! And therefore, the final *heh* is patterned after the first *heh* [of the Tetragrammaton]—since the first *heh* is the source of spirit <by which all the other spirits above are sustained. And the final *heh* follows its pattern, since it is [also] a spirit, by which all the other spirits below are sustained. And in this way, the spirits are sustained>[111] spirit in spirit. And therefore, everything is held, one by another, everything being bound in a single secret. And truly, the secret of the final spirit is called "the holy spirit," and this is a [lower] soul subsisting spirit-in-spirit with the [upper] soul (*nefesh ha-ʿomed ruaḥ be-ruaḥ ba-neshamah*), everything being one in a strong bond.[112] And truly, the secret of this subject pertains to the holy

[108] On the patterning of the lower world after the upper, compare Moses de León, *Shushan ha-ʿedut*, 343.

[109] On pneumatology and psychology in de León and the Zohar, see Tishby, *Wisdom of the Zohar*, 2:677–722; and Avishai Bar-Asher, "The Soul Bird: Ornithomancy and Theory of the Soul in the Homilies of Zohar Pericope Balak" [in Hebrew], in *The Zoharic Story: Studies of Zoharic Narrative*, ed. Jonatan M. Benarroch, Yehuda Liebes, and Melilla Hellner-Eshed (Jerusalem: Ben-Zvi Institute, 2017), 354–392.

[110] See Moses de León, *Sod Darkhe ha-otiyyot*, 207–211, printed in Avishai Bar-Asher, "From the Vaults of Thebes: Moses de León's Pseudepigraphic Writings on the Letters, Vowel Signs, Theonyms, and Magical Practices and the Origin of Zoharic Fiction" [in Hebrew], *Kabbalah* 51 (2022): 157–248, there 200–248. See Farber, "On the Sources," 79; Wolfson, "Letter Symbolism," 204. For the identification of the holy spirit with *malkhut*, see Moses de León, *Shushan ha-ʿedut*, 337 and (vis-à-vis *ḥokhmah*), 343.

[111] MS New York, Jewish Theological Seminary of America 1777, fol. 23b, provides language to fill a lacuna in the Munich text.

[112] On the bonding of "spirit in spirit," see Tanja Werthmann, "'Spirit to Spirit': The Imagery of the Kiss in the Zohar and Its Possible Sources," *Harvard Theological Review* 111 (2018): 586–609.

> spirit, that is, spirit from that holiness above [i.e., the *ḥokhmah-binah* conjunction], and thus is the secret of a spirit that is derived from a spirit, and is sustained one in the other; and behold the secret of the final *heh* that is sustained by the spirit above.[113]

This topos comes closer to aligning gender with the differentiated economic functions of the sefirot than the other speculative topoi we have discussed. Though the female world acts as a benefactor in facilitating prophetic phenomena, she depends upon her male benefactor in both imitating and channeling the upper spirit from *ḥokhmah*. In contrast to the Solomon's Sea topos, which emphasizes female superordination, this model does the opposite, perpetuating a framework of female dependency, even where the text deems the male to be reciprocally dependent on the female.

This paradigm of dependency is reinforced by the shifting indices of the lower female. When she is endowed in conjunction with her male benefactor, she embodies the *heh*—the completion of the Tetragrammaton. But when she is alienated from the male, she is signified by *dalet*, the image of deficiency.

> And you should know the reason it is *dalet*, and the reason it is *heh*. You should contemplate that she [i.e., the female world] is *dalet* when she is in her [state of] poverty (*dalutah*). She does not shine at all—a mirror that does not shine. Should you ask yourself, at what time? You should know it is when she does not contain the <male> (*she-enah kelulah min ha-zakhar*) [i.e., *tif'eret*].[114] For when the sun is removed from the moon, then she is called *dalet*. But at the time that the sun is drawn close to the moon,[115] then she contains the male (*she-hi kelulah min ha-zakhar*); [then] she is surely called by the letter *heh*, since she brought forth "every living creature after its kind" (Genesis 1:26).[116]

[113] MS Munich, Bayerische Staatsbibliothek, Cod. hebr. 47, fols. 374b–375a.

[114] Here MS Munich, Bayerische Staatsbibliothek, Cod. hebr. 47, fol. 375a, preserves a corrupt reading: "You should know it is when she does not contain the *heavens*." The correct reading of "the male" (*ha-zakhar*, not *shamayim*) is provided on the basis of MS New York, Jewish Theological Seminary of America 1777, fol. 23b.

[115] MS New York, Jewish Theological Seminary of America 1777, fol. 23b, again proves the better witness in this context, where the preposition *el* appears instead of *min*: "But at the time that the sun is drawn close *to* [*el*; MS Munich, Bayerische Staatsbibliothek, Cod. hebr. 47 = *by*; *min*] the moon."

[116] MS Munich, Bayerische Staatsbibliothek, Cod. hebr. 47, fol. 375a; here the proof text is Genesis 1:26, where this life-giving function is applied to the earth; hence, de León equates the female world with the womb of the earth.

If we read this characterization of the female world as beholden to the principle of feminine perpetuity upheld elsewhere in the text, then it would be false to suppose that the female's conjunction with the male causes her to become contained by or even assimilated into the male.[117] Thus, we have rendered the language of conjunction in terms of her containment of the male—that is, she contains the endowment transmitted to her by the male, who, in turn, lifts her from poverty. In this, she is integrated into the Tetragrammaton, but in some manner that does not curtail her perpetual femininity.

At the culmination of its excursus on *heh* and *dalet* as the alternating signs of the female, our text enters into an explanation of an arcane feature of the Masoretic text of Deuteronomy 22.[118] In that context, wherever the Bible introduces legislation concerning "a young woman who is a virgin" (*na'arah betulah*), the Masoretic text has *na'ar*, instead of *na'arah* with the final *heh*. According to de León's account, this scribal convention comes to disclose the secret that the *heh* does not appear, that is, the Tetragrammaton is not unified, unless male and female appear in conjunction. Accordingly, the absence of the final *heh* from the word *na'ar(ah) betulah* is due to the virginity of the subject in question, in contradistinction to her conjunction with the male.[119]

> You have known the secret of the scriptural language, "if there be a young woman who is a virgin" (*na'arah betulah*). [Whenever this language is found,] it is written as "youth" (*na'ar*). And the *heh* stands from without. Thus, in every [instance] young woman (*na'arah*) [is intended], youth

[117] On the supposed containment of the female by the male, see Wolfson, *Circle in the Square*, 80–85.

[118] For parallels to this teaching, see Moses de León, *Sefer ha-Rimmon*, 115; and Zohar 1:51b; 2:38b, 3:156b.

[119] In advancing this line of exegesis, de León is not deterred by the fact that, in terms of the scriptural mandate, the desired outcome of most cases involving a *na'arah betulah* would be to find evidence of intact virginity rather than the opposite. For the suggestion that a zoharic parallel to this de León text involves the transformation of the female into the male, see Wolfson, *Language, Eros, Being*, 326–327: "When *Shekhinah* is united with Israel from below, she is united with the male above, and this unification transforms her semiotic status from *dalet* to *he*. Underlying this linguistic symbolism is an ontological presumption: *Shekhinah* is transformed from the impoverished feminine . . . to the enriched feminine, the virgin that has united with *and transformed into the male*" (our emphasis). The chief obstacle to such a reading, at least with respect to the "Nameless Composition," is our text's insistence on the tenacity of the female world to remain so perpetually. On the polemical character of the theosophical representation of virginity, see Daniel Abrams, "The Virgin Mary as the Moon That Lacks the Sun: A Zoharic Polemic Against the Veneration of Mary," *Kabbalah* 21 (2010): 7–56.

> (*na'ar*) appears. Though it is not read [as such]. But a *heh* is not written. [And] the matter returns to its root and to its foundation. Whenever the female does not contain the male,[120] the *heh* is absent from there to indicate that the *shekhinah* is not found except in a place where male and female are conjoined together. And since a "young woman that is a virgin" is not found in conjunction with a male, it is written *na'ar*, without *heh*. And this matter comes to teach a secret, that the *heh* is not pronounced except when male and female conjoin. And because of this secret, this letter [*heh*] is in the secret of the unified name, when it [the name] is conjoined together, male and female [unite] in a single conjunction. And then the moon is illuminated by the sun, and it gives her spirit. And *heh* is called the holy spirit. . . . And without this, she is called *dalet*. And truly, when *gimel* approaches the *dalet*, and they are found together, *heh* is read. . . . And thus, YHV is a secret of the male world, [and] the final *heh* conjoins to it. And considering this, you should know the matter of the four letters of the unified name, and they are the secret of His name, exalted and blessed be He, to teach that He and His name are one. And there is no separation between those attributes at all. And He, may He blessed and exalted, is they, and they are like "a flame bound to a coal."[121]

In reiterating the idea that the conjugal union of male and female brings forth the outpouring of the holy spirit, de León reverts to the principle of male bestowal. As the text affirms here, the male benefactor is identified with *gimel*, and the female beneficiary with *dalet*.[122] This allocation of economic functions to the sefirot is based upon ancient rabbinic lore concerning the alphabetical apposition of *gimel* and *dalet*, which expresses the charitable mandate of giving to the poor (*gemol dalim*).[123] The benevolent transmission of resources from male to female, *gimel* to *dalet*, produces the alternation from *dalet* to *heh*. This action restores the primordial unity of the Tetragrammaton.[124] The shifting index assigned to the female world conveys an image of the sefirah as fluctuating between modalities. It is a picture of *malkhut* that may be hard to reconcile with the image of a steadfast "eternal

[120] This phrase is rendered according to MS New York, Jewish Theological Seminary of America 1777, fol. 23b, because the term *ha-zakhar* is omitted from the corrupt Munich witness.

[121] MS Munich, Bayerische Staatsbibliothek, Cod. hebr. 47, fol. 375a–b. The expression "a flame bound to a coal" is found in *Sefer Yeṣirah*, §. 6.

[122] See Moses de León, *Sefer ha-Rimmon*, 229; Zohar 1:3a, 51b, 234b, 244b.

[123] B. Shabbat 104b, where a similar explanation supports the apposition of *samekh* and *'ayin*.

[124] Cf. Zohar 3:90b–91a.

femininity." It is nonetheless consistent with the topos of the *dalet* turning upward at the base of the *alef* and also that of the upward-downward oscillation of the female standing between two males. In the case of the *alef*, it is important to recall that the *vav*, the cipher for the male world, also personified such oscillation. Just as this movement did not nullify the masculinity of the male, we may conclude that it does not limit the femininity of *malkhut*.

4.8 *Sub Rosa*: Migrations of de León's Earliest Speculation on Gender

What is the legacy of the gendered ontology advanced in our text? Though the fullness of its dynamism was largely overshadowed through the development of subsequent speculation—especially through the privileging of less nuanced and more ideologically opportune paradigms—de León had significant recourse to his early thinking on the topos of "male and female" throughout the course of his writings. Support for this assertion may be found already in the rhymed-prose preface of 1286's *Shushan ha-'edut*, which, per our chronology, follows on the heels of de León's earliest theosophical work.

In fact, the titular symbol of *Shushan ha-'edut*, "the rose of testimony" (Psalms 60:1) proves to be de León's axis for coordinating a double-thirteenfold order that is largely faithful to the paradigm we elicited from the Munich fragment. There, the author elaborated at least two, if not three, sets of thirteen spanning the divine, angelic, and cosmic orders. In *Shushan ha-'edut*, one thirteenfold is, just as in our text, identified with *binah*, or the hidden world, resting atop twelve supports corresponding to the six medial sefirot (which are doubled, as in our text, to reach the sum of twelve supports). Also, just as in our text, this thirteenfold, which traverses the hiatus between the hidden world of *binah* and the domain of the medial sefirot, is interpreted in light of "female shall compass male." Here, again, this prophecy calls to mind the crossing of a gendered threshold obtaining between *binah* and the "six extremities." Such flexibility does not, however, characterize the complete femininity of the lower thirteenfold. The latter is identified, as in our text, with *malkhut* and the twelvefold supporting her (here, the twelvefold pattern is instantiated by angelic, astrological, and political structures). As in the Munich fragment, de León circumscribes this domain as "the female world," which encompasses *malkhut* and the "world of separation." Perhaps most interestingly, *Shushan ha-'edut* even appears to ascribe to this domain the same steadfast femininity we encountered above. But instead of employing the terms "perpetual female" (*neqevah temidit*), or "eternal femininity" (*neqevut 'olamit*) adduced above, *Shushan ha-'edut* opts for the biblical phrase "unblemished female" (*neqevah temimah*, Leviticus 4:28, 32),[125] which—in contrast to its contextual meaning of a female animal fit for sacrifice—suggests a female whose femininity is wholly uncompromised. Her female quality is deemed perfect in roughly the same sense that Psalm 19:8 affirms that "the Torah of the Lord is perfect (*temimah*)." This epithet for the female world is juxtaposed to the characterization of *binah* as "female shall compass male," apparently to establish a functional contrast between the lower and upper females along the lines of the "Nameless Composition."

According to the rhymed-prose passage at hand, the "rose of testimony" refers specifically to *malkhut* in her fruitful embrace with *tiferet*. She is "the rose of testimony who stands in love." As a result of her union with the groom, who, in turn, embodies knowledge of the upper thirteenfold, the bride testifies to the supernal pattern (which is rooted in "the Eden of divinity," that is, the hidden world of *binah*). She thus bears witness to a divine pattern that she reproduces within the idealized ordering of creation and society.

> And thus he [i.e., *tiferet*] is known by her [i.e., *malkhut*] / like the gladness of a groom over a bride (Isaiah 62:5). / And she dwells with him in oneness. / The rose of testimony / upon the enlightened's rose of testimony is the song of friendship (Psalms 60:1). / A rose appears upon the summit of the sky / and is also revealed in ideas of delight, / in six petals according to the secret of six extremities, plus one petal in the Eden of divinity [i.e., according to the pattern of the upper thirteen [= 6 < × 2 > + *binah*)]. / . . . The rose of testimony / who stands in love [i.e., *malkhut*] / is the secret of the female world (*sod 'olam ha-neqevah*) / to unite with the seal of His glory [i.e., the covenant of circumcision sealed upon the divine], / to apprehend and know the secret of its unity. / For everything is one and there is nothing more apart from it. / And from thenceforth the worlds separated, which were mentioned (*niqqevu*) by names [of the twelve tribal chieftains; Numbers 1:17], / according to the secret of holy, scintillating stones [i.e.,

[125] Compare the use of *temimah* in MS Munich, Bayerische Staatsbibliothek, Cod. hebr. 47, fol. 372a, and MS New York Jewish Theological Seminary of America 1777, fol. 22b.

> the twelve stones of the Urim and Tummim]. / . . . All of them are engraved like seals [i.e., the twelve stones corresponding in number "to the names of the sons of Israel" (Exodus 28:21)]. / Twelve princes [are appointed over] their peoples, / a person over his camp and a person over his banner, / to establish His praise. / And the rose is above [all of] them in study, / standing upon twelve oxen.[126]

The "rose of testimony" is thus the speculative axis for doubling the upper thirteenfold pattern at the lower threshold of divinity—a motif based upon de León's earlier teachings about Solomon's Sea. The primary function of the *hieros gamos* described in the passage just adduced is the thirteenfold testimony it reproduces, which, due to the reducibility of the thirteen to one (13 = ד + ח + א), is chiefly a testimony to God's unity.[127] Though de León shifted the emphasis of his thirteenfold imagery from the sea to the rose, the two domains of symbolism dovetail in the biblical accounts of Solomon's Sea, which describe the laver's brim in terms of a rose: "Its lip was made like the lip of a rose-blossom cup" (1 Kings 7:26; 2 Chronicles 4:5; Fig. 4.2).

The rose also adorns de León's 1287 *Sefer ha-Rimmon*.[128] There the author returned to the motif that carried much of his earliest theosophical speculation, this time in conversation with earlier "commentators," apparently a reference to Ezra of Girona. The latter went no further than identifying the flora (*shushan*) with the six (*shesh*) medial sefirot, or, per de León's representation of Ezra's teaching, as the six extremities contained by *malkhut*. However, the above-cited passage from *Shushan ha-'edut* already helps us to anticipate that de León will take issue with Ezra's position. There the author had intimated that the thirteenfold rose ("standing upon twelve oxen") recapitulates the upper pattern of the six medial sefirot (implicitly doubled) with the addition of *binah* ("in six petals according to the secret of six extremities [× 2], plus one petal in the Eden of divinity"). Not only does Ezra's paradigm fail

[126] Moses de León, *Shushan ha-'edut*, 332.

[127] See Daniel Abrams, ed., *R. Asher ben David: His Complete Works and Studies in His Kabbalistic Thought (Including the Commentaries to the Account of Creation by the Kabbalists of Provence and Gerona)* [in Hebrew] (Los Angeles, CA: Cherub Press, 1996), 174; Zohar 3:233a–b (*Piqqudin*); compare *Tiqqune Zohar*, 71a; see Jonatan M. Benarroch, "'The Mystery of Unity': Poetic and Mystical Aspects of a Unique Zoharic Shema Mystery," *AJS Review* 37, no. 2 (2013): 231–256, 244. And see our discussion in Chapter 5 of a text attributed to Joseph Gikatilla called the "Secret of the Thirteen Attributes That Flow from the Supernal Crown, which are called 'Springs of Salvation'"; and Brown, *World of Piety*, chap. 3 ("Thirteen Attributes of Compassion: Judeomorphism and the Fidelity of Mimesis").

[128] Moses de León, *Sefer ha-Rimmon*, 183–184 (see the editor's s.v. *mefarshim*).

to account for the inclusion of *binah*, but Ezra explicitly identifies the species in the vernacular as a lily.[129] For de León, the species corresponding to "the rose of testimony" is truly a fragrant "rose among the thorns," rather than an odorless lily.[130]

> One must understand the content of the secret of the rose that testifies to the oneness (*shushan ha-ʿoseh ʿedut ʿal ha-aḥdut*).[131] All of the commentators enlightened in their knowledge detailed the fact that the rose indicates a single rose containing six petals, which refers to the bride [i.e., *malkhut*], and that she comprises . . . six extremities. "Behold, how good and how pleasant" (Psalms 133:1).
>
> However, one must ask, if this is so, then why is "a rose among the thorns" (Song 2:2) referred to [in Scripture], because the other [six-petaled flower] is not found "among the thorns." And moreover, if it were so that she [the bride] were composed of six extremities [based on the model of six petals], where is the "rose [among the thorns" that is mentioned in Song of Songs]? For the flower [of six petals, namely, the lily] has naught but petals alone. And what is more, it has no scent. I [nonetheless] saw that all the matters are true and there is no contradiction. But the secret of the rose that is among the thorns is [precisely] that rose which is found among them! And the petals are thirteen in number. And above her are five sepals protecting [and] surrounding her, all of them strong and shielding her.

[129] Ezra of Girona, "Perush Shir ha-Shirim," 481 (and 504): "'The shepherd among the lilies' (Song 6:3), 'hedged about by lilies' (Song 7:3), 'a lily of the valleys' (Song 2:1), and 'to gather lilies' (Song 6:2) refer to that plant known as *lliri*, which possesses six leaves and symbolizes the six supernal extremities" (adapted from Ezra ben Solomon of Girona, *Commentary on the Song of Songs and Other Kabbalistic Commentaries*, trans. Seth Brody [Kalamazoo, MI: Medieval Institute Publications, 1999], 32; our adaptation of Brody's translation is based upon our emendation of לי״די [Chavel's reading of Ezra's transliteration into Hebrew] to לי״רי; the latter transliteration is clearly attested in MS Vatican, Biblioteca Apostolica Vaticana, ebr. 86, fol. 6b, and conforms to the Catalan *lliri*).

[130] Did the lily's identification with the Virgin Mary (see Miri Rubin, *Mother of God: A History of the Virgin Mary* [New Haven, CT: Yale University Press, 2009], 344) inform León's discomfort with Ezra's reading (and de León's preference for the passionate rose as a symbol of Israel's emphatically married divine female)? This line of questioning may be suggested by the scholarship on the polemical deployment of conjugal imagery in the face of Christendom's foremost personification of virginity (see, e.g., sec. 4.7, above); nonetheless, Mary figures as a rose also in contemporaneous material; to cite one example from de León's Castilian milieu, the "Cantiga de loor" calls Mary "Rosa das rosas, flor das flores, / dona das donas, sennor das sennores." See Alfonso X, *"Cantigas de Santa Maria": An Anthology*, ed. Stephen Parkinson (Cambridge, UK: Modern Humanities Research Association, 2015), 52–53. If we may then dispense with the question of polemical motivations, it would seem that the main impetus for de León's disagreement with Ezra was the former's commitment to a thirteenfold divine pattern.

[131] Playing on Psalms 60:1 and Genesis 1:11.

This passage, again, draws on the rose speculation developed in *Shushan ha-'edut*, which was, in turn, steeped in de León's earliest androgynology. It does so to resolve an ostensible contradiction between Ezra's tradition that the flower (which for Ezra corresponds to a lily) alludes to the six extremities and de León's thirteenfold paradigm. How so? It seems that de León's discovery of the five protective sepals encasing the rosebud, perhaps an empirical observation made outside of the study house,[132] prompted a novel calibration of his thinking that is only discernible if we take stock of the trajectory of his speculation.

But how would the addition of these five structures help to reconcile six with thirteen? It seems that the thirteen petals reduce to one as a function of the 13 = 1 equation already mentioned. Hence "the secret of the [thirteenfold] rose that furnishes a testimony to the oneness." Adding this oneness to the five sepals yields six. In this manner, de León can reconcile his thirteenfold speculation with Ezra's sixfold schema. But only tentatively so. We have already anticipated the problem that a sixfold that refers only to *malkhut*'s containment of the six medial sefirot does not square with de León's view that the rose reproduces the upper thirteenfold, which most crucially includes *binah*. The solution arises from de León's observation of the calyx of five sepals protecting the rosebud from "above." Thus, *malkhut* receives protection from the maternal *binah*, who appears here in her fivefold guise—an image supported by her identification with the fiftieth year (5 × 10), namely, the Jubilee (*yovel*, which is orthographically identical to *yuval*—the uterine stream with which *binah* is also identified), and the source of five ([1] *ḥesed*, [2] *gevurah*, [3] *tiferet*, [4] *neṣaḥ*, and [5] *hod*—i.e., the six medial sefirot minus *yesod*).[133]

However, the reconciliation with Ezra's framework is only successful at the numerical level. It not only fails botanically, but, more importantly, theosophically. Though conciliatory in the tone of his response to Ezra, de León was dissatisfied with the model he had inherited for calibrating gender

[132] On extracurricular Torah study in Castilian kabbalah, see David Greenstein, *Roads to Utopia: The Walking Stories of the Zohar* (Stanford, CA: Stanford University Press, 2014).

[133] See, for example, Moses de León, *Sod 'Eser sefirot belimah*, 372: "The five sefirot that emerge from *teshuvah* [i.e., *binah*] and below . . . are the secret of the five hundred years that the Tree of Life was latent within them." When this is read according to the account of divine self-parturition recovered from the "Nameless Composition," these five gradations may be glossed as an extension of *binah*'s femininity, that is, until the appearance of *yesod* (at which point the five assume a masculine character).

to the divine realities.[134] Ultimately, he insisted on upholding his earliest androgynology—the speculation he reinscribed in *Shushan ha-'edut*—by affirming that the marriage of *malkhut* and *tif'eret* testifies to a theosophical pattern that is rooted ultimately in *binah*. The latter point is conveyed graphically when the text describes the consummation of the divine marriage, the procreative act yielding the seed for duplicating the upper pattern within the female world:

> And you will find that by means of all of the rose's sepals [the five outgrowths of *binah*—*ḥesed, gevurah, tif'eret, neṣaḥ,* and *hod*], the secret of the covenant enters [i.e., the circumcised penis; *yesod*]. And [this union is] truly according to the [testimonial] pattern of the covenant. It enters within, [yielding] its seed therein, to bear fruit with the rose, according to the verse: "[a fruit-tree bearing fruit after its kind], wherein is the seed thereof upon the earth" (Genesis 1:11).[135]

The force of the author's exegesis is to emphasize that the divinity entrusts the mundane realm with resources for instantiating its supernal archetype "upon the earth." Just as we saw in *Shushan ha-'edut*, de León's account of the divine marriage as the testimonial axis of the upper world's reproduction did not derail his efforts to carry forward his early thinking. On the contrary, the union of male and female that constitutes "the rose of testimony" is productive precisely because it testifies to the thirteenfold pattern.

By far the most important piece of evidence for demonstrating the resilience of de León's early discourse of "male and female" is a passage that is, without exaggeration, one of the most familiar examples of kabbalistic literature. Notwithstanding its familiarity, its relevance to the present discussion has fittingly remained sub rosa. As intimated above, we are referring to the medieval text selected by early modern editors to beguile any reader adventurous enough to inspect the printed Zohar's opening folia. Though scholarship has demonstrated the resemblance between this text—a homily

[134] If we are indeed correct that de León was, compared to the earlier discourse of Girona, more invested in upholding the superordination of *binah*, it will be necessary to overturn the opposing view—namely, that Girona was host to the promotion of *binah* as a maternal symbol that the Castilian kabbalists subsequently undermined. As we see here, de León's recasting of Geronese models hinged on his emphasis on the superordination of *binah*. For the opposing view, see Haviva Pedaya, "The Great Mother: The Struggle Between Nahmanides and the Zohar Circle," in *Temps i espais de la Girona jueva*, ed. Silvia Planas Marcé (Girona, Spain: Patronat del Call de Girona, 2011), 311–328.

[135] Moses de León, *Sefer ha-Rimmon*, 184.

attributed to Rabbi Hezekiah on the "rose among the thorns"—and *Sefer ha-Rimmon*'s "secret of the rose that furnishes a testimony to the oneness," its instantiation of a speculative pattern dating back to de León's earliest androgynology has eluded previous accounts.[136]

> Rabbi Hezekiah opened, "'Like a rose among the thorns, so is my beloved among the maidens' (Song 2:2). Who is a rose? Assembly of Israel. For there is a rose, and then there is a rose. Just as a rose among the thorns is colored red and white, so the Assembly of Israel includes judgment and compassion. Just as a rose has thirteen petals, so the Assembly of Israel has thirteen attributes of compassion surrounding Her on all sides. Similarly, from the moment אלהים (Elohim), God, is mentioned [in the Torah, until it appears a second time], it generates thirteen words to surround the Assembly of Israel and protect Her; then it is mentioned again. Why again? To produce five sturdy sepals surrounding the rose. These five are called 'salvation'; they are five gates. Concerning this mystery, it is written: 'I raise the cup of salvations' (Psalms 116:13). This is the cup of blessing, which should rest on five fingers—and no more—like the rose, sitting on five sturdy sepals, the paradigm of five fingers. This rose is the cup of blessing. From the second אלהים (Elohim) till the third, five words appear. From here on: light—created, concealed, contained in the covenant, entering the rose, emitting seed into Her. This is the 'tree bearing fruit [after its kind], wherein is the seed thereof.' That seed endures in the actual sign of the covenant. Just as the image of the covenant [i.e., the Tetragrammaton] is sown in forty-two couplings of that seed, so the engraved, explicit name is sown in forty-two letters of the act of creation."[137]

The Aramaic text at hand significantly embellishes the thinking articulated in the above-cited passage from *Sefer ha-Rimmon*, adding several motifs that require our attention. To begin with, the rose, which is here "the rose among the thorns" (and implicitly "the rose of testimony"), is identified with the Assembly of Israel (the archetypal aspect of the holy community, that is,

[136] For a late harmonization of the Zohar's thirteen-petaled rose and Solomon's Sea, see, for example, Ḥayyim ben Joseph Vital, *Sha'ar ma'amare Rashbi* (Tel Aviv: Hoṣa'at Kitve Rabbenu ha-Ari, 1961), 12a–17b.

[137] Zohar 1:1a; translation adapted from Matt, ad loc. The placement of this text appears on the first page of the introduction to the Zohar, following the editorial tradition of the Mantua edition of 1558; whereas it appears on fol. 5b, col. 17, of the Cremona printing of 1558/9, where it is integrated into the body of the zoharic homilies on Parashat Bereshit.

malkhut, surrounded by its thorny detractors). The idealized identification of the people with *malkhut* is based, however tacitly, on Ezra of Girona's theosophical enhancement of the older midrashic characterization of the Song's bride as God's beloved Israel. However, the Zohar's account of the rose fits well with the notion that Israel's twelve tribes are integral to the thirteenfold female world. The rose's red-and-white, variegated petals reflect the instantiation of judgment and mercy within both *malkhut* and the storied people shepherded by the divine exemplar of those qualities.[138] These ostensibly oppositional qualities, however, are sublimated by the quality of compassion (*raḥamim*), whose thirteen attributes surround the rose. The assertion that this thirteenfold appears on "all sides" recalls the language of our early text, "All of the worlds accord with the secret of thirteen."[139] The language of "all sides" suggests, again, a double-thirteenfold structure, which surrounds the bride from both above and below.[140]

The reader is thus confronted with another iteration of the pattern we have observed, where the lower thirteenfold comprises *malkhut* presiding over the created order (with Israel, in this case, as the implicitly twelvefold representative of that order). The upper thirteen are, again, *binah* plus the medial sefirot.[141] This reading not only receives support from our examination of the earlier discourse. But the text's fastening of the theo-cosmic order to *binah* and *malkhut* respectively is again attested in the highly technical continuation of the passage. The text proceeds by prompting its reader to take careful note of the number of words found between, initially, the first and second, and later, the second and third appearances of the name Elohim in the first chapter of Genesis. The term, meaning both "God" (in fact, one of God's names) and "angels" in the Hebrew Bible, is associated with both *binah* and *malkhut* in the onomastic conventions of de León's thinking. Between the first and second appearance of the term, then, one counts thirteen words, which allude to the corresponding quantity of divine gradations

138 See Matt's note on the *rosa gallica versicolor*, ad loc.

139 MS Munich, Bayerische Staatsbibliothek, Cod. hebr. 47, fol. 370b.

140 This architectural insight lies in the deeper theological background of what is, more overtly, a contra-Maimonidean affirmation that the thirteen attributes of compassion are God's own essential attributes—realities internal to the divinity, which, nonetheless, govern God's comportment with Israel. See Brown, *World of Piety*, chap. 3 ("Thirteen Attributes of Compassion: Judeomorphism and the Fidelity of Mimesis").

141 On the basis of a convention known from the writings of Gikatilla and the *Idra* literature of the Zohar, readers have suggested (e.g., Daniel Matt ad loc.) that the thirteen attributes of compassion referred to in this text are rooted in *keter*, but this suggestion is harder to maintain when the thirteen-petaled rose text is viewed as the culmination of the vector of de León's thinking we have reconstructed. On de León's reluctance to apply thirteenfold speculation to *keter*, see Chapter 5.

from *binah*—the first "Elohim"—to the cusp of *malkhut*—the second "Elohim." Between the second and third iterations of the term, one counts five words. The second and third appearances of "Elohim" refer to *malkhut* and the angelic hierarchy respectively, and the five words appearing between them refer to the protective grip of *binah*, in her fivefold guise, encompassing the lower domain by means of the medial sefirot she engenders save for *yesod* (6 – 1 = 5). The lower domain, again, circumscribes the lower female and "the world of separation," here typified by the angels.

The text goes on to translate the calyx that encircles the rose into a parallel domain of symbolism. The five sepals of the calyx are associated with the five fingers that grasp the cup of blessing; the text's rose-cup association is apparently based on the aforementioned accounts of Solomon's Sea's brim ("like the lip of a rose-blossom cup"; 1 Kings 7:26; 2 Chronicles 4:5; Fig. 4.2). Here the cup of the rose corresponds to *malkhut*, the lower female; she is identified with the cup that is traditionally held by the male when reciting the Sabbath eve liturgy of the sanctification. The sanctification is significant insofar as it commemorates the account of creation at the outset of the time sanctioned for procreative intercourse (see Chapter 2). Just as the liturgy functions as a prelude to intercourse, so, too, the intimate reference to the five fingers grasping the female cup of blessing prefigures the *hieros gamos*. If we read this passage in light of de León's earliest thinking about "male and female," the five extensions of *binah*—figured both as the sepals about the rose and the fingers securing the cup—would become male with the appearance of the sixth gradation, the sefirah of *yesod*, corresponding to the covenant of circumcision. In de León's androgynology and elsewhere in the Zohar, the intermediate world's individuation from the hidden world occurs at this moment. Though the passage at hand makes no overt reference to such a crossing of gendered thresholds, it is clear that, just as in the text from *Sefer ha-Rimmon*, the five-sepaled calyx, which is male, comes to the aid of the covenant-signifying *yesod*. The latter serves as the instrument for disseminating testimony to the supernal gradations through its conception of the created order with the female rose. Attending to the precise language of the text substantiates this point:

> That seed endures in the actual sign of the covenant (*ha-hu zera' qayyama be-ot berit mamash*). Just as the image of the covenant [i.e., the Tetragrammaton] is sown in forty-two couplings of that seed, so the engraved, explicit name (*shema gelifa*) is sown in forty-two letters of the act of creation.

The text understands the "sign" in which the ṣeed inheres hyperliterally; the generative-testimonial principle is precisely the "*letter* of the covenant," a reference to the punctiform *yod* of the Tetragrammaton (i.e., the first stroke of the explicit name and, as we saw in Chapter 3, the concentrated potentiality of all testimony).[142] It is, then, the letter *yod* that fructifies the generative-testimonial process of creation precisely through the insignia of the upper world sealed upon the groom's body. The *yod* therefore couples in forty-two different divinity-disclosing ways with the rose blossom. The latter is the vulnerable image of the impassioned bride's tender place of receptivity.[143]

We have focused on this prominent example from the zoharic anthology to establish the relevance of de León's earliest discourse on gender to some of the most traditionally authoritative and hermeneutically privileged texts. Several other examples could enable a similar demonstration. The Zohar's Aramaic homilies on Genesis 47:28–50:26 (Vayeḥi) present a compelling illustration. As one might expect, this pericope, which deals in large part with Jacob's blessing of the twelve tribes, occasions the most extensive exposition within the zoharic corpus of de León's early thirteenfold speculation. The Aramaic homilies include speculation on Solomon's Sea,[144] an account of *binah*'s parturition of the circumcised infant,[145] as well as the trope of the lower female as the "unblemished female (*neqevah temimah*)," who remains resolutely feminine ("from this place upward all is male [until *binah*], but from female downward all is female").[146]

[142] On the midrashic identification of the sign of the covenant with the letter *yod* and its adoption by de León and others, see Wolfson, "Circumcision and the Divine Name"; and Elliot R. Wolfson, "Circumcision, Vision of God, and Textual Interpretation: From Midrashic Trope to Mystical Symbol," *History of Religions* 27, no. 2 (1987): 189–215.

[143] The forty-two-letter name associated with the creation of the world is traditionally constructed by rearranging the first forty-two letters of Genesis (the number forty-two being equal to the sum of the initials of ***ma'aseh bereshit***); see t. Ḥagigah 11b; b. Qiddushin 71a; Maimonides, *Guide*, 1:62; see, for example, Pinchas Giller, "The Forty-Two-Letter Divine Name in the Later Strata of the *Zohar*," *Kabbalah* 39 (2017): 53–77.

[144] Zohar 1:241a; for example: "Standing upon twelve oxen—certainly so! For this sea is arrayed by twelve in two worlds; by twelve above, appointed chariots; by twelve below, twelve tribes"; compare Zohar 2:164b.

[145] Zohar 1:246a: "[The] consummation of the body demonstrates that the whole body is male. [But the] head of the body is female, until descending to consummation; when consummation appears, it renders everything male. But [even] here, head and end are female, for the entire array of the body is female." Matt's commentary clarifies: "Binah is surely female, because She is known as Divine Mother. However, Rabbi Shim'on explains, the female aspect of Binah is simply the head, or beginning, of the sefirotic configuration that culminates in Yesod, the phallus. The consummation renders the entire body male. Shekhinah, on the other hand, is entirely female from beginning to end, encompassing Her own being and the angelic realms beneath Her (pictured as maidens or daughters)."

[146] Zohar 1:245b–6a.

Lastly, the zoharic composition known as *Piqqudin*, whose close resemblance to de León's *Sefer ha-Rimmon* has been duly observed by scholars,[147] furnishes an additional example of the endurance of de León's early speculation on gender, here integrated into the "rationales of the commandments" genre that we discussed at the outset of the chapter. The rationale in question concerns the commandment of exempting a newlywed groom from all obligations during his first year of marriage for the stated purpose of giving "happiness to the woman he has wed."[148] This yearlong period is dedicated entirely to satisfying the conjugal rights of his spouse (*ʿonah*). The zoharic text treats the dedication of this year to the wife's pleasure as a temporal expression of the Solomon's Sea archetype. The pattern of the female sea supported by twelve oxen is iterated by the bride as resting, as it were, atop twelve months.[149] Suffice it to say that vestiges of the early speculation on gender are numerous and important within the anthology that generations after de León would come to regard as canonical.

[147] Ephraim Gottlieb, *Studies in the Kabbalah Literature* [in Hebrew], ed. Joseph Hacker (Tel Aviv: Tel Aviv University Press, 1976), 226–227; Neta Sobol, "The Pikudin Section of the Zohar" [in Hebrew] (MA thesis; Tel Aviv University, 2001), 45–48, 70–73.

[148] Deuteronomy 24:5.

[149] Zohar 3:277b–78a (translation adapted from Matt, ad loc.):

> The fifteenth commandment: a groom must delight with his wife for one year. . . . Those twelve months are hers, for the year is the bride—and there should no bride without twelve months, as is written: "standing upon twelve oxen" (1 Kings 7:25). Since there is no arraying of the bride other than with twelve, the groom must delight her and her house—her and her adornments, corresponding to the supernal pattern. Accordingly, it is written of Jacob: "he took of the stones of the place" (Genesis 28:11)—the stones of the place were twelve. One who delights the bride delights her maidens—her maidens are twelve. All is the mystery of the year, and that is why the groom must delight with his wife for one year.

5

Light of the West

Moses de León of Guadalajara

We have argued that the "Nameless Composition"—whose attribution to Moses de León we have verified through detailed philological and thematic analyses—attests to discursive patterns that pervade the theosophical kabbalah of late thirteenth-century Castile. In many respects, these patterns typify the conceptual topography of the Zohar. In other respects, they are distinctive. Our presentation hinges on the supposition that de León composed this work before *Shushan ha-ʿedut*, which he dated to 1286 and located in the city of Guadalajara. Thus we place its composition at the very outset of his writings that may be properly deemed "kabbalistic" and after his anonymous corpus of cosmo-theological speculation. This early corpus had yet to embrace the identification of the sefirot with the gradations of divinity—the theosophical wisdom espoused most famously by Naḥmanides. The "Nameless Composition," which was wrongly attributed to Naḥmanides, thus marks the transformative entrée of this signature understanding of divinity into de León's Hebrew corpus, where it dovetailed in unique ways with the author's pretheosophical speculation. We observed this, for example, in the text's adaptation of earlier speculation on the Hebrew letters to a theosophical paradigm. We also saw this in the text's accommodation of a three-worlds cosmology to a threefold division of the divinity, introducing earlier speculation into a novel discourse of gender.

Our placement of this highly distinctive composition at a pivotal moment in de León's transition to theosophical kabbalah gives readers access to the most formative phase in the development of the Zohar's celebrated theology. The chronology lends significant hermeneutical stability to the study of central problems related to the intellectual, religious, and textual history of the most representative and represented work of kabbalah. Our text contains exact Hebrew parallels—and a host of other precise correspondences of a conceptual, terminological, and exegetical nature—to the Aramaic homilies

Light is Sown. Avishai Bar-Asher and Jeremy Phillip Brown, Oxford University Press.
© Oxford University Press 2025. DOI: 10.1093/oso/9780197744819.003.0005

of the Zohar. These features help to both contextualize and sequence the zoharic material with a relative degree of precision.

In terms of genre, another result of the foregoing study is the realization that the "Nameless Composition" is not, as Scholem suggested, a symbolic lexicon in the style of Joseph Gikatilla's well-known, albeit significantly later, *Sha'are orah*; nor is it typical of a broader genre of commentaries on the ten sefirot. While the text's extant chapters are loosely structured as expositions of individual sefirot (or pairings thereof), these discussions are intersected by long excurses on topics diverging from the straightforward delineation of divine gradations.[1] Moreover, commentaries on the sefirot typically follow a ten-part structure, whereas per our hypothesis, de León's earliest theosophical work comprised thirteen parts. The work not only frustrates the expectation of a ten-chapter form, but its contents are brimming with constructive challenges to the trend in speculative theology of reducing all things divine to ten.

5.1 The Thirteenfold Pattern

One of the most distinctive features of the "Nameless Composition" is its fascination with the numerical figure of thirteen. "All the worlds accord with the secret of thirteen," the text affirms.[2] Though earlier thinkers such as Ezra of Girona, Naḥmanides, Asher ben David, and Ṭodros ben Joseph Abulafia sought to calibrate God's classical thirteen attributes of compassion (following Exodus 34:6–7) to the ten sefirot, no previous composition is as saturated with thirteenfold patterns as our text. Interest in thirteenfold patterns—especially the reconciliation of the thirteen attributes of compassion with God's oneness—is attested already in de León's pretheosophical writings.[3] Central to the text is the scriptural image of Solomon's Sea (1 Kings

[1] De León may have modeled the use of such excurses after Ezra of Girona, who, for example, collated an early theosophical account of creation into his commentary on the Song of Songs. In 1287's *Sefer ha-Rimmon*, de León inserted just such an excursus on creation into his account of the sanctification of the moon, an excursus that not only follows Ezra's style—i.e., reading Genesis 1 in light of Psalm 104—but actually sources material from the Song commentary directly.

[2] MS Munich, Bayerische Staatsbibliothek, Cod. hebr. 47, fol. 370b.

[3] Consider, for example, de León's early musings on the Shema (Deuteronomy 6:4) and the traditional thirteen attributes of compassion (Exodus 34:6); Avishai Bar-Asher, "*Sefer ha-Ne'lam*, New Parts of *Sefer Or Zarua* and Clarifications regarding the Early Writings of R. Moses de León: Studies and Critical Editions" [Hebrew], *Tarbiz* 83, nos. 1–2 (2015): 197–329, with the edition of the text on 256–318 = Moses de León, *Or zarua'*, 265–266; and its reworking in Avishai Bar-Asher, "From the Vaults of Thebes: Moses de León's Pseudepigraphic Writings on the Letters, Vowel Signs, Theonyms,

7:23–26; 2 Chronicles 4:2–5; see Figure 4.2), the singular priestly laver shouldered by twelve brass oxen who are, in turn, arrayed in groups of three facing the four cardinal directions (13 = 1 + 12 [= 3 × 4]). Our text treats the laver of Solomon's Temple as an archetype that is reflected in the divine order, the array of angelic ranks, and the political order of Israel. When discussing de León's initial foray into gendered speculation, we established that the Solomon's Sea is notable in calling to mind the superordination of female elements within the divine world vis-à-vis subordinate elements. The text consistently understands the laver as a female principle (whereas it is inconsistent when gendering the twelve elements supporting the female; sometimes these are male, sometimes female). The text even speculates that the archetype of Solomon's Sea patterns all reality. Accordingly, the vast expanse of being constitutes three successive iterations of thirteen. The first iteration delineates the succession of intradivine structures from *binah* (or *teshuvah*) to *yesod* (where *binah* corresponds to the basin resting atop the twelve oxen, that is, the six gradations from *ḥesed* to *yesod*—which are doubled to yield twelve). The second iteration transitions from divinity to angelic being (where the laver symbolizes *malkhut* or *shekhinah*—the "world of the female"—that rests atop twelve ranks of angels). The third iteration bridges the angelic and human realities, where the angelic world rests atop the twelve tribes of Israel (who, like the oxen arrayed about the laver, encamped in four divisions of three at the four cardinal directions surrounding the Tabernacle).

Speculation on the figure of thirteen also organizes the composition's novel penitential discourse—in both formal structure and content. The text, as discussed at length, contains an important thirteen-part excursus adumbrating thirteen attributes of repentance (*middot shel teshuvah*). Unlike other classical thirteenfold motifs, this one is effectively novel, though its formulation may be indebted to the language of Naḥmanides's account of the thirteen attributes of compassion.[4] The thirteenfold excursus is called the "Order of Penitents" (*Siddur ba'ale teshuvah*; see Figure 2.1), the likes of which exist nowhere in the previous literature of kabbalah. This portion of

and Magical Practices and the Origin of Zoharic Fiction" [in Hebrew], *Kabbalah* 51 (2022): 157–248, with the edition of the text on 200–248 = Moses de León, *Sod Darkhe ha-otiyyot*, 246–247.

[4] Naḥmanides on Exodus 34:6: "YHVH, YHVH, El: These three words are holy Names that the Sages call attributes (*middot*), since they constitute the attribute of the penitent (*middat ba'al ha-teshuvah*), the attribute of His compassions (*middat raḥamav*) and the attribute of His goodness (*u-middat ṭuvo*)." This may be added to the various factors informing the scribal attribution of the Munich fragment to Naḥmanides discussed in Chapter 1.

the text exhorts the reader to assimilate thirteen supererogatory behaviors and temperaments that correspond to a divine model. More specifically, they correspond to the intradivine iteration of the thirteenfold pattern in which the superordinate principle of the thirteen attributes of repentance is the upper female sefirah called *teshuvah* or, alternately, *binah*. At the start of the chapter containing the excursus,[5] the penitents (or perhaps their souls) are characterized as birds chirping and flitting about an oasis, presumably the sefirah of *teshuvah*, in which a single spring is said to flow into twelve channels. Following the pattern of the oxen of Solomon's Sea, the channels are arrayed in groups of three, with each facing one of the four cardinal directions. Finally, another important example of the thirteenfold motif, found in one of the composition's two extant appendices, is a theosophical commentary on Rabbi Ishmael's thirteen principles for interpreting the Torah (*middot she-ha-torah nidreshet ba-hen*). Here, again, the text resists the tenfold paradigm in both content and form.

When considering formal attributes, one can do better than merely adducing the excurses and appendices in our text that exhibit a thirteenfold organization. In fact, it is possible—through careful reconstruction and attention to the organization of other texts by de León—to posit a thirteenfold form for the entire composition. Although there are extant only four and a half "gates" or "parts" (i.e., chapters) and two appendices (the second of which is only partially preserved in the Munich version of our text but fully preserved in another codicological context; see Figure 1.3, in Chapter 1),[6] we hypothesize that de León organized the original composition into thirteen sections—ten chapters plus three appendices. The original work may have included an additional third appendix, which would bring the sum of the work's parts to thirteen. Of course, in the absence of textual evidence regarding this structure, this suggestion is conjectural. However, de León's pattern of supplementing his longer compositions with shorter textual units is exemplified by the author's 1290 composition *Sefer ha-Nefesh ha-ḥakhamah* (alternately titled *Sefer ha-Mishqal*), which features an appendix containing a large number of episodic "secrets." 1287's *Sefer ha-Rimmon* likewise contains an additional textual unit, namely, a responsum concerning the

5 MS Munich, Bayerische Staatsbibliothek, Cod. hebr. 47, fol. 348a.

6 Ronit Meroz, "Kabbalah, Science and Pseudo-Science in Ramdal's Commentary on the Thirteen Attributes," in *And This Is for Yehuda: Studies Presented to Our Friend, Professor Yehuda Liebes, on the Occasion of His Sixty-Fifth Birthday*, ed. Maren R. Niehoff, Ronit Meroz, and Jonathan Garb (Jerusalem: Mossad Bialik, 2012), 123–143.

soul addressed to de León's benefactor (and perhaps student as well) Joseph ben Ṭodros ha-Levi Abulafia. The most relevant example for our purposes of de León's penchant for including addenda is his 1292 *Sheqel ha-qodesh*—precisely because the work's inclusion of shorter textual units yields a sum of thirteen parts. In a "Table of Contents" extant in some manuscripts, we read: "This book is divided into thirteen and not [ten]."[7] The thirteenfold division of *Sheqel ha-qodesh* may shed light on the enigma of the original structure of our fragmentarily preserved work. The extant evidence is enough to show that the original composition was a work comprising at least twelve sections (not counting excurses), and thus irreducible to a simple tenfold division.

Why such concern with thirteen? This pervasive pattern presents an alternative to the decadic structure of the divinity. Though he was evidently beholden to the conventions of tenfold speculation exemplified by his predecessors, it seems that de León, ever eager to integrate novelty and complexity, took it upon himself to challenge its standardization. Did the author wish to hold a tension within our text between the ten and the thirteen to express the overarching dynamism of a divinity that, per his theology, is not reducible to a stable quantum? Did he assume that by shuttling between individually unstable patterns one could discern a unity that surpasses numerical fixity? Thoughtful as this line of theological questioning may be, one would expect on its basis to find little preference for this or that delineation of quantity. But this is not the case for de León, who privileged certain numerical patterns over others. Our text does not merely destabilize tenfold speculation but strives in a positive vein to foreground the thirteenfold patterns. Thirteen is a numerical figure that, unlike ten, does not lend itself to facile symmetries. Whereas the decad boasted a range of universal arithmetical

[7] The parchment bearing the final word is worm eaten; MS Jerusalem, National Library of Israel, Heb. 8°2066, fol. 102a–b; Charles Mopsik, ed., *R. Moses De Leon's Sefer Sheqel ha-Qodesh* (Los Angeles, CA: Cherub Press, 1996) = Moses de León, *Sheqel ha-qodesh*, 107. This statement is missing from the tables of contents preserved in MS London, British Library, Add. 27044, fol. 97a–b; MS Paris, Bibliothèque nationale de France, héb. 823, fol. 166b; and MS Moscow, Russian State Library, Guenzburg 362, fol. 209b. All three manuscripts nonetheless contain, like the Jerusalem MS, the same thirteenfold chapter divisions. It is important to ascertain that none of the above-cited versions of the chapter index—which, according to Mopsik (107n769), de León composed himself—count the infamous responsum concerning the Trinity that closes *Sheqel ha-qodesh* ("The Final Question"; *ha-she'elah ha-aḥaronah*) as a *fourteenth* division of the text that follows the commentary on the ten divine names (a version of which appeared first, as we established, in the "Nameless Composition"; MS Munich, Bayerische Staatsbibliothek, Cod. hebr. 47, fols. 381a–385b); rather, both the commentary on the ten names and the responsum concerning the Trinity are counted together as the thirteenth division. Moreover, the inclusion of both texts—one dealing with a tenfold and one dealing with a threefold—figures sensibly within a single division that is fittingly numbered the thirteenth.

properties that recommended its adoption for a rabbinic discourse on divine oneness, thirteen furnished an emphatically Hebraic witness to unity that was proven, again, by the numerical value of the Hebrew word for "one," and its scriptural-rabbinic resonances with the various motifs we have seen. Moreover, the thirteenfold pattern emphasizes horizontal asymmetry and an especially top-heavy hierarchy, with its repeated superordination of one over twelve. The figure of thirteen is not divisible by two into whole numbers; it is thus not given to easy oppositions that are readily assimilable to binary patterns of mentation. In this sense, thirteen is a number that gives rise to thinking about the divinity's transcendence of binarity. Moses de León returned to the thirteenfold infrastructure that framed his thinking on a range of topics—from the concrete mandates of his penitential program to the sublime ontology of God's exemplary attributes—throughout his subsequent Hebrew and zoharic writings.

Our composition's use of the number nine also illustrates how its author resisted the default of kabbalistic speculation to tenfold patterns.[8] That is, de León refused to enumerate the supernal crown (*keter 'elyon*) as a tenth sefirah. The crown, rather, transcends numeration, abiding above the nine—not ten—sefirot. The nine sefirot, in turn, conform to the ninefold pattern of the nine concentric spheres of Farabian-cum-Maimonidean cosmology.[9]

> Behold that they [i.e., the sefirot] are nine in [accord with] the secret of nine spheres . . . for the supernal crown is not contained in the sum; even though it is that which bestows existence and brings forth being and all things return to it, and from thence they go out, and all things are contained within it.[10]

[8] For another case of de León's challenge to inherited tenfold patterns, see Avishai Bar-Asher, "Decoding the Decalogue: Theosophical Re-Engraving of the Ten Commandments in Thirteenth-Century Kabbalah," in *Accounting for the Commandments in Medieval Judaism: Studies in Law, Philosophy, Pietism, and Kabbalah*, ed. Jeremy Phillip Brown and Marc Herman (Leiden: Brill, 2021), 156–174. For another example of ninefold speculation in the "Nameless Composition," consider the speculative topos of the first nine letters of the alphabet discussed above in Chapter 3. For a harmonization of sevenfold, ninefold, and thirteenfold frameworks, see Gershom Scholem, "Shene quntresim le-R. Moshe de León," *Kobez al Yad* 8, no.18 (1976): 325–384, esp. 330–370 = Moses de León, *Shushan ha-'edut*, 364.

[9] Maimonides, Mishneh Torah, Hilkhot yesode ha-Torah, 3:1 (this may be contrasted with the delineation of five concentric spheres in *Guide of the Perplexed*, 2:9). On the nine primary spheres of Farabian cosmology, see Thérèse-Anne Druart, "Al-Farabi and Emanationism," in *Studies in Medieval Philosophy*, ed. John F. Wippel (Washington, DC: Catholic University of America Press, 1987), 23–43. On earlier Andalusi vacillation between nine and ten spheres, see Adena Tanenbaum, "Nine Spheres or Ten? A Medieval Gloss on Moses Ibn Ezra's 'Be-shem El asher amar,'" *Journal of Jewish Studies* 47 (1996): 294–310.

[10] MS Munich, Bayerische Staatsbibliothek, Cod. hebr. 47, fol. 378b.

Elsewhere, the composition's appendix on ten divine names demonstrates a similar dynamic, at one point subtracting one of the ten names discussed to yield nine.[11] "Behold the secret of nine names," implores the text, "even though we said that they are ten, the tenth is not from the sum, because the secret of nine conforms with the nine existent spheres."[12] By the tenth name, however, the author seems to refer to the first name on his list, namely Ehyeh, meaning "I will be" (Exodus 3:14), which corresponds to the supernal crown.[13] It is described as a name that outstrips all other theonyms in terms of its absolute concealment. This name alludes to a facet of God that is "like one who stands in a hidden essence"; God says, "I will be," as if to say, "I am He who stands in my essence without revealing a thing."[14] The text goes on to distinguish the name Ehyeh from Ehyeh asher Ehyeh, "I will be what I will be," which is understood in terms of the essence *keter* will surreptitiously impart to *ḥokhmah*.[15] Suffice it to say that the name corresponding to the supernal crown is surely no ordinary name. Again, the text suggests that the pattern of the nine spheres conforms with the existence of nine countable tiers of divinity; this implies that the supernal crown (*keter ʿelyon*) transcends the sefirot in a manner analogous to the divinity's transcendence of the cosmos. Again, this speculation—here ninefold rather than thirteenfold—functions to spur thinking about the divinity beyond the ordinary parameters of a tenfold structure.

With both patterns, the ninefold and thirteenfold, de León sought to ensure the transcendental ultimacy of the supernal crown, or, as he often called it, the primordial ether. What the thirteenfold does by positively demarcating the upper limits of cataphatic discourse with *binah* (or, in some cases, *binah* in her conjunction with *ḥokhmah*), the ninefold does negatively, by subtracting the purely apophatic domain from the field of nameability.[16] As shown in Chapter 4, our author identified this ultimate reality as "a pure

[11] Maimonides's list in Mishneh Torah, Hilkhot yesode ha-Torah, 6:2 (based on y. Megillah 1:9 and b. Shevuʿot 35a) contains only seven names that one may not erase; it may be that de León innovated the list of ten. See Avishai Bar-Asher, "From Alphabetical Mysticism to Theosophical Kabbalah: A Rare Witness to an Intermediate Stage of Moses de León's Thought," *Revue des études juives* 179, nos. 3–4 (2020): 351–384, here 374n.84.

[12] The better witness to this portion of the text is preserved in MS New York, Jewish Theological Seminary of America 1777, fol. 27a; compare MS Munich, Bayerische Staatsbibliothek, Cod. hebr. 47, fol. 385a.

[13] MS Munich, Bayerische Staatsbibliothek, Cod. hebr. 47, fols. 381b–382a.

[14] MS Munich, Bayerische Staatsbibliothek, Cod. hebr. 47, fol. 382a.

[15] MS Munich, Bayerische Staatsbibliothek, Cod. hebr. 47, fol. 382a.

[16] See Eitan P. Fishbane, "Mystical Contemplation and the Limits of the Mind: The Case of *Sheqel ha-Qodesh*," *Jewish Quarterly Review* 93, nos. 1–2 (2002): 1–27.

ether that is never perceptible whatsoever; its level is elevated above everything. And it becomes elevated through the elevation of all levels, and it is concealed through the concealment of everything because it is the Lord of everything."[17] The thirteenfold speculation, in fact, helps our author to schematize the field of nine perceptible gradations that he delineates from the supernal crown as the legitimate domain of cataphatic discourse. We find no evidence that de León anywhere, whether in his Hebrew writings or in the zoharic material bearing his fingerprints,[18] subjected the apophatic crown to any kind of thirteenfold delineation. What apophatic descriptions of *keter* that we do possess from this author suggest that he would have trembled at the prospect. As we already saw in our account of de León's earlier pretheosophical speculation on language, the author directly contradicted Joseph Gikatilla's early idea, expressed already in the mid-1270s, that the primordial point indicates the ultimate term of reality. He did so by endorsing only the penultimacy of the primordial point. In our text, de León assimilated this position into his theosophical account of the vowels, where even the primordial point—which he aligned with the ninth gradation, *ḥokhmah*—is too determinate an image to ascribe to the imperceptible ether.

In a text convincingly ascribed to Gikatilla, which suggests its author's familiarity with de León's discourse on thirteens and nines, we read about a thirteenfold pattern exemplified by the crown itself.[19] According to this text, "The Secret of the Thirteen Attributes That Flow from the Supernal Crown, Which Are Called 'Springs of Salvation,'"[20] the crown is the site of God's thirteen attributes of compassion (*middot shel raḥamim*), knowledge of which is all but identical with Israel's redemption.[21]

> From this crown spring the sources of compassion, and the good, and the pleasure of eternal things that do not change or reverse, and there is

[17] MS Munich, Bayerische Staatsbibliothek, Cod. hebr. 47, fol. 366a.

[18] Compare the account of Ehyeh in Zohar, 3:11a.

[19] See Jeremy Phillip Brown, *A World of Piety: The Aims of Castilian Kabbalah* (Stanford, CA: Stanford University Press, 2025), chap. 3 ("Thirteen Attributes of Compassion: Judeomorphism and the Fidelity of Mimesis").

[20] See "Sod Shelosh ʿesre middot ha-noveʿot min ha-keter," in Gershom Scholem and Bernhard I. Joel, *Catalogus codicum hebraicorum quot conservator in Bibliotheca Hierosolymitana* (Jerusalem: Hebrew University of Jerusalem, 1930), 219–225.

[21] Indeed, this is a motif attested throughout the mature Gikatilla's writings, and the *Idra* literature of the Zohar as well; see, for example, Ephraim Gottlieb, "The Concluding Portion of R. Joseph Chiqatella's *Sha'arei Ẓedeq*" [in Hebrew], *Tarbiz* 39, no. 4 (1970): 359–389; and Jeremy Phillip Brown, "The Reason a Woman Is Obligated: Women's Ritual Efficacy in Medieval Kabbalah," *Harvard Theological Review* 116, no. 3 (2023): 422–446, esp. 443–444.

> no harm in their wake, no trouble, no darkness, no lack; and that place is called "neither day nor night" (Zechariah 14:7) since there is no day without night and no night without day—and that [i.e., the correlativity of day and night] is the secret of all nine sefirot below the crown. But the crown is called "neither day nor night." And at the time that it appears, then there will be complete redemption, after which [time] there will be neither trouble nor sorrow. And this is the secret of "but there shall be a continuous day—only YHVH knows when—of neither day nor night" (ibid.); and this is the secret of "and there shall be light at eventide" (ibid.) . . . and this is the secret of "on that day YHVH will be one and His name will be one" (Zechariah 14:9).[22]

The author of this text took pains to disambiguate the thirteenfold crown from the nine sefirot, and, therewith, took flight into exegetical speculation on the non-binarity of the most concealed facet of divinity. Basing himself on the prophecy of Zechariah, the author distinguished the nature of the nine sefirot, which are given to the polarity of oppositional characteristics (whether diurnal or nocturnal), from the crown, which both encompasses and transcends polarity. The text suggests that the equanimous consciousness of this "eventide" is precisely the long-awaited consciousness of redemption.

Appended to a truncated version of the same text exemplified in a Vatican manuscript is a personal note composed by the author, presumably Gikatilla, addressed to a fellow student of divine wisdom concerning various iterations of the thirteenfold pattern:

> Behold, I wrote for you, my brother, some of the paths of the enigmas of wisdom in the depth of the crown (*derakhim mi-ta'alumot ḥokhmah be-'emeq ha-keter*). And know that from this source all of the worlds are emanated; in accord with the secret of one, the thirteen hermeneutical principles proceed. In accord with the secret of one, proceed the four elements and eight celestial spheres, and spheres of *'aravot* above [i.e., 4 + 8 + 1 (*'aravot*) = אח"ד (= 13)]. In accord with the secret of one, proceed the thirteen attributes of compassion. And with God's help, if you merit

[22] Scholem and Joel, *Catalogus codicum hebraicorum*, 225.

Eden, you will behold the paths and the passageways to these matters as is fitting.[23]

This note is a rare personal testimony to the intimacy of the epistolary medium used by late-thirteenth-century Castilian authors to share the discoveries of their learning and perhaps an indication of the kind of correspondence in which de León and Gikatilla incubated their innovations. But more specifically, the artifact shows that another author—an author from Castile with whom de León engaged in fruitful and contentious dialogue—likewise sought to integrate a host of thirteenfold motifs,[24] indeed some of the same motifs marshaled by de León, for a similar purpose, namely, to push speculation about the divinity beyond the conventional doctrine of ten sefirot and therewith to prolong "the paths of the enigmas of wisdom" to unforeseen lengths. The text's repeated emphasis on the comportment of the thirteenfold pattern with the "secret of one" may be decoded, as in de León's thinking, by recalling the numerical value of the Hebrew word for "one" (אח"ד = 1 + 8 + 4 = 13). Nonetheless, this text confidently advances an agenda that de León was reluctant to embrace. For the latter, the thirteenfold pattern reaches no higher than *binah*, and the primordial point, associated with *ḥokhmah*, is too definite a notion to attribute to *keter*. Though "The Secret of the Thirteen Attributes" is clearly sensitive to de León's intention to secure the ultimacy of *keter*, it dares to introduce thirteenfold speculation into this subtlest of domains and even touts the redemptive promise of such knowledge. Suffice to say that de León was not the prophet of this particular vision of redemption. Studying the distinct yet intersecting paths of Gikatilla and de León in the thirteenfold wisdom sheds light on the positioning of the authors in their exchange over such ultimate concerns. The thirteenfold pattern furnishes a vantage point from which to survey the authors' intellectual itineraries generally and, recalling the author's early disagreement (sec. 3.9), gives further indication of a dialogical mechanism propelling the cultivation of kabbalah in medieval Castile.

[23] MS Vatican, Biblioteca Apostolica Vaticana, ebr. 214, fol. 75a, and a second witness bound in the same codex, fols. 238b–239a; compare Scholem, *Kitve yad ba-qabbalah*, 55.

[24] See Joseph Gikatilla, *Sha'are ṣedeq* (Krakow: Fischer & Deutscher, 1881), 1b, where Gikatilla names some of the same motifs in connection with "the secret of thirteen." Also see Gikatilla, *Sha'are orah*, ed. Joseph Ben-Shlomo (Jerusalem: Mossad Bialik, 1996), 1:163, where it is said that Hannah directed her prayer to "the secret of the thirteen attributes of compassion in the sefirah of Ehyeh, which is the secret of *keter*."

5.2 *Sabios Antiguos*: Wisdom and Its Contexts

What kind of knowledge is this? Rather than directly classifying the distinctive type of learning honed by de León in pursuit of "the enigmas of wisdom," we propose to assess the multiple contexts relevant to our text, beyond the immediate context we have explored extensively, namely, de León's corpus. Careful readers do well to address multiple wisdom contexts when assessing de León's formidable contribution to Jewish theology, whether de León's writings are examined in light of their reception by Christian Hebraists, as a northerly vector of Andalusi wisdom, against the background of the Alfonsine corpus, as elaborations of and reactions to Catalonia's cultures of rabbinic wisdom, or in conversation with earlier and contemporaneous authors in Castile.

With respect to Christian Hebraism, one can only concede that our text owes its survival, though partial, to the interest of Renaissance scholars in kabbalah. In some cases, such interest arose within a broader cultural project of accounting for the occult sciences, such as astronomy, magic, hermeticism, alchemy, and so on. An ideology of esotericism animated such interest, even inspiring the collection of a global repository of disparate and decontextualized knowledge for the apparent purpose of recovering lost testimonia to the ostensible universality of Christian doctrine. The most conspicuous representative of this ideology, Giovanni Pico della Mirandola, fancied himself a student of the kabbalah literature produced in medieval Iberia, including the work of de León.[25] Pico considered this material to be rife with "the ancient mysteries of the Hebrews," mysteries that he arrogated to "cite

[25] Note, for example, *Anima scientiae*, the translation into Latin of de León's *Sefer ha-Nefesh ha-ḥakhamah*, preserved in MS Vatican, Biblioteca Apostolica Vaticana, ebr. 191, fols. 125a–208a, which Flavius Mithridates prepared for Pico. Benjamin Richler, ed., *Hebrew Manuscripts in the Vatican Library*, with palaeographical and codicological descriptions by Malachi Beit-Arié in collaboration with Nurit Pasternak (Vatican City: Biblioteca Apostolica Vaticana, 2008), 134; Jochanan H. A. Wijnhoven, "Sefer ha-Mishkal: Text and Study" (PhD diss., Brandeis University, 1964), 15; Moritz Steinschneider, "Jochanan Alemanno, Flavius Mithridates und Pico de la Mirandola," *Hebraeische Bibliographie* 21, no. 125 (1881–1882): 109–115, here 114. Additionally, scholarship has indicated that the source material for Pico's *Conclusiones* often derives from Castile (esp. Gikatilla and the Zohar) or from authors closely related thereto (e.g., Recanati). See, for example, Chaim Wirszubski, *Pico della Mirandola's Encounter with Jewish Mysticism* (Cambridge, MA: Harvard University Press, 1989), 19–52. Apropos of this trajectory of de León's reception is the fact that the fourteenth-century Sephardic manuscript (MS New York, Jewish Theological Seminary of America, 1609) preserving the earliest witness to de León's commentary on Rabbi Ishmael's thirteen hermeneutical principles (which also appears as an appendix to the "Nameless Composition") was acquired by Agostino Giustiniani and circulated among Christian Hebraists. See Avishai Bar-Asher, "Isaac ben Solomon Ibn Sahula's Commentary on Psalms" [in Hebrew], *Kobez al Yad* 26, no. 36 (2018): 1–45, here 3–4; and Saverio Campanini, "Transmission and Reception of Isaac ibn Sahula's Kabbalistic Commentary on Two Psalms," *European Journal of Jewish Studies* 16, no. 1 (2022): 28–53.

as confirmation of the sacrosanct and Catholic faith"; by the same token, he purported to explain "how divine, how necessary they [the mysteries] are to our men [of the Catholic faith] for the safeguard of religion against the importunate calumnies of the Jews (ad propugnandum religionem contra Hebraeorum importunes calumnias)."[26] This, to be sure, was an ideology that exploited the kabbalists' rhetoric of secrecy to harmonize Israel's hidden wisdom with Christian doctrine—all the while demonizing the Jews and their overt faith.

Such misplaced esteem for kabbalah contributed to its prestige. Its status alongside other domains of Hebrew learning led Johann Jakob Fugger of Augsburg to invest in its reproduction and acquisition. Thus, in sixteenth-century Venice, Fugger's collaborator Cornelio Adelkind hired several scribes to copy a great many works eventually acquired by the Bavarian State Library (see sec. 1.6), among them the larger extant portion of the "Nameless Composition." The high appraisal of this and many other cherished works of kabbalah in the Christian intellectual marketplace cannot be explained without reference to widespread ideological assumptions regarding the Christian significance of kabbalistic writing. We can thus speak not only of the monetary price expended by Fugger for preserving our text, among others, but also the ideological cost paid by our text, as it were, for its survival in Christian Europe.

If the harmonization of kabbalah with Christianity is indicative of an ideology basic to "Western esotericism," it must be clarified in no uncertain terms what will nonetheless be obvious to lucid readers: Moses de León's theosophical writings are transcriptions of a confessionally decisive expedition into the heart of Torah. To the great extent that his writings avail themselves of a rhetoric of secrecy, there is no indication that their author harbored a clandestine belief in the Gospel or any other creed that he might have considered heterodox to the rabbinic tradition.[27] On the contrary, his zealous writings may be aptly described as "hyperconfessional."[28] As we discussed in Chapter 2, de León did not hesitate to conscript ancient rabbinic heresiology into the service of his kabbalah, notwithstanding his

[26] Pico della Mirandola, *Oration on the Dignity of Man: A New Translation and Commentary*, ed. Francesco Borghesi, Michael Papio, and Massimo Riva (Cambridge, UK: Cambridge University Press, 2012), 250–251 (§. 234).

[27] See discussion in Chapter 2 of de León's adoption of rabbinic heresiology. See, too, Jeremy Phillip Brown, "What Does the Messiah Know? A Prelude to Kabbalah's Trinity Complex," *Maimonides Review of Philosophy and Religion* 2 (2023): 1–49.

[28] We propose this characterization in conversation with Steven M. Wasserstrom, "Jewish-Muslim Relations in the Context of Andalusian Emigration," in *Christians, Muslims, and Jews in Medieval and Early Modern Spain* (Notre Dame: University of Notre Dame Press, 1999), 69–87.

express competition with Franciscan piety. It would thus be fallacious to peg de León—whether as the author of the "Nameless Composition," a sizable Hebrew corpus, or even zoharic texts—as a forerunner of the kind of occultist ideology espoused by Giovanni Pico della Mirandola. This must be said notwithstanding the cornucopia of fascinations the Zohar (and other works of medieval kabbalah) provoked for Latin occultists, including the androgynous divinity,[29] the threefold speculation on the Godhead,[30] various para-alchemical motifs,[31] as well as linguistic and numerological speculation.[32] In this sense, "Western esotericism" *à la renaissance* is but one horizon of Westernism that de León acquires at a great and distorting distance from his *Sitz im Leben.*

If this Western horizon is belated and radically decontextualizing, should de León's writings be classed as a different kind of "Western," or specifically, *maghrebi* esotericism? We are supported in this line of questioning by various considerations. Not only did a seventeenth-century Moroccan codex preserve a sizable fragment of the "Nameless Composition" (see Figure 1.2) and, more generally, did the Zohar find an eager reception in North Africa,[33] but, perhaps most compellingly, de León's designated himself the "light of the West" (*ner ha-ma'aravi*).[34] This honorific expressed the author's self-assurance. Indeed, he reserved it for only one other authority: Maimonides![35] Thus, by *maghrebi,* we have in mind a broader cultural geography straddling the Strait of Gibraltar to al-Andalus,[36] one that would include the discourse of esotericism that Maimonides developed by fostering a rapprochement between ancient rabbinic categories of secrecy and medieval Islamic philosophy, especially the thought of al-Farabi. Through our readings of texts from before

[29] Leah DeVun, *The Shape of Sex: Nonbinary Gender from Genesis to the Renaissance* (New York: Columbia University Press, 2021), esp. 163–199.

[30] Brown, "What Does the Messiah Know?"

[31] Gershom Scholem, "Alchemie und Kabbala: Ein Kapitel aus der Geschichte der Mystik," *Monatsschrift für Geschichte und Wissenschaft des Judentums* 69, nos. 1–2 (1925): 13–30.

[32] Moshe Idel, "Ramon Lull and Ecstatic Kabbalah: A Preliminary Observation," *Journal of the Warburg and Courtauld Institutes* 51 (1988): 170–174.

[33] See, for example, Harvey E. Goldberg, "The Zohar in Southern Morocco: A Study in the Ethnography of Texts," *History of Religion* 29, no. 3 (1990): 233–258; Moshe Idel, "The Kabbalah in Morocco: A Survey," in *Morocco: Jews and Art in a Muslim Land*, ed. Vivian B. Mann (New York: Merrell, 2000), 105–124; Moshe Hallamish, *The Kabbalah in North Africa: A Historical and Cultural Survey from the 16th Century* [in Hebrew] (Tel Aviv: Hakibbutz Hameuhad, 2001).

[34] Avishai Bar-Asher, ed., *R. Moses de León's Sefer Mishkan ha-'edut* [in Hebrew] (Los Angeles, CA: Cherub Press, 2013) = Moses de León, *Mishkan ha-'edut*, 1. The epithet is based on b. Shabbat 22b.

[35] Moses de León, *Mishkan ha-'edut*, 123.

[36] Joshua Blau, "At Our Place in al-Andalus, at Our Place in the Maghreb," in *Perspectives on Maimonides: Philosophical and Historical Studies*, ed. Joel L. Kraemer (Oxford: Oxford University Press for the Littman Library, 1991), 293–294.

and during de León's transition to theosophical speculation, we have seen that Maimonides is rarely far from de León's mind. More broadly, however, than a strictly Maimonidean context, the designation of *maghrebi* might also include the discourses of secrecy forged by other Andalusi theologians, such as Judah Halevi, the first known Iberian author to quote from *Sefer Yeṣirah*,[37] and Abraham Ibn Ezra, an author especially interested in the mathematical significance of divine names.[38] Solomon Ibn Gabirol also figures within this legacy.[39] We note his poetic interest in the topos of Solomon's Sea, to which he likened the design of an Andalusi court fountain.

> . . . and a full sea: It resembles Solomon's Sea,
> but it does not stand upon cattle,
> and the lions' standing-place is on its edge,
> as if young lions were roaring for prey,
> whose bellies, like wells, emit
> through their mouths streams like rivers[40]

Scholars have debated whether it was the famous Patio de los Leones of the Alhambra Palace that Ibn Gabirol intended to compare with the laver of Solomon's Temple (see Figure 5.1).[41] Whatever the precise reference to Islamic architecture, it is clear that the Sea of Solomon, which was also adopted variously in contemporaneous Christian iconography,[42] held

[37] Avishai Bar-Asher, "The *Kuzari* and Early Kabbalah: Between Integration and Interpretation Regarding the Secrets of the Sacrificial Rite," *Harvard Theological Review* 116, no. 2 (2023): 228–253.

[38] See, for example, Carlos del Valle Rodríguez, "Abraham ibn Ezra's Mathematical Speculations on the Divine Name," in *Mystics of the Book: Themes, Topics, and Typologies*, ed. R. A. Herrera (New York: Peter Lang 1993), 159–176; and Norman Roth, "Abraham Ibn Ezra—Mysticism," *Iberia Judaica* 4 (2012): 141–150.

[39] See Isaiah Tishby, ed., *The Wisdom of the Zohar: An Anthology of Texts*, trans. David Goldstein (London: Littman Library, 1991), 1:75–77, 82.

[40] Solomon Ibn Gabirol, *The Secular Poetry of Solomon Ibn Gabirol* [in Hebrew], ed. Dov Jarden (Jerusalem: Kiryat Noar, 1975), 1:86, 2:18–20; translated in Raymond P. Scheindlin, "El poema de Ibn Gabirol y la fuente del Patio de los Leones," *Cuadernos de la Alhambra* 29–30 (1993–1994): 185–189, here 186.

[41] Scheindlin, "El poema de Ibn Gabirol."

[42] Two famous examples are the twelfth-century baptismal font at St. Batholomew's Church in Liège, attributed to Renier de Huy (see Clemens M. M. Bayer, "Les fonts baptismaux de Liège: Qui les bœufs soutenant la cuve figurent-ils? Étude historique et épigraphique," in *Cinquante années d'études médiévales: À la confluence de nos disciplines. Actes du colloque organisé à l'occasion du cinquantenaire du CESM, Poitiers, 1–4 septembre 2003*, ed. Claude Arrignon and Caludio Galderisi [Turnhout, Belgium: Brepols, 2005], 665–726); and the Klosterneuburg Altar of Nicholas of Verdun, which features a panel depicting a gilded Solomon's Sea holding fish-filled water composed in various shades of brilliant blue enamel. On the inscription surrounding the panel, see Wilhelm Seelbach, "Bemerkungen zu τύπος, ἀντίτυπος und ἀρχέτυπος sowie zu den Inschriften des Verduner Altars," *Glotta* 62, nos. 3–4 (1984): 175–186. On the dating of the altar, see Helmut Buschhausen, "Die Geschichte der Inschriften auf dem Verduner Altar des Nikolaus: Überlegungen zu einer Neudatierung," *Wiener Studien* 100 (1987): 265–309.

Figure 5.1 Patio de los Leones, Alhambra Palace, Granada, Spain; lithograph by Francisco Javier Parcerisa Boada; Francisco Pi y Margall, *Recuerdos y bellezas de España: Reino de Granada* (Madrid: Jose Repullés, 1850), 384–385 (interleaf).

currency in an Iberian repertoire of scriptural images for paradisiacal gardens. Lastly, the discernment of para-Akbarian elements within de León's linguistic speculation also bespeaks a unique aspect of the author's Andalusi heritage, begging the question of interreligious acculturation.

By de León's time, *maghrebi* centers of learning formerly under Muslim rule, like the Cordoba that nourished the likes of Maimonides and Averroës, were firmly established as capitals of Christian Castile. We can thus reflect on the cultural politics of Castile during the second half of the thirteenth century, in which milieu, recalling our discussion in Chapter 1, de León received resources stemming from the court of Alfonso's son Sancho IV. By de León's lifetime, only the Nasrid Kingdom of Granada remained as a last stronghold of Muslim Iberia; the rest of Muslim-ruled al-Andalus had been appropriated by Castile during the campaigns of Alfonso's father Fernando III ("el Santo"). The upbuilding and expansion of a Castilian empire proceeded apace with the Alfonsine literary project of producing a politically Christian and linguistically Castilian ("Castiella") culture of wisdom that encompassed many of the religious, linguistic, literary, and historical vectors traversing its recently annexed territories south of Toledo.

An outstanding exemplar of this project is *La Estoria de Espanna*, a vernacular chronicle composed under the supervision of Alfonso X ("el Sabio"; the sage). Like Joseph Gikatilla and Moses de León, the chronicle affirms an ancient wisdom that is predicated on the view that scripted letterforms constitute the primordial essence of discursive knowledge.[43] The work begins with an account of legendary adepts living at the dawn of history who possessed this wisdom and preserved it for future generations. This immediately recalls de León's writings, which refer, for example, to "ancient sages of the supernal who knew all matters and made them known" for those to come.[44] The chronicle's opening genealogy of written language effectively grounds a universal history culminating with the reign of Fernando III in the wisdom of the ancients. How to read this genealogy against the background of its Hebrew and Arabic precursors actively studied throughout the territories of greater Castile? It seems that adapting and adopting an Andalusi legacy of language speculation—developed analogously by Jews and Muslims based

[43] For a general overview of Alfonsine thinking about language, see Hans J. Niederehe, *Alfonso X y la lingüística de su tiempo* (Madrid: Historiografía de la lingüística española, Sociedad General Española de Librería, 1987).
[44] Moses de León, *Mishkan ha-'edut*, 127.

on their respective languages of revelation—for the comparatively unlettered Castilian vernacular was instrumental to consolidating Alfonso's reign.

> The ancient sages (*los sabios antiguos*), who [lived] in primeval times and discovered wisdom (*fallaron los saberes*) and other things, maintained that they would be lacking in their deeds and loyalty if they did not have regard for those [who would live in times] to come, just as they did for themselves or for others in their own time. Understanding through the deeds of God, which are spiritual, that the wisdom (*los saberes*) is lost when those who know it die and leave no record (*no dexando remenbrança*).... Those who understand (*los entendudos*) had ... to seek out pathways for arriving at it and apprehending it, and after finding it, not forgetting it. And in [their] search for this, they discovered the shapes of the letters (*fallaron las figuras de las letras*). And joining these, they made syllables from them, and from joined syllables they made words (*partes*). And joining the words they produced discourse (*razon*), and through discourse they came to understand wisdom ... and to know as well how to recount what was in the times before, how it was in their season, and so that those who would come after them could also know the deeds they did, and also so that they could approximate it [i.e., the behavior of the ancients], and so that the crafts of the sciences and the other forms of knowledge that were discovered through it [i.e., discourse] by the [ancient] men would be guarded in script so that they would not fall into oblivion but be known by those yet to come.[45]

The Alfonsine corpus goes beyond a general theory of language's origins to furnish specific examples of linguistic and onomastic correspondences, exhibiting an agenda that is at once Christian, Castilian, and dynastic. One example is the *Setenario*, which scholars place during Alfonso's final decade (ca. 1274–1284; suggesting its composition overlapped with the earliest linguistic speculation of de León and Gikatilla). As its title announces, the work, part of Alfonso's legal corpus, highlights the theme of sevenfold perfection,

[45] MS Madrid, Real Biblioteca del Monasterio de San Lorenzo de El Escorial, Y-I-2, fol. 2a–b (from the first redaction or *versión primitiva*, edited in 1270–1274); compare Alfonso el Sabio, *Primera crónica general: Estoria de España que mandó componer Alfonso el Sabio y se continuaba bajo Sancho IV en 1298*, vol. 1, *Texto*, ed. Ramón Menéndez Pidal (Madrid: Bailly-Bailliere é Hijos, 1906), 3. On the redaction history of this work, see Rosa María Rodríguez Porto, "The Pillars of Hercules: The *Estoria de Espanna* (Escorial, Y.I.2) as Universal Chronicle," in *Universal Chronicles in the High Middle Ages*, ed. Michele Campopiano and Henry Bainton (Rochester: Boydell & Brewer; York Medieval Press, 2017), 223–254, es228 (for a stemma).

through speculation on seven (rather $7 \times 7 = 49$) names of God (in Latin, Hebrew, and Greek—including the Tetragrammaton),[46] seven gifts of the Holy Spirit, seven pious virtues of Fernando III, seven perfections of Seville (the great Andalusi city annexed by Fernando), seven liberal arts (trivium + quadrivium), seven planets, seven stages of life, and so on. At one instance, the text muses on the seven-letter composition of the terms "ALFA ET O" (Alpha and Omega, i.e., Jesus Christ,[47] and, perhaps implicitly, *alfa(b)eto*, that is, the alphabetic totality that is already suggested by the Greek), the name "ALFONSO" (whose orthography conveys the ruler's divine mandate by beginning and ending with the same letters as the previous term), "ESPANNA" (or, more specifically, its language), and the name of Alfonso's late father, the virtuous "FERNA[N]DO." The sevenfold pattern uniting these four terms underscores the apparent agenda of appropriating for the Castilian vernacular the same kind of primordial resonance and legislative gravitas that Muslims and Jews residing under his Christian rule ascribed to Arabic and Hebrew respectively.[48] This largely unexamined context in which theoretical knowledge about language leveraged an imperial project raises questions about the dynamics of power at work in the early writings of authors like Gikatilla and de León—latter-day continuators in Alfonsine Castile of an Andalusi legacy of Judeo-Islamic wisdom claiming the authority of hoary antiquity—who confronted a politics of cultural annexation. As adventurous innovators in such traditional wisdom, it seems that these authors competed not only with their predecessors, with one another, and even with earlier iterations of their own creativity (recall de León's references

[46] MS Toledo, Biblioteca Capitular, 43–20, fol. 1b; Alfonso el Sabio, *Setenario*, ed. Kenneth H. Vanderford (Buenos Aires: Facultad de Filosofía y Letras de la Universidad de Buenos Aires, Instituto de Filología, 1945), 5: "Thetagramaton en griego quiere dezir nonbre de Dios ascondido, e por esto, porque algunas gentes lo nonbrauan por ssennal de letras, e non por uoz; porque tenı́en que lengua de omne mortal non era digna de nonbrar a él nin ponerle nonbre ssennalado." For an overview of the manuscript tradition of the text, see ibid., xxvi–lxxvi.

[47] Revelations 1:8, 21:6, and 22:13; Paolo Cherchi, "'Alfa et O' en el 'Setenario' de Alfonso el Sabio," *Revista de Filología Española* 78, no. 3 (1998): 373–377.

[48] Our account here is much indebted to Ryan Szpiech, "From Founding Father to Pious Son: Filiation, Language, and Royal Inheritance in Alfonso X, the Learned," *Interfaces* 1 (2015): 209–235. Szpiech also discusses the Trinitarian underpinnings of the *Setenario*, which also figure in the text's understanding of language; see esp. 221–222, where the text accounts for the components of spoken language, as opposed to the above-cited account of the genesis of written language (adapted from Szpiech's translation): "For the will sends forth the voice; and the voice sends forth the letter; and the letter, the syllable; and the syllable, the word; and word, the statement; and the statement, language."

to *ba'ale sod ha-otiyyot* and *ba'ale sod ha-ḥeshbon*), but also, daringly, with the law of the land.[49]

As we saw in the prologue to the *Estoria de Espanna*, the anxiety of forgetting is a driving rhetorical motif, which emphasizes the fragility of oral forms of knowledge and mandates their preservation through the craft of written discourse. The same motif occupied Ezra ben Solomon of Girona during the first half of the thirteenth century. This is evident from the epigram with which we began this book—words from the prologue to the *Commentary on the Song of Songs*. According to Ezra, it was the obliviating passage of his days that justified the written disclosure of hidden wisdom. Ezra's account was likely indebted to an earlier Maimonidean rationale for the disclosure of secrets,[50] though it is evident that the content of his wisdom differed substantially from that of his Andalusi predecessor.[51] We began this book by reinscribing Ezra's words, not only to dramatize our own scholarly story of recovering a critical phase of de León's intellectual development—the earliest developmental snapshot, so to speak, of the zoharic kabbalah—from the vast reserves of forgotten knowledge. Beginning with Ezra also set the contextual stage for our project, by positioning de León as an eager yet independently minded student of the kabbalah of Girona. Even before the appearance of kabbalistic writing by the likes of Ezra and Naḥmanides, two

[49] On the Alfonsine context of kabbalah, see Yitzhak Baer, *A History of the Jews in Christian Spain*, trans. Louis Schoffman (Philadelphia: Jewish Publication Society, 1978), 1:118–130, 244; Marc Saperstein, "The Preaching of Repentance and the Reforms in Toledo of 1281," in *Models of Holiness in Medieval Sermons*, ed. Beverly Mayne Kienzle (Louvain-la-Neuve: Fédération Internationale des Instituts d'Études Médiévales, 1996), 157–174; Hartley Lachter, *Kabbalistic Revolution: Reimagining Judaism in Medieval Spain* (New Brunswick: Rutgers University Press, 2014), 15–20; and Eitan P. Fishbane, *The Art of Mystical Narrative: A Poetics of the Zohar* (Oxford: Oxford University Press, 2018), 401–411.

[50] On this Maimonidean rationale, see, most recently, Omer Michaelis, "'For the Wisdom of Their Wise Men Shall Perish': Forgotten Knowledge and Its Restoration in Maimonides's *Guide of the Perplexed* and Its Karaite Background," *Journal of Religion* 99, no. 4 (2019): 432–466. Compare the justification for revealing secrets for the purpose of ending a controversy in Eleazar of Worms, cited by the editor of Abraham ben Azriel, *'Arugat ha-bosem*, ed. Ephraim Urbach (Jerusalem: Mekize Nirdamim, 1964), 4:74; Ṭodros Abulafia adopts this rhetorical strategy when divulging secrets of the soul in his *Sha'ar ha-razim*, 104–105. For a general overview, see Jonathan Dauber, *Secrecy and Esoteric Writing in Kabbalistic Literature* (Philadelphia: University of Pennsylvania Press, 2022), 1–60, and 134–172 ("Ezra ben Solomon of Gerona as an Esoteric Writer").

[51] See Moshe Idel, "Maimonides and Kabbalah," in *Studies in Maimonides*, ed. Isadore Twersky (Cambridge, MA: Harvard University Press, 1990), 31–79. Though the study is largely compelling, the narrative suggesting that Maimonides's philosophical claim to the content of *ma'aseh bereshit* and *ma'aseh merkavah* served as the negative catalyst spurring the beginning of kabbalist writing does not square with Ezra's express rationale for his composition. Also, a difference between the account of Ezra versus that of Maimonides is that the former represented himself as the last link in a still unbroken chain of tradition, whereas, for the latter, the living chain of transmission had already broken, in which case the author portrayed himself as one who had succeeded, per m. Ḥagigah 2:1, at accessing the hidden knowledge independently.

authors with whom de León's earliest theosophical speculation demonstrates an acute degree of engagement, Catalonia was host to the development of a distinctive context of wisdom. In the development of sciences associated with the Greco-Arabic heritage, such as the psychology, cosmology, and astronomy elaborated by Abraham bar Ḥiyya, but also, and perhaps especially, in the intensive study of rabbinic lore that Maimonidean thought had either neglected, denigrated, or subjected to allegorical interpretation. In this context, the *Tanḥuma-Yelammedenu* literature is first attested, closely linked to the figure of Judah ben Yaqar (who authored a forerunner to the liturgical commentaries of Azriel of Girona).[52] Other late midrashic compendia, such as Exodus Rabbah, first appear to the light of history in Catalonia.[53]

This context boasts the first pre-kabbalistic commentary on *Sefer Yeṣirah* in northern Spain. Written by Judah ben Barzilai of Barcelona, the text amplifies the meaning of various motifs in *Sefer Yeṣirah* by reading them in light of the wisdom literature of the Bible and rabbinic legends (especially exemplars of the esoteric genres of *ma'aseh bereshit* and *ma'aseh merkavah*). One sapiential motif that became so central to kabbalistic speculation of all stripes is the "thirty-two paths of wisdom" that frames *Sefer Yeṣirah*'s delineation of ten digits (*sefirot*) and twenty-two Hebrew letters (of which the Torah is composed), that is, the primary alphanumeric constituents of the wisdom with which God formed the world. Barzilai insists that Torah is truly the heart (thirty-two = *lamed bet* = *lev* [heart]) of all wisdom: "The thirty-two paths are literally thirty-two paths, which are the letters and the numbers (*ha-otiyyot ve-ha-ḥeshbon*) but they really allude to heart in the overt sense and not [merely] to the number [thirty-two]."[54] This motif, which became the starting place for so much subsequent linguistic and theosophical speculation, is closely related to the identification of God's wisdom with a kind of hypostasized primordial Torah. The idea is, of course, an early forebear to de León's association of the Hebrew letters of the Torah with *ḥokhmah*.[55] Barzilai reminds us of the equation of God's wisdom with the Torah by,

[52] Shalem Yahalom, "Tanhuma in Masquerade: Discovering the Tanhuma in the Latter Midrash Rabbah Texts," in *Studies in the Tanhuma-Yelammedenu Literature*, ed. Ronit Nikolsky and Arnon Atzmon (Leiden: Brill, 2021), 222–245.

[53] See Brown, "What Does the Messiah Know?," 27n79.

[54] Judah ben Barzilai, *Commentar zum Sepher Jezira* [in Hebrew], ed. Solomon Halberstam (Berlin: Mekize Nirdamim, 1885), 106.

[55] In fact, Barzilai had already adduced traditions related to the creation of the world by means of the letters of the Tetragrammaton, with detailed attention (just as de León did; MS Munich, Bayerische Staatsbibliothek, Cod. hebr. 47, fol. 361a) to the exedra-like form of the letter *heh* (Barzilai, *Commentar*, 113).

for example, emphasizing that the entire Torah is the heart of wisdom, encompassed as it is by the letters *lamed*, the final letter of the final word (*Yisrael*) that seals the Book of Deuteronomy, and *bet*, the first letter of the first word (*bereshit*) of Genesis.[56] The Amoraic midrash in which God is said to consult the Torah as a blueprint when creating the world is a classic example of the Platonic predilection of rabbinic creation lore to idealize the Torah as a preexistent hypostasis.

The anonymous *Sefer ha-Bahir*, which was first cited by Catalonian authors, imports this ancient midrash into the earliest literature of kabbalah. The Bahir, as well as the writings of the Catalonian authors who referred to its wisdom, also contains some of our earliest theosophical speculation on gender. In the main, however, the Geronese corpus is beholden to a framework in which only the lowest gradation is singled out as female. In the Bahir, one finds the following language, first referring to the female as the last of God's seven anthropoid forms (1/7), and likening it, later, to an etrog, or cedrate tree (*citrus medica*) planted by a king in the middle of nine male date palms (1/10):

> [The blessed Holy One possesses] seven holy forms (*ṣurot qedoshot*), all of which correspond to the human, as is stated, "for in the image of Elohim He created him [the human]; male and female He created them" (Genesis 1:27). And these are they: right and left leg [= 2], right and left arm [= 2], torso and covenant [i.e., circumcised penis = 1], and head [= 1]. Thus six.... Seven is his wife.... A parable for which the matter is likened to a king who planned to plant nine male trees in his garden and all of them were date palms. What did he do? He said, "When they are all one sex, it is impossible for them to sustain." What did he do? He planted an etrog among them. And it is one among the nine ... males.... An etrog is female.[57]

In this much-studied passage from the Bahir, the rationale for including a single female "form" within the divine world is that her inclusion is required

[56] Barzilai, *Commentar*, 107; this is very likely one of the traditions the author elaborated from a tenth-century Babylonian commentary found in the Cairo Geniza. See Avishai Bar-Asher, "The Bahir as It Once Was: Transmission History as a Tool for Reconstructing and Reassessing the Text, Format, and Ideas of the Original Composition" [in Hebrew], *Tarbiz* 89, no. 1 (2022): 73–225, here 151–152n.335, which appears in a long citation from the Eastern source (Barzilai, *Commentar*, 166).

[57] Bar-Asher, "Bahir as It Once Was," 208; compare this topos with the parable of the one out of ten kings called "poor," discussed in Jeremy Phillip Brown, "Espousal of the Impoverished Bride in Early Franciscan Hagiography and the Kabbalah of Gerona," *History of Religions* 61, no. 3 (2022): 279–305, here 285–289.

for the perpetuation of a predominantly male divinity. The Bahir's gendered distribution of God's forms anticipates what one finds in the speculation on "male and female" in texts from Catalonia. If one views de León's early discourse on gender alongside the comparatively primitive androgynology from Girona, one finds that our Castilian author creatively expanded the assignment of femininity to various aspects and functions of the divinity, contributing substantially to the maternal personification of *binah*, and the projection of femininity from the lower "perpetual female" into the world of separation, where all of the angelic ranks, even the tribes of Israel, are posited as female.

To recall another example from our analysis of gender, we observed how de León took issue with Ezra's reading of the six-petaled lily. The latter, notwithstanding de León's attempted rapprochement, could not accommodate the double-thirteenfold pattern of female superordination. Taking Ezra and de León as exemplars of the wisdom developed in their respective regions, it would be patently false to endorse the view that Castilian kabbalah undermined an earlier Catalonian discourse of divine maternality. Just the opposite is the case. Moses de León emerges from our analysis as the foremost exponent of a Great Mother archetype in postbiblical Judaism.[58] The contrasts produced, however, by viewing de León's creativity against the rich background of Catalonia's culture of rabbinic wisdom should not minimize the great debt owed by de León to Ezra and Naḥmanides. The many illustrations of this debt we have observed could very well be multiplied. Our text helps scholarship to track the moment when de León intercepted the wisdom disseminated from Girona and began to synthesize it with his pretheosophical project already underway.

Within the domain of theosophical speculation, de León oriented himself toward the esoteric wisdom of Catalonia, apparently more so than did earlier authors from Castile. One finds within the "Nameless Composition," for example, no trace of the ontology of impurity associated with Isaac ha-Kohen of Soria, Moses ben Simeon Çinfa of Burgos, and Ṭodros ben Joseph ha-Levi Abulafia of Toledo. This doctrine is well attested in the Zohar, and in the late

[58] That is, our author labored quite consciously to collect a scripturally sourced array of maternal images for the divinity and its processes that would function as an archetypal schema for the ordering of reality. It is not, however, our intention to present de León's fascination with uterine and birth-giving imagery as a tradition-specific, or evolutionarily specific, expression of an archetype of the collective unconscious; we do not, in other words, commit ourselves, and much less de León, to Erich Neumann's Jungian epistemology. Erich Neumann, *The Great Mother: An Analysis of the Archetype*, trans. Ralph Manheim (Princeton, NJ: Princeton University Press, 1955).

writings of Gikatilla and de León, but not in the latter's early theosophical writings.[59] The doctrine held no sway over our text's penitential discourse, in contrast to the chapter on repentance in *Mishkan ha-'edut* (1293). Nor did it shape de León's earliest constructions of gender. Nonetheless, even after the penetration of the doctrine and its bestiary symbolism into de León's thinking, the author labored to bring it into conformity with elements of his early thirteenfold speculation. This may be gleaned from a passage in *Sheqel ha-qodesh* (1292) where the belated appearance of such knowledge in de León's oeuvre is dramatized. The passage recounts the doctrine's climactic revelation by Jacob the Patriarch. The latter is said to gather his twelve sons about him in an apotropaic configuration when delivering his final disclosure concerning the "end of days," a term that is glossed as a reference to *malkhut*. The gradation is the "end," as it were, of the days, or gradations, of divinity (and correspondingly, the end of Jacob's days on the earth and the beginning of his apotheosis).[60] This beatific "end" is contrasted with another "end," namely, "the cause of the 'end of all flesh' [that God inflicted on the generation of Noah,[61] which] is the secret of the cursed primordial serpent, cursed is he more than all of the beasts of the field."[62] The divine gradation of *malkhut* thus parallels its negative counterpart, the pernicious serpent, which we can identify with Lilith, the bride of Samael, the malevolent source of impurity, and the personification of the demonic feminine.[63] To prevent any such impurity from prevailing over the end of Jacob's earthly

[59] See Avishai Bar-Asher, "'Samael and His Female Counterpart': R. Moses de León's Lost Commentary on Ecclesiastes" [in Hebrew], *Tarbiz* 80, no. 4 (2012): 539–566. It appears that Gikatilla came to this doctrine late in his writing but, like de León, composed numerous texts dedicated to expositing the ontology of evil and its symbolism, all while integrating this body of knowledge into his earlier thinking. See Naama Ben Shachar, *Israel and the Archons of the Nations: War, Purity and Impurity. Three Commentaries on the Ten Sefirot Attributed to R. Joseph Giqatilla* (Los Angeles, CA: Cherub Press, 2022). A close parallel to de León's exegesis of Jacob's valediction can be found in a text ascribed to Moses of Burgos, where the motif likewise fuels thirteenfold speculation, printed in Gershom Scholem, "An Inquiry in the Kabbala of R. Isaac ben Jacob Hacohen: III. R. Moses of Burgos, the Disciple of R. Isaac (Concluded)" [in Hebrew], *Tarbiz* 5, nos. 3–4 (1934): 305–323, here 320–321; on the correspondence of Jacob and his sons to the thirteen attributes, see, too, Ṭodros Abulafia, *Sha'ar ha-razim*, ed. Michal [Kushnir-]Oron (Jerusalem: Mossad Bialik, 1989), 115.

[60] Though it is attested already in Catalonian sources, the theosophical motif of Jacob's immortality appears for the first time in de León's corpus in our text, MS Munich, Bayerische Staatsbibliothek, Cod. hebr. 47, fol. 336a.

[61] Genesis 6:13.

[62] Moses de León, *Sheqel ha-qodesh*, 81; compare the earlier accounts in Elliot R. Wolfson, ed., *The Book of the Pomegranate: Moses de Leon's* Sefer ha-Rimmon (Atlanta, GA: Scholars Press, 2020) = Moses de León, *Sefer ha-Rimmon*, 73–74. See, too, Moses de León, *Sefer ha-Mishqal*, 158.

[63] See the comparatively reserved formulation of MS Munich, Bayerische Staatsbibliothek, hebr. 47, fol. 368b: "The female is from the left side," where the left side is aligned with judgment and might, but not yet the full-blown doctrine of the *siṭra ahra*.

days, the patriarch arrays his sons according to the model of Solomon's Sea, over which he presides from on high through the mediation of *malkhut*. The sons act accordingly, pronouncing two theological statements of unification,[64] which have the effect of unifying both the world below (the lower thirteenfold headed by *malkhut*) and the world above (the domain headed by *binah* and supported by Jacob's divine aspect): "And thus there transpired there two unifications: a secret of the supernal world, and a secret of the lower world, and all is one."[65]

5.3 Wisdom of the Zohar from Rav Hamnuna Saba

Moses de León dated most of his major works. This is something virtually no kabbalistic authors from his period did. We are thus able to chart chronological and developmental trajectories by tracing the author's elaboration of central themes, which we explored in the foregoing chapters. Our readings, which synthesize philological and thematic analyses, are founded upon the methodological premise that the pathways of de León's ideational development serve as a reliable gauge for sequencing those of his texts whose dates are unknown. The primary test case for demonstrating the productivity of this premise has been the composition at the heart of our study, de León's earliest theosophical work, for which no authorial indication of date survives. But what about the copious material from the homilies (and other compositions) of the Zohar that can be traced to de León? The fact that this large quantity of material is undated need not flummox scholars to the dramatic degree that it has. From a strictly scientific perspective, the outlook for organizing de León's zoharic creativity in terms of chronology is far rosier than, for example, the prospect of arranging the corpus of kabbalistic writings from Catalonia around a fixed set of points on a timeline. To conclude, we highlight the confidence our study of the "Nameless Composition" lends to the historical-critical interpretation of the Zohar, the most traditionally authoritative repository of kabbalistic wisdom. We will demonstrate, to a degree heretofore unprecedented in the research, the interdependence and mutually constitutive character of the zoharic anthology and de León's Hebrew writings.

64 Based on b. Pesaḥim 56a.
65 Moses de León, *Sheqel ha-qodesh*, 81.

There is indeed good reason for confidence when it comes to ordering de Léon's zoharic writings according to the developmental, and, in some cases, datable progression of the author's thought. The evidence supports our supposition that de León engaged in the composition of zoharic texts from at least as early as 1286, the terminus ante quem of our focal text, and we presume that he continued to enlarge the scope of his zoharic project throughout the period of his dated Hebrew writings, the last of which is dated 1293. This means that de León's Hebrew corpus remains our best point of reference for outlining the beginnings of the project that was already called "The Book of the Zohar" (*Sefer ha-Zohar*) in the writings of Menaḥem ben Benjamin Recanati around the turn of the fourteenth century. Coordinating the corpora may proceed, then, by emploting zoharic passages that bear the telltale signs of de León's authorship into the longitudinal pathways tracked by the author's changing elaboration of key themes. Though the themes we isolated derive from the earliest traceable phase of de León's theosophical speculation, they are themes that occupied the writer throughout the course of his discernible journey, with roots in his pretheosophical speculation and branches extending into his latest known writings.

Our analysis of the zoharic "rose among the thorns" exemplified this method of emplotment; we charted de León's ideational development from the "Nameless Composition" through *Shushan ha-'edut* (1286) and *Sefer ha-Rimmon* (1287), culminating in the passage chosen by early modern editors to ornament the first page of the printed Zohar, a literary gem apparently cut by de León. Locating this famous passage within an obscure pathway of ideational growth not only allowed us to locate the rose passage in the wake of a comparable passage in *Sefer ha-Rimmon*, but also to furnish a case history for the text that is indispensable for its contextual interpretation.

For another example of how this method may be employed, we return to the above-mentioned "end of all flesh" passage from 1292's *Sheqel ha-qodesh*. We saw how the passage, which dramatizes the belated appearance of ontological speculation about impurity within de León's corpus, integrated the thirteenfold speculation that distinguished his earliest theosophy into his late thinking about evil. What does this teach us about the Zohar? The latter's lengthy and detailed account of Jacob's farewell discourse is found in its homilies to Parashat Vayeḥi, where one observes, as seen in Chapter 4, some of the most striking examples of the Zohar's indebtedness to the "Nameless Composition." But the extensive parallels to the latter contained in the Vayeḥi homilies bear nary a trace of the thinking about defilement that scholarship has often ascribed to Castilian kabbalah in a generic manner. In the zoharic context, that is, there is no indication that such thinking is reflected in Jacob's valediction. These factors recommend placing the Vayeḥi material prior to the composition of *Sheqel ha-qodesh* in 1292, and after the theosophical composition that preceded 1286's *Shushan ha-'edut*. Additional variations on the "end of days" motif that appear in *Sefer ha-Rimmon* (1287) and *Sefer ha-Nefesh ha-ḥakhamah/ Sefer ha-Mishqal* (1290) can further nuance our dating of the zoharic narrative of the Patriarch's farewell.

We can adduce an additional text from the Zohar that can be similarly positioned, namely, an explanation of divine names found in the zoharic homilies to Parashat Vayiqra,[66] an account that we propose to emplot on a developmental trajectory leading from (a) the appendix of the early "Nameless Composition" on the divine names to (b) the parallel appendix of the later *Sheqel ha-qodesh*. Here, too, the sequence of texts demonstrates a definite direction of ideational development. But there is more yet to learn from the collation of related material within the two corpora than the sequencing, dating, and interpretive contextualization that the method of emplotment produces.

Close attention to parallels between the two corpora has aided a critical breakthrough that emboldens a more radical rethinking of the status quo in Zohar–de León scholarship.

At the end of the appendix on the divine names in *Sheqel ha-qodesh*, one finds the responsum addressing a questioner's fears about the para-Trinitarian character of theosophical speculation on the Shema. In this context, de León refers his reader to a title whose appearance is utterly unique within the known Hebrew works of de León. When concluding its discussion of the divine names with a delineation of the three names mentioned in the Shema, the text refers the reader to a book that contains an account of the triunity of God's intellectual attributes (see Figure 5.2).[67]

> The secret of *ḥokhmah* and *binah* and *da'at* is the entirety of all of the sefirot, the entirety of all of the unity and the secret of His truth, and this is the secret of the name YHV, the unique name that is one, and . . . *ḥokhmah* and *tevunah* (understanding) and *da'at* (knowledge) are likewise the secret

[66] Zohar 3:10b–11a.
[67] See Brown, "What Does the Messiah Know?," esp. 2–8.

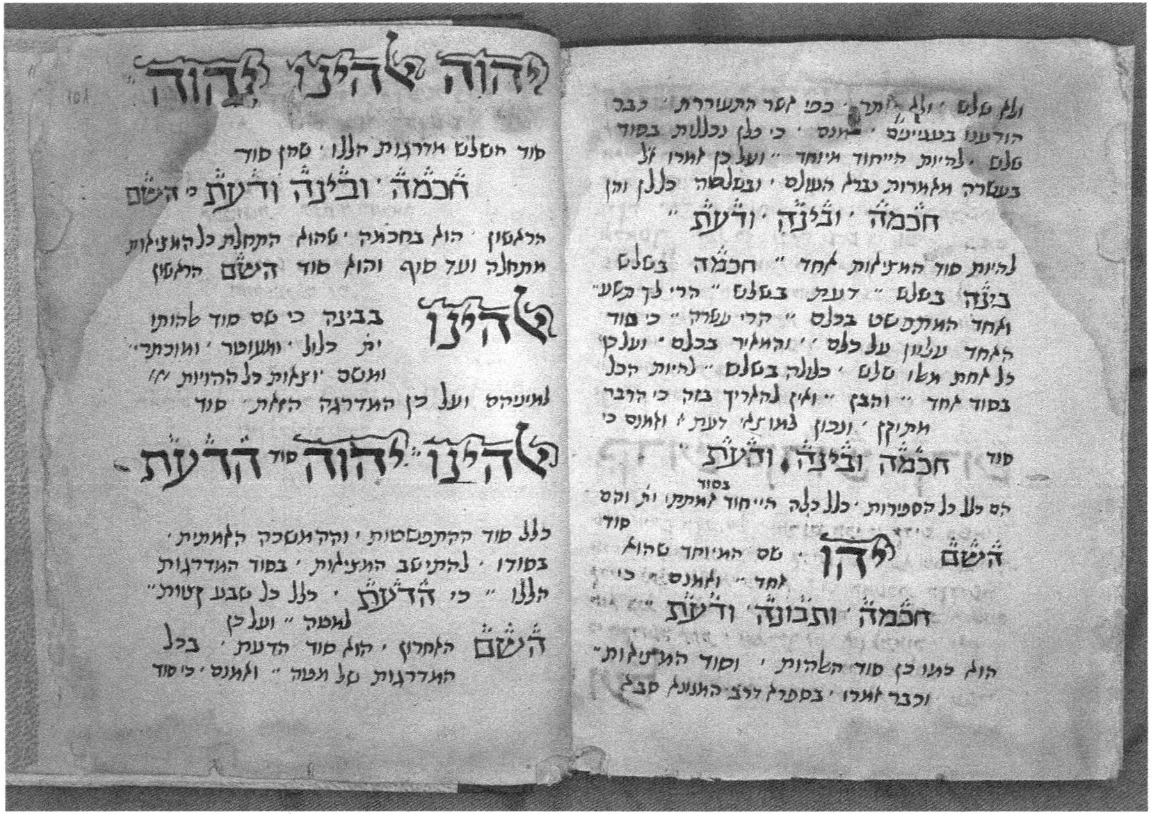

Figure 5.2 "And it is already stated in the Book of Rav Hamnuna Saba," presumably referring to the "Nameless Composition"; from the final part of Moses de León's 1292 *Sheqel ha-qodesh*; MS Jerusalem, National Library of Israel, Heb. 8°2066, fols. 100b–101a.

> of divinity and the secret of existence, and it is already stated in the *Book of Rav Hamnuna Saba* (*Sifra de-Rav Hamnuna Saba*): "YHWH, Our God, YHWH is one"; this is the secret of these three gradations that are *ḥokhmah*, *binah* and *da'at*.[68]

How to understand de León's enigmatic citation in this context? Nowhere else in his Hebrew writings does this title appear, but the Zohar makes many references to it, as a book attributed to an ancient master from the East who, in the anachronistic hagiography of the Zohar, traveled from Babylonia to the Land of Israel to teach the forebears of Simeon bar Yoḥai (though the historical personage lived several generations after the Galilean rabbi).[69] The Zohar's numerous references to this book have puzzled traditional and modern scholars for centuries. The scholarly consensus has counted this title among the holdings of a fanciful library of imaginary books mentioned by the Zohar, titles with no clear point of reference. Attitudes toward such titles have typically ranged from skeptical of their objective existence, to overtly cynical, regarding the citation of such titles as a merely rhetorical strategy of self-authorization.[70] A traditional view holds that these books were actual works that Israel lost through the vicissitudes of exile. We have nonetheless reached the surprising conclusion that when the zoharic homilies allude to Hamnuna's book,[71] they refer precisely to the wisdom preserved in de León's earliest theosophical composition.

As for the reference in *Sheqel ha-qodesh* cited above, a perusal of the "Nameless Composition" turns up a corresponding stratification of the divinity into the same three intellectual attributes that the text from *Sheqel ha-qodesh* assigns to the three names mentioned in the Shema:

[68] Moses de León, *Sheqel ha-qodesh*, 105; see below in sec. 5.3 for the synoptic presentation of this passage alongside MS Munich, Bayerische Staatsbibliothek, Cod. hebr. 47, fols. 378b–379a.

[69] See, for example, Zohar 3:72b and 2:79a.

[70] Tishby, *Wisdom of the Zohar*, 1:81–82: "Many passages are quoted [in the Zohar] from various strange sources that never existed at all." Daniel Matt, *Zohar: The Book of Enlightenment* (Mahwah: Paulist Press, 1983), 25: "An entire imaginary library provides proof texts whenever necessary." See Avishai Bar-Asher, *Journeys of the Soul: Concepts and Imageries of Paradise in Medieval Kabbalah* [in Hebrew] (Jerusalem: Magnes Press, 2019), 295–299.

[71] On the characterization of Hamnuna in the Zohar, see Tishby, *Wisdom of the Zohar*, 1:60; Pinchas Giller, *Reading the Zohar: The Sacred Text of the Kabbalah* (New York: Oxford University Press, 2001), s.v. "Hamnuna Sabba"; Jonatan M. Benarroch, "God and His Son: Christian Affinities in the Shaping of the Sava and Yanuka Figures in the Zohar," *Jewish Quarterly Review* 107, no. 1 (2017): 38–65; and Yakov Z. Mayer, "Rashbi and Rav Hamnuna: Between Sepharad and Ashkenaz" [in Hebrew], in *The Zoharic Story*, ed. Jonatan M. Benarroch, Yehuda Liebes, and Melilla Hellner-Eshed (Jerusalem: Ben-Zvi Institute, 2017), 2:445–462.

MS Munich, Bayerische Staatsbibliothek, Cod. hebr. 47	***Sheqel ha-qodesh***
All of the attributes in their entirety interpenetrate and become bound with one another. . . . For *ḥokhmah* is bound with *binah* and *binah* is bound with *da'at* [i.e., the set of seven gradations descending below *binah*], and *da'at* is bound with all that is below [the threshold of divinity].[72]	The secret of *ḥokhmah* and *binah* and *da'at* is the entirety of all of the sefirot, the entirety of all of unity and the secret of His truth . . . ; *ḥokhmah* and *tevunah* and *da'at* are likewise the secret of divinity and the secret of existence, and it is already stated in the *Book of Rav Hamnuna Saba*.[73]

If we turn to the account of divine names from the Zohar that parallels those found in the appendices to *Sheqel ha-qodesh* and our text, we find another reference to Rav Hamnuna Saba's elusive book. In this case, the reference appears amid a nexus of linguistic, onomastic, and gender speculation closely resembling that of our text:

> We have learned: Ten names are fashioned, issuing from . . . *yod*—*yod*, the tenth of the letters—and it [i.e., the *yod*] conveyed all of them [i.e., the letters] into that holy river when she [i.e., *binah*] conceived. All ten names are concealed within one, all concealed in *yod*; *yod* contains them, *yod* generates them—this is the father of all, father of fathers—from him they issued, to Him they return.
>
> [Additionally,] *vav*, *dalet*—alluding to ten by adding [the sum of] of letters [i.e., 6 (*vav*) + 4 (*dalet*) = 10 (*yod*)] *yod* includes them; *dalet* [and] *vav*, consummation of all; *vav*, *dalet*—male and female, called *du* [i.e.,

72 MS Munich, Bayerische Staatsbibliothek, Cod. hebr. 47, fols. 378b–379a.

73 Moses de León, *Sheqel ha-qodesh*, 105. Compare the secret of the Shema to that mentioned in Zohar 3:7b (where Rav Hamnuna's book is referenced) and 216b (on which, see discussion below in the same section [sec. 5.3]); also compare the secrets of the Shema apparently authored by de León, which are preserved in MS Paris, Bibliothèque nationale de France, héb. 806, fol. 226a–b, and their close parallels discussed in Avishai Bar-Asher, "*Kabbalah* and *Minhag*: Geonic Responsa and the Kabbalist Polemic on *Minhagim* in the Zohar and Related Texts" [in Hebrew], *Tarbiz* 84, no. 1 (2016): 195–263, here 238–239; Mopsik was evidently hasty in his explanation of this reference: "Un ouvrage qui porte ce titre est mentionné plus de vingt-cinq fois dans le Zohar, mais la présente citation ne s'y trouve pas. Moïse de León se réfère sans doute ici à Zohar III, 216b, où est développée une explication du *Chéma* attribuée à 'Rav Hamenouna l'Ancien qui l'avait apprise de son père, et son père de son maître [qui l'avait obtenue] de la bouche d Èlie.' Le texte du *Zohar* est en fait succinctement résumé ici, Moïse de León n'en retenant que le sens général" (Mopsik, *Le Sicle du sanctuaire*, 296n.1082).

two in Greek, which is transliterated by juxtaposing the *dalet* and *vav*], two. Therefore, Adam was created androgynous (*du parsufin*), with two facets, and those facets were male and female, corresponding to the pattern above: *vav*, *dalet*—and they are *dalet*, *vav* from below to above, but all is one matter. Thirteen attributes depend upon it, and thus *yod* includes *vav*, *dalet*, as has been said and established.

Come and see: There are ten names corresponding to ten letters. And in the *Book of Rav Hamnuna Saba*, they are eight, and two rungs corresponding to two firmaments. And the names change: ten, nine, eight, seven. The first [name] is Yah (spelled *yod* + *heh*), because the *yod* encompasses the *heh* and the *heh* is drawn forth from the *yod*. For this reason, *ḥokhmah* is called Yah.[74]

One is immediately impressed with the speculative parallels between this passage and the "Nameless Composition": the description of *yod* as the source of all letters and hence all being; the *yod* personified here as the paterfamilias (a personification that is absent from de León's earliest theosophy) who conceives with the maternal *binah*, the life-giving stream;[75] the discussion of the male and female letters—*vav* and *dalet*; and the dependency of a lower thirteenfold pattern on their unity.

But it is perhaps more impressive still to find within the "Nameless Composition" precise correspondences to the riddling details attributed to Hamnuna's book. Corresponding to the mysterious assertion that the letters "are eight and two rungs corresponding to two firmaments," de León's earliest theosophical composition mentions, as described in Chapter 3, a twofold division of the first eight letters of the alphabet that is linked to the value of the theonym Yah: "As for 'BGDHVZḤ, you find YH [= 15] on the one side of the letter *vav* ['(1) + B (2) + D (3) + G (4) + H (5)] and YH [= 15] on other [Z (7) + Ḥ (8)]; *vav* is in the middle to govern through the

[74] Zohar 3:10b–11a.

[75] An examination of the earliest attestations of the text in question from the zoharic homilies to Vayiqra supports the version rendered above on the basis of Matt's translation, suggesting, in particular, that the paternity of the yod is not an idea that has been interpolated into the text. See especially the earliest known copy of the passage in question, in MS Vatican, Biblioteca Apostolica Vaticana, ebr. 202, fol. 27a (a manuscript produced in Spain ca. 1300); consider also the earliest documented translation of this text into Hebrew, found in MS Vatican, Biblioteca Apostolica Vaticana, 226, fol. 149b. For the significance of these attestations to the transmission history of the Zohar, see Avishai Bar-Asher, "Emendation, Editing, Elucidation: Preliminary Remarks on the Historical Edition of Zoharic Texts," in Editing Kabbalistic Texts: New Philological and Digital Approaches, ed. Bill Rebiger and Gerold Necker (Wiesbaden: Harrassowitz), 173–186.

secret of YH."[76] In Chapter 3, we also examined our text's musings on the theosophico-numerical significance of various sets of letters; these include sets of ten, nine, and eight (due to the attenuation of the *vav*, the set of eight is also a set of seven).[77] This correlates directly with the claim that "their names change: ten, nine, eight, seven," allegedly found within Hamnuna's book. This is an assertion whose meaning has eluded centuries of commentators.[78] Whereas the arithmetic exercise just adduced is designed to yield fifteen (i.e., Yah), the zoharic exposition on the book of Ruth mentions an alphanumeric operation based on the *atbash* cipher (see Chapter 3) that reproduces the sum of fourteen (i.e., *yad*). The latter is similar in style to the techniques of letter pairing articulated in the "Nameless Composition," which the zoharic text attributed, once again, to the allegedly ancient, and ostensibly oriental, book of the Babylonian elder.[79]

In Chapter 3, we observed how de León transposed the speculation on the letters and vowels from his earliest pretheosophical *Sefer ha-Ne'lam* corpus into the theosophical framework of his earliest para-zoharic composition. Correspondingly, we find attributed to Rav Hamnuna Saba one of the most famous and extensive examples of zoharic discourse on the Hebrew letters,[80] namely, the theosophical adaptation of the pretheosophical account of the letters in the "Alphabet of Rabbi Aqiba" (*Midrash Otiyyot de-Rabbi Aqiba*). Elsewhere, the Zohar relays arcane knowledge of the letters *ḥet* and *ṭet* from Hamnuna's book, and this too resembles the specific lore found in our text.[81]

In Chapter 4, we made special note of the fact that the zoharic homilies on Parashat Vayeḥi contain speculation on gender that exhibits the same motifs found in the "Nameless Composition," including the double-thirteenfold pattern of female superordination, the account of divine self-parturition, and the notion of the "unblemished female," inter alia. Additionally, the zoharic homilies on Parashat Vayeḥi articulate a fourfold psychology that tracks perfectly with de León's earliest theosophical discourse. Compellingly, when

[76] MS Munich, Bayerische Staatsbibliothek, Cod. hebr. 47, fol. 373a; see the discussion in Chapter 3.

[77] MS Munich, Bayerische Staatsbibliothek, Cod. hebr. 47, fol. 364a.

[78] Compare MS Munich, Bayerische Staatsbibliothek, Cod. hebr. 47, fol. 384a, for language of changing names.

[79] *Midrash ha-Ne'lam* on the book of Ruth, in *Zohar ḥadash*, ed. Reuven Margaliyot (Jerusalem: Mossad ha-Rav Kook, 1953), fol. 87a.

[80] The ascription appears at the outset of this passage, sometimes called *Otiyyot de-Bereshit*, on Zohar 1:2b;. See Michal Oron, "The Narrative of the Letters and Its Source: A Study of a Zoharic Midrash on the Letters of the Alphabet" [in Hebrew], *Jerusalem Studies in Jewish Thought* 3, nos. 1–2 (1983–1984): 97–109.

[81] Zohar 2:152a.

embarking on its respective discussions of the soul and gender, this section of the Zohar alludes in each case to the *Book of Rav Hamnuna Saba*.

As a prelude to the account of the soul in the homilies on Vayeḥi, Rabbi Simeon exhorts his students to be silent in preparation to receive a precious pearl of wisdom he is about to disclose from Hamnuna's book.

> Rabbi Simeon was silent for a while. He said, "Silence is necessary everywhere—except for the silence of Torah. I have one treasure, treasured away, and I do not want it to be lost to you. It is a supernal word. I found it in the *Book of Rav Hamnuna Saba*."[82]

If de León is the author of this exhortation, which we presume he is, and the elusive book it mentions somehow refers to the "Nameless Composition," which we likewise posit, then the language of Rabbi Simeon's exhortation would bespeak de León's highest esteem for his first foray into kabbalah; he did not wish to abandon his earliest theosophical composition whatsoever, but rather to enshrine its memory within the Zohar's hagiography.

The teaching that Rabbi Simeon goes on to divulge from Hamnuna's book corresponds to a passage in the "Nameless Composition" in which the three divine sources of the soul correspond pictographically to the superscript, medial, and subscript positions of three Hebrew vowel points: the superscript *ḥolem* (וֹ) signifies *neshamah*, whose source is *binah*; the medial *shuruq* (וּ) signifies *ruaḥ*, whose source is *tif'eret*; and the subscript *ḥiriq* (וִ) signifies *nefesh*, whose source is *malkhut*. Sustaining all of these psychic gradations is the ungraspable pneumatic faculty called "the primordial ether," which de León, as we have seen, identified with *keter* (or here *ayin*, i.e., "nothing"), the most sublime of divine realities that transcends even the supernal point of the *ḥolem*.[83] Though the wisdom drawn by Rabbi Simeon from Hamnuna's book is not focused on the Hebrew vowel points,[84] it nonetheless evinces the same psycho-theosophical framework.

[82] Zohar 1:245b. Rabbi Simeon proceeds to urge his students to marvel at the counterintuitive inversion of gender roles within the divinity to be found in Hamnuna's book—a theme obviously suggestive of the "Nameless Composition."

[83] See sec. 3.9, in Chapter 3, on de León's account of the *ḥolem* vis-à-vis Gikatilla.

[84] Though the text's language of the descending pearl drops is redolent of the ink drops that constitute the upper, middle, and lower vowel points.

Zohar	MS Munich, Bayerische Staatsbibliothek, Cod. hebr. 47
Come and see: There are three souls, ascending by certain rungs, and as for their being three, they are four. One: transcendent soul that cannot be grasped.... This is the soul of all souls, concealed, eternally unrevealed, unknowable—and all of them depend upon it. This envelops itself in a wrapping of crystal radiance within radiancy, and drips pearls, drop by drop, all linking as one, like joints of limbs of one body—one. It enters into them, displaying through them its activity; this and they are one, inseparable. This supernal soul is hidden from all.[85]	And truly, [the superscript] *ḥolem*, which is the supernal one [i.e., *neshamah*, corresponding to *binah*], sustains the other spirits [i.e., *ruaḥ* and *nefesh*, corresponding to *tif'eret* and *malkhut*], and it is sustained by that which is invisible and unrevealed. And this is the secret of *ayin* [i.e., *keter*], an ether that one never grasps. And therefore, those three gradations of the soul are three ethers (*avirim*), one above the other and one above the other. And thus they [constitute] a single pattern, and all of them are bound in a single bond.[86]

The two passages exhibit an exceedingly subtle degree of equivalence in expressing, through the use of alternate images, the convergence of psychology and ontology within the ungraspable depth of divinity. That is, above and beyond the coordination of a tripartite understanding of the soul with three dimensions of God's being, both texts articulate a negative psychology that is coordinated with the apophatic dimension of the author's theology.[87]

From this demonstration we can proceed to the subsequent reference to Hamnuna's book, which appears shortly after the previous. It is here that Rabbi Simeon invokes the lofty title when expounding how the two loaves served on the Sabbath allude to the two primary female attributes.[88]

> In the *Book of Rav Hamnuna Saba*,[89] it said thus: "From Asher [i.e., *binah*], rich is his bread, [he will provide delicacies of a king]" (Genesis 49:20)—the bread of Sabbath, which is a double pastry, as it says: "They gathered double bread" (Exodus 16:22). What does "double" mean? Two breads: "bread from heaven" (Exodus 16:4) and "bread from earth" (Psalms

85 Zohar 1:245a–b.

86 MS Munich, Bayerische Staatsbibliothek, Cod. hebr. 47, fol. 369b.

87 See Jeremy Phillip Brown, "Glimmers of the World Soul in Kabbalah," in *World Soul: A History*, ed. James Wilberding (New York: Oxford University Press 2021), 124–150, esp. 131–137.

88 For another tradition attributed to Hamnuna concerning the heavenly bread consumed in purity by the ministering angels, see *Midrash ha-Ne'lam* on the book of Ruth, in *Zohar ḥadash*, fol. 86d, where the angelic model of purity is the example to be emulated by Israel in their sanctifications before and after meals.

89 Though Daniel Matt rendered the title "The Book of Yeiva Sava," our reading is well attested in both print and manuscript witnesses.

> 104:14)—one is a pastry; one is a "bread of poverty" (Deuteronomy 16:2). On Sabbath lower bread is interbraided with higher bread, one blessed through the other; this is "double bread." It said further: "double bread"—for the Sabbath [i.e., *malkhut*] receives from the supernal Sabbath [i.e., *binah*], who flows and illumines all; so bread joins with bread, becoming "double." In every instance, the mystery of bread is a female.[90]

The explication of this double-braid pattern of female gradations leads to the lengthy disquisition of God's gender in Zohar on Parashat Vayeḥi that recaps the distinctive theologoumena we examined in Chapter 4, albeit on the basis of some alternate images and scriptural language. Especially noteworthy are the students' objections anticipated by Rabbi Simeon, since they suggest the inherited opinions, notably, opinions indicative of the earlier Catalonian discourse on "male and female," that the author, presumably de León, wished to redress. Thus, after emphasizing the superordinate identification of *binah* as the supernal "bread," the text gives voice to this rhetorical objection:

> Now, you might say, "The bread is gone [indicating the masculine verb form, אזל] from our sacks" (1 Samuel 9:7)—and not אזלת [the female verb form]! Well, we call other food "bread," and it is well known which is other food and which is actual bread. Bread from above is always male; lower bread is female. And we have found that sometimes it is written as male and sometimes as female. All is one entity, whether this or that, and all is fine.[91]

But Rabbi Simeon rejects the line of argumentation that leads to the conclusion that "bread from above is always male." He does so by reinforcing his earlier teaching about the double female pattern with another tradition, one supposed sourced from the wisdom of Hamnuna's revered book, concerning a double thirteenfold pattern that proves the supernal position of the female.

> Come and see: Asher [i.e., *binah*] is inscribed above and inscribed below in the adornments of the bride [i.e., *malkhut*]. The sea rests upon all twelve tribes and is arrayed in them, as is written: "with the sea resting upon them from above" (1 Kings 7:35). Mystery of the matter: arrayed above, arrayed below on earth. Arrayed above, in certain adornments corresponding to

[90] Zohar 1:246a; compare the attestations of the double-braid motif discussed in Bar-Asher, "Kabbalah and Minhag," 208–212.

[91] Zohar 1:246a.

> the supernal world. Arrayed below, in these twelve tribes, corresponding to the pattern above. So *shekhinah* above, *shekhinah* below, by virtue of Israel; she is encompassed and arrayed on both sides.[92]

Chapter 4 already established the importance of the Zohar's theosophical speculation on Solomon's Sea for observing the legacy of de León's earliest thinking about gender, noting the attestation, within the continuation of the above-cited passage, of additional topoi related to the pattern of the one resting atop twelve.

One such topos is attested elsewhere in the Zohar, where it is again cited by Rabbi Simeon on the authority of Rav Hamnuna, namely, the identification of *binah* as the source of life. This uterine motif is embellished through the symbol of the river issuing from Eden, which is named "Yuval," meaning stream.

Zohar	**MS Munich, Bayerische Staatsbibliothek, Cod. hebr. 47**
Come and see: "A river issues from Eden to water the garden" (Genesis 2:10). We have learned: What is the name of that river? As had been established, its name is Yuval [i.e., *binah*], as is written: "spreading its roots by a stream (*yuval*)" (Jeremiah 17:8). And in the *Book of Rav Hamnuna Saba*, its name is Life, because life issues from there to the world, and that is called Life of the King. We have established that the grand and mighty tree, containing food for all, is called the Tree of Life [i.e., *tif eret*]—a tree whose roots are planted in that Life [i.e., *binah*].[93]	The secret of the existence [extending] from below *ḥokhmah* is never known and revealed save when the concealment of its existence from the supernal world is the stream (*yuval*), which is the secret of "female shall compass male" (Jeremiah 31:22). And thus the supernal world being [the] "issue of life" (Proverbs 4:23) to all is the source of all rivers going forth within the female who brings forth fruit for its purpose.[94] . . . When everything began from this [process of] extension, all of the matters began [according to the hyperliteral reading of Genesis 2:4: בהבראם]: "By means of *heh* He created them," whether above or below, but all of them were planted in the stream (*yuval*), and therefore "the issue of life" is by the letter *heh* (i.e., *binah*).[95]

[92] Zohar 1:246a.

[93] Zohar 3:58a.

[94] MS Munich, Bayerische Staatsbibliothek, Cod. hebr. 47, fol. 366a; for another description of *binah* as the river issuing from Eden, see fol. 338b; de León had recourse to the name *yuval* for *binah* throughout his writings. See his *Shushan ha-'edut*, 335; *Sefer ha-Rimmon*, 106; *Sheqel ha-qodesh*, 56, and there n. 439 (for zoharic iterations). But its earliest appearance is in our text; see too another description of *binah* as the life-giving stream, fol. 359a–b, and the fuller use of the phrase "spreading its roots by a stream," fol. 379a.

[95] MS Munich, Bayerische Staatsbibliothek, Cod. hebr. 47, fol. 372a.

These parallels further cement the association of our text with the wisdom attributed to the *Book of Rav Hamnuna Saba*. We will briefly mention but a few additional pieces of evidence.

In Chapter 2, we analyzed the development of de León's penitential discourse. While, in the main, the Zohar lacks the formal instructional genre exemplified by the "Order of Penitents," the zoharic homilies generally take a different tack to inculcate pious behavior. How does the ethos of de León's regimens vitae present within the Zohar? It is sufficient for our purposes to note that the transposition of this ethos from a didactic framework to a hagiographical-homiletical genre occurs through the exhortations of Rabbi Simeon and his associates and the stories of their exemplary virtues.[96] In one instance, the Zohar recounts a teaching conveyed to the Prophet Elijah by none other than Rav Hamnuna, which, as with the third behavioral mandate of the "Order of Penitents,"[97] urges upon its reader the importance of making a verbal—presumably liturgical—confession of sins so that atonement will be efficacious.[98] Additionally, when surveying de León's broader concept of pietism in Chapter 2, we elucidated the moralistic basis of the author's delineation of the right and left "sides" of the Godhead, that is, as the theological fulcrum of a mimetic ethics, and foundation of the axiom: "by the attribute with which a person conducts himself so will he be conducted."[99] In a parallel attestation of this teaching attributed to Rav Hamnuna, we see how a zoharic composition adopts our text's moralistic outlook for the promotion of ritual praxis:

> Thus said Rav Hamnuna Saba: "Two attributes stand before a person's table—one is the attribute of good, and one is the attribute of evil. If a person sanctifies his hands and recites the blessing, the attribute of good declares: 'This is the table of the blessed Holy One!' And it [i.e., the attribute of good] rests its hands upon his [i.e., the person's] head and says, '"You are my servant" (Isaiah 49:3)—servant of the Lord.' . . . But if one does not lave his hands before eating, the attribute of evil says, 'That one is mine!' It rests upon him at once, rendering him impure, and his food is called 'Bread from the Evil Eye.'"[100]

[96] See, however, Brown, *World of Piety*, chap. 4 ("Making Other People: The Formative Aspirations of Zoharic Piety").

[97] MS Munich, Bayerische Staatsbibliothek, Cod. hebr. 47, fol. 351a–b.

[98] Zohar 3:231a.

[99] MS Munich, Bayerische Staatsbibliothek, Cod. hebr. 47, fol. 347b.

[100] From the zoharic midrash on the book of Ruth; *Zohar ḥadash*, fol. 87a.

Our appraisal of de León's earliest theosophical pietism also considered the austere characterization of scholars as the "eunuchs who keep the Sabbath"; the latter are thus named because the conjugal rights (*'onah*) they owe their wives are limited to Sabbath Eve. In our discussion, we noted that a fuller account of conjugal rights appears to comprise a portion of the "Nameless Composition" that we do not possess. Correspondingly, the Zohar recounts an episode in which Rabbi Simeon adduces a mystery found in the *Book of Rav Hamnuna Saba* concerning the verse "He must not withhold her food, her clothing, or her conjugal rights."[101]

Further allusions to Hamnuna's book in the Zohar may correspond to other material from the portion of our text that is no longer extant. This is suggested, to cite another example, by a tradition related by Rabbi Judah on the authority of "The Aggadah of the House of Rav Hamnuna Saba," namely, a theosophical interpretation of Resh Laqish's ancient list of seven firmaments.[102] According to this interpretation, the seven are contained within the singular designation of the blessed Holy One by the name "Heaven" (i.e., *tiferet* = *shamayim*, a heaven encompassing seven firmaments, that is, the seven lower sefirot).[103] Since our text employs the *tiferet* = *shamayim* equivalence often and assumes that its reader is already familiar with this equivalence, it is probable that some such discussion preceded the beginning of our extensive fragment.[104]

In conclusion, the traditions pseudepigraphically attributed to Rav Hamnuna and his book allow us to track attestations of de León's earliest theosophical speculation within the Zohar. Do we thus have a name for our nameless composition? Not exactly. Though it is cited in *Sheqel ha-qodesh*, the title *Book of Rav Hamnuna Saba* is a rubric that de León likely contrived for the artfully antiquated atmosphere of the Zohar. It designates wisdom associated with a work that, in all likelihood, once possessed a proper Hebrew title. At the very least, the discovery that de León, as the author of much of the material comprising the zoharic anthology, availed himself of a highly idiosyncratic convention for alluding to his thirteenth-century Hebrew work within writings ostensibly set in the ancient Galilee opens unforeseen

[101] Zohar 3:268a.
[102] B. Ḥagigah 12b.
[103] Zohar 3:287a.
[104] In this case, a corresponding account appears in *Shushan ha-'edut*, 338–339 (and 338n.56), but like much material in that work, the account of the seven firmaments may have (had) a precursor in our text; compare also Gershom Scholem, "Shene quntresim le-R. Moshe de León," *Kobez al Yad* 8, no. 18 (1976): 371–384 = Moses de León, *Sod 'Eser sefirot belimah*, 379–380.

opportunities for correlating the twin corpora engendered by the same author. This is not only a sure indication of the intersecting chronologies of their respective compositions, but also a clearer demonstration than heretofore in the history of scholarship of their mutually constitutive character. The finding is an important development for the historical and philological study of a masterpiece of theology and a classic of literature, which may, in fact, prompt additional identifications of the legendary titles held in the Zohar's putatively "imaginary" library.

We have learned that Moses de León remained creatively committed to commemorating the richly generative text that remains nameless to us, and to propagating its wisdom throughout his zoharic writings. Scholars have long postulated that the allusions in de León's Hebrew corpus to the supposedly ancient wisdom attested in the Zohar served to promote the antiquity or at least prestige of the latter. Now we understand that hidden within the Zohar is also a reciprocal literary mechanism for the promotion of de León's "modern," so to speak, Hebrew writings. The two corpora are mutually interreferential, each augmenting the legend, content, and truth value of the other through a dynamic mirroring of what is ostensibly old in what is contemporaneous—and what is contemporaneous in the prehistory of what is supposed to be ancient. The disorienting temporal effects produced by the interaction of the corpora raise new questions for interrogating the Zohar's uses of pseudepigraphy, its citation practices, and its provocative collisions of temporal and spatial horizons. Scholarship is only beginning to account for the ingenuity of this duly celebrated but still underestimated rabbinic intellectual from Guadalajara—the self-proclaimed "light of the West."

Bibliography

Manuscripts

MS Jerusalem, National Library of Israel, Heb. 8°2066.
MS Jerusalem, Schocken Institute, 13161.
MS London, British Library, Add. 27044.
MS Madrid, Biblioteca Nacional de España, S. 34.
MS Madrid, Real Biblioteca del Monasterio de San Lorenzo de El Escorial, Y-I-2.
MS Moscow, Russian State Library, Guenzberg 362.
MS Munich, Bayerische Staatsbibliothek, Codices bavarici monacenses Cat. 36.
MS Munich, Bayerische Staatsbibliothek, Codices bavarici monacenses Cat. 36 m.
MS Munich, Bayerische Staatsbibliothek, Codices bavarici monacenses Cat. 37.
MS Munich, Bayerische Staatsbibliothek, Cod. hebr. 47.
MS Munich, Bayerische Staatsbibliothek, Cod. hebr. 54.
MS New York, Jewish Theological Seminary of America, 1609.
MS New York, Jewish Theological Seminary of America, 1777.
MS New York, Jewish Theological Seminary of America, 1886.
MS Oxford, Bodleian Library, Opp. 228 (Neubauer 1618).
MS Oxford, Bodleian Library, Opp. Add. 4°4 (Neubauer 1565).
MS Paris, Bibliothèque nationale de France, héb. 770.
MS Paris, Bibliothèque nationale de France, héb. 817.
MS Paris, Bibliothèque nationale de France, héb. 823.
MS Paris, Bibliothèque nationale de France, héb. 839.
MS Ramat Gan, Bar Ilan University 1038 (Moussaieff 63).
MS St. Petersburg, Institute of Oriental Manuscripts, The Russian Academy of Sciences D 21 (Guenzburg 606).
MS Toledo, Biblioteca Capitular, 43–20.
MS Vatican, Biblioteca Apostolica Vaticana, ebr. 86.
MS Vatican, Biblioteca Apostolica Vaticana, ebr. 202.
MS Vatican, Biblioteca Apostolica Vaticana, ebr. 212.
MS Vatican, Biblioteca Apostolica Vaticana, ebr. 214.
MS Vatican, Biblioteca Apostolica Vaticana, ebr. 226.

Primary Sources

Abraham ben Azriel. *'Arugat ha-bosem.* 4 vols. Edited by Ephraim Urbach. Jerusalem: Mekize Nirdamim, 1964.

Abulafia, Ṭodros ben Joseph he-Levi. *Oṣar ha-kavod.* Satmar: M. L. Hirsch, 1926.

Abulafia, Ṭodros ben Joseph he-Levi. *Sha'ar ha-razim.* Edited by Michal Kushnir-Oron. Jerusalem: Mossad Bialik, 1989.

Actus beati Francisci et sociorum ejus. Edited by Paul Sabatier. Paris: Fischbacher, 1902.

Alfonso X. *Cantigas de Santa Maria* = Stephen Parkinson, ed., *Alfonso X, the Learned: Cantigas de Santa Maria: An Anthology.* Cambridge, UK: Modern Humanities Research Association, 2015.

Alfonso X. *Primera crónica general: Estoria de España que mandó componer Alfonso el Sabio y se continuaba bajo Sancho IV en 1298.* Vol. 1, *Texto.* Edited by Ramón Menéndez Pidal. Madrid: Bailly-Bailliere é Hijos, 1906.

Alfonso X. *Setenario.* Edited by Kenneth H. Vanderford. Buenos Aires: Facultad de Filosofía y Letras de la Universidad de Buenos Aires, Instituto de Filología, 1945.

Asher ben David. *R. Asher ben David: His Complete Works and Studies in His Kabbalistic Thought (Including the Commentaries to the Account of Creation by the Kabbalists of Provence and Gerona).* [In Hebrew.] Edited by Daniel Abrams. Los Angeles, CA: Cherub Press, 1996.

Azriel of Girona. *Commentarius in Aggadoth auctore R. Azriel Geronensi.* [In Hebrew.] Edited by Isaiah Tishby. Jerusalem: Mekize Nirdamim, 1945.

David ben Judah he-Ḥasid. *The Book of Mirrors: Sefer Mar'ot ha-Ẓove'ot.* Edited by Daniel C. Matt. Chico, CA: Scholars Press, 1982.

de León, Moses [Moïse]. *La résidence du témoignage: Mishkan ha-'Edut.* Translated by Simon Bouskila. Paris: Hermann, 2020.

de León, Moses [Moïse]. *Le Sicle du sanctuaire: Chéqel ha-Qodech.* Translated by Charles Mopsik. Lagrasse, France: Éditions Verdier, 1996.

de León, Moses. *Mishkan ha-'edut = R. Moses de León's Sefer Mishkan ha-'edut.* [In Hebrew.] Edited by Avishai Bar-Asher. Los Angeles, CA: Cherub Press, 2013.

de León, Moses. *Responsa* = Isaiah Tishby. "She'elot u-teshuvot le-Rabbi Moshe de León be-'inyene qabbalah." [In Hebrew.] In *Studies in Kabbalah and Its Branches: Research and Sources,* 1:40–75. Jerusalem: Magnes, 1982. Reprinted from *Kobez al Yad* 5, no. 15 (1950): 9–38.

de León, Moses. *Sefer ha-Mishqal* = Jochanan H. A. Wijnhoven. "Sefer ha-Mishkal: Text and Study." PhD diss., Brandeis University, 1964.

de León, Moses. *Sefer ha-Ne'lam* = Avishai Bar-Asher. "*Sefer ha-Ne'lam,* New Parts of *Sefer Or Zarua* and Clarifications Regarding the Early Writings of R. Moses de León: Studies and Critical Editions." [In Hebrew.] *Tarbiz* 83, nos. 1–2 (2015): 318–329.

de León, Moses. *Sefer ha-Pardes* = Avishai Bar-Asher. "R. Moses de León's Sefer haPaRDeS and the Zoharic Commentaries on Biblical Narratives." *JSIS* 24 (2024): 1–71, there 43–71.

de León, Moses. *Sefer ha-Rimmon = The Book of the Pomegranate: Moses de Leon's* Sefer ha-Rimmon. Edited by Elliot R. Wolfson. Atlanta, GA: Scholars Press, 2020.

de León, Moses. *Sefer Maskiyyot Kesef* = Jochanan H. A. Wijnhoven. "*Sefer Maskiyyot Kesef:* Text and Translation with Introduction and Notes." MA thesis, Brandeis University, 1961.

de León, Moses. *Sefer Or zarua'* = Alexander Altmann. "*Sefer Or Zarua'* by R. Moses de Leon: Introduction, Critical Text, and Notes." [In Hebrew.] *Kobez al Yad* 9, no. 19 (1980): 219–293.

de León, Moses. *Sefer Or zarua'* = Avishai Bar-Asher. "*Sefer ha-Ne'lam,* New Parts of *Sefer Or Zarua* and Clarifications Regarding the Early Writings of R. Moses de León: Studies and Critical Editions." [In Hebrew.] *Tarbiz* 83, nos. 1–2 (2015): 256–318.

de León, Moses (probable author; Eliezer ben Hyrcanus [attr.]). *Sefer Orḥot ḥayyim* = "The 'Paths of Life' by R. Eleazar [*sic*] the Great." [In Hebrew and translation.] In *Hebrew Ethical Wills,* edited by Israel Abrahams, 1:31–50. Philadelphia: Jewish Publication Society of America, 1926.

de León, Moses. *Sefer Sheqel ha-qodesh = R. Moses de León's* Sefer Sheqel ha-Qodesh. [In Hebrew.] Edited by Charles Mopsik. Los Angeles, CA: Cherub Press, 1996.

de León, Moses (Jacob ha-Kohen [attr.]). "Sefer Sod darkhe ha-otiyyot ve-ha-nequddot." In *Yalqut ha-Ro'im ha-Gadol,* edited by Shraga Bauer and Shraga Eisenbach, 1–58 [seventh pagination.] Jerusalem: Nezer Shraga, 2000.

de León, Moses. *Shushan ha-'edut* = Gershom Scholem. "Shene quntresim le-R. Moshe de León." *Kobez al Yad* 8, no. 18 (1976): 325–384, esp. 330–370.

de León, Moses. *Sod Darkhe ha-otiyyot* = Avishai Bar-Asher. "From the Vaults of Thebes: Moses de León's Pseudepigraphic Writings on the Letters, Vowel Signs, Theonyms, and Magical Practices and the Origin of Zoharic Fiction." [In Hebrew.] *Kabbalah* 51 (2022): 157–248, with edition 200–248.

de León, Moses. *Sod 'Eser sefirot belimah* = Gershom Scholem. "Shene qunṭresim le-R. Moshe de León." *Kobez al Yad* 8, no. 18 (1976): 325–384, esp. 371–384.

Ezra ben Solomon of Gerona. *Commentary on the Song of Songs and Other Kabbalistic Commentaries.* Translated by Seth Brody. Kalamazoo, MI: Medieval Institute Publications, 1999.

Ezra ben Solomon of Gerona. *Le Commentaire d'Ezra de Gérone sur le Cantique des cantiques, traduction et notes annexes.* Edited by Georges Vajda. Paris: A. Montaigne, 1969.

Ezra ben Solomon of Girona. *Perush ha-Aggadot = Abraham ben Judah Elmalik: Liqquṭe shikheḥah u-fe'ah.* Ferrara, Italy: Abraham Ibn Usque, 1556.

Ezra ben Solomon of Girona (Moses Naḥmanides [attr.]). "Perush Shir ha-Shirim." In *Kitve Ramban*, edited by Charles B. Chavel, 2:473–518. Jerusalem: Mossad ha-Rav Kook, 1964.

Gikatilla, Joseph ben Abraham. *David et Bethsabée: Le Secret du marriage.* Edited by Charles Mopsik. Paris: Éditions de l'Éclat, 2003.

Gikatilla, Joseph ben Abraham. *Ginnat egoz.* Jerusalem: Yeshivat ha-Ḥayyim ve-ha-Shalom, 1989.

Gikatilla, Joseph ben Abraham. *Ginnat egoz.* In Asi Farber. "Qeṭa' ḥadash me-haqdamat R. Yosef Gikatilla le-Sefer Ginnat egoz." *Jerusalem Studies in Jewish Thought* 1 (1981): 158–176, esp. 166–176.

Gikatilla, Joseph ben Abraham. *R. Joseph Gikatilla's Commentary to Ezekiel's Chariot.* [In Hebrew.] Edited by Asi Farber. Los Angeles, CA: Cherub Press, 1998.

Gikatilla, Joseph ben Abraham. *Sefer ha-Niqqud.* In *Yosef Giqatilla, The Book of Punctuation: Flavius Mithridates' Latin Translation, the Hebrew Text, and an English Version*, edited by Annett Martini, 13–85 in "Hebrew Section." Turin: Nino Aragno Editore, 2010.

Gikatilla, Joseph ben Abraham. *Sha'are orah.* 2 vols. Edited by Joseph Ben-Shlomo. Jerusalem: Mossad Bialik, 1981.

Gikatilla, Joseph ben Abraham. *Sha'are ṣedeq.* Krakow: Fischer & Deutscher, 1881.

Gikatilla, Joseph ben Abraham. *Sha'are ṣedeq.* In Ephraim Gottlieb. "The Concluding Portion of R. Joseph Chiqatella's *Sha'arei Ẕedeq.*" [In Hebrew.] *Tarbiz* 39, no. 4 (1970): 359–389, esp. 363–389.

Gikatilla, Joseph ben Abraham [attr.]. "Sod Shelosh 'esre middot ha-nove'ot min ha-keter." [In Hebrew.] In *Catalogus codicum hebraicorum quot conservantor in Bibliotheca Hierosolymitana quae est Judaeorum Populi et Universitatis Hebraicae*, edited by Gershom Scholem and Bernhard I. Joel, 219–225. Jerusalem: Hebrew University of Jerusalem, 1930.

Ibn al-'Arabī, Muḥammad ibn 'Ali. *Al-Futūḥāt al-makkiyya.* 4 vols. Cairo: Bulaq Press, 1911.

Ibn Gaon, Shem Ṭov ben Abraham. *Sefer Badde ha-aron u-migdal Ḥananel.* Edited by D. S. Loewinger. Jerusalem: Mizraḥ u-ma'arav, 1977.

Ibn Gabirol, Solomon. *The Secular Poetry of Solomon Ibn Gabirol.* [In Hebrew.] Edited by Dov Jarden. 2 vols. Jerusalem: Kiryat Noar, 1975.Ibn Sahula, Isaac ben Solomon. *Commentary on Psalms* = Avishai Bar-Asher, "Isaac ben Solomon Ibn Sahula's Commentary on Psalms." [In Hebrew.] *Kobez al Yad* 26, no. 36 (2018): 1–45.

Ibn Sahula, Isaac ben Solomon. *Meshal Haqadmoni: Fables from the Distant Past.* 2 vols. Edited and translated by Raphael Loewe. Portland, OR: Littman Library of Jewish Civilization, 2004.

Jacob ben Jacob ha-Kohen. "Jacob ben Jacob ha-Kohen's Commentary to Ezekiel's Chariot." [In Hebrew.] Edited by Asi Farber. MA thesis, Hebrew University of Jerusalem, 1978.

Jacob ben Jacob ha-Kohen [attr.] "Perush ha-otiyyot." In Gershom Scholem. "Qabbalot R. Yiṣḥaq ve-R. Ya'aqov bene R. Ya'aqov ha-Kohen: meqorot le-toledot ha-qabbalah lifne hitgallut ha-Zohar." *Madda'e ha-Yahadut* 2 (1927): 201–219.

Jacob ben Meir (Rabbenu Tam) [attr.]. *Sefer ha-Yashar.* Jerusalem: Eshkol, 1978.

John of Perugia [attr.]. "Anonymous of Perugia" = "The Beginning or Founding of the Order and the Deeds of Those Lesser Brothers Who Were the First Companions of Blessed Francis in Religion." In *Francis of Assisi: Early Documents*, edited by Regis J. Armstrong, 2:34–58. Hyde Park, NY: New City Press, 2000.

Juan Manuel. *Don Juan Manuel y el Libro de la caza*. Edited by José Manuel Fradejas Rueda. Tordesillas, Spain: Instituto de Estudios de Iberoamérica y Portugal, Seminario de Filología Medieval, 2001.

Juan Manuel. *El libro dela caza*. Edited by Gottfried Baist. Halle: Max Niemeyer, 1880.

Judah ben Barzilai. *Commentar zum Sepher Jezira*. [In Hebrew.] Edited by Solomon Halberstam. Berlin: Mekize Nirdamim, 1885.

Maimonides, Moses. *The Code of Maimonides*. 13 vols. New Haven, CT: Yale University Press, 1949–2004.

Maimonides, Moses. *The Guide of the Perplexed*. Translated by Shlomo Pines. Chicago: University of Chicago Press, 1963.

Maimonides, Moses. *Haqdamot ha-Rambam la-Mishnah*. Translated by Isaac Shailat. Jerusalem: Hoṣa'at Ma'aliyot, 1992.

Maimonides, Moses. *Mishnah 'im perush rabbenu Mosheh ben Maimon*. 3 vols. Edited by Yosef Qafiḥ. Jerusalem: Mossad ha-Rav Kook, 1963.

Maimonides, Moses. *Sefer Mishneh Torah le-ha-Rambam*. 15 vols. Edited by Shabse Frankel. Jerusalem: Hoṣa'at Shabse Frankel, 1975–2007.

Meiri, Menaḥem ben Solomon. *Ḥibbur ha-Teshuvah*. Edited by Abraham Sofer. New York: Hoṣa'at Talpiyot, 1950.

Naḥmanides, Moses. *Commentary on the Torah*. 5 vols. Edited by Charles B. Chavel. Jerusalem: Mossad ha-Rav Kook, 1959–1963.

Naḥmanides, Moses [and attr.]. *Kitve Ramban*. 2 vols. Edited by Charles B. Chavel. Jerusalem: Mossad ha-Rav Kook, 1963.

Neḥunya ben ha-Qanah [attr.] *Sefer ha-Bahir* = Avishai Bar-Asher. "The Bahir as It Once Was: Transmission History as a Tool for Reconstructing and Reassessing the Text, Format, and Ideas of the Original Composition." [In Hebrew.] *Tarbiz* 89, no. 1 (2012): 73–225.

Pico della Mirandola, Giovanni. *Oration on the Dignity of Man: A New Translation and Commentary*. Edited by Francesco Borghesi, Michael Papio, and Massimo Riva. Cambridge, UK: Cambridge University Press, 2012.

Recanati, Menaḥem ben Benjamin. *Perush Recanati*. 2 vols. Edited by Amnon Gross. Tel Aviv: Aharon Barzani, 2003.

Recanati, Menaḥem ben Benjamin. *Sefer Ṭa'ame ha-miṣvot ha-shalem*. Edited by Simḥah Lieberman. London: Mekhon Oṣar ha-ḥokhmah, 1962.

Simeon bar Yoḥai [attr.]. *Sefer ha-Zohar*. Cremona, 1559.

Simeon bar Yoḥai [attr.]. *Sefer ha-Zohar*. 3 vols. Mantua, 1558.

Simeon bar Yoḥai [attr.]. *Sefer ha-Zohar*. 3 vols. Edited by Reuben Margaliyot. Jerusalem: Mossad Harav Kook, 1964.

Simeon bar Yoḥai [attr.]. *Tiqqune ha-Zohar*. Edited by Reuben Margaliyot. Jerusalem: Mossad ha-Rav Kook, 1978.

Simeon bar Yohai [attr.]. *Zohar ḥadash*. Edited by Reuben Margaliyot. Jerusalem: Mossad ha-Rav Kook, 1953.

Simeon bar Yohai [attr.]. *The Zohar: Pritzker Edition*. 12 vols. Translated by Daniel Matt, Joel Hecker, and Nathan Wolski. Stanford, CA: Stanford University Press, 2004–2017.

Zacuto, Abraham. *Sefer Yuḥasin*. Edited by A. H. Fraymann. Frankfurt am Main: A. Vohrmann, 1925.

Secondary Sources

Abbas, Claude. "Andalusī Mysticism and the Rise of Ibn 'Arabī." In *The Legacy of Muslim Spain*, edited by Salma Khadra Jayyusi, 2:909–933. Leiden: Brill, 1992.

Abbas, Claude. *Ibn 'Arabī, ou, La quête du soufre rouge*. Paris: Gallimard, 1989.

Abrahams, Israel, ed. *Hebrew Ethical Wills*. 2 vols. Philadelphia: Jewish Publication Society of America, 1926.

Abrams, Daniel. "'The Book of Illumination' of R. Jacob ben Jacob ha-Kohen: A Synoptic Edition from Various Manuscripts." [In Hebrew.] PhD diss., New York University, 1993.

Abrams, Daniel. "Divine Jealousy: Kabbalistic Traditions of Triangulation." *Kabbalah* 35 (2016): 7–54.

Abrams, Daniel. "Divine Yearning for *Shekhinah*—'The Secret of the Exodus from Egypt: R. Moses de León's *Questions and Answers* from Unpublished Manuscripts and Their Zoharic Parallels.'" *Kabbalah* 32 (2014): 7–34.

Abrams, Daniel. *The Female Body of God in Kabbalistic Literature: Embodied Forms of Love and Sexuality in the Divine Feminine*. [In Hebrew.] Jerusalem: Magnes, 2004.

Abrams, Daniel. "From Germany to Spain: Numerology as a Mystical Technique." *Journal of Jewish Studies* 47 (1996): 85–101.

Abrams, Daniel. "Gershom Scholem's Methodologies of Research on the Zohar." In *Scholar and Kabbalist: The Life and Work of Scholem, Gershom*, edited by Mirjam Zadoff and Noam Zadoff, 3–16. Leiden: Brill, 2018.

Abrams, Daniel. *Kabbalistic Manuscripts and Textual Theory: Methodologies of Textual Scholarship and Editorial Practice in the Study of Jewish Mysticism*. Jerusalem: Magnes, 2010.

Abrams, Daniel. "'A Light of Her Own': Minor Kabbalistic Traditions on the Ontology of the Divine Feminine." *Kabbalah* 23 (2006): 7–29.

Abrams, Daniel. "The Only Sefirotic Diagram of the Zohar Manuscript Witnesses and Its Absence in Print." *Daat* 87 (2019): 7–20.

Abrams, Daniel, ed. *R. Asher ben David: His Complete Works and Studies in His Kabbalistic Thought (Including the Commentaries to the Account of Creation by the Kabbalists of Provence and Gerona)*. [In Hebrew.] Los Angeles, CA: Cherub Press, 1996.

Abrams, Daniel. "'The Secret of Secrets': The Concept of the Divine Glory and the Intention of Prayer in the Writings of R. Eleazar of Worms." [In Hebrew.] *Daat* 34 (1994): 61–81.

Abrams, Daniel. "The Secret of the Upper and Lower Waters: An Unknown Work from Early Castilian Kabbalah." [In Hebrew.] In *And This Is for Yehuda: Studies Presented to Our Friend, Professor Yehuda Liebes on the Occasion of His Sixty-Fifth Birthday*, edited by Maren Niehoff, Ronit Meroz, and Jonathan Garb, 311–325. Jerusalem: Mossad Bialik, 2012.

Abrams, Daniel. "The 'Zohar' as Palimpsest: Dismantling the Literary Constructs of a Kabbalistic Classic and the Turn of the Hermeneutics of Textual Archeology." *Kabbalah* 29 (2013): 7–60.

Altmann, Alexander. "*Homo Imago Dei* in Jewish and Christian Theology." *Journal of Religion* 48 (1968): 235–259.

Altmann, Alexander. "*Sefer Or Zarua'* by R. Moses de Leon: Introduction, Critical Text, and Notes." [In Hebrew.] *Kobez al Yad* 9, no. 19 (1980): 219–293.

Asulin, Shifra. "The Stature of the *Shekhina*: The Place of the Feminine Divine Countenance (*Parzuf*) in *Idra Rabba* and *Idra Zuta*." [In Hebrew.] In *Spiritual Authority: Struggles over Cultural Power in Jewish Thought*, edited by Howard Kreisel, Boaz Huss, and Uri Ehrlich, 103–183. Beer Sheva: Ben-Gurion University Press, 2009.

Baer, Yitzhak. "The Historical Background of the Raya Mehemna." [In Hebrew.] *Zion* 5 (1940): 1–44.

Baer, Yitzhak. *A History of the Jews in Christian Spain*. 2 vols. Translated by Louis Schoffman. Philadelphia, PA: Jewish Publication Society, 1978.

Baer, Yitzhak. "Religious Social Tendency of the Sefer Hasidism." [In Hebrew.] *Zion* 3 (1938): 1–50.

Bar-Asher, Avishai. "The *Bahir* and Its Historiography: A Reassessment." *Journal of Religion* 103, no. 2 (2023): 115–144.

Bar-Asher, Avishai. "The *Bahir* as It Once Was: Transmission History as a Tool for Reconstructing and Reassessing the Text, Format, and Ideas of the Original Composition." [In Hebrew.] *Tarbiz* 89, no. 1 (2022): 73–225.

Bar-Asher, Avishai. "Concepts and Imageries of Paradise in Medieval Kabbalah." [In Hebrew.] PhD diss., Hebrew University, 2014.

Bar-Asher, Avishai. "Decoding the Decalogue: Theosophical Re-Engraving of the Ten Commandments in Thirteenth-Century Kabbalah." In *Accounting for the Commandments in Medieval Judaism: Studies in Law, Philosophy, Pietism, and Kabbalah*, edited by Jeremy P. Brown and Marc Herman, 156–174. Leiden: Brill, 2020.

Bar-Asher, Avishai. "The Earliest Citation from *Sefer ha-Zohar* and from Whence the *Book of Zohar* Received Its Name." [In Hebrew.] *Kabbalah* 39 (2017): 79–156.

Bar-Asher, Avishai. "The Earliest *Sefer ha-Zohar* in Jerusalem: Early Manuscripts of Zoharic Homilies and an Unknown Homily from the *Midrash ha-Ne'elam* (?)." [In Hebrew.] *Tarbiz* 84, no. 4 (2016): 575–614.

Bar-Asher, Avishai. "Emendation, Editing, Elucidation: Preliminary Remarks on the Historical Edition of Zoharic Texts." In *Editing Kabbalistic Texts: New Philological and Digital Approaches*, edited by Bill Rebiger and Gerold Necker, 173–186. Wiesbaden: Harrassowitz, 2024.

Bar-Asher, Avishai. "From Alphabetical Mysticism to Theosophical Kabbalah: A Rare Witness to an Intermediate Stage of Moses de León's Thought." *Revue des études juives* 179, nos. 3–4 (2020): 351–384.

Bar-Asher, Avishai. "From the Vaults of Thebes: Moses de León's Pseudepigraphic Writings on the Letters, Vowel Signs, Theonyms, and Magical Practices and the Origin of Zoharic Fiction." [In Hebrew.] *Kabbalah* 51 (2022): 167–178.

Bar-Asher, Avishai. "Illusion Versus Reality in the Study of Early Kabbalah: The *Commentary on Sefer Yetzirah* Attributed to Isaac the Blind and Its History in Kabbalah and Scholarship." [In Hebrew.] *Tarbiz* 86, nos. 2–3 (2019): 340–349.

Bar-Asher, Avishai. "Isaac ben Solomon Ibn Sahula's Commentary on Psalms." [In Hebrew.] *Kobez al Yad* 26, no. 36 (2018): 1–45.

Bar-Asher, Avishai. *Journeys of the Soul: Concepts and Imageries of Paradise in Medieval Kabbalah*. [In Hebrew.] Jerusalem: Magnes Press, 2019.

Bar-Asher, Avishai. "*Kabbalah* and *Minhag*: Geonic Responsa and the Kabbalist Polemic on *Minhagim* in the Zohar and Related Texts." [In Hebrew.] *Tarbiz* 84, no. 1 (2016): 195–263.

Bar-Asher, Avishai. "The *Kuzari* and Early Kabbalah: Between Integration and Interpretation Regarding the Secrets of the Sacrificial Rite." *Harvard Theological Review* 116, no. 2 (2023): 228–253.

Bar-Asher, Avishai. "New Fragments from *Sefer Or zarua'* and *Sefer ha-Ne'lam*." [In Hebrew.] *Tarbiz* 83, no. 4 (2016): 635–642.

Bar-Asher, Avishai. "Penance and Fasting in the Writings of Rabbi Moses de León and the Zoharic Polemic with Contemporary Christian Monasticism." *Kabbalah* 25 (2011): 293–319.

Bar-Asher, Avishai. "The Punctiform Deity: Theological Debates Among the Masters of Niqqud in the Works of Joseph Gikatilla's 'Disciples.'" [In Hebrew.] *Kabbalah* 53 (2022): 103–236.

Bar-Asher, Avishai, ed. *R. Moses de León's Sefer Mishkan ha-'edut*. [In Hebrew.] Los Angeles, CA: Cherub Press, 2013.

Bar-Asher, Avishai. "'Samael and His Female Counterpart': R. Moses de León's Lost Commentary on Ecclesiastes." [In Hebrew.] *Tarbiz* 80, no. 4 (2012): 539–566.

Bar-Asher, Avishai. "*Sefer ha-Ne'lam*, New Parts of *Sefer Or Zarua'*, and Clarifications Regarding the Early Writings of R. Moses de León: Studies and Critical Editions." [In Hebrew.] *Tarbiz* 83, nos. 1–2 (2014–2015): 197–329.

Bar-Asher, Avishai. "*Sefer ha-Nequddah*, the Short *Sefer ha-Yiḥud*, and Fragments from *Sefer Or zarua'* and *Sefer Toledot Adam*." [In Hebrew.] *Kabbalah* 35 (2016): 307–321.

Bar-Asher, Avishai. "The Soul Bird: Ornithomancy and Theory of the Soul in the Homilies of Zohar Pericope Balak." [In Hebrew.] In *The Zoharic Story*, edited by Jonatan M. Benarroch, Yehuda Liebes, and Melilla Hellner-Eshed, 354–392. Jerusalem: Ben-Zvi Institute, 2017.

Bar-Asher, Avishai. "The Zohar and Its Aramaic: The Dynamic Development of the Aramaic Dialect[s] of the Zoharic Canon." [In Hebrew.] *Leshonenu* 83 (2021): 221–287.

Baskin, Judith. "From Separation to Displacement: The Problem of Women in *Sefer Hasidim*." *AJS Review* 19 (1994): 1–18.

Baskin, Judith. "Images of Women in Sefer Hasidim." In *Mysticism, Magic and Kabbalah in Ashkenazi Judaism*, edited by Karl Erich Grözinger and Joseph Dan, 93–105. Berlin: Walter de Gruyter, 1995.

Baumgarten, Elisheva. "Appropriation and Differentiation: Jewish Identity in Medieval Ashkenaz." *AJS Review* 42 (2018): 39–63.

Bayer, Clemens M. M. "Les fonts baptismaux de Liège: Qui les bœufs soutenant la cuve figurant-ils? Étude historique et épigraphique." In *Cinquante années d'études médiévales: À la confluence de nos disciplines; actes du colloque organisé à l'occasion du cinquantenaire du CESM, Poitiers, 1–4 septembre 2003*, edited by Claude Arrignon and Caludio Galderisi, 665–726. Turnhout, Belgium: Brepols, 2005.

Ben-Sasson, Hillel. "The Concept of Repentance in the Zohar." *Jerusalem Studies in Jewish Thought* 26 (2021): 97–125.

Ben-Sasson, Hillel. "Transgressions and Punishments: The Special Contribution of Rabenu Jonah Gerondi's *Sha'are teshuvah*." [In Hebrew.] *Tarbiz* 86, no. 1 (2018): 63–106.

Ben-Sasson, Hillel. *Y-HWH: Its Meanings in Biblical, Rabbinic, and Medieval Jewish Thought.* [In Hebrew.] Jerusalem: Magnes Press, 2019.

Ben Shachar, Naama. *Israel and the Archons of the Nations: War, Purity and Impurity: Three Commentaries on the Ten Sefirot Attributed to R. Joseph Giqatilla.* Los Angeles, CA: Cherub Press, 2022.

Ben-Shlomo, Joseph. "Gershom Scholem on Pantheism in the Kabbala." In *Gershom Scholem: The Man and His Work*, edited by Paul Mendes-Flohr, 56–72. Albany: State University of New York Press, 1993.

Ben-Shlomo, Joseph. "On Pantheism in Jewish Mysticism According to Gershom Scholem and His Critics." [In Hebrew.] *Daat* 50–52 (2003): 461–482.

Benarroch, Jonatan M. "'The Mystery of Unity': Poetic and Mystical Aspects of a Unique Zoharic Shema Mystery." *AJS Review* 37, no. 2 (2013): 231–256.

Benarroch, Jonatan M. "'Son of an Israelite Woman and an Egyptian Man'—Jesus as the Blasphemer (Lev. 24:10–23): An Anti-Gospel Polemic in the Zohar." *Harvard Theological Review* 110, no. 1 (2017): 100–124.

Benjamin, Richler, ed. *Hebrew Manuscripts in the Vatican Library: With Palaeographical and Codicological Descriptions by Malachi Beit-Arié in Collaboration with Nurit Pasternak.* Vatican City: Biblioteca Apostolica Vaticana, 2008.

Berman, Lawrence. "Maimonides on the Fall of Man." *AJS Review* 5 (1980): 1–15.

Biale, David. *Eros and the Jews.* Berkeley: University of California Press, 1992.

Biti, Roi. *Love of the Shekhina: Mysticism and Poetics in Tiqqune ha-Zohar.* [In Hebrew.] Ramat-Gan: Bar Ilan University Press, 2017.

Blau, Joshua. "At Our Place in al-Andalus, at Our Place in the Maghreb." In *Perspectives on Maimonides: Philosophical and Historical Studies*, edited by Joel L. Kraemer, 293–294. Oxford: Littman Library, 1991.

Blickstein, Shlomo. "Between Philosophy and Mysticism: A Study of the Philosophical-Kabbalistic Writings of Joseph Giqatila (1248–ca. 1322)." PhD diss., Jewish Theological Seminary of America, 1983.

Brody, Seth. "Human Hands Dwell in Heavenly Heights: Contemplative Ascent and Theurgic Power in Thirteenth-Century Kabbalah." In *Mystics of the Book*, edited by R. A. Herrera, 123–158. New York: Peter Lang, 1993.

Brody, Seth. "Human Hands Dwell in Heavenly Heights: Worship and Mystical Experience in Thirteenth-Century Kabbalah." PhD diss., University of Pennsylvania, 1991.

Brown, Jeremy Phillip. "Distilling Depths from Darkness: Forgiveness and Repentance in Medieval Iberian Jewish Mysticism." PhD diss., New York University, 2015.

Brown, Jeremy Phillip. "Espousal of the Impoverished Bride in Early Franciscan Hagiography and the Kabbalah of Gerona." *History of Religions* 61, no. 3 (2022): 279–305.

Brown, Jeremy Phillip. "Gazing into Their Hearts: On the Appearance of Kabbalistic Pietism in Thirteenth-Century Castile." *European Journal of Jewish Studies* 14 (2020): 177–214.

Brown, Jeremy Phillip. "God as Androgyne in Medieval Kabbalah." *Traditio* 80 (forthcoming).

Brown, Jeremy Phillip. "Glimmers of the World Soul in Kabbalah." In *World Soul: A History*, edited by James Wilberding, 124–150. New York: Oxford University Press, 2021.

Brown, Jeremy Phillip. "La Perversión de la Cábala Judía: Gershom Scholem and Anti-Kabbalistic Polemic in the Argentine Catholic Nationalism of Julio Meinvielle." In *All Religion Is Inter-Religion: Engaging the Work of Steven M. Wasserstrom*, edited by Kambiz Ghanea Bassiri and Paul Robertson, 65–73, 218–223. London: Bloomsbury, 2019.

Brown, Jeremy Phillip. "Of Sound and Vision: The Ram's Horn in Medieval Kabbalistic Rituology." In *Qol Tamid: The Shofar in Ritual, History, and Culture*, edited by Jonathan Friedman and Joel Gereboff, 83–113. Claremont, CA: Claremont Press, 2017.

Brown, Jeremy Phillip. "The Reason a Woman Is Obligated: Women's Ritual Efficacy in Medieval Kabbalah." *Harvard Theological Review* 116, no. 3 (2023): 422–446.

Brown, Jeremy Phillip. "Review of Jonathan Garb's Yearnings of the Soul: Psychological Thought in Modern Kabbalah." *Aries: Journal for the Study of Western Esotericism* 18 (2018): 131–136.

Brown, Jeremy Phillip. "What Does the Messiah Know? A Prelude to Kabbalah's Trinity Complex." *Maimonides Review of Philosophy and Religion* 2 (2023): 1–49.

Brown, Jeremy Phillip. *A World of Piety: The Aims of Castilian Kabbalah*. Stanford, CA: Stanford University Press, 2025.

Brown, Jeremy Phillip, and Avishai Bar-Asher. "The Enduring Female: Differentiating Moses de León's Early Androgynology." *Jewish Studies Quarterly* 28, no. 1 (2021): 21–53.

Buschhausen, Helmut. "Die Geschichte der Inschriften auf dem Verduner Altar des Nikolaus: Überlegungen zu einer Neudatierung." *Wiener Studien* 100 (1987): 265–309.

Campanini, Saverio. "Transmission and Reception of Isaac ibn Sahula's Kabbalistic Commentary on Two Psalms." *European Journal of Jewish Studies* 16, no. 1 (2022): 28–53.

Casewit, Yousef. *The Mystics of Al-Andalus: Ibn Barrajān and Islamic Thought in the Twelfth Century*. Cambridge, UK: Cambridge University Press, 2017.

Cherchi, Paolo. "'Alfa et O' en el 'Setenario' de Alfonso el Sabio." *Revista de Filología Española* 78, no. 3 (1998): 373–377.

Clark, Elizabeth A. *Reading Renunciation: Asceticism and Scripture in Early Christianity*. Princeton, NJ: Princeton University Press, 1999.

Cohen, Jeremy. *The Friars and the Jews: The Evolution of Medieval Anti-Judaism*. Ithaca, NY: Cornell University Press, 1982.

Cohen-Mushlin, Aliza. *Selected Hebrew Manuscripts from the Bavarian State Library*. Wiesbaden: Harrassowitz, 2020.

Cusato, Michael F. *The Early Franciscan Movement (1205–1239): History, Sources and Hermeneutics*. Spoleto: Centro Italiano di Studi Sull'alto Medioevo, 2009.

Cusato, Michael F. "To Do Penance / *Facere poenitentiam*." *The Cord* 57 (2007): 3–24.

Dal Bo, Federico. *Emanation and Philosophy of Language: An Introduction to Joseph ben Abraham Giqatilla*. Los Angeles, CA: Cherub Press, 2019.

Dalarun, Jacques. *À l'origine des Fioretti: Les actes du bienheureux François et de ses compagnons*. Translated by Aremelle Le Huërou. Paris: Cerf, 2008.

Dan, Joseph. *The Esoteric Theology of Ashkenazi Hasidism*. [In Hebrew.] Jerusalem: Bialik Institute, 1968.

Dan, Joseph. *The History of Jewish Mysticism and Esotericism*. [In Hebrew.] Vols. 6 and 10. Jerusalem: Shazar Center, 2011, 2014.

Dauber, Jonathan. *Knowledge of God and the Development of Early Kabbalah*. Leiden: Brill, 2012.

Dauber, Jonathan. *Secrecy and Esoteric Writing in Kabbalistic Literature*. Philadelphia: University of Pennsylvania Press, 2022.

Del Valle Rodríguez, Carlos. "Abraham ibn Ezra's Mathematical Speculations on the Divine Name." In *Mystics of the Book: Themes, Topics, and Typologies*, edited by R. A. Herrera, 159–176. New York: Peter Lang, 1993.

Despres, Denise L. "Exemplary Penance: The Franciscan 'Meditations on the Supper of Our Lord.'" Franciscan Studies 47 (1987): 123–137.
DeVun, Leah. *The Shape of Sex: Nonbinary Gender from Genesis to the Renaissance.* New York: Columbia University Press, 2021.
Druart, Thérèse-Anne. "Al-Farabi and Emanationism." In *Studies in Medieval Philosophy*, edited by John F. Wippel, 23–43. Washington, DC: Catholic University of America Press, 1987.
Dweck, Yaacob. *The Scandal of Kabbalah: Leon Modena, Jewish Mysticism, Early Modern Venice.* Princeton, NJ: Princeton University Press, 2011.
Ebstein, Michael. *Mysticism and Philosophy in al-Andalus: Ibn Masarra, Ibn al-'Arabī and the Ismā'īlī Tradition.* Leiden: Brill, 2014.
Elbaum, Yaakov. *Repentance of the Heart and the Acceptance of Suffering.* [In Hebrew.] Jerusalem: Magnes, 1993.
Farber, Asi. "'The Husks Precede the Fruit'—on the Question of the Origin of Evil in the Early Kabbalah." [In Hebrew.] *Eshel Beer Sheva* 4 (1996): 118–142.
Farber, Asi. "Jacob ben Jacob ha-Kohen's Commentary to Ezekiel's Chariot." [In Hebrew.] MA thesis, Hebrew University of Jerusalem, 1978.
Farber, Asi. "On the Sources of Rabbi Moses de Leon's Early Kabbalistic System." [In Hebrew.] *Jerusalem Studies in Jewish Thought* 3 (1983–1984): 67–92.
Farber, Asi. "Qeṭa' ḥadash me-haqdamat R. Yosef Gikatilla le-Sefer Ginnat egoz." *Jerusalem Studies in Jewish Thought* 1 (1981): 158–176.
Farber, Asi. "Traces of the Zohar in the Writings of R. Joseph Gikatilla." [In Hebrew.] *'Alei Sefer* 9 (1981): 70–83.
Felix, Iris. "Theurgy, Magic and Mysticism in the Kabbalah of R. Joseph of Shushan." [In Hebrew.] PhD diss., Hebrew University of Jerusalem, 2005.
Fine, Lawrence. "Penitential Practices in a Kabbalistic Mode." In *Seeking the Favor of God*, vol. 3, *The Impact of Penitential Prayer Beyond Second Temple Judaism*, edited by Mark Boda, Daniel Falk, and Rodney Werline, 127–148. Atlanta, GA: Society of Biblical Literature, 2008.
Fine, Lawrence. *Physician of the Soul, Healer of the Cosmos: Isaac Luria and His Kabbalistic Fellowship.* Stanford, CA: Stanford University Press, 2003.
Fine, Lawrence. "Purifying the Body in the Name of the Soul: The Problem of the Body in Sixteenth-Century Kabbalah." In *People of the Body: Jews and Judaism from an Embodied Perspective*, edited by Howard Eilberg-Schwartz, 117–142. Albany: State University of New York Press, 1992.
Fishbane, Eitan P. *The Art of Mystical Narrative: A Poetics of the Zohar.* Oxford: Oxford University Press, 2018.
Fishbane, Eitan P. "Mystical Contemplation and the Limits of the Mind: The Case of *Sheqel ha-Qodesh.*" *Jewish Quarterly Review* 93, nos. 1–2 (2002): 1–27.
Fishbane, Eitan P. "The Speech of Being, the Voice of God: Phonetic Mysticism in the Kabbalah of Asher ben David and His Contemporaries." *Jewish Quarterly Review* 98 (2008): 485–521.
Fishman, Talya. "The Penitential System of Hasidei Ashkenaz and the Problem of Cultural Boundaries." *Journal of Jewish Thought and Philosophy* 8 (1999): 201–229.
Flood, David. *Francis of Assisi and the Franciscan Movement.* St. Bonaventure, NY: Franciscan Institute Publications, 2017.
Franks, Paul. "The Midrashic Background of the Doctrine of Divine Contraction: Against Gershom Scholem on Tsimtsum." In *Tsimtsum and Modernity*, edited by Agata Bielik-Robson and Daniel Weiss, 39–60. Berlin: de Gruyter, 2020.
Garb, Jonathan. *Yearnings of the Soul: Psychological Thought in Modern Kabbalah.* Chicago: University of Chicago Press, 2015.
Garcı́a Avilés, Alejandro. "Alfonso X y el *Liber Razielis*: Imágenes de la magia astral judı́a en el *scriptorium* alfonsı́." *Bulletin of Hispanic Studies* 74, no. 1 (1997): 21–40.
Gardiner, Noah D. "Esotericism in a Manuscript Culture: Aḥmad al-Būnī and His Readers Through the Mamlūk Period." PhD diss., University of Michigan. 2014.

Garrido Clemente, Pilar. "Edición crítica del *K. jawāṣṣ al-ḥurūf* de Ibn Masarra." *Al-Andalus Magreb* 14 (2007): 51–89.

Giller, Pinchas. *The Enlightened Will Shine: Symbolization and Theurgy in the Later Strata of the Zohar*. Albany: State University of New York Press, 1993.

Giller, Pinchas. "The Forty-Two-Letter Divine Name in the Later Strata of the *Zohar*." *Kabbalah* 39 (2017): 53–77.

Giller, Pinchas. *Reading the Zohar, the Sacred Text of the Kabbalah*. Oxford: Oxford University Press, 2001.

Giller, Pinchas. *Shalom Shar'abi and the Kabbalists of Beit El*. New York: Oxford University Press, 2008.

Ginsburg, Elliot. *The Sabbath in Classical Kabbalah*. Albany: State University of New York, 1989.

Goetschel, Roland. "The Conception of Prophecy in the Works of R. Moses de León and R. Joseph Gikatilla." [In Hebrew.] *Jerusalem Studies in Jewish Thought* 8 (1989): 217–237.

Goldberg, Harvey E. "The Zohar in Southern Morocco: A Study in the Ethnography of Texts." *History of Religion* 29, no. 3 (1990): 233–258.

Goldreich, Amos. "*Sefer Me'irat 'einayim* by Isaac of Acre." PhD diss., Hebrew University of Jerusalem, 1981.

González Diéguez, Guadalupe. "Kabbalistic Traditions in the Castilian Vernacular: R. Moshe Arragel's Glosses to the Alba Bible." *eHumanista* 50 (2022): 538–557.

Gottlieb, Ephraim. "The Concluding Portion of R. Joseph Chiqatella's *Sha'arei Ẕedeq*." [In Hebrew.] *Tarbiz* 39, no. 4 (1970): 359–389.

Gottlieb, Ephraim. *Kabbalah at the End of the Thirteenth Century*. [In Hebrew.] Edited by Yehuda Liebes. Jerusalem: Kiryat Sefer, 1969.

Gottlieb, Ephraim. *Kabbalah in the Writings of R. Baḥya ben Asher Ibn Halawa*. [In Hebrew.] Jerusalem: Kiryat Sefer, 1970.

Gottlieb, Ephraim. *Studies in the Kabbalah Literature*. [In Hebrew.] Edited by Joseph Hacker. Tel Aviv: Tel Aviv University Press, 1976.

Green, Arthur. "Kabbalistic Re-Vision." *History of Religions* 36 (1997): 265–274.

Green, Arthur. "R. Isaac ibn Sahula's Commentary on the Song of Songs." [In Hebrew.] *Jerusalem Studies in Jewish Thought* 6, nos. 3–4 (1987): 393–491.

Green, Arthur. "Shekhinah, the Virgin Mary, and the Song of Songs: Reflections on a Kabbalistic Symbol in Its Historical Context." *AJS Review* 26 (2002): 1–52.

Gries, Zeev. *Conduct Literature (Regimen Vitae): Its History and Place in the Life of the Beshtian Hasidism*. [In Hebrew.] Jerusalem: Bialik Institute, 1989.

Gries, Zeev. "The Fashioning of Conduct Literature at the Turn of the Sixteenth Century and in the Seventeenth Century and Its Historical Significance." [In Hebrew.] *Tarbiz* 56, no. 4 (1987): 527–581.

Grözinger, Karl E. *Jüdisches Denken: Theologie, Philosophie, Mystik*. Vol. 2. Frankfurt am Main: Campus, 2004.

Grözinger, Karl E. "The Names of God and the Celestial Powers: Their Function and Meaning in the *Hekhalot* Literature." In *Early Jewish Mysticism: Proceedings of the First International Conference on the History of Jewish Mysticism*, edited by Joseph Dan, 53–70. Jerusalem: Hebrew University of Jerusalem, 1987.

Halbertal, Moshe. *Nahmanides: Law and Mysticism*. Translated by Daniel Tabak. New Haven, CT: Yale University Press, 2020.

Hallamish, Moshe. *The Kabbalah in North Africa: A Historical and Cultural Survey from the Sixteenth Century*. [In Hebrew.] Tel Aviv: Hakibbutz Hameuhad, 2001.

Hames, Harvey. *Like Angels on Jacob's Ladder: Abraham Abulafia, the Franciscans and Joachimism*. Albany: State University of New York Press, 2007.

Hartig, Otto. *Die Gründung der Münchener Hofbibliothek durch Albrecht v. und Johann Jakob Fugger*. Munich: Verlag der Königlich Bayerischen Akademie der Wissenschaften, 1917.

Harvey, L. P. "The Alfonsine School of Translators: Translations from Arabic into Castilian Produced Under the Patronage of Alfonso the Wise of Castile (1221–1252–1284)." *Journal of the Royal Asiatic Society of Great Britain and Ireland* 1 (1977): 109–117.
Harvey, Warren Zev. "Maimonides on Genesis 3:22." [In Hebrew.] *Daat* 12 (1984): 15–21.
Haskell, Ellen Davina. *Suckling at My Mother's Breasts: The Image of a Nursing God in Jewish Mysticism*. Albany: State University of New York Press, 2012.
Hecker, Joel. *Mystical Bodies, Mystical Meals: Eating and Embodiment in Medieval Kabbalah*. Detroit, MI: Wayne State University Press, 2005.
Hellner-Eshed, Melila. *A River Flows from Eden: The Language of Mystical Experience in the Zohar*. Translated by Nathan Wolski. Stanford, CA: Stanford University Press, 2009.
Huss, Boaz. *The Zohar: Reception and Impact*. Translated by Y. Nave. Oxford: Littman Library of Jewish Civilization, 2016.
Idel, Moshe. *Absorbing Perfections: Kabbalah and Interpretation*. New Haven, CT: Yale University Press, 2002.
Idel, Moshe. "Androgyny and Equality in the Theosophical-Theurgical Kabbalah." *Diogenes* 208 (2005): 27–38.
Idel, Moshe. "Between Ashkenaz and Castile: Incantations, Lists, and 'Gates of Sermons' in the Circle of Rabbi Neḥemiah ben Shlomo the Prophet, and Their Influences." [In Hebrew.] *Tarbiz* 77, nos. 3–4 (2008): 475–554.
Idel, Moshe. "Defining Kabbalah: The Kabbalah of the Divine Names." In *Mystics of the Book: Themes, Topics, and Typologies*, edited by Robert A. Herrera, 97–122. New York: Peter Lang, 1993.
Idel, Moshe. "The Divine Female and the Mystique of the Moon: Three-Phases Gender-Theory in Theosophical Kabbalah." *Studia Archaeus* 19–20 (2015–2016): 151–182.
Idel, Moshe. "The Feminine Aspect of Divinity in Early Kabbalah." [In Hebrew.] In *Tov Elem: Memory, Community and Gender in Medieval and Early Modern Jewish Societies*, edited by Roni Weinstein, Elisheva Baumgarten, and Amnon Raz-Krakotzkin, 91–110. Jerusalem: Bialik Institute, Mandel Institute of Jewish Studies, 2001.
Idel, Moshe. *Kabbalah: New Perspectives*. New Haven, CT: Yale University Press, 1990.
Idel, Moshe. *Kabbalah and Eros*. New Haven, CT: Yale University Press, 2005.
Idel, Moshe. "The Kabbalah in Morocco: A Survey." In *Morocco: Jews and Art in a Muslim Land*, edited by Vivian B. Mann, 105–124. New York: Merrell, 2000.
Idel, Moshe. "Kabbalistic Materials from the School of Rabbi David ben Yehudah he-Ḥasid." [In Hebrew.] *Jerusalem Studies in Jewish Thought* 2 (1983): 169–207.
Idel, Moshe. *Language, Torah, and Hermeneutics in Abraham Abulafia*. Albany: State University of New York Press, 1989.
Idel, Moshe. "Maimonides and Kabbalah." In *Studies in Maimonides*, edited by Isadore Twersky, 31–79. Cambridge, MA: Harvard University Press, 1990.
Idel, Moshe. "The Mud and the Water: Towards a History of a Simile in Kabbalah." *Zutot* 14 (2017): 64–72.
Idel, Moshe. *The Mystical Experience in Abraham Abulafia*. Albany: State University of New York Press, 1988.
Idel, Moshe. "On R. Neḥemiah ben Shlomo the Prophet's 'Commentaries on the Name of Forty-Two' and *Sefer ha-Ḥokhmah* Attributed to R. Eleazar of Worms." [In Hebrew.] *Kabbalah* 14 (2006): 157–261.
Idel, Moshe. "On the Concept of Ẓimẓum in Kabbalah and Its Research." [In Hebrew.] *Jerusalem Studies in Jewish Thought* 10 (1992): 59–112.
Idel, Moshe. "On the Genre of Commentaries on the Forty-Two Letter Divine Name and Its Later History." [In Hebrew.] *Kabbalah* 42 (2018): 131–191.
Idel, Moshe. "On the Meanings of the Term 'Kabbalah': Between the Ecstatic and the Sefirotic Schools of Kabbalah in the 13th Century." [In Hebrew.] *Pe'amim* 93 (2001): 39–76.
Idel, Moshe. *Primeval Evil in Kabbalah: Totality, Perfections, Perfectibility*. New York: Ktav Publishing, 2020.

Idel, Moshe. *The Privileged Divine Feminine in Kabbalah*. Berlin: de Gruyter, 2018.

Idel, Moshe. "Ramon Lull and Ecstatic Kabbalah: A Preliminary Observation." *Journal of the Warburg and Courtauld Institutes* 51 (1988): 170–174.

Idel, Moshe. "Reification of Language in Jewish Mysticism." *Mysticism and Language*, edited by Steven T. Katz, 42–79. Oxford: Oxford University Press, 1992.

Idel, Moshe. "*Sefer Yetzirah*: Twelve Commentaries on *Sefer Yetzirah* and the Extant Remnants of R. Isaac of Bedresh's Commentary." [In Hebrew.] *Tarbiz* 79, nos. 3–4 (2010): 471–556.

Idel, Moshe. *Studies in Ecstatic Kabbalah*. Albany: State University of New York Press, 1988.

Idel, Moshe. "The World of Angels in Human Form." [In Hebrew.] *Jerusalem Studies in Jewish Thought* 3 (1984): 1–66.

Idel, Moshe. "The Writings of Abraham Abulafia and His Teaching." [In Hebrew.] 2 vols. PhD diss., Hebrew University of Jerusalem, 1976.

Jacobs, Louis. *Holy Living: Saints and Saintliness in Judaism*. Northvale, NJ: Jason Aronson Press, 1990.

Jellinek, Adolph. *Moses Ben Schem-Tob de Leon und sein Verhältnis zum Sohar: Eine historisch-kritische Untersuchung über die Entstehung des Sohar*. Leipzig: Heinrich Hunger, 1851.

Kanarfogel, Ephraim. *Peering Through the Lattices: Mystical, Magical, and Pietistic Dimensions in the Tosafist Period*. Detroit, MI: Wayne State University Press, 2000.

Kaplan, Lawrence. "An Introduction to Maimonides' 'Eight Chapters.'" *Edah Journal* 2, no. 2 (2002): 2–23.

Kara-Kaniel, Ruth. "King David and Jerusalem from Psalms to the Zohar." In *Psalms in/on Jerusalem*, edited by Ophir Münz-Manor and Ilana Pardes, 67–107. Berlin: de Gruyter, 2019.

Katz, Steven T. "Mysticism and the Interpretation of Sacred Scripture." In *Mysticism and Sacred Scripture*, edited by Steven T. Katz, 21–32. Oxford: Oxford University Press, 2000.

Kiener, Ronald C. "The Image of Islam in the Zohar." *Jerusalem Studies in Jewish Thought* 8 (1989): 43–65.

Klein-Braslavy, Sarah. *Maimonides' Interpretation of the Adam Stories in Genesis: A Study in Maimonides' Anthropology*. [In Hebrew.] Jerusalem: Reuben Mass, 1986.

Klein-Braslavy, Sarah. "On Maimonides' Interpretation of the Story of the Garden of Eden in the *Guide of the Perplexed* I.2." In *Maimonides as Biblical Interpreter*, edited by Sarah Klein-Braslavy, 21–69. Boston: Academic Studies Press, 2011.

Koch, Patrick B. "Approaching the Divine by *Imitatio Dei*: *Tzelem* and *Demut* in R. Moshe Cordovero's *Tomer Devorah*." In *Visualizing Jews Through the Ages: Literary and Material Representations of Jewishness and Judaism*, edited by Hannah Ewence and Helen Spurling, 48–61. New York: Routledge, 2015.

Koch, Patrick B. *Human Self-Perfection: A Re-Assessment of Kabbalistic Musar-Literature of Sixteenth-Century Safed*. Los Angeles, CA: Cherub Press, 2015.

Koch, Patrick B. "Of Stinging Nettles and Stones: The Use of Hagiography in Early Modern Kabbalah and Pietism." *Jewish Quarterly Review* 109, no. 4 (2019): 534–566.

Koren, Sharon Faye. *Forsaken: The Menstruant in Medieval Jewish Mysticism*. Waltham, MA: Brandeis University Press, 2011.

Kozma, Emese. "The Practice of Teshuvah (Penance) in the Medieval Ashkenazi Jewish Communities." PhD diss., Eötvös Loránd University, 2012.

Krentzman-Ossi, Adeena. "The Implications of the Metaphysics of Light of Abraham Bar Ḥiyya." *Granot* 2 (2002): i–xvii.

Lachter, Hartley. "Charity and Kabbalah in Medieval Spain: Possible Evidence from Isaac ibn Sahula's *Meshal ha-Kadmoni*." *Iberia Judaica* 6 (2014): 119–126.

Lachter, Hartley. "Kabbalah, Philosophy, and the Jewish-Christian Debate: Reconsidering the Early Works of Joseph Gikatilla." *Journal of Jewish Thought and Philosophy* 16, no. 1 (2008): 1–58.

Lachter, Hartley. *Kabbalistic Revolution: Reimagining Judaism in Medieval Spain*. New Brunswick, NJ: Rutgers University Press, 2014.

Lambert, Malcolm. *Franciscan Poverty: The Doctrine of the Absolute Poverty of Christ and the Apostles in the Franciscan Order, 1210–1323*. London: Society for Promoting Christian Knowledge, 1961.

Langermann, Y. Tzvi. "Gradations of Light and Pairs of Opposites: Two Theories and Their Role in Abraham Bar Ḥiyya's *Scroll of the Revealer*." In *Texts in Transit in the Medieval Mediterranean*, edited by Y. Tzvi Langermann and Robert G. Morrison, 47–66. University Park: Pennsylvania State University Press, 2016.

Lapanski, Duane. *Evangelical Perfection: An Historical Examination of the Concept in the Early Franciscan Sources*. St. Bonaventure, NY: Franciscan Institute, 1977.

Lasker, Daniel J. *From Judah Hadassi to Elijah Bashyatchi: Studies in Late Medieval Karaite Philosophy*. Leiden: Brill, 2008.

Lehmann, O. H. "The Theology of the Mystical Book Bahir and Its Sources." *Studia Patristica* 1 (1957): 477–483.

Liebes, Yehuda. *Ars Poetica in Sefer Yetsira*. [In Hebrew.] Jerusalem: Schocken, 2000.

Liebes, Yehuda. "The Date of Rabbi Moshe de Leon's Death." [In Hebrew.] In *Meir Benayahu Memorial*, vol. 2, *Studies in Kabbalah, Jewish Thought, Liturgy, Piyut, and Poetry*, edited by Moshe Bar-Asher, Yehuda Liebes, Moshe Assis, and Yosef Kaplan, 745–750. Jerusalem: Carmel, 2019.

Liebes, Yehuda, ed. *Gershom Scholem's Annotated Zohar (Jozefow 1873)*. [In Hebrew.] 6 vols. Jerusalem: Magnes Press, 1992.

Liebes, Yehuda. "How the Zohar Was Written." In *Studies in the Zohar*, translated by Arnold Schwartz, Stephanie Nakache, and Penina Peli, 85–161. Albany: State University of New York Press, 1993.

Liebes, Yehuda. "Review of Charles Mopsik, *Moses de León's Sefer Sheqel ha-Qodesh*, with an Introduction by Idel, Moshe. Los Angeles, 1996." [In Hebrew.] *Kabbalah* 2 (1997): 275.

Liebes, Yehuda. "Sections of the Zohar Lexicon." [In Hebrew.] PhD diss., Hebrew University of Jerusalem, 1976.

Liebes, Yehuda. *Studies in Jewish Myth and Jewish Messianism*. Translated by Batya Stein. Albany: State University of New York Press, 1992.

Liebes, Yehuda. "Zohar ve-eros." *Alpayyim* 9 (1994): 67–119.

López, Atanasio. *La Provincia de España de los Frailes Menores: Apuntes histórico-críticos sobre los orígenes de la Orden Franciscana en España*. Santiago: El Eco Franciscano, 1915.

Marcus, Ivan. "*Hasidei Ashkenaz* Private Penitentials: An Introduction and Descriptive Catalogue of Their Manuscripts and Early Editions." In *Studies in Jewish Mysticism*, edited by Joseph Dan and Frank Talmage, 57–83. Cambridge, MA: Association for Jewish Studies, 1982.

Marcus, Ivan. "A Jewish-Christian Symbiosis: The Culture of Early Ashkenaz." In *Cultures of the Jews*, vol. 2, *Diversities of Diaspora*, edited by David Biale, 146–214. New York: Schocken, 2002.

Marcus, Ivan. "Jews and Christians Imagining the Other in Medieval Europe." *Prooftexts* 15 (1995): 209–226.

Marcus, Ivan. *Piety and Society: The Jewish Pietists of Medieval Germany*. Leiden: Brill, 1981.

Marcus, Ivan. "The Recensions and Structure of *Sefer Hasidim*." *Proceedings of the American Academy for Jewish Research* 45 (1978): 131–153.

Marcus, Ivan. *"Sefer Hasidim" and the Ashkenazic Book in Medieval Europe*. Philadelphia: University of Pennsylvania Press, 2018.

Margoliouth, George. "The Doctrine of the Ether in the Kabbalah." *Jewish Quarterly Review* 20 (1908): 825–861.

Martini, Anette. *Yosef Giqatilla, The Book of Punctuation; Flavius Mithridates' Latin Translation, the Hebrew Text, and an English Version*. Turin, Italy: Nino Aragno Editore, 2010.

Matt, Daniel C. "David ben Yehudah Heḥasid and His Book of Mirrors." *Hebrew Union College Annual* 51 (1980): 129–172.

Matt, Daniel C. "New-Ancient Words: The Aura of Secrecy in the Zohar." [In Hebrew.] In *Gershom Scholem's Major Trends in Jewish Mysticism: 50 Years After*, edited by Peter Schäfer and Joseph Dan, 181–207. Tübingen: J. C. B. Mohr, 1993.

Mayer, Yakov Z. "Rashbi and Rav Hamnuna: Between Sepharad and Ashkenaz." [In Hebrew.] In *The Zoharic Story*, edited by Jonatan M. Benarroch, Yehuda Liebes, and Melilla Hellner-Eshed, 2:445–462. Jerusalem: Ben-Zvi Institute, 2017.

McGaha, Michael. "The *Sefer ha-Bahir* and Andalusian Sufism." *Medieval Encounters* 3 (1997): 20–57.

Mel, Conrad. הים מוצק, *dissertatio theologico-philologica, de Mari Aeneo, seu labro magno Templi Salomonis, 1 Reg. VII. & II. Chron. IV.* Regiomontum [= Königsberg]: Reusnerus, 1702.

Meroz, Ronit. "An Anonymous Commentary on Idra Raba by a Member of the Saruq School." *Jerusalem Studies in Jewish Thought* 12 (1996): 307–378.

Meroz, Ronit. "Kabbalah, Science and Pseudo-Science in Ramdal's Commentary on the Thirteen Attributes." In *And This Is for Yehuda: Studies Presented to Our Friend, Professor Yehuda Liebes, on the Occasion of His Sixty-Fifth Birthday*, edited by Maren R. Niehoff, Ronit Meroz, and Jonathan Garb, 123–143. Jerusalem: Mossad Bialik, 2012.

Meroz, Ronit. "R. Joseph Angelet and His Zoharic Writings." [In Hebrew.] In *Ḥiddushe Zohar: Meḥqarim ḥadashim be-sifrut ha-Zohar*, edited by Ronit Meroz, 334–340. *Te'udah* 21–22. Tel Aviv: Tel Aviv University Press, 2007.

Meroz, Ronit. *The Spiritual Biography of Rabbi Simeon bar Yochay: An Analysis of the Zohar's Textual Components.* [In Hebrew.] Jerusalem: Mossad Bialik, 2018.

Michaelis, Omer. "'For the Wisdom of Their Wise Men Shall Perish': Forgotten Knowledge and Its Restoration in Maimonides's *Guide of the Perplexed* and Its Karaite Background." *Journal of Religion* 99, no. 4 (2019): 432–466.

Montefusco, Antonio. "The History as a Pendulum: The 'Actus' and the 'Fioretti.'" *Franciscan Studies* 71 (2013): 361–373.

Moorman, John. *A History of the Franciscan Order from Its Origins to the Year 1517.* Oxford: Clarendon Press, 1968.

Mopsik, Charles. *Les grands textes de la Cabale: Les rites qui font Dieu.* Paris: Lagrasse Verdier, 1993.

Mopsik, Charles, trans. *Moses de León (Moïse de León), Le Sicle du sanctuaire: Chéqel ha-Qodech.* Lagrasse: Éditions Verdier, 1996.

Mopsik, Charles. *Sex of the Soul: The Vicissitudes of Sexual Difference in Kabbalah.* Edited by Daniel Abrams. Los Angeles, CA: Cherub Press, 2005.

Morlok, Elke. *Rabbi Joseph Gikatilla's Hermeneutics.* Tübingen: Mohr Siebeck, 2011.

Morlok, Elke. "Visual and Acoustic Symbols in Gikatilla, Neoplatonic and Pythagorean Thought." In *Lux in Tenebris: The Visual and the Symbolic in Western Esotericism*, edited by Peter Forshaw, 21–49. Leiden: Brill, 2016.

Neubauer, Adolf. "The Bahir and the Zohar." *Jewish Quarterly Review* 4 (1892): 361–363.

Neumark, David. *Geschichte der jüdischen Philosophie des Mittelalters.* Vol. 2. Berlin: Verlag von Georg Reimer, 1910.

Niederehe, Hans J. *Alfonso X y la lingüística de su tiempo.* The Madrid: Sociedad General Española de Librería, 1987.

Orduna, Germán. "Los prólogos a la *Crónica abreviada* y al *Libro de la caza*: La tradición alfonsí y la primera época en la obra literaria de don Juan Manuel." *Cuadernos de historia de España* 51–52 (1970): 123–144.

Oron, Michal. *Samuel Falk: The Baal Shem of London.* [In Hebrew.] Jerusalem: Mossad Bialik, 2003.

Oron, Michal. *Sefer ha-Shem Attributed to R. Moses de León.* [In Hebrew.] Los Angeles, CA: Cherub Press, 2010.

Oron, Michal. "Three Commentaries on the Story of Genesis and Their Significance for the Study of the 'Zohar.'" [In Hebrew.] *Daat* 50–52 (2003): 183–200.

Pachter, Shilo. "'A Sin Without Repentance': On a Disagreement Between Moses de León and the Zohar." [In Hebrew.] In *And This Is for Yehuda: Studies Presented to Our Friend, Professor Yehuda Liebes, on the Occasion of His Sixty-Fifth Birthday*, edited by Maren R. Niehoff, Ronit Meroz, and Jonathan Garb, 144–163. Jerusalem: Mandel and Bialik Institutes, 2012.

Paz, Yakir, and Tzahi Weiss, "From Encoding to Decoding: The AṬBḤ of R. Hiyya in Light of a Syriac, Greek, and Coptic Cipher." *Journal of Near Eastern Studies* 74 (2015): 45–65.

Pazzelli, Raffaele. *St. Francis and the Third Order: The Franciscan and Pre-Franciscan Penitential Movement.* Chicago: Franciscan Herald Press, 1989.

Pedaya, Haviva. "The Great Mother: The Struggle Between Nahmanides and the Zohar Circle." In *Temps i espais de la Girona jueva*, edited by Silvia Planas Marcé, 311–328. Girona: Patronat del Call de Girona, 2011.

Pedaya, Haviva. *Name and Sanctuary in the Teaching of R. Isaac the Blind.* [In Hebrew.] Jerusalem: Magnes Press, 2001.

Pedaya, Haviva. *Vision and Speech: Models of Revelatory Experience in Jewish Mysticism.* [In Hebrew.] Los Angeles, CA: Cherub Press, 2002, 134–135.

Pi y Margall, Francisco. *Recuerdos y bellezas de España: Reino de Granada.* Madrid: Jose Repullés, 1850.

Pines, Shlomo. "Truth and Falsehood Versus Good and Evil." In *Studies in Maimonides*, edited by Isadore Twersky, 95–157. Cambridge, MA: Harvard University Press, 1990.

Pinto, Idan. "Universe–Sanctuary–Man: On a Threefold Analogy in Two Anonymous Texts and Their Traces in Thirteenth-Century Kabbalah." [In Hebrew.] *Tarbiz* 88, no. 3 (2022): 371–417.

Ray, Jonathan. *The Sephardic Frontier: The "Reconquista" and the Jewish Community in Medieval Iberia.* Ithaca, NY: Cornell University Press, 2013.

Rodríguez Porto, Rosa María. "The Pillars of Hercules: The Estoria de Espanna (Escorial, Y.I.2) as Universal Chronicle." In *Universal Chronicles in the High Middle Ages*, edited by Michele Campopiano and Henry Bainton, 223–254. Rochester, NY: Boydell & Brewer; York Medieval Press, 2017.

Roest, Bert. *Franciscan Literature of Religious Instruction Before the Council of Trent.* Leiden: Brill, 2004.

Rojo Alique, Francisco Javier. "Para el estudio de conventos franciscanos en Castilla y León: San Francisco de Valladolid en la Edad Media." In *El Franciscanismo en la Península Ibérica: Balance y Perspectivas, Congreso Internacional*, edited by Maria del Mar Graña Cid, 419–428. Barcelona: Griselda Bonet Girabet, 2005.

Roth, Norman. "Abraham Ibn Ezra—Mysticism." *Iberia Judaica* 4 (2012): 141–150.

Rubenstein, Jeffrey. *Stories of the Babylonian Talmud.* Baltimore, MD: Johns Hopkins University Press, 2010.

Rubin, Asher. "The Concept of Repentance Among Hasidey Ashkenaz." *Journal of Jewish Studies* 16 (1965): 161–176.

Rubin, Miri. Mother of God: A History of the Virgin Mary. New Haven, CT: Yale University Press, 2009.

Sack, Bracha. "R. Moses of Cordovero's Doctrine of Ẓimẓum." [In Hebrew.] *Tarbiz* 58, no. 2 (1989): 207–237.

Sachs-Shmueli, Leore. "'I Arouse the Shekhina': A Psychoanalytic Study of Anxiety and Desire of the Kabbalah in Relation to the Object of Taboo." *Kabbalah* 35 (2016): 227–266.

Sachs-Shmueli, Leore. "The Image of the Prophetess Miriam as a Feminine Model in Zoharic Literature." [In Hebrew.] *Kabbalah* 33 (2015): 183–210.

Sachs-Shmueli, Leore. "The Rationale of the Negative Commandments by R. Joseph Hamadan: A Critical Edition and Study of Taboo in the Time of the Composition of the Zohar." [In Hebrew.] 2 vols. PhD diss., Bar Ilan University, 2019.

Sagerman, Robert. *The Serpent Kills or the Serpent Gives Life: The Kabbalist Abraham Abulafia's Response to Christianity.* Leiden: Brill, 2011.

Saperstein, Marc. "The Preaching of Repentance and the Reforms in Toledo of 1281." In *Models of Holiness in Medieval Sermons: Proceedings of the International Symposium (Kalamazoo,*

4–7 May 1995), edited by Beverly Mayne Kienzle, 157–174. Louvain-la-Neuve: Fédération Internationale des Instituts d'Études Médiévales, 1996.

Saward, John. *Perfect Fools: Folly for Christ's Sake in Catholic and Orthodox Spirituality*. Oxford: Oxford University Press, 2000.

Schäfer, Peter. *Jesus in the Talmud*. Princeton, NJ: Princeton University Press, 2007.

Schäfer, Peter. *Mirror of His Beauty: Feminine Images of God from the Bible to the Early Kabbalah*. Princeton, NJ: Princeton University Press, 2004.

Scheindlin, Raymond P. "El poema de Ibn Gabirol y la fuente del Patio de los Leones." *Cuadernos de la Alhambra* 29–30 (1993–1994): 185–189.

Schimmel, Annemarie. "The Primordial Dot: Some Thoughts About Sufi Letter Mysticism." *Jerusalem Studies in Arabic and Islam* 9 (1987): 350–356.

Scholem, Gershom. "Alchemie und Kabbala: Ein Kapitel aus der Geschichte der Mystik." *Monatsschrift für Geschichte und Wissenschaft des Judentums* 69, nos. 1–2 (1925): 13–30.

Scholem, Gershom. "A Charter of the Students of R. Isaac Luria." [In Hebrew.] *Zion* 5 (1940): 133–160.

Scholem, Gershom. *Das Buch Bahir: Ein Text aus der Frühzeit der Kabbala*. Berlin: Arthur Scholem, 1923.

Scholem, Gershom [Gerhard]. "Eine unbekannte mystische Schrift des Mose de Leon." *Monatschrift für Geschichte und Wissenschaft des Judentums* 71, nos. 3–4 (1927): 109–123.

Scholem, Gershom. "Farben und ihre Symbolik in der jüdischen Überlieferung." *Eranos Jahrbuch* 41 (1972): 46–47.

Scholem, Gershom. "The First Quotation from the Zohar's *Midrash ha-Ne'lam*." [In Hebrew.] *Tarbiz* 3, no. 2 (1931–1932): 181–183.

Scholem, Gershom. "Ha-im ḥibber R. Moshe de León et Sefer ha-Zohar?" [In Hebrew.] *Madda 'e ha-Yahadut* 1 (1926): 16–29.

Scholem, Gershom. "He'arot ve-tiqqunim li-reshimat kitve ha-yad she-be-Minkhen." *Kiryat Sefer* 1 (1925): 284–293.

Scholem, Gershom. "An Inquiry in the Kabbala of R. Isaac ben Jacob Hacohen, II: Evolution of the Doctrine of the Worlds in the Early Kabbala." [In Hebrew.] *Tarbiz* 3, no. 1 (1931): 33–66.

Scholem, Gershom. "An Inquiry in the Kabbala of R. Isaac ben Jacob ha-Kohen, III: R. Moses of Burgos, the Disciple of R. Isaac (Continued)." [In Hebrew.] *Tarbiz* 4, nos. 2–3 (1932): 207–225.

Scholem, Gershom. "An Inquiry in the Kabbala of R. Isaac ben Jacob ha-Kohen, III: R. Moses of Burgos, the Disciple of R. Isaac (Continued)." [In Hebrew.] *Tarbiz* 5, no. 2 (1934): 180–198.

Scholem, Gershom. "An Inquiry in the Kabbala of R. Isaac ben Jacob Hacohen, III: R. Moses of Burgos, the Disciple of R. Isaac (Concluded)." [In Hebrew.] *Tarbiz* 5, nos. 3–4 (1934): 305–323.

Scholem, Gershom. *Kabbalah*. Jerusalem: Keter, 1974.

Scholem, Gershom. "A Key to the Commentaries on the Ten Sefirot." [In Hebrew.] *Kiryat Sefer* 10 (1933–1934): 498–515.

Scholem, Gershom. *Kitve yad ba-qabbala*. Jerusalem: Hebrew University Press, 1930.

Scholem, Gershom. *Major Trends in Jewish Mysticism*. New York: Schocken, 1995.

Scholem, Gershom. "The Name of God and the Linguistic Theory of the Kabbala." *Diogenes* 20, no. 79 (1972): 59–80.

Scholem, Gershom. "The Name of God and the Linguistic Theory of the Kabbala (Part 2)." *Diogenes* 20, no. 80 (1972): 164–194.

Scholem, Gershom. "A New Document Concerning the History of the Beginning of the Kabbalah." [In Hebrew.] In *Sefer Bialik*, edited by Jacob Fichman, 141–162. Tel Aviv: Omanut, 1934.

Scholem, Gershom. "A New Passage from the *Midrash ha-Ne'lam* of the Zohar." [In Hebrew.] In *Louis Ginzberg: Jubilee Volume*, edited by Alexander Marx et al., 2:425–446. New York: American Academy for Jewish Research, 1946.

Scholem, Gershom. *On the Kabbalah and Its Symbolism*. New York: Schocken, 1965.

Scholem, Gershom. *On the Mystical Shape of the Godhead.* New York: Schocken, 1991.

Scholem, Gershom. *The Origins of Kabbalah.* Princeton, NJ: Princeton University Press, 1992.

Scholem, Gershom. "Qabbalot R. Yiṣḥaq ve-R. Ya'aqov bene R. Ya'aqov ha-Kohen: Meqorot le-toledot ha-qabbala lifne hitgallut ha-Zohar." *Madda'e ha-Yahadut* 2 (1927): 201–219.

Scholem, Gershom. "Remnants of R. Shem Tob Ibn Gaon's Work on the Elements of the Sefirot Theory." [In Hebrew.] *Kiryat Sefer* 8 (1932): 534–542.

Scholem, Gershom. *Reshit ha-qabbalah.* Jerusalem: Schocken, 1948.

Scholem, Gershom. "Review of Carlo Bernheimer, *Codices Hebraici Bybliothecae Ambrosianae.*" [In Hebrew.] *Kiryat Sefer* 11 (1934): 188.

Scholem, Gershom. "Shene qunṭresim shel R. Moshe de Leon." *Kobez Al Yad* 8, no. 18 (1976): 325–384.

Scholem, Gershom. *Zohar: The Book of Splendor: Basic Readings from the Kabbalah.* New York: Schocken, 1949.

Scholem, Gershom, and Bernhard I. Joel, eds. *Catalogus codicum hebraicorum quot conservantor in Bibliotheca Hierosolymitana quae est Judaeorum Populi et Universitatis Hebraicae.* [In Hebrew.] Jerusalem: Hebrew University, 1930.

Schwartz, Dov. *Religion or Halakha: The Philosophy of Rabbi Joseph B. Soloveitchik.* 2 vols. Translated by Batya Stein. Leiden: Brill, 2007–2013.

Seelbach, Wilhelm. "Bemerkungen zu τύπος, ἀντίτυπος und ἀρχέτυπος sowie zu den Inschriften des Verduner Altars." *Glotta* 62, nos. 3–4 (1984): 175–186.

Sendor, Mark. "The Emergence of Provençal Kabbalah." 2 vols. PhD diss., Harvard University, 1994.

Shokek, Shimon. *Jewish Ethics and Jewish Mysticism in Sefer ha-Yashar.* Translated by Roslyn Weiss. Lewiston, ME: Edwin Mellon Press, 1991.

Shokek, Shimon. "The Relationship Between 'Sefer ha-Yashar' and the Gerona Circle." [In Hebrew.] *Jerusalem Studies in Jewish Thought* 6, nos. 3–4 (1987): 337–366.

Simon, Larry. "Intimate Enemies: Mendicant-Jewish Interaction in Thirteenth-Century Mediterranean Spain." In *Friars and Jews in the Middle Ages and Renaissance,* edited by Steven McMichael, 53–80. Leiden: Brill, 2004.

Sirat, Colette. *Hebrew Manuscripts of the Middle Ages.* Translated by Nicholas de Lange. Cambridge, UK: Cambridge University Press, 2002.

Sobol, Neta. "The Pikudin Section of the Zohar." [In Hebrew.] MA thesis, Tel Aviv University, 2001.

Soloveitchik, Haym. "Piety, Pietism and German Pietism: 'Sefer Hasidim I' and the Influence of 'Hasidei Ashkenaz.'" *Jewish Quarterly Review* 92 (2002): 455–493.

Soloveitchik, Haym. "Three Themes in Sefer Hasidim." *Association for Jewish Studies Review* 1 (1976): 311–358.

Steimann, Ilona. "Jewish Scribes and Christian Patrons: The Hebraica Collection of Johann Jakob Fugger." *Renaissance Quarterly* 70 (2017): 1235–1281.

Steinschneider, Moritz. *Die hebräischen Handschriften der K. Hof- und Staatsbibliothek in München.* Munich: Commission der Palm'schen Hofbuchhandlung, 1895.

Steinschneider, Moritz. "Hebräische Handschriften in Parma." *Hebräische Bibliographie* 10 (1870): 96–104.

Steinschneider, Moritz. "Zur kabbalistischen Literatur." *Hebräische Bibliographie* 17 (1877): 36–38.

Stern, Gregg. *Philosophy and Rabbinic Culture: Jewish Interpretation and Controversy in Medieval Languedoc.* London: Routledge, 2014.

Stern, S. M. "'The First in Thought Is the Last in Action': The History of a Saying Attributed to Aristotle." *Journal of Semitic Studies* 7, no. 2 (1962): 234–252.

Stewart, Robert M. "The Rule of the Secular Franciscan Order: Origins, Development, Interpretation." PhD diss., Graduate Theological Union, 1990.

Szpiech, Ryan. "From Founding Father to Pious Son: Filiation, Language, and Royal Inheritance in Alfonso X, the Learned." *Interfaces* 1 (2015): 209–235.

Tanenbaum, Adena. "Nine Spheres or Ten? A Medieval Gloss on Moses Ibn Ezra's 'Be-shem El asher amar.'" *Journal of Jewish Studies* 47 (1996): 294–310.

Tishby, Isaiah. *Messianic Mysticism: Moses Hayim Luzzatto and the Padua School.* London: Littman Library of Jewish Civilization; Liverpool: University of Liverpool Press, 2008.

Tishby, Isaiah. "She'elot u-teshuvot le-Rabbi Moshe de León be-'inyene qabbalah." [In Hebrew.] In *Studies of Kabbalah and Its Branches: Researches and Sources,* 1:36–75. Jerusalem: Magnes Press, 1982. Reprinted from *Kobez al Yad* 5, no. 15 (1950): 9–38.

Tishby, Isaiah. *Studies in Kabbalah and Its Branches: Researches and Sources.* 3 vols. [In Hebrew.] Jerusalem: Magnes Press, 1982.

Tishby, Isaiah, ed. *The Wisdom of the Zohar: An Anthology of Texts.* 3 vols. Translated by David Goldstein. Portland, OR: Littman Library of Jewish Civilization; Oxford: Oxford University Press, 1989. Reprinted 2002.

Travis, Yakov M. "Kabbalistic Foundations of Jewish Spiritual Practice: Rabbi Ezra of Gerona—on the Kabbalistic Meaning of the Mitzvot." PhD diss., Brandeis University, 2002.

Vajda, Georges. *L'Amour de dieu dans la théologie juive du moyen age.* Paris: J. Vrin, 1957.

Vajda, Georges. *Le Commentaire d'Ezra de Gérone sur le Cantique des cantiques, traduction et notes annexes.* Paris: A. Montaigne, 1969.

Wasserstrom, Steven M. "Jewish-Muslim Relations in the Context of Andalusian Emigration." In *Christians, Muslims, and Jews in Medieval and Early Modern Spain,* edited by Mark D. Meyerson and Edward D. English, 69–87. Notre Dame, IN: University of Notre Dame Press, 1999.

Weiler, Moshe C. "Issues in the Kabbalistic Terminology of Joseph Gikatilla and in His Relationship to Maimonides." [In Hebrew.] *Hebrew Union College Annual* 37 (1966): 13–44.

Weiler, Moshe C. "The Kabbalistic Doctrine of R. Joseph Gikatilla in His Works." [In Hebrew.] *Ṭemirin* 1 (1972): 157–186.

Weinstein, Roni. *Kabbalah and Jewish Modernity.* Portland, OR: Littman Library of Jewish Civilization, 2016.

Weinstock, Israel. *Perush Sefer Yeṣirah "Almoni."* Jerusalem: Mossad ha-Rav Kook, 1984.

Weiss, Tzahi. *Cutting the Shoots: The Worship of the Shekhinah in the World of Early Kabbalistic Literature.* [In Hebrew]. Jerusalem: Magnes Press, 2015.

Wiener, Orna R. "The Mysteries of the Vocalization of the Spanish-Castilla Kabbalah in the 13th Century." [In Hebrew.] PhD diss., Bar-Ilan University, 2009.

Wijnhoven, Jochanan H. A. "*Sefer ha-Mishkal*: Text and Study." PhD diss., Brandeis University, 1964.

Wijnhoven, Jochanan H. A. "*Sefer Maskiyyot Kesef*: Text and Translation with Introduction and Notes." MA thesis, Brandeis University, 1961.

Wirszubski, Chaim. *Pico della Mirandola's Encounter with Jewish Mysticism.* Cambridge, MA: Harvard University Press, 1989.

Wolfson, Elliot R. *Abraham Abulafia—Kabbalist and Prophet: Hermeneutics, Theosophy and Theurgy.* Los Angeles, CA: Cherub Press, 2000.

Wolfson, Elliot R. *Alef, Mem, Tau: Kabbalistic Musings on Time, Truth, and Death.* Berkeley: University of California Press, 2005.

Wolfson, Elliot R. *Along the Path: Studies in Kabbalistic Myth, Symbolism, and Hermeneutics.* Albany: State University of New York Press, 1995.

Wolfson, Elliot R. "Anthropomorphic Imagery and Letter Symbolism in the Zohar." [In Hebrew.] *Jerusalem Studies in Jewish Thought* 8 (1989): 150–152.

Wolfson, Elliot R. "Biblical Accentuation in a Mystical Key: Kabbalistic Interpretations of the *Te'amim*." *Journal of Jewish Music and Liturgy* 12 (1989–1990): 1–16.

Wolfson, Elliot R. "Bifurcating the Androgyne and Engendering Sin: A Zoharic Reading of Gen. 1–3." In *Hidden Truths from Eden: Esoteric Readings of Genesis 1–3,* edited by Caroline Vander Stichele and Susanne Scholz, 83–115. Atlanta, GA: Society for Biblical Literature, 2014.

Wolfson, Elliot R., ed. *The Book of the Pomegranate: Moses de Leon's Sefer ha-Rimmon*. Atlanta, GA: Scholars Press, 2020.
Wolfson, Elliot R. "By Way of Truth: Aspects of Naḥmanides' Kabbalistic Hermeneutic." *AJS Review* 14, no. 2 (1989): 103–178.
Wolfson, Elliot R. *Circle in the Square: Studies in the Use of Gender in Kabbalistic Symbolism*. Albany: State University of New York Press, 1995.
Wolfson, Elliot R. "Circumcision and the Divine Name: A Study in the Transmission of Esoteric Doctrine." *Jewish Quarterly Review* 78 (1987): 77–112.
Wolfson, Elliot R. "Circumcision, Vision of God, and Textual Interpretation: From Midrashic Trope to Mystical Symbol." *History of Religions* 27, no. 2 (1987): 189–215.
Wolfson, Elliot R. *A Dream Interpreted Within a Dream: Oneiropoiesis and the Prism of Imagination*. Cambridge, MA: Zone Books, 2011.
Wolfson, Elliot R. "The Face of Jacob in the Moon: Mystical Transformations of an Aggadic Myth." In *The Seduction of Myth in Judaism: Challenge or Response?*, edited by S. Daniel Breslauer, 235–270. Albany: State University of New York Press, 1997.
Wolfson, Elliot R. "God, the Demiurge and the Intellect: On the Usage of the Word *Kol* in Abraham ibn Ezra." *Revue des études juives* 149 (1990): 77–111.
Wolfson, Elliot R. "Hai Gaon's Letter and Commentary to *'Aleynu*: Further Evidence of de Leon's Pseudepigraphic Activity." *Jewish Quarterly Review* 81, nos. 3–4 (1991): 365–410.
Wolfson, Elliot R. "Hebraic and Hellenic Conceptions of Wisdom in *Sefer ha-Bahir*." *Poetics Today* 19 (1998): 147–176.
Wolfson, Elliot R. "The Image of Jacob Engraved upon the Throne: Further Speculation on the Esoteric Doctrine of the German Pietism." [In Hebrew.] In *Massu'ot: Studies in Kabbalistic Literature and Jewish Philosophy in Memory of Prof. Ephraim Gottlieb*, edited by Michal Oron and Amos Goldreich, 131–185. Jerusalem: Mossad Bialik, 1994.
Wolfson, Elliot R. *Language, Eros, Being: Kabbalistic Hermeneutics and Poetic Imagination*. New York: Fordham University Press, 2005.
Wolfson, Elliot R. "Left Contained in the Right: A Study in Zoharic Hermeneutics." *AJS Review* 11, no. 1 (1986): 27–52.
Wolfson, Elliot R. "Letter Symbolism and *Merkavah* Imagery in the Zohar." In *Alei Shefer: Studies in the Literature of Jewish Thought; Presented to Dr. Alexander Safran*, edited by Moshe Hallamish, 195–236. Ramat-Gan: Bar Ilan University, 1990.
Wolfson, Elliot R. *Luminal Darkness: Imaginal Gleanings from Zoharic Literature*. New York: Oxford University Press, 2007.
Wolfson, Elliot R. "Martyrdom, Eroticism and Asceticism in Twelfth-Century Ashkenazi Piety." In *Jews and Christians in Twelfth-Century Europe*, edited by John Van Engen and Michael Signer, 171–220. Notre Dame, IN: University of Notre Dame Press, 2001.
Wolfson, Elliot R. "Moisés de León y el Zohar." In *Pensamiento y mística hispanó judía y sefardí*, edited by Judit Targarona Borrás, Angel Sáenz-Badillos, and Ricardo Izquierdo Benito, 167–192. Cuenca, Spain: Ediciones de la Universidad Castilla-La Mancha, 2001.
Wolfson, Elliot R. "Mystical Rationalization of the Commandments in *Sefer ha-Rimmon*." *Hebrew Union College Annual* 59 (1988): 217–251.
Wolfson, Elliot R. *Open Secret: Postmessianic Messianism and the Mystical Revision of Menaḥem Mendel Schneerson*. New York: Columbia University Press, 2012.
Wolfson, Elliot R. "Sacred Space and Mental Iconography: *Imago Templi* and Contemplation in Rhineland Jewish Pietism." In *Ki Baruch Hu: Ancient Near Eastern, Biblical, and Judaic Studies in Honor of Baruch A. Levine*, edited by Robert Chazan, William Hallo, and Lawrence Schiffman, 593–634. Winona Lake, IN: Eisenbrauns, 1999.
Wolfson, Elliot R. "Textual Flesh, Incarnation, and the Imaginal Body: Abraham Abulafia's Polemic with Christianity." In *Studies in Medieval Jewish Intellectual and Social History: Festschrift in Honor of Robert Chazan*, edited by David Engel, Lawrence Schiffman, and Elliot R. Wolfson, 189–226. Leiden: Brill, 2012.

Wolfson, Elliot R. "The Tree That Is All: Jewish-Christian Roots of a Kabbalistic Symbol in *Sefer ha-Bahir*." *Journal of Jewish Thought and Philosophy* 3 (1994): 31–76.

Wolfson, Elliot R. *Through a Speculum That Shines: Vision and Imagination in Medieval Jewish Mysticism*. Princeton, NJ: Princeton University Press, 1994.

Wolfson, Elliot R. "Woman—the Feminine as Other in Theosophic Kabbalah: Some Philosophical Observations on the Divine Androgyne." In *The Other in Jewish Thought and Identity*, edited by Laurence Silberstein and Robert Cohn, 166–204. New York: New York University Press, 1994.

Wolski, Nathan. "Metatron and the Mysteries of the Night in *Midrash ha-Ne'lam*: Jacob ha-Kohen's *Sefer ha-Orah* and the Transformation of a Motif in the Early Writings of Moses de León." *Kabbalah* 23 (2010): 69–94.

Wolski, Nathan. "Moses de León and *Midrash ha-Ne'elam*: On the Beginnings of the Zohar." *Kabbalah* 34 (2016): 27–116.

Yahalom, Shalem. "Tanhuma in Masquerade: Discovering the Tanhuma in the Latter Midrash Rabbah Texts." In *Studies in the Tanhuma-Yelammedenu Literature*, edited by Ronit Nikolsky and Arnon Atzmon, 222–245. Leiden: Brill, 2021.

Hebrew Bible Index

Genesis
1:1–3, 157–58
1:11, 153n.130, 155
1:24, 94n.71
1:26, 147
1:27, 118n.9, 181
2:4, 195
2:10, 94n.71, 195
3:19, 34–35n.3
3:22, 38
6:13, 182–84
24:1, 9–10, 22n.59
47:28–50:26, 159
49:20, 193–94

Exodus
3:14, 167
5:22, 25
16:4, 193–94
16:22, 193–94
28:21, 151–52
33:21, 49n.48
34:6-7, 41–42, 162–63

Leviticus
4:28, 130–32n.63, 150–51
4:32, 130–32n.63, 150–51
19:18, 53

Numbers
1:17, 151–52
10, 83
10:2, 86
10:18, 87n.48
11:7, 35
15:31, 49n.48
17:11, 23–24
17:11–13, 23–24
31:21, 58–59
31:53, 58–59

Deuteronomy
6:4, 162–63n.3, 186, 188, 189n.73
16:2, 180–81, 193–94
22, 148–50
29:9–10, 23–24
30:15, 55–56
30:19, 55–56

Judges
6:12, 57

1 Samuel
9:7, 194

1 Kings
7:23–26, 57, 162–63
7:25, 134, 141–42
7:26, 158
7:35, 194–95

Isaiah
11:10, 134–35
49:3, 196
54:16, 129n.57
56:4-5, 50–52
57:15, 46n.35
62:5, 151–52

Jeremiah
3:12, 59
17:8, 127n.48, 195
31:22, 127–28, 128n.51, 130n.61, 195

Ezekiel
1:5, 13-15, 19, 22 (and 3:13), 81–82
1:26, 127n.49
10:20, 94n.71
43:2, 145

Micah
7:18-20, 41–42

Zechariah
14:7-9, 168–69

Psalms
2:4, 134–35, 136, 141–42
19:8, 150–51
31:13, 46n.35
60:1, 150–52
68:18, 57
89:3, 59–60
104, 163n.4
104:14, 193–94
116:13, 156
133:1, 153
141:2, 23–24

Proverbs
3:12, 46
4:23, 129n.56, 195
10:25, 138
27:5, 69n.134
27:9, 23–24
31:29, 129n.59

Job
40:19, 92–93

Song of Songs
2:2, 153,
156–58
6:3, 57
6:11, 57

Esther
8:4, 57

Daniel
9:17, 25
12:3, 58–59, 105–6

2 Chronicles
4:2–5, 57, 162–63
4:4, 134, 141–42
4:5, 158

Index

Figures are indicated by an italic *f* following the page number.

1 Kings, 57, 134, 141–42, 158, 162–63, 194–95
1 Samuel, 194
2 Chronicles, 57, 134, 141–42, 158, 162–63

Abraham ben Maimonides, 33–34
abstinence (*perishut*). *See* asceticism
Abulafia, Abraham, 11–12n.18, 75–77, 111n.127
Abulafia, Joseph ben Ṭodros ha-Levi, 9, 12–13, 15, 16, 47–48, 164–65
Abulafia, Ṭodros ben Joseph ha-Levi, 9, 11–12n.18, 12, 14, 15, 22n.60, 40n.13, 47–48, 53n.67, 55n.74, 76–77, 104n.107, 126n.43, 127n.49, 162–63, 179n.50, 182–84
  Oṣar ha-kavod, 40n.13, 53n.67, 55n.74, 119n.14
  Sha'ar ha-razim, 40n.13, 76n.12, 104n.107, 126n.43, 127n.49, 179n.50, 183n.59
active intellect, 81–82, 102–3, 112, 115
Adam, 36–39, 189–90
  and Eve, 38
  prelapsarian knowledge of, 36–39, 42–43, 56–57
Adelkind, Israel Cornelio, 29–31, 172
Aemilius, Paulus, 30n.84
Akbarism, 174–76. *See* Ibn ʿArabī
al-Andalus, 31–32, 33–34, 107–8, 109, 110, 171, 173–80. *See* Iberia
Albrecht V, Duke of Bavaria, 2–3
al-Farabi, 166, 173–74
Alfonso de Valladolid, 18n.36, 47n.41
Alfonso X, 14, 16–18, 176–79
  Alfonsine culture, 16–18, 31–32, 171, 176–79
  Estoria de Espanna, 176–80
  Setenario, 177–80
  translations, 16–18
Alhambra Palace, 174–76, 175*f*
almsgiving (*ṣedaqah*), 119–20
Alphabet of Rabbi Aqiba, 73–74, 191
ancient hidden wisdom, 176–77
  lost knowledge, 108–9
  written preservation of, 1, 177, 179–80, 192
  See also kabbalah, as new-ancient wisdom
androgynology, 118–19, 120–21, 135, 154–55, 158, 181–82
angelification, 58–59
angelology, 9–10, 13–14, 38–39, 79–82, 84–86, 87–90, 102–5, 110, 112–13, 115, 121–22, 136–37, 139–41, 157–58, 162–63, 181–82
  bridesmaids, angels as, 135
  gender and, 134–35, 137–38, 141
  See also active intellect; fourfold angelology; thirteenfold, angelology; tenth intellect
apophasis and cataphasis, 93, 98–99, 167–68, 193. *See* supernal crown, concealment of
Aristotle, 53, 88–89, 90, 101n.96, 102, 110, 115
asceticism, 50–52, 60, 64, 65. *See* poverty
Asher ben David, 44n.25, 77–78, 162–63
Ashkenaz, 42–43, 61n.106, 68–69, 70, 75–76, 108n.121, *See* pietism, Ashkenazi
Assembly of Israel, 156–57
Assisi, 65–66
asymmetry of divine order (*see* divine order, asymmetry)
Averroës (Ibn Rushd), 176
avir qadmon. *See* primordial ether

baʿale teshuvah. *See* penitents
Babylonia, 188
Baḥya Ibn Paquda, 33–34, 54n.69, 65n.117, 69n.134
Bar Ḥiyya, Abraham, 65n.117, 110, 179–80
Bavarian State Library, 2–3, 172
belimah, 73–74, 97–98
Beshtian ḥasidism, 54n.69
binah (sefirah), 19–20, 35–36, 41–42, 43–46, 56–58, 62–63, 82–83, 90–92, 95–96, 105–6, 122, 126, 128, 136–37, 150–51, 162–64, 167–68, 170, 181–84, 186–88, 192, 193–94
  freedom (*ḥerut*), 18–19, 46–47, 126
  gender instability of, 126, 127–28, 129–32

binah (sefirah) (*cont.*)
mother or uterus, 57–58, 64n.113, 71–72, 127–28, 129–32, 154, 181–82, 189, 190, 196 (*see also* three divine worlds)
stream (*yuval*), 57n.87, 94n.71, 127–28, 129, 154, 195 (*see also* Jubilee)
teshuvah, 18–19, 31–32, 35–36, 40, 43–46, 56–57, 58–59, 62–63, 71–72, 163–64 (*see also* repentance)
birds, 163–64
homeward, 56–57
wayward, 46–47, 48–49, 51–52

cabala. *See* kabbalah, Romanization of
Cairo Geniza, 181n.56
Castile, 4–8, 10, 20–22, 29–32, 33–34, 60n.101, 70–71, 76–78, 107–8, 161, 170, 171, 177–79
Alfonsine, 176–79
See also Iberia
Castilian language, 16–18, 65n.120, 176–79
Catalonia, 14, 15, 21–22, 31–32, 55n.74, 74–75, 87–88, 171, 179–84, 194. *See* Girona
celestial spheres, 9–10, 18–19, 74–75, 79–81, 89–90, 103–5, 110, 115, 121–22
chariot, 58–59, 79–81, 145
angelic, 81–82, 84–85, 87, 92, 98
divine, 81–82, 84–85, 88–89, 98
double, 83, 85, 114–15
See also Merkavah/Hekhalot literature; *ma'aseh bereshit* and *ma'aseh merkavah*
Christian Hebraists. *See* Christianity
Christianity
anti-Christian rhetoric, 16, 64–65, 153n.130
Christian Europe, 63–64, 66, 172–73
Christian Hebraists, 31–32, 171–72
Christian iconography, 174–76
Christian knowledge of kabbalah, 16–18, 30n.84, 31–32, 171–72
Christian piety, 50n.55, 63–66
harmonization of kabbalah with, 171–73
intra-Christian polemics, 65–66
Jewish knowledge of, 16
polemical positioning of Judaism in relation to, 64–66
Christology, 66n.122, 121, 127–28, 177–79
circumcision, 129–32, 155, 158, 159
coming world. *See 'olam ha-ba*
commandments, 43, 45–46, 53, 59–60, 98–99, 119–20, 138–39. *See* rationales of the commandments
compassion. *See raḥamim*
concatenation of divine gradations, 105–6
Cordoba, 176
Cosmogony. *See* linguistic speculation, on cosmogony
cosmology 140–41, 179–80
of de León 20–21, 86, 112–13, 114–15, 166
of Gikatilla 110
See also cosmology *under* threefold, fourfold, ninefold; thirteenfold
covenant
berit/ṣaddiq (divine attribute), 129–32, 151–52, 155, 156, 158–59 (*see also* divine righteousness)
of God with Israel, 51, 53
creation, 31–32, 58–59
crown rabbi, 9, 12–13, 14
cutting of the shoots, 47, 48–49

Daniel, 25, 58–59, 105–6
de León, Moses, 2–3, 4–8, 9–18, 19–22, 184
anonymous/unsigned works, 78–81, 103–5, 112, 113
and Ashkenazi pietism, 41–43, 68–70
chronology of works, 4–8, 9–14, 78, 117–18, 184
on "commentators," 152–53
context of, 171, 172–74, 176–79, 182
on "custodians of secrets," 11–12n.18, 21n.52, 83–84, 94–95, 96, 99, 103–5, 114n.140
dating and sequencing the works of, 78–79, 117–18, 184–86, 197–98
and Franciscans, 65, 70–72, 159, 172–73
gender speculation (*see* gender of divinity)
and Gikatilla, 18n.37, 21–22, 31–32, 60n.101, 76–78, 110–13, 152–53, 162, 167–70, 182–84
Hebrew corpus, 2–3, 18–19, 22–23, 29–31, 43, 50, 105–6, 116–18, 138n.83, 161–62, 167–68, 172–73, 184–85, 186, 188, 197–98
on hidden knowledge and repentance, 38–39, 41–42n.18, 42–43
interreferentiality of works, 12–13, 31–32, 78–79, 83–84, 188, 198 (*see also* the "Nameless Composition," parallelism with Zohar)
linguistic speculation of (*see* linguistic speculation)
Maskiyyot kesef, 94–95
Mishkan ha-'edut, 2–3n.6, 18n.37, 29–31, 41–42, 56n.80, 62, 63–64, 63n.111, 65, 68–69, 70–71, 94n.72, 173n.34, 182–84
on "Muslim sages," 107–9
Or zarua', 9–10, 34–35, 36, 39–41, 59n.95, 78–82, 83–86, 87, 95
penitential writings, 34–43, 68–69, 182–84

pretheosophical works, 9–10, 11–12n.18, 12–14, 21–22, 34–35, 42–43, 44–45, 55–57, 58–59, 68, 73, 77–82, 83–86, 89–90, 94–95, 103–5, 110, 113, 121–22, 146, 150, 152, 161, 162–63, 167–68, 177–79, 182, 185, 191
pseudepigraphy of/attribution to ancient sages, 12–13, 23–26, 79–81, 83–84, 87–88n.49, 96, 97, 111, 113, 176–77, 186–92, 197–98
regimens vitae, 31–32, 33–43, 51–52, 56–57, 63–64, 69–71, 196
Sefer ha-Nefesh ha-ḥakhamah or *Sefer ha-Mishqal* (*Anima scientiae*), 78–79, 103n.104, 164–65, 171n.25, 185–86
Sefer ha-Ne'lam (and corpus of), 9–10, 11–12, 13–14, 79–81, 83–84, 84–85nn.36–37, 86, 87–88, 87n.48, 89–90, 92, 103–5, 113, 121–22, 191
Sefer ha-Rimmon, 21–22, 24n.67, 29–31, 39–41, 57–58, 58n.88, 59n.95, 60n.103, 69n.134, 118–19, 130n.61, 138–39, 152–53, 155–57, 158, 160, 163n.4, 164–65, 185–86, 195n.94
Sefer Orḥot ḥayyim (or *The Testament of R. Eliezer the Great*), 34–35n.3
Sha'ar ḥeleq ha-nequddah, 112
Sheqel ha-qodesh, 9–10, 12, 19–20, 25, 29–31, 52n.59, 59n.95, 59n.98, 88–89, 94n.72, 105, 105n.110, 106–7, 130n.61, 164–65, 182–84, 185–86, 188–89, 195n.94, 197–98
Shushan ha-'edut, 2n.4, 10–13, 22–23, 29–32, 39–41, 47n.40, 47nn.42–43, 57–58, 68, 132–34, 150, 152–53, 154–55, 161, 185–86, 197n.104
social aims of, 31–32, 63–64, 65–66, 67–72
Sod Darkhe ha-otiyyot ve-ha nequddot, 79–81, 107–8, 111
students of, 15, 68
theosophical speculation of (*see* theosophy, de León)
theosophical turn, 11–12n.18, 12–13, 31–32, 55–56, 68, 73, 77–78, 82, 83–84, 85–86, 90, 93, 94–96, 102–3, 105–6, 114–15, 122, 172, 173–74, 179–80, 182, 191
theosophical writings of, 2–3, 29–32, 34–35, 38, 41–42, 88–89, 102–3, 114–15, 142, 185
transitional phase, 11–12, 13–14, 22–24, 28–29, 31–32, 77–78, 83, 105–6, 114–15
vowels, 111–13, 115
on the wisdom of (ancient) sages, 12–13, 20–22, 40, 44–45, 53, 60, 79–82, 97, 138, 162, 188, 190–91, 194
zoharic writings, 79–82, 115, 182–98 (*see also* Zohar)
Deuteronomy, 23–24, 55–56, 148–50, 162–63n.3, 180–81, 193–94
divine attributes, 18–19, 27, 28–29, 43, 45–46, 53, 186, 188
divine body/divine limbs, 130–32. *See also* gender of divinity, male body; female body
divine judgment, 19n.42, 44–45, 53, 54–56, 98n.83, 156–57, 183n.63
divine marriage (or *hieros gamos*), 47–48, 51–52, 118–19, 142–43, 147–48, 151–52, 154–55, 158
divine names, 13–14, 19–20, 21–22, 25, 167, 186, 189–90. *See also* divine attributes
Elohim, 19n.42, 97n.82, 105–6, 156, 157–58, 181
forty-two-letter name, 156, 158–59
incomplete name (*see* Hebrew letters and divinity, incomplete name)
nine/ten names and sefirot, 98n.83
Tetragrammaton, 84–85, 92, 148–50, 156, 158–59, 163n.4, 168–69, 177–79, 186–88 (*see also* linguistic speculation, letters of Tetragrammaton)
divine order, 9–10, 13–14, 18–20, 38–39, 44–45, 47–50, 52, 57, 60, 61, 73–74, 81–82, 85, 86, 87–89, 90, 93, 98, 100–1, 103, 104n.105, 114–15, 161, 162, 182–84. *See also* sefirot; theosophy
asymmetry of, 165–66
divine righteousness, 137–39. *See* King Solomon
divine worlds. *See* divine order; sefirot; theosophy

Egypt, 33–34
Eleazar of Worms, 41–43, 68–69, 179n.50
Yoreh ḥaṭṭa'im, 42
emanation, 13–14, 55–56, 81–82, 103–6, 110, 112–13, 123–24, 169–70
emanationist language, 124n.33
emet (truth), 19–20, 62
encryption, 99
end of all flesh, 185–86
Enelow, Hyman, 29–31
enlightened. *See maskil*
esotericism, 16–18, 20–21, 31–32, 43–44, 79–81, 171–74
pre-kabbalistic, 16, 180–81
Western, 171–74

Esther, 57
eternal femininity (*neqevut 'olamit*), 31–32, 120, 129–34, 136, 149–51
perpetual female (*neqevah temidit*), 137–39, 148
unblemished female (*neqevah temimah*), 130–32n.63, 150–51, 159, 191–92
even temperament, 54
evil, 21–22, 182–84, 185, 196
evil inclination, 36–39, 42–43, 55–56, 61
impurity, 182–84, 185–86
Lilith, 182–84
serpent, 182–84
sinister emanations, 21–22
exile, 188
Exodus, 25, 26, 41–42, 49n.48, 151–52, 162–63, 167, 193–94
Exodus Rabbah, 179–80
extension of divine worlds, 123–24
Ezekiel, 81–82, 94n.71, 127n.49, 145
Ezra ben Solomon of Girona, 1, 21–22, 48–50, 55n.74, 55–56n.78, 58n.88, 71n.140, 88n.52, 94n.71, 119–20, 135n.71, 138n.81, 143n.97, 145n.104, 152–55, 156–57, 162–63, 179–80, 182

Farber, Asi, 82
female shall compass male, 120, 127–28, 129–32, 150–51, 195. *See* Jeremiah
femininity. *See* eternal femininity; gender of divinity, female
Fernando III, 70n.135, 176–79
fivefold speculation, 154, 158
fingers grasping cup of blessing, 156, 158
gates, 156
sepals, 154, 155, 156, 158
and thirteenfold paradigm, 154
See also Jubilee
flame bound to a coal, 20–21, 27, 148–49
form of life, 70–72
fourfold speculation, 85–89, 140–42
angelology, 139–40
cardinal directions, 87, 88–89, 132–34, 139–40, 141–42, 162–64
corners of the earth, 134–35, 139–40, 141–42
cosmology, 85–90, 114–15, 139–40
four elements, 20–21, 85–89, 169–70
metallurgical, 88–89
political body of Israel, 140 (*see also* Israelite banners)
psychology, 191–92
on sefirot, 87–89, 92
and twelvefold, thirteenfold speculations, 140–42

France, 108n.121, *See also* Provence
Francis of Assisi, 70–71
Franciscans (Minorites), 64, 65–66, 70–72
Franco-German Jewish culture, 75–76. *See* Ashkenaz; pietism, Ashkenazi
Freedom. *See binah*
Fugger, Johann Jakob (of Augsburg), 29–31, 172

Gabriel (archangel), 84–85, 87–88
Galilee, 197–98
Garden of Eden, 36–38, 168, 195
gender of created world, 136–39
female, 138–39 (*see also* angelic intellect, gender, Israel)
male, 137–39 (*see* King Solomon)
gender of divinity, 31–32, 73, 92, 116–17, 124–27, 165–66, 189–90, 192n.82, 194
of attributes and sefirot, 8, 25, 31–32, 100–1, 130–32, 161–63, 181–82, 189, 193–94 (*see binah,* as mother or uterus; three divine worlds)
as the basin of Solomon's Sea, 132–34, 139–40 (*see also* thirteenfold, superordination)
in Castilian kabbalah, 137
conventions of speculation about, 134, 142
demonic feminine, 182–84
divine androgyny, 119–20, 127–32, 137, 159, 181–84
divine self-parturition, 129, 191–92
divine marriage (*see* divine marriage)
in early kabbalah, 130–32, 142, 154–55
economic functions and, 126, 138–39, 147, 149–50
female, 31–32, 71–72, 100–1, 120, 142, 162–64, 181–82, 191–92, 193 (*see* eternal femininity)
female body, 71–72, 126, 129–32, 154, 182n.58, 195
female-female pattern, 135–36
gender permeability, 126, 127–28, 129–32
in the "Nameless Composition," 31–32, 116–18, 119–22, 154, 172–73, 181–82
male body, 126, 129–32
nine males and one female, 181
paterfamilias, 189, 190
personifications, 128
reciprocity, 144–45, 147, 148–49
and soul, 191–92
subordination/dependence of female, 124, 134, 144–45, 146–47
superordination of female, 64n.113, 83, 120–21, 135–36, 142, 147, 162–63, 164–65, 182, 191–92, 194–95 (*see* thirteenfold,

double thirteenfold forms of female superordination)
and thirteenfold paradigm (*see* thirteenfold, and androgynology)
triads, 137–39
unblemished female (*see* eternal femininity, unblemished female)
in the Zohar and Hebrew corpus of de León, 154–56, 158, 159–60
See also Hebrew letters and divinity
gender of Israel, 135–36
Genesis, 9–10, 22n.59, 34–35n.3, 38, 77–79, 94n.71, 105–6, 147, 155, 157–58, 159, 163n.4, 180–81, 182–84, 193–94, 195
Genesis Rabbah, 58n.88
geometrical speculation, 103
Germany, 42n.24, 108n.121, *See* Ashkenaz
Gerondi, Jonah, 69n.134
Gibraltar, 173–74
Gikatilla, Joseph ben Abraham, 2–3n.6, 18–19, 21–22, 31–32, 60n.101, 78–79, 157n.141, 162, 176–77
early works of, 76–78, 110, 177–79
Ginnat egoz, 76–77, 78–79
late writings of, 182–85
linguistic speculation, (*see* linguistic speculation, of Gikatilla)
and Moses de León, (*see* de León, and Gikatilla)
pretheosophical speculation, 77–78
Sha'are orah, 2–3n.6, 18–19, 76–77, 162, 170n.24
Sha'are Ṣedeq, 170n.24
theosophical turn of, 76–78
theosophy of, (*see* theosophy, of Gikatilla)
vowels, 110–13
Girona, 15, 21–22, 47–48, 64n.113, 155n.134, 179–84. *See* Catalonia
Giustiniani, Agostino, 171n.25
gradations of divinity. *See* divine order; sefirot; theosophy
Granada, 175*f*, 176. *See* Alhambra Palace
Greek letters, 177–79
Guadalajara, 16, 161, 198

hagiography
Christian, 65–66
zoharic, 29–31, 188, 192, 196
ha-Kohen, Isaac ben Jacob, 22n.60, 76–77, 102–3n.102, 121n.20, 182–84
ha-Kohen, Jacob ben Jacob, 76–77, 80n.22
Halevi, Judah, 173–74
Hanhagot (conduct literature), 67–68
ḥasidut, 35–36, 53
divine, 52–53, 59
See also pietism
Heavens (*shamayim*), 147n.114, 197
Hebrew Bible, 9–10, 47–48, 51n.56, 148, 154–55, 157–58
Hebrew letters and divinity,
alef, 83, 84–85, 87–88, 89–92, 99–101, 120, 121–22 (*see also* threefold speculations, structure of *alef*)
dalet (*see* three divine worlds)
Hebrew letters and divine attributes, 189–90
Hebrew letters and divine names, 79–81, 190–91
heh, 82–83, 84–85, 92, 95–97, 99–101, 112–13 (*see also* three divine worlds, letter *heh*)
incomplete name, 95–97, 102, 149–50
letters of Tetragrammaton, 74–75, 82–83, 84–85, 92, 95–98, 112, 142–43, 144 (*see also* three divine worlds, first *heh* of Tetragrammaton; last *heh* of Tetragrammaton)
ten letters and sefirot, 87–88, 90–92, 95–96, 97–98, 99–100, 189–90
vav, (*see* three divine worlds)
yod, 75–76, 82–83, 84–85, 89–92, 95, 96, 99–102, 110, 112–13, 159 (*see also* three divine worlds)
Hebrew letters, modes of speculation on, 9–10, 11–12n.18, 13–14, 18–21, 31–32, 82–83, 89–95, 99–106, 108–9, 167–68, 172–73, 180–81
archaic Hebrew letterforms, 108–9
cantillation marks, 103–5
gender of letters, 189–90, 195 (*see also* three divine worlds)
on shapes of letters/graphemic of, 73–74, 76–77, 81–82, 83, 89–90, 92, 94–95, 100–1, 103–5, 108–9, 110, 115
on sounds of letters/phonology of, 81–82, 83, 95–96, 97, 110, 115
vowels, 31–32, 79–81, 82–83, 85–86, 94–95, 103–5, 106n.117, 108, 110–13, 191, 192 (*see also* fourfold speculations)
heresiology, 43–50, 69–70, 172–73. *See* birds, wayward
Ḥibbur ha-teshuvah. *See* Meiri, Menaḥem ben Solomon
hidden point, 105–6
hieros gamos. *See* divine marriage
ḥokhmah. *See* sefirot
ḥolem (vowel), 110, 111–13, 167–68, 170, 192
as *ḥokhmah* versus active intellect, 103–5, 115

ḥolem (vowel) (*cont.*)
as subordinate to *qamaṣ*, 111–13
See also noetic point
holy spirit, 76–77, 146–47, 148–50
as *malkhut*, 146n.110
human body, 35, 38–39

Iberia, 4–8, 29–31, 42n.20, 42n.24, 64, 70n.135, 73, 113, 171–72, 173–76, 175*f*, 180–81, 190n.75
Muslim Iberia, 176
See al-Andalus; Castile; Catalonia; Spain
Ibn ʿArabī, 109n.123, 113–14n.139
Ibn Ezra, Abraham, 49n.49, 73–74, 110, 173–74
Ibn Gabirol, Solomon 110, 173–76
Ibn Gaon, Shem Ṭov, 104n.107
Ibn Tibbon, Samuel, 53–54n.68
Idra literature, 60n.101, 104n.105, 157n.141, 168n.21
ʿilm al-ḥurūf. *See* lettrism
image of all images, 48–50, 51–52
imitatio Christi, 71–72
imitatio Dei, 16, 34–35n.3, 35, 52, 53–54n.68, 54, 55–57, 59, 71–72, 137
intellects. *See* angelology
Isaac ben Samuel of Acre, 9
Isaac ben Ṭodros, 2–3n.6
Isaac Ibn Latif, 110
Isaac Ibn Sahula, 22–23, 77–78
Isaac of Corbeil, 66n.122
Isaac the Blind, 21–22, 74–75
Isaiah, 46n.35, 50–52, 129n.57, 134–35, 151–52, 196
Islam, 16
Castilian knowledge of, 16
Islamic architecture, 174–76
Islamic philosophy, 173–74, 179–80
Qurʾān, 16–18, 109n.123
Islamic philosophy. *See* Islam
isomorphism, 87–89, 114–15, 139–42, 145–46
Israel, 23–24, 26, 27–28, 41n.16, 47–48, 50, 51, 53, 63–64, 65–66, 75–76, 83, 85–86, 127–28, 132–35, 141–42, 151–52, 156–58, 162–63, 168, 171–72, 181–82, 188, 193n.88, 194–95
Israelite banners, 85–90, 132n.66, 134–35, 140, 151–52
Italy, 10, 29–32. *See* Venice

Jacob, 55n.74, 55–56n.78, 159, 182–84, 185–86
Jacob (student of de León), 15
Jacob ben Meir Tam, 64
Jacob ben Sheshet, 11–12n.18
Jeremiah, 59, 127–28, 127n.48, 128n.51, 130n.61, 195, *See* female shall compass male
Jesus of Nazareth, 44–45, 52, 71–72
Jewish Theological Seminary of America, 7*f*, 29–31
Job, 92–93
Joseph of Hamadan, 60n.101
Joshua ben Peraḥiah, 52
Juan Manuel, 16
Jubilee, 154
Judah ben Barzilai of Barcelona, 180–81
Judah ben Moses ha-Darshan, 127–28
Judah ben Yaqar, 179–80
Judah of Regensburg, 68–69
Judges, 57

kabbalah, 14, 15
Castilian, 8, 26n.69, 31–32, 33–34, 50–51, 63–64, 73, 76–78, 82, 104n.107, 113–15, 126, 130–32, 153n.130, 169–70, 171, 181–84, 185–86
of divine names, 11–12, 13–14, 21–22, 186
earlier, 11–12, 13–14, 16–18, 21–22, 47–48, 67–68
early *regimen vitae* of, 33–34, 35–36, 37*f*, 67–68
kabbalistic fellowships, 33–34, 67–68
Lurianic, 31–32, 102–3
as new-ancient wisdom, 8, 47–48, 66
as oral Torah/ rabbinic tradition, 1, 14, 47–48, 55–56, 60, 172–73
orthodoxy of, 46, 47–48, 67–68, 69–70, 172–73
in Ottoman Galilee, 33–34
as penitential-pietistic movement, 31–32, 33–34, 43–57, 66, 67–68
prophetic, 75–76
Romanization of (cabala), 16–18, 17*f*
of sefirot, 8, 9–11, 11–12n.18, 47–48, 67–68, 76–77, 82, 161
as a social project of piety, 31–32, 63–64, 67–72
zoharic kabbala, 22–23, 114–15, 161, 179–80, 184
Karaites, 47–48, 47n.41
karet (punishment of), 48–52, 69–70
King Solomon, 137–38
Kingdom of the House of David (final *heh* of Tetragrammaton), 144–45
Klosterneuburg Altar (Nicholas of Verdun), 174n.42

Land of Israel, 188
Languedoc, 64–65

Law (Jewish), 16, 68–69
left. *See* right and left
lettrism, Islamic science of (*'ilm al-ḥurūf*), 31–32, 78, 107–8, 176–79
  de León, 107–9, 113
levirate marriage, 49n.49, 50
Levites, 54
Leviticus, 53, 130–32n.63, 150–51
Leviticus Rabbah, 44n.28, 46n.35, 53n.63
light, 34–35, 58–59
  sensible and intellectual, 27, 142–43, 144
  white, indigo, and black, 27–28
"Light of the West" (*ner ha-ma'aravi*), 173–74
linguistic speculation, 8, 9–10, 11–12, 13–14, 19n.43, 31–32, 73–74, 102–3, 161, 176–79
  in Alfonsine corpus, 176–79
  context of, 106–9 (*see also* lettrism, Islamic science of)
  on cosmogony, 9–10, 73–76, 79–82, 86
  in early kabbalah 73–74, 104n.107
  Franco-German, 75–76
  of Gikatilla, 78, 104n.107 (*see also* Gikatilla, vowels)
  in the "Nameless Composition," 78, 82–83, 85–86, 87–88, 90, 95–96, 98n.83
  in pretheosophical works of de León, 78–85, 114–15
  pre-Zoharic, 95–97, 190–91
  in prophetic kabbalah, 73–75
  theosophical, 11–12, 19–20, 31–32, 56–57, 73, 86, 87–88, 90, 95–96, 97, 103–5, 161, 167–68, 170, 190–91
  in Zohar, 75–76, 98n.83
  See also Abulafia, Abraham; Hebrew letters and divinity
liturgy and worship, 23–24, 53, 158, 196
luminous point, 105–6. *See also* noetic point
  punctus scientificus, 106–7
Luria, Isaac, 103n.103

ma'aseh bereshit and *ma'aseh merkavah*, 179n.50, 180–81
Maghreb, 173–76
Maimonides, Moses, 9, 20–22, 43–44, 53, 60n.103, 75–76, 81–82, 103–5, 157n.140, 166, 173–74, 176, 179–80
  on Adam, 36
  on character change, 39n.10
  The Guide for the Perplexed, 36
  Mishneh Torah, 39n.10, 65nn.117–18, 69n.134, 167n.11
Marcus, Ivan, 68–69
Mary (mother of Jesus), 127–28, 153n.130
maskil (enlightened person), 13–14, 15, 40–41, 127n.49
Matthew, 44–45
median way, 53–54
  and Aristotelian golden mean, 53
Mediterranean, 75–76
Meir ben Isaac ha-Levi of Prague, 5*f*, 29–31, 134
Meir Ibn Gabbai, 30n.83
Meiri, Menaḥem ben Solomon, 64–65
Merkavah/Hekhalot literature, 73–74, 180–81
Metatron (archangel), 81–82, 84–85, 92, 102–5, 115. *See* active intellect
Micah, 41–42
Michael (archangel), 84–85, 87–88
midrash, 20–21, 25, 57n.85, 73–74, 86, 87–88, 156–57, 179–81
Midrash ha-Ne'lam, 22–23, 58n.88, 77–79, 121–22
might, attribute of (*middat ha-gevurah*), 54, 183n.63, *See also* sefirot, *gevurah*
Minorites. *See* Franciscans
Mishnah, 43–44
Mithridates, Flavius, 171n.25
Moors, 16. *See also* Islam
Mopsik, Charles, 60n.100, 106–7
Moroccan manuscript, 4–8, 6*f*, 29–31, 134n.69, 173–74
Moses, 41n.16
  as *tif'eret*, 26
Moses ben Simeon of Burgos, 11–12n.18, 22n.60, 49n.48, 55n.74, 63n.111, 182–84, 183n.59
Muḥammad, 16
Munich manuscript (Venice), 2–8, 7*f*, 10–11, 11–12n.18, 20–21, 22–25, 27, 28–31, 37*f*, 150–51, 163n.4, 164–65, 172
  textual corruption, 134–37
musar, 67–68

Naḥmanides, 5*f*, 21–22, 45n.31, 64–65, 77–78, 128n.53, 161, 162–64, 179–80, 182
"Nameless Composition," 2–8, 5*f*–7*f*, 10–15, 18–19, 21–22, 172, 190–91
  attribution to Naḥmanides, 5*f*, 21–22, 161, 163n.4
  as a commentary on ten sefirot, 18–20, 73, 162, 180–81
  as de León's earliest speculation on male and female, 118–19 (*see also* three divine worlds)
  as the earliest theosophical work of de León, 2–3, 5*f*, 8, 10–11, 12–13, 15, 16–18, 22–23, 31–32, 35–36, 41–42, 43, 47–48, 51–52,

"Nameless Composition" (*cont.*)
67–68, 73, 78, 83, 89–90, 95–96, 99, 103–5, 113, 114–15, 121–22, 161, 162, 167–68, 170, 179–80, 182–88, 190, 191–92, 194–95, 197–98 (*see also* de León, transitional phase)
linguistic speculation (*see* linguistic speculation, in the "Nameless Composition")
number of chapters of, 162, 164–65
and *Or zarua'* (*see Or zarua'*; "Nameless Composition")
on oral and written Torah, 46–48
parallelism with Zohar, 22–29, 47–48, 88–89, 121–22, 129, 135, 161–62, 184–98
penitential pietism, 34, 35–36, 38–39, 43, 50–52, 60, 63–64, 67–70
and (The Book of) Rav Hamnuna Saba (*see* Rav Hamnuna Saba)
reception of, 29–32, 142, 155–60, 194–95, 198
regimen vitae, 35–36, 37*f*, 41–43, 56–63, 67–68 (see also "Order of Penitents")
and *Shushan ha-'edut* (*see Shushan ha-'edut*; "Nameless Composition")
sources of, 20–22, 182–84
structure of, 18–20, 162–65
theosophy and penitent in, 35–36, 41–43, 57–58, 67–71, 113 (*see also* "Order of Penitents")
thirteenfold speculation in (*see* thirteenfold)
title of, 197–98
See also Moroccan manuscript; Munich fragment
Neḥemiah of Erfurt, 75–76
Neoplatonism, 49n.49, 143n.97
Neo-Pythagoreanism, 74–75
neqevut 'olamit. See eternal femininity
new soul. *See* soul
ninefold
cosmology, 166, 169–70
sefirot (nine versus ten), 97–99, 166–69
Noah, 182–84
noetic point, 31–32, 78, 101–3, 105–6, 107–8, 110, 115. *See also* Hebrew letters and divinity, *yod*; *ḥolem*; luminous point
North Africa, 173–74
nothingness, 101–2. *See also* sefirot, *ayin*
Numbers, 23–24, 35, 49n.48, 58–59, 83, 86, 87n.48, 151–52
Numbers Rabbah, 87–88
numerological speculation, 74–75, 99–100, 154–55, 165–66, 172–74. *See also* linguistic speculation
Numerological value of letters, 74–75, 81–82, 83, 95–98, 99–100, 167–68, 170, 172–73, 190–91
letter pairing, 99–100
one, 99–101, 123
primordial numbers, 74–75

occult sciences, 171–73
'olam ha-ba (the coming world), 19–20, 43–44, 46–47, 56–57
as *binah*, 43–44, 46–47, 48–49, 56–57
and the "Nameless Composition," 11–12n.18, 68, 83–86, 89–90, 92, 98
Order of Penitents (Franciscan), 70–71
"Order of Penitents" (*Siddur ba'ale teshuvah*), 35–36, 37*f*, 40–42, 61–63, 67–69, 70–72, 163–64, 196. *See also* "Nameless Composition"
Orḥot ḥayyim, 34–35n.3

paradise, 57, 58–59, 132–34, 174–76. *See also* Garden of Eden
Parenti, Giovanni, 70n.135
Patriarchs, 145
penitenciados, 65–66. *See also* Franciscans
penitents, 15, 19–20, 55–56, 57–58, 60, 132–34
afflictions of love and, 46, 52, 57–58
as broken vessels, 45–48, 52
and kabbalah (*see* kabbalah, as penitential-pietistic movement)
as manifestation/exemplification of divinity, 46, 55–56, 71–72
mimetic knowledge of, 34–35n.3, 35, 42–43, 52, 71–72, 196
penitents and theosophy, 35, 41–42n.18, 52, 67–68 (*see also* pietism, theosophical paradigm of)
regimens, 35–36, 39–42, 41n.16, 56–58, 67–68 (*see also* "Order of Penitents"; thirteenfold)
as testimony, 33–34, 43, 45–46, 52, 67–68, 70, 71–72, 158
Pico della Mirandola, Giovanni, 171–73
pietism, 33–34, 46, 50–51, 196
Ashkenazi, 33–34, 41–43, 54n.69, 61n.106, 61–62n.108, 68–70
Jewish-Christian rivalry, 38, 63–66, 70–71, 172–73
kabbalah as (*see* kabbalah, as penitential-pietistic movement)
mendicant piety, 33–34, 63–66
rabbinic, 33–34, 44–45, 50–51, 55–56, 62, 63–64, 66

theosophical paradigm of, 13–14, 15, 33–34, 43, 44–45, 50–51, 62–63, 67–68
poverty, 64
of lower female world, 144–45, 147
primordial ether (*avir qadmon*), 19–20, 81–82, 92–93, 128, 130–32, 167–68, 192
and *binah*, 128n.53
See also supernal crown
primordial grapheme, 31–32
primordial letters, 73, 74–75, 81–82
primordial sin, 36–39
procreation, 50–52, 124, 154–55, 158
Prommer, Wolfgang, 30n.84
prophetic kabbalah. *See* kabbalah, prophetic
prophetology, 142–45, 146–47
Provence, 35–36, 74–75
Proverbs, 23–24, 46, 69n.134, 129n.56, 129n.59, 138, 195
providence, 44–45, 55–56, 59–60, 95
Psalms, 23–24, 46n.35, 57, 59–60, 134–35, 136, 141–42, 150–52, 153, 156, 163n.4, 193–94
psychology, 55–56. *See also* threefold; fourfold
and divine ontology 93–95
punishment, 19n.42, 48–50, 55–56

Qalonymide family, 75–76
qamaṣ, 85–86, 87–88
as all-encompassing nature of God, 111–13

Rabbi Abraham (teacher of Gikatilla), 111
Rabbi Eleazar, 98n.83
Rabbi Hezekiah, 155–56
Rabbi Isaac (*ha-parush*), 111
Rabbi Ishmael, 7*f*, 11–12n.18, 19–20
Rabbi Judah, 65
Rabbi Simeon 23–24, 192, 194, 195, 196, 197
Rabbi Yoḥanan, 41n.16
rabbinic tradition (and kabbalah), 14, 20–21, 22–26, 43–44, 47–48, 50–51, 52, 55–56, 60, 68–69, 73–74, 94–95, 122, 149–50, 165–66, 171, 172–74, 179–81. *See also* Torah, oral
raḥamim (compassion), 19–20, 34–35, 48–49, 53–56, 156–57. *See also* thirteenfold, attributes of compassion
Raphael (archangel), 84–85, 87–88
Rashi, 127–28
rationales of the commandments (*ṭa'ame ha-miṣvot*), 21–22, 39, 49n.48, 50, 114n.140, 118–20, 137, 160
Rav Hamnuna Saba, 98n.83, 184–98
Recanati, Menaḥem ben Benjamin, 21n.53, 55–56n.78, 185
Reconquista, 70n.135
Redemption, 62–63, 127–28, 168–69, 170
Regula Bullata, 70–71
Renaissance, 31–32, 171–73
repentance (*teshuvah*), 21–22, 38–40, 43–44, 47, 58–59, 60, 62, 69–70
binah as *teshuvah* (*see under binah*)
and the coming world, 43–44
and hidden knowledge, 38–39
teshuvah (human), 8, 18–19, 34–35, 36–40, 51–52, 55–57, 63–66
teshuvah and *gan'eden*, 58–59
teshuvah as penance vs. repentance, 41–42n.18
Resh Laqish, 65
resurrection, 57, 58–59
right and left, 21–22, 23–24, 52–56, 86, 87–88
left-side of divinity, 19–20, 28–29, 39
right-side of divinity, 19n.42, 40
subordination of left to right, 52–56, 181, 183n.63, 196
rose among the thorns, 152–53, 155–57, 185. *See* Song of Songs
rose of testimony, 31–32, 150–54, 155–57, 158, 159. *See also* Psalms

Saadia Gaon, 65n.117
Sabbath, 50–52, 158, 193–94, 196
Sadducees, 47n.41
Safed, kabbalistic fraternities of, 33–34, 54n.69
Sancho IV of Castile, 10, 12–13, 15, 176
Scheler, Max 39n.10
Scholem, Gershom, 64n.113, 117–18
on the "Nameless Composition," 2–8, 9–11, 18–19, 22–23, 162
secret of faith, 28–29, 47–48
ṣedeq, 62–63
Sefer ha-Bahir, 21–22, 73–74, 94n.71, 104n.107, 122, 181–82
Sefer Ḥasidim, 44n.29, 46n.34, 62, 66n.122, 68–69
Sefer ha-Yashar, 64, 65–66
Sefer ha-Zohar. *See* Zohar
Sefer Yeṣirah, 20–21, 27n.70, 57n.83, 73–75, 90, 98–99, 173–74, 180–81
sefirot, 18–21, 23–24, 43, 47–48, 51–52, 56–57, 62, 92–93, 161, 162–63, 186–88, 197
ayin, *keter* as, 18–20, 82–83, 90–93, 98–99, 101–2, 104n.105, 110, 192 (*see also* supernal crown)
binah (*see binah*)
commentary on, 18–19, 162
concatenation of, 103
din 130–32

sefirot (*cont.*)
gender of (*see* three divine worlds)
gevurah (or *paḥad*), 19–20, 54, 87–89, 130–32, 154, 155
ḥesed, 52–53, 55–56, 57–58, 59–60, 62, 87–89, 90, 130–32, 154, 155, 162–63
hod, 130–32, 154, 155
ḥokhmah, 18–20, 31–32, 82–83, 85, 90, 92–93, 95–96, 97–101, 102–6, 123, 126, 128, 132n.66, 145–46, 167–68, 170, 180–81, 186–88, 190, 195
ḥokhmah and *binah*, conjunction of, 146–47
keter (*see* supernal crown)
malkhut, 25, 26, 27, 31–32, 47–49, 51–52, 58–59, 62–63, 87–89, 90, 92, 100–1, 122, 130–34, 136–37, 162–63, 182–84, 192, 193–95 (*see also* three divine worlds, lower)
neṣaḥ, 130–32, 154, 155
as numerical ciphers, 74–75
ten sefirot, 8, 18–19, 23–24, 73–74, 97–99, 123, 162–63, 165–66, 170, 189–90
tiferet, 19–20, 25, 26, 27, 47–49, 51–52, 62, 87–89, 130–32, 142–43, 144–45, 147, 151–52, 154, 155, 192, 195, 197
upper and lower *ḥokhmah*, 100–1, 115, 128n.53
yesod, 57–58, 62, 87–89, 90, 142–43, 154, 155, 157–58, 162–63
See also divine marriage; *ḥokhmah* and *binah*, conjunction
Segovia, 76–77
seven divine anthropoid forms, 181
Seville, 16–18
sexual abstinence, 51–52
sexuality, kabbalistic/pietistic, 50–52, 197
shalshelet ha-qabbalah (chain of transmission), 14
shekhinah, 25, 122, 137, 138n.83, 141–42, 148–49, 162–63, 194–95
double, 100–1
as moon, 138–39
See also eternal femininity; sefirot, *malkhut*; three divine worlds, lower female world
Shema, 162–63n.3, 186, 188
Simeon bar Yoḥai, 88–89, 188
ṣimṣum, 31–32, 103
Sinai, 14, 23–24, 47–48
six extremities, 20–21, 90, 150–52, 153, 154
six-petaled flower, 153
lily 152–54, 182
rose versus, 151–53
Solomon's Sea, 133*f*, 147, 173–76
Christian iconography, 174–76
gender of, 134–37, 141–42
isomorphism of worlds, 139–42
See also thirteenfold, Solomon's Sea
Soloveitchik, Joseph, 41n.16
on self-creation, 39n.10
Song of Songs, 57, 153, 156–58
soul, 35, 50, 51–52, 191–93
new soul, 39, 57–58
radiance of, 35, 38, 39–40
See also psychology
Spain. *See* Iberia
St. Bartholomew's Church, Liège, 174n.42
Steinschneider, Moritz, 2–3, 2–3n.6
supernal crown (*keter 'elyon*), 19–20, 60n.101, 82–83, 92–93, 128n.53, 166–70
transcendence or concealment of, 92–93, 128, 165–66, 167–68, 169, 192–93

ṭa'ame ha-miṣvot. *See* rationales of the commandments
Tabernacle, 162–63
Talmud, 16–18, 73–74. *See* rabbinic tradition; Torah, oral
aggadot, 15, 21n.53
Babylonian, 20–21
Tanḥuma-Yelammedenu Literature, 179–80
Temple, 25, 162–63
tenfold speculation and ten commandments, 98–99
tenth intellect, 84–85, 87, 98, 112–13
teshuvah. *See* binah; repentance
The Testament of R. Eliezer the Great. *See* de León, *Sefer Orḥot ḥayyim*
testimony, 151–53, 155, 158–59
See also penitents, as testimony
theogony, 104n.105, 105–6
theosophical transition, 76–78, 82
of androgynology, 121–22, 129
of threefold worlds (cosmology to theosophy), 121–22
See also de León, theosophical turn; de León, transitional phase; Gikatilla, theosophical turn
theosophy, 14, 31–32, 43, 59–60, 186. *See also* Hebrew letters and divinity; sefirot; thirteenfold; three divine worlds
of de León, 1, 2–3, 8, 10–13, 14, 16–19, 21–22, 29, 31–32, 43, 44–45, 47–48, 52, 56–57, 81–82, 113, 142, 161, 165–68, 170, 172–73, 182–84, 194–95
of Gikatilla, 76–77, 168–70, 171n.25
and heresy (*see* heresiology)

and linguistic speculation (*see* linguistic speculation, theosophical)
and penitents (*see* penitents, and theosophy)
and pietism (*see* pietism, theosophical paradigm of)
and psychology, 192
and thirteenfold attributes, 19–20, 41–42, 180–81
theurgy, 59–60
thirteen attributes. *See* thirteenfold; attributes
thirteenfold
and androgynology, 120, 141–42, 154, 156–57
angelology, 56–57, 120–21, 137–38, 162–63
attributes, 18–20, 31–32, 35–36, 41–42, 41n.16, 56–57, 170, 183n.59, 189–90
attributes of compassion (*raḥamim*), 19–20, 41–42, 53, 156–57, 162–64, 168, 169–70
attributes of repentance (*middot shel teshuvah*), 31–32, 40–42, 53, 56–57, 71–72, 163–64, 165–66
cosmology, 56–57, 120–21, 151
the covenant of the thirteen, 53
duplication of the thirteen pattern, 152, 154–55, 156–57
female superordination and, 118–37, 139–42, 150–51, 156–58, 182, 190, 191–92, 194–95
penitential attributes, 35–36, 41–42, 53, 56–57, 61, 62, 71–72, 163–64, 196
penitential regimens, 19–20, 34, 35–36, 40–41, 56–63
political order of Israel, 140–41, 151, 162–63, 194–95
Solomon's Sea, 19–20, 31–32, 56–58, 120, 132–34, 139–42, 152, 159, 160, 162–64, 182–84, 195
speculation, 18–20, 31–32, 56–57, 139–42, 150–55, 162–66, 168–70, 182–84, 185–86, 194–95
structure of de León's works, 162, 164–65 (*see also* "Nameless Composition," structure)
tenfold speculation and, 18–19, 162, 163–66, 167–68, 170
thirteen hermeneutical principles (of Rabbi Ishmael), 7*f*, 11–12n.18, 19–20, 163–64, 169–70, 171n.25
thirteen-petaled rose, 120–21, 132–34, 150–51, 153, 157–58n.141 (*see also* rose of testimony)
triple thirteenfold, 136–37, 140–42
three divine worlds, 90–95, 100–1, 121–23, 136–37, 161, 192–93, 194–95
binary/non-binary genders, 126–27
divine bride, 126, 135, 151, 160
divine groom, 51–52, 153, 156–57, 159, 160
divine newborn, 129–32, 159
female between two males, 137–38, 149–50
female world as moon, 138–39, 140, 142–44, 145, 147, 148–49
first *heh* of Tetragrammaton (*binah*, supernal female), 142–43, 145–47
gender-determination /sexual differentiation of, 126–27
gender stability of the lower female world (*see* eternal femininity)
hidden/upper world (*binah*), 122–23, 126, 128, 130n.61, 135–37, 140–42, 145–46–, 150–51, 152–53, 154–55, 157–58, 159
individuation of, 123–24
last *heh* of Tetragrammaton (*malkhut,* lower female), 120, 142–43, 144–46, 147, 148–49
letter *dalet* (*malkhut, lower female*), 122–23, 124–26, 142–43, 144–45, 147, 148–49
letter *vav*, 122–23, 124–26, 144–45, 149–50
letter *yod*, 122–23, 124–25
lower female world, 122–23, 124–25, 126–27, 129–34, 136–42, 144–47, 149–53, 154–55, 156–58, 159 (*see also* eternal femininity; *malkhut*; sefirot, *shekhinah*)
male between two females, 137–39
male world, 124–25, 126–27, 138–39, 142–43, 144–45
maternal world, 154
middle world (six intermediate sefirot, son), 122–23, 124–25, 127–28, 129, 130–32, 135–37, 139–40, 141, 145–46, 150–51, 152–53, 154, 157–58
patriarchy, 126–27
son from mother, 129–32
threefold family, 124–25, 126–27, 135, 142–43
upper female world, 124–25, 159
threefold speculation 93, 94–95, 140, 162–64, 172–73
androgynology, 120, 140–42
Arabic writing system, 109
attributes of divine intellect, 186–88
divine worlds (*see* three divine worlds)
psychology, 93–95, 146–47, 192–93
structure of *alef*, 89–90, 121–22, 123, 124–26, 138–39, 144–45, 149–50
three worlds, 28–29, 83, 87–88n.49, 89–90, 93, 103–5, 114–15, 121–22, 161, 182–84
vowels, 103–5, 106n.117
See also three divine worlds
Togarmi, Baruch, 87–88n.49

Toledo, 176
Torah, 21–23, 53, 65, 73–74, 172–73, 192
 kabbalah as oral Torah (*see* kabbalah, as oral Torah)
 oral, 1, 14, 46–48, 52 (*see also* rabbinic tradition)
 primordial Torah (as a preexistent hypostasis), 180–81
 secrets of, 15, 38 (*see also* secrets of faith)
 unity of oral and written Torah, 44–45, 47–48, 77–78, 105–6, 150–51, 156
 written, 47–48
translation of kabbalah, 16–18
Tree of Life, 87–88, 195
Trinity, 121, 165n.7, 186
Truth. *See emet*
twelvefold, 57–58, 130n.61, 132–37, 139–42, 150–53, 157–58, 160, 162–63, 165–66, 194–95

Ulrich of Strasbourg (Ulricus de Argentina), 106–7
Uriel (archangel), 87–88
Urim and Tummim, 151–52

Venice, 4–8, 5*f*, 29–31, 172
virtue ethics, 53

wisdom
 cultures of, 171–84
 ḥokhmah (*see* sefirot, *ḥokhmah*)
 thirty-two paths of, 73–74, 180–81
 wisdom literature, 180–81
world of separation, 142–43, 150–52, 157–58

Zechariah, 168–69
Zohar 8, 11–12n.18, 16, 22–29, 171n.25, 172–74, 185, 196, 197–98
 Aramaic, 20–21, 22–23, 42, 88–89
 Ashkenazi penitential culture and, 42–43, 68–69, 156n.137
 authorship, 2–3, 4–8, 22–23, 68, 77–120, 161–62, 184–85
 background of, 68, 78, 161–62, 184–98
 Cremona edition, 42, 112n.133, 156n.137
 ethical teachings, 67–68
 imaginary library, 184–98
 Mantua edition, 42, 112n.133, 120–21, 156n.137
 Midrash Ruth (zoharic composition), 163–64, 193n.88
 and the "Nameless Composition," 9–10, 22–32, 58–59, 67–68, 88–89, 94–95, 105–6, 120, 132n.66, 142, 155–60, 161–62, 165–66, 171n.25, 182–86, 196–98 (*see also* "Nameless Composition," parallelism with Zohar)
 on *Parashat Vayeḥi*, 159, 185–86, 191–92, 194
 on *Parashat Vayiqra*, 186, 190n.75
 Piqqudin, 160
 Printing, 4–8, 155–56
 zoharic homilies, 12–13, 22–23, 26, 28–29, 42–43, 77–78, 98–99, 105–6, 161–62, 184, 185–86, 190n.75, 191–92, 196
 See also Rav Hamnuna Saba; *Idra* literature; Jacob; *Midrash ha-Ne'lam*; rose among thorns